OUR GRAND MISSIONARY ADVENTURE

Our Family's Journey of Faith
to the Belgian Congo, Africa

Jeanette Spainhower Rudder
Marian Spainhower Ammons

RudderHaven
3014 Washington Ave
Granite City, IL 62040

Our Grand Missionary Adventure
Our Family's Journey of Faith to the Belgian Congo, Africa

First softcover printing, December 2015, RudderHaven
(ISBN 978-1-932060-17-1)

Copyright © 2015 by Jeanette Rudder and Marian Ammons

All rights reserved.

Scripture quotations are from the King James Bible.

Cover art and design by Douglas and Sheri Rudder

Published by Rudderhaven
Printed in the United States of America

ISBN: 978-1-932060-17-1

No portion of this publication may be reproduced, stored in a retrieval system, or transmitted in any form or by any means—whether electronic, mechanical, photocopying, recording, or otherwise—except for brief quotations in articles or reviews—without the prior written permission of the both the copyright owner and the publisher of this book.

RudderHaven
www.rudderhaven.com

Dedication

*In memory of Leslie J. and Gertrude F. Spainhower
for the foundation they laid
for our families.*

*To our children and grandchildren –
May you enjoy the legacy
they've left for you.*

My Path

Thy will, O Lord, and not mine be done,
    No matter how difficult it may be;
Thy way, O Lord, is always the best,
    Choose Thou the path for me.
Whether it be smooth or rough,
    Your way will always be best;
Through hills or by still waters matters not,
    Only that my soul may be blest.

I dare not choose the path I take,
    I would not, even if I might;
But choose Thou the path for me,
    And grant that my burden may be light.
Go Thou before and show me the way,
    For my footsteps are so prone to stray;
Let me not turn to the left nor the right,
    That I may walk by faith and not by sight.

Leslie J. Spainhower

Acknowledgments

We rejoice in the opportunity to tell you the story of one decade of our lives. More importantly, it is the story of a family who learned to trust God's provision and protection in both the good times, as well as the bad.

Working together to bring you the story of our decade of missionary adventure has drawn us closer than ever. Oh, we wasted some good years in bickering when we were little kids, but we've learned to really appreciate each other as adults. We're different—but we are both grounded in the values that Dad and Mom taught us. And we have those values to pass on to our children and grandchildren—and any others who may read this book.

We truly appreciate the encouragement of our husbands and children while facing the daunting task of compiling these letters and writing down memories of our decade as missionary kids.

We want to thank Douglas Rudder for his help in publishing this book. Without his knowledge and expertise, all we'd have would be a pile of prayer letters and bits and pieces of memories. We also really appreciate the graphic artistry of Sheri Rudder.

Most of all, we thank God for giving us parents who loved us and cared for us, who were there in good times and bad, who knew when to speak and when to just pray. And we thank God for giving us the opportunity to share our story with you—family and friends, both old and new. We pray you will be blessed by seeing how God can work in the lives of those who love and trust Him.

—Jeanette and Marian

Table of Contents

The Legacy..1

Beginning the Adventure...9

Off to France (1953)..53

Marseille, France (1953-1954) 91

Africa – First Term (1954-1956)...155

Starting Again (1956-1958)...277

Africa – Second Term (1958-1960)..313

The Final Chapter (1960)..397

Appendixes

    A. A Brief History of Berean Mission in the Belgian Congo
    B. Map of Station Locations

Authors' Bios

Part One

The Legacy

"And thou shalt teach [these words] diligently unto thy children, and shalt talk of them when thou sittest in thine house, and when thou walkest by the way, and when thou liest down, and when thou risest up."
Deuteronomy 6:7

The Legacy

Gertrude and Leslie Spainhower

The Beginning

They came from two different worlds.

Dad had a rough beginning. He was born in East St. Louis, Illinois, to a severely crippled father and a cold, unloving mother. Both were heavy smokers and drinkers. Dad and his older brother, Lloyd, basically raised themselves. Dad started smoking when he was seven years old by stealing cigarettes from his parents. He often finished up the beer and other drinks left from his parents' parties. To this wild boy, *Jesus* was nothing but a curse word.

Mom was raised in a noisy, but happy home in East St. Louis. Her stepfather was a kind, hard-working, generous man. Her mother was a strong Christian woman who had faced much adversity in her early life and found comfort in her church. Grandma Wilson's three children—Robert, Francis, and Gertrude—regularly attended Sunday School and church with her as long as they lived at home.

Dad traveled the country with his family when he was young. His father, a Pulitzer Prize-winning journalist, started in St. Louis but spent years in Idaho and Montana where Dad learned to hunt and shoot—and to play the trumpet. By the time Dad graduated from high school at age sixteen, he was so good that he traveled with a dance band that played across the country.

Mom's early life was difficult in another way. She contracted muscular polio when she was two that left her with slightly deformed feet and a withered left arm. Several surgeries gave her movement in her left hand, but she was never able to lift or move her left arm. Because Grandma Wilson was so determined that she would have as normal a life as possible, however, Mom grew up with a strong, sweet courage that gave her the ability to conquer problems throughout her life.

Although both of them were born in East St. Louis, Dad and Mom didn't meet until they attended Margaret Hickey School of Business. Dad was extraordinarily handsome and debonair—and quite a ladies' man. Mom was beautiful and vivacious—and handicapped. But Dad was drawn to her quiet strength and generous nature.

And this lonely, wild young man finally found a real family. Grandma Wilson just added him to her lively brood. Dad discovered that Mom's brother, Bob, was a great poker player—but Grandma didn't allow them to play for money, only peanuts. He had to obey the rules of her household when he was there, and Dad found the first security he'd ever known under Grandma Wilson's firm but loving hand. He always said that Grandma Wilson was the only real mother he ever had—and Mom always laughed and declared that he'd married her just to get Grandma Wilson for a mother!

They were married at the Wilson house on November 24, 1937, in the midst of the Great Depression. Dad was not quite 20 years old; Mom was 18. He couldn't even afford a suit for the wedding. Grandma Wilson bought him one—with two pairs of trousers—and she sewed a pretty dress for Mom to wear.

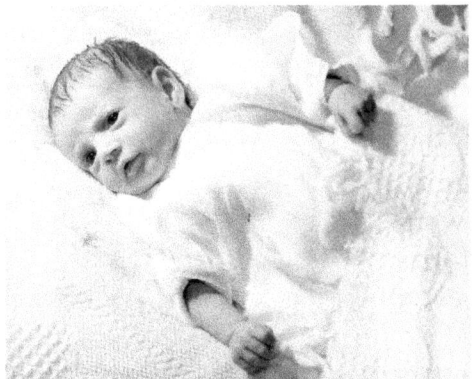

Jeanette was born on November 14, 1941—just three weeks before World War II began. Marian was born prematurely on April 19, 1945, a few months before it ended.

That's the background of our family heritage. Even more important, however, is to know about our spiritual heritage.

The Called Ones

From sin to salvation. Although Mom had received Christ as her Savior when she was young, she had wandered away from the Lord during her teen years because the church her family attended had "modernized." She went to church because her mother said she had to, but she could party with the best (or worst) of them. Dad, of course, was not a Christian. Although he deeply loved Mom, a bottle of beer and a pack of cigarettes were never far from his reach.

After Jeanette was born, Mom decided that she needed to take her to Sunday School and church—that's how Mom had been brought up, and that's how she intended to raise her family. She had to take a bus across town to the church she had attended growing up. Carrying a toddler, a diaper bag, and a purse was almost too much for her with only one good arm.

Dad saw her struggle and decided that he would go with her. But he asked if Mom would be willing to attend a new little church that was meeting in a basement out in the Edgemont area of East St. Louis, near to where they lived. He would go with her for three Sundays, so she could feel comfortable with the people. So they started attending the Edgemont Bible Church where Rev. G. Joseph Wright was the pastor.

The Holy Spirit began working in Dad's heart, and by the close of that third Sunday morning service, Dad was ready to give his life to Christ. Mr. Ed Lieb, an elder at Edgemont, led him to the Lord.

Dad immediately began studying the Bible. He was a highly intelligent man, and that's how he always tackled anything new. But he was totally untaught in the Scriptures—a "rank heathen," by his own account—so Mom was startled to see him sitting at the kitchen table poring over his Bible, a cigarette in one hand and a bottle of beer in the other. But she said it was as if God told her to remain quiet—He would handle the situation. It only took a couple of weeks, and Dad suddenly jumped up from the table where he was studying, went over to the sink, and poured the beer down the drain. "These just don't go together," he told Mom.

Giving up cigarettes was harder. Dad said that one of the deacons at Edgemont mentioned to him that, as a Christian, he shouldn't be smoking, so Dad tried to stop—and failed, tried—and failed, tried—and failed. He said he finally realized that he couldn't break the habit just because someone told him he ought to. It had to come from his own heart. God helped him succeed—it didn't happen immediately, as it does with some people. He still had to fight his cravings for them, but with the Lord's help, he finally won that battle.

Dad purchased three city lots in Edgemont, and at the back of this huge property, built a large, two-car garage. As a trained draftsman, he drew up plans for the dream home he would build in front.

In the meantime, the four of us happily lived in that little garage house only about two or three blocks from the church. So Dad and Mom settled into their new life as growing Christians, active in the church, enjoying their lives together with their girls.

To the ministry. Faculty members from Midwest Bible and Missionary Institute in St. Louis, Missouri, held college-credit Bible classes at Edgemont Bible Church on Monday nights, and Dad began taking classes. By 1948, Dad felt strongly that God was calling him to the ministry and enrolled full-time at Midwest in 1949 through 1952. He took classes in the morning, then worked full-time in the afternoons and evenings with half-days on Saturday as a draftsman for J.D. Falvey, an architect, in St. Louis.

It is only by the grace of God that Dad was able to keep up this rough schedule. Living in that tiny garage house, he didn't even have a quiet room in which to study. He had an upright desk (called a secretary) in one corner of the main room that contained the tiny kitchen, plus a table with six chairs. In the opposite corner stood a large coal-burning stove that heated the whole house. Dad wore out a couple of linoleums by pacing around the table while memorizing Scriptures or Hebrew and Greek. Mom said it wasn't at all unusual for Marian and Jeanette to be pacing right behind him—and he never even noticed.

Mom took a few classes at Midwest, generally on a Saturday morning. Marian and Jeanette usually stayed with Grandma Wilson, but a few times Dad and Mom took us with them to Midwest. It seemed so huge with so many people, all of them hurrying someplace. On a few special occasions—mission conferences, skit nights, that sort of thing—we went on the bus and the streetcar out to Midwest at night. That was even more exciting!

After World War II came an explosion of missionary activity from the United States. Edgemont Bible Church supported many missionaries and had a big missions conference every year. We always got to meet the missionaries and often played with their children. Midwest Bible and Missionary Institute had a strong emphasis on missions, so it was not surprising when one night during a missions conference at Edgemont, Dad and Mom went forward to dedicate their lives as missionaries. Jeanette thought it was very exciting and joined them at the front where the congregation came by to shake the hands of those who had committed their lives that night to be missionaries. Little did we girls really understand what all the excitement was about—just that something big had happened in our lives.

Dad finished Bible School in June 1952 and, along with three other students from Midwest sat before a panel of local pastors who questioned them for several hours on their doctrinal beliefs. Their answers had to be backed up with Scripture. All four men passed the oral examination and were officially ordained for ministry before the congregation.

Left: The four Bible students at Edgemont Bible Church as they were being questioned. Dad is on the far left.

Right: After the Ordination Service, each man was presented with a Bible. Reverend Leslie J. Spainhower is on the far left.

Below: The congregation shaking their hands and expressing their congratulations. Dad is in the center with a big smile on his face.

Edgemont Bible Church supported missionaries who had gone out to a number of different fields, many of them from Berean Mission, headquartered in St. Louis. That summer, Dad and Mom attended the annual conference of Berean Mission, which was held in Denver, Colorado, while Marian and Jeanette stayed with Grandma Wilson.

When Dad and Mom returned, the decision had been made—we were going to the Belgian Congo (now the Democratic Republic of Congo). Mom said she knew their calling to Africa was real the day Dad took his carefully drawn blueprints of our future house out to the burn pit and, with tears streaming down his face, lit a match to them. Our future was in God's hands, not his.

To the mission field. The garage house and the three city lots were sold, and we moved into Grandma Wilson's basement for a few weeks before we left for Norman, Oklahoma, for the Summer Institute of Linguistics, where Dad learned the principles of learning an unwritten language and then translating Scriptures into that language.

From Oklahoma, we went to California where we did deputation work to raise support for our five-year term in Africa. But we were called back to East St. Louis in December when Dad's father was dying of cancer.

We finished our preparations that spring, attended Camp Tadmor for a week for new-missionary orientation, and sailed for France in August 1953. After spending a year there learning French, the colonial language of the Belgian Congo, we finally set sail in 1954 for Mombasa, Kenya.

After driving across East Africa to the Congo, we finally arrived in Kivu Province, B.A.M.S. Katanti Station. As we drove up the curving road, past the African village, past the church and schools, to the missionary compound, the Africans swarmed out of every building and hurried up to where Dad had stopped the car in front of one of the houses. We stepped onto the wide veranda of the house as the schoolboys marched smartly up to the front of the house. The rest of the Africans filled in around them, and they sang a welcome song to us—we recognized the tune but not the words. After the elders welcomed us to the station, the missionary who was translating told Dad that the Africans wanted him to talk to them.

That's when Dad told them through a translator how God had called him from a life of sin to salvation through Jesus Christ. Then God called him into the ministry. And finally, God had called him and his family to Berean Mission—and to the church on Katanti. It was not surprising a couple of weeks later, when the Africans gave us Balega names, that they called Dad *Tata Wemaninua*—the called one.

A Ministry Interruption. In late 1955, Mom became deathly ill with respiratory malaria. It was finally decided that the only way to save her life was for our family to return to the United States, far away from the malaria-infested jungles of the Belgian Congo.

Mom and Dad deeply grieved the loss of their ministry in the Congo. Our family slowly began building a new life back in East St. Louis, Illinois.

And then, Mom got well—really, truly well—and hope blossomed again.

Back to the mission field. We headed off to California in the fall of 1957 for deputation work. In late August 1958, Jeanette and Marian flew alone to the Belgian Congo in order to enter school on time. Mom and Dad followed by ship, arriving four months later.

We served nearly two more years in the Congo. Then in June 1960, Belgium granted the Congo its independence. Less than a month later, the U. S. State Department ordered all American citizens out of the Congo as violence erupted across the country.

Our decade of missionary adventure had ended.

To Glory. Many decades have passed since then, decades that have added spouses, grandchildren, and great-grandchildren to Mom and Dad's family.

Mom went home to Glory on October 21, 2000. Dad followed on February 1, 2012. Safe in the arms of Jesus, they are waiting to be reunited with the rest of their family.

The Bequest

Mom and Dad weren't wealthy, according to this world's standards, but they left a rich inheritance for all of us.

The love of God. As you will see from the words written in the rest of this book, first and foremost, Mom and Dad loved God with all their "hearts, souls, mind, and strength." They were willing to sacrifice everything to serve Him—to love others.

Their bequest to the family was to teach Jeanette and Marian to love God the same way—and for us to teach our children—and to carry this trust throughout the generations.

The love of family. When Dad and Mom married, it was for life—till death parted them. With God's help, they were faithful to each other and faithful to their family. There was never a time when Jeanette and Marian lost a sense of their love, no matter how difficult circumstances might become. It didn't matter if we were on board a ship, in a cramped apartment in France, in a mud hut in Africa, or even separated from them half a world away, we knew we could depend on God, first, but also on Mom and Dad's unflagging love.

Prayer Letters. All the time we were preparing for the mission field and especially while we were away from the United States, Dad and Mom sent back a prayer letter almost every month to the secretary at the Edgemont Bible Church, Adele Cruikshank. She would mimeograph the letter and send it to everyone on our prayer list who was supporting us, either financially or by prayer. And she saved a copy of almost every letter. After our final return from Africa, she gave the letters to Mom and Dad, along with letters Dad had sent to Pastor and Mrs. Wright over the years.

Dad and Mom turned the letters over to Jeanette and Marian when they moved to smaller living quarters. We're giving those letters to all of you now, along with our comments and thoughts about this special decade in our lives—our grand missionary adventure.

Part Two

Beginning the Adventure

"Commit thy way unto the Lord; trust also in him; and he shall bring it to pass."
Psalm 37:5

Beginning the Adventure

Marian's Comment: Early Memories

In 1952, when I was seven years old, our parents came to my sister, Jeanette—then ten years old—and me to tell us that the Lord was calling them to go to the Belgian Congo, Africa as missionaries. This meant we would be moving there to tell Africans about Jesus. Well, that sounded like a fun adventure!

I didn't fully understand the magnitude of this decision. The idea of leaving my beloved Grandma and Grandpa Wilson (my mom's mother and step-father) and not being able to see them for five years didn't register in my young mind. Leaving our other family members and friends just seemed more like an extended vacation.

However, my vivid imagination did start to take hold. My first thought was that we would be in the jungle, surrounded by lions and tigers all the time. I actually ended up having recurring dreams about trying to walk outside my front door but couldn't because there was a lion sitting on the front steps! Little did I know that half of that imaginary scene was true—no, not the lions and tigers -- just the part about living in the jungle. But I'm getting too far ahead in our story so I better get back on track.

As I quickly found out, though, the move to Africa did not happen right away. A lot had to take place before that would occur. The first thing we had to do was to raise monthly financial support. Our support was divided into "units," and each unit was in the amount of $2.50. Individuals within churches would make a faith promise to prayerfully give us a certain number of units each month.

Our home church, Edgemont Bible Church in East St. Louis, Illinois, was our strongest support base. The church was located one block from where Grandma and Grandpa Wilson lived.

We also had to raise $4,500 to purchase needed equipment and then transport the four of us, our vehicle, and part of the equipment to France and then on to Africa, as well as shipping everything else to the Congo at the right time.

Dad made a tall wooden thermometer that was placed in front of the sanctuary at Edgemont. A red line representing the mercury of the thermometer was painted on it and moved upward as passage and equipment money started coming in. But Edgemont couldn't possibly handle the entire support needed for four people, plus passage and equipment, so we set out in faith to California where we would present our future work in Africa to other churches.

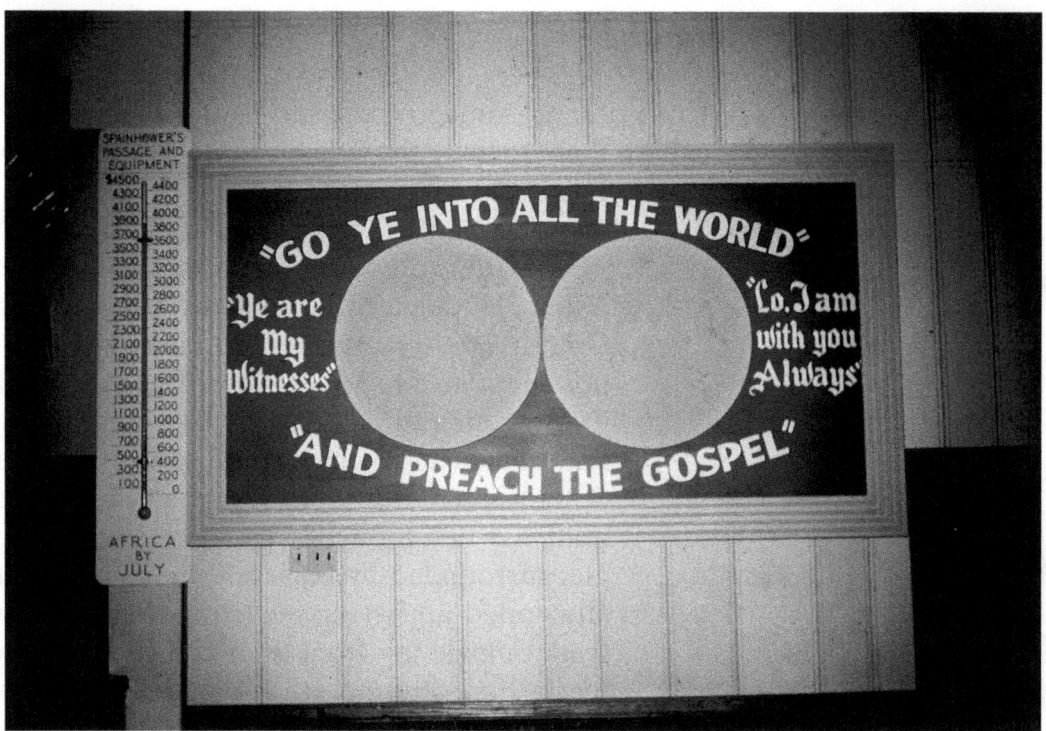

Jeanette's Comment

I vividly remember the night Dad and Mom went forward at the missions conference at Edgemont Bible Church to dedicate themselves to the Lord as foreign missionaries. I had been raised in church—and I knew what this meant. I wanted to show people that I was not going to be dragged along but would be going with them as a very young missionary.

I got many pats on the head that night, but I could tell that people just thought that I wanted to be standing with my parents. I was a very shy little girl, and I really had no idea what lay ahead for us. But I knew it was thrilling—and I got to be a part of it.

The people at Edgemont knew that I'd been taking piano lessons since I was seven years old with our church organist—and, at that time, also the church secretary—Ruth Herin. Every day I would go from Edgemont School about a block away directly to the church and knock on the office door. Ruth would let me in and turn on the lights in the auditorium for me. Only once a week did I have a piano lesson—but my teacher was there every day as I practiced! No nonsense allowed. And I practiced on a baby grand piano!

If I had trouble with something, Ruth was right there to come in and help me with the problem. Since there weren't any courses in music theory for children at that time, she worked through a college theory course with me. Although I've long forgotten much of the terminology, what I learned from Ruth has stood me in good stead throughout the years as Larry and I have written our own music.

But we didn't think there would be any pianos in the Congo—the extreme humidity would ruin them. So Ruth, wanting me to be able to continue with my music, spoke to someone who started a campaign to buy me an accordion before we left for deputation work out West to raise funds for our missionary venture.

Along with everything else Edgemont Bible Church did for us, they gave me an accordion just shortly before we left for Oklahoma. It was slightly smaller than full size, but it's all I could handle at that time. Ruth didn't know much about an accordion, but she helped me to at least play on it with my right hand. She also gave my folks some money to get me a few lessons while we were in California so that I'd learn to properly play the left hand as well.

I ended up with ten accordion lessons overall. I could already read music and knew a lot about theory—which actually helped in learning the bass chords—so the accordion teacher could concentrate on proper movement of the bellows, plus exercises for the bass. Before we left California, he told Mom and Dad about music books that would help me progress on my own. They purchased them to take with us, and I spent hours practicing my accordion over the next years. Music was always my refuge when I felt homesick or frightened, discouraged—or happy.

By the time we returned to Edgemont from California, I would occasionally play an accordion solo for the evening service or played the piano accompaniment for Dad's trumpet solos. It was a start to a long musical life.

BEREAN MISSION, INC.
AFRICA
"THE DARK CONTINENT"

Prayer Letter   * * * * *   April 1952

Dear Christian friends:

"And when he putteth forth his own sheep, he goeth before them, and the sheep follow him: for they know his voice" (John 10:4).

    How good it is to know that as Christians we have One who goes before and runs the interference for us. All we have to do is to follow. And then, lest we should turn to the right hand or to the left, we may hear His voice saying, "This is the way, walk ye in it."

    Since writing our prayer letter last January, our plans have been changed many times over. At first this seemed very disconcerting, and at times we wondered if we were really in the center of God's will for us. But finally the Lord opened our eyes and caused us to see that when we walk with Him we do not lay plans a year in advance—instead, we follow Him one step at a time.

> He does not lead me year by year
>   Nor even day by day,
> But step by step my path unfolds;
>   My Lord directs my way.
> Tomorrow's plans I do not know,
>   I only know this minute;
> But He will say, "This is the way,
>   By faith now walk ye in it."
> And I am glad that it is so,
>   Today's enough to bear;
> And when tomorrow comes, His grace
>   Shall far exceed its care.

> What need to worry then, or fret?
> The God who gave His Son
> Holds all my moments in His hand
> And gives them, one by one.

The Lord has intervened, and it will not be necessary for us to spend a year in Belgium as we had anticipated. Instead, we will be able to go directly to Africa as soon as the necessary funds are provided. "Pray ye therefore the Lord of the harvest, that He will send forth…" (Matthew 9:38).

Our God is supplying our needs in a wonderful way. Praise His name! Since writing you last, we have received forty five units of support. This represents approximately one-third of the necessary units. In addition, the Lord has sent in several love-gifts as a partial provision toward the expense of attending the Summer Institute of Linguistics, where we will undertake some special courses in Bible translation. These courses are conducted during the months of June, July and August by the Wycliffe Bible Translators, Inc. at the University of Oklahoma.

This schooling will complete our formal training for the mission field, and we shall then enter upon full time deputation work until all needs of support, passage and equipment are fully met. In this respect, the Lord graciously laid it upon the heart of a loved one to provide us with a projector for showing slides, and a large screen, which we will be able to use in presenting the work which Berean Mission is doing in the heart of the Belgian Congo. We were also given a splendid 35 mm. camera with which we trust to obtain some interesting first-hand pictures upon our arrival in Africa.

The more we cast ourselves upon the Lord, the more we are made to realize "that all things work together for good to them that love God, to them who are the called according to his purpose" (Romans 8:28). At the close of the last war, when the housing shortage was so acute, the house which we had been renting was sold, and we were faced with eviction. It was impossible to find a house to rent, and we could not pay the inflated prices to buy a home. At the time we certainly could not see how these circumstances were working together for our good.

But God had His purpose in it all because out of necessity we purchased a lot, and I erected a garage to be used as temporary living quarters until we could build a permanent home. This garage-home has proved to be a real blessing of the Lord during these past three years at Bible School. And now, as we are "pulling up roots" and making ready to "thrust out into the deep," we have sold our little garage-home, and have realized sufficient from this investment to purchase an automobile to be used as we travel about in deputation work. How we praise the Lord for His wonderful provision. Truly, "His ways are past finding out!"

In closing, let me express our sincere appreciation to each and every one of you for your fellowship in the gospel, and our heartfelt thanks for your many prayers in our behalf. And so, until you hear from us again, our prayer is,

The Lord bless thee and keep thee,

Leslie and Gertrude Spainhower

*Our Plymouth Suburban parked in front of
Berean Mission, Inc. St. Louis, Missouri*

Marian's Comment: Oklahoma

In June, July and August of 1952, before we went to California, we attended the Summer Institute of Linguistics in Norman, Oklahoma where Dad took some special training in Bible translation from Wycliffe Bible Translators, Inc. So that is how we spent our first summer as prospective missionaries.

Dad's classes were held in this building to the left. None of the buildings were air conditioned back then which made for some very hot classrooms and living quarters. As young as I was, I can remember the sultry heat of Oklahoma!

Missionary families stayed in the dormitory below during the summer months. Our rooms were on the second floor. The men's restroom was on the second floor; the women's on the first—a long trek, especially at night!

The second-floor windows above the entrance normally lighted a student lounge during the college year. It became a bright nursery for babies and toddlers where Mom worked many hot days while Dad and the other missionaries were in class.

My most vivid memory was that living in a dormitory afforded us the adventure of eating our meals in a noisy cafeteria with everyone else. My parents detested doing that, but I thought it was a lark. Imagine being able to pick and choose what I wanted to eat!

Unfortunately, Dad took a dim view of eating all three meals in the cafeteria with a bunch of other people. Finally, my parents worked it out so that one of them would go over to the cafeteria just to get milk and some butter in the morning. We had our own toaster and, with

the cereal and bread we bought at the grocery store, we had our very own private breakfast each morning in Dad and Mom's room—just the four of us together without all the noise of the cafeteria. So we ended up having one meal in our room and two in the cafeteria every day for three months.

Jeanette and I made friends with other kids, and we always had someone to play with—but I really can't remember much about it. However, I do remember Dad and Mom would spend as much time with us away from their classes and work as they could. Occasionally we would leave the campus and take rides into the mountains for a time of family togetherness and, I'm sure, to give Dad and Mom a breather from their tasks. Those were special times. As we were growing up, Dad and Mom always made sure that no matter where we were, or what was happening, Jeanette and I were secure in their love for us and in the joys of being a family together. We had the greatest gift parents can give their children—LOVE and LAUGHTER.

One very special treat was when Grandma Wilson drove to Oklahoma to spend a few days with us that summer. We took a drive to the mountains where we had the best picnic lunch ever!

(Not sure why we are all wearing hairnets! Rather creepy-looking if you ask me!)

Norman, Oklahoma
June 20, 1952

Dear Brother and Sister Wright:

We have been praying for your Daily Vacation Bible school, realizing what a drain it is on the teachers physically, and realizing too what great opportunities it presents for leading precious little ones to Christ. By the time you receive this letter, the first week will be over, and one to go. May the Lord continue to richly bless your combined efforts to His glory. Jeanette and Marian miss being able to go to Bible School as they do not have one here. However, they do have a nice Sunday School right here on the Campus of the University. It is conducted by the First Baptist Church of Norman with the help of Wycliffe students as teachers.

You mentioned in your letter that it has been so hot there. We have been hitting over the 100% mark too, although the evenings have been reasonably cool. Personally, we enjoy it very much, being rather sensitive to the cool weather. The staff members say that it gets too hot for comfort later in the summer, so we are all set for a warm ol' time of it. Good training for the tropics!

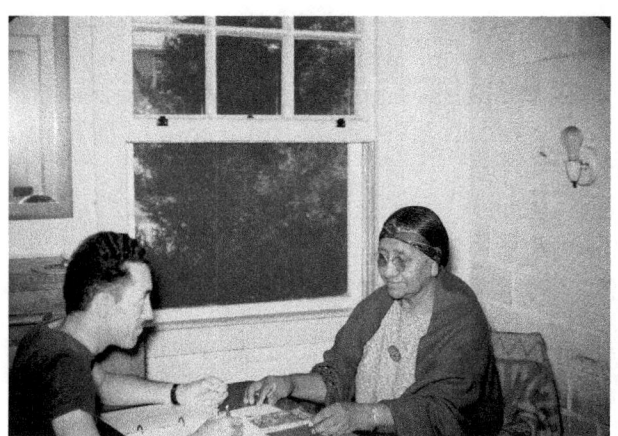

I have now begun working with a Kiowa Indian for an informant. Her name is Myrtle Paudlety (pronounced, "Bawldee"). We begin our informant work by asking for the Kiowa words for many simple nouns, such as, man, woman, boy, girl, coyote, prairie dog, etc. Next we ask for such things as, "his horse", "their horse", "my horse", "our horse", etc. Then we secure a few verb forms; and so on and on and on. As we proceed with the securing of words and expressions we must also begin analyzing the forms we are writing down phonetically. When the eleven weeks are over we should have a reasonably accurate analysis of the Kiowa language set up in a practical orthography which in turn could be taught to the Indians so they could read and write their own language. Naturally, the extent of our lexicon would be limited in so short a time. Now, these same principles and methods can be applied to any unwritten language, whether it be American Indian, African, Eskimo, or English, with a resultant lexicon, grammar, etc. My earnest prayer is that the Lord will so enable me that I may give His precious Word to those who have it not because their language is unwritten. God's Word will only speak to their hearts when it is in their own native tongue.

Thinking of you both, and praying for you and all the dear ones at Edgemont as you continue to "hold forth the Word of Life."

The Lord bless you — real good!

Les, Gertie, and the girlies

Jeanette's Comment: Tales from Oklahoma

As missionary candidates, we couldn't afford many luxuries. But Dad believed there had to be something special once in a while so that life didn't become burdensome. Talking to one of the cafeteria workers, he found out about a local dairy that had an ice cream bar. So almost once a week, we went to the dairy for a treat. That ice cream was rich and creamy and tasted so wonderful—especially on a very hot night in Oklahoma.

Sometimes, all we could afford was a small ice cream cone—one for each of us. A few times Mom tried to say that she really didn't want anything, but Dad refused to accept her sacrifice. We all enjoyed a treat or no one did.

Once in a while, we could afford a small hot fudge sundae for each of us. Now that was true luxury! The taste of that delicious ice cream, the sound of a clinking spoon against a pretty glass bowl, and the happy smile on Dad's face—those are good memories.

Since Wycliffe Bible Translators conducted the Summer Institute of Linguistics, a large number of their missionaries and candidates also attended the Institute. In the two rooms next to ours was a family that had spent several years in the jungles around the Amazon River, far from civilization. When the wife was several months pregnant with their first child, her husband became deliriously ill. The only way to save him was to get to a mission station that had a short-wave radio and call for help. The nearest station was many miles downriver. The natives helped the woman build a raft and put her husband on it. She brought a few supplies and pushed off into the middle of the river. She poled that raft for two or three days to reach the mission station that had the radio—and a landing strip for a small airplane. After the husband had recuperated and she had their baby, they headed back into the jungles again. Until their furlough, they came out only once more—when she had a second child.

They had lived as much like the natives as possible while learning their language, putting it into writing, teaching the Indians to read and write, and beginning to translate the Gospel of John into that language. They had only been back in America a few weeks when they came to Oklahoma.

The first thing we discovered about living as much like the natives as possible is that the little boy and girl refused to wear clothes. They were used to running around without any clothes in the jungle and took the slightest opportunity to shed their clothes. They were also used to being called "boy" and "girl." Apparently, these natives did not name their children until close to adulthood and, even though the missionary parents had given their children American names, they followed the native custom and simply called them by their gender.

The children spoke some English but were fluent in the native language. It was at this point that Mom decided that no matter what the policy may be on the Berean mission field, her children would not be raised like the natives! Of course, both Marian and I were older than these other two children—but Mom held fast to her resolution to raise us like young Americans because she knew we would be returning to the States at some point. She didn't want us to be misfits in American society.

Even though it's getting ahead of our story, I remember one time at the beginning of our first term that Mom insisted that she wanted to be at home when Marian and I returned from school or when we came home for lunch. One of the other missionaries told her that the African cook could take care of us. Mom's instant reply was, "I came out here to bring Christ to the Africans, not to have the Africans raise my children." And that was that!

BEREAN MISSION, INC.
AFRICA
"THE DARK CONTINENT"

Prayer Letter   * * * * *   July 1952

Dear Christian friends:

"I will go in the strength of the Lord God" (Psalm 71:16).

In our last letter to you, we told of the Lord's gracious provision of various items of equipment, including a much-needed Plymouth Suburban to be used in deputation work and, Lord willing, to be taken to Africa for use in the field. We thank the Lord for its fine performance and for a comfortable, uneventful trip of some 600 miles from East St. Louis to Norman, Oklahoma, where we are now taking the Wycliffe course in Bible translation.

Here at the Summer Institute of Linguistics we are privileged to fellowship daily with missionaries from all over the world, as well as scores of missionary candidates, all taking the courses in linguistics in order that they may be better prepared to learn the language of their respective people with the view of ultimately translating God's precious Word into their native tongue.

Missionaries are here on furlough from Africa, China, New Guinea, South America, and Mexico. There is also one native of Liberia, West Africa, who is being sent here by the government of Liberia to receive linguistic training in order that he may do language work for his government among the aboriginal tribes of his country. Praise the Lord, Byron is a Christian and will not only be a representative for the government of Liberia to these tribes, but above all will be an Ambassador for Christ.

Another family here for the course in linguistics are on furlough from the Belgian Congo, and what a joy it has been to fellowship with them. Their children are about the same ages as our Jeanette and Marian, and they have become quite chummy in these few weeks. We were very pleased to learn that their station in the Congo is near Costermansville, which is only about 140 miles to the east of our station at Ikozi. Brother Bothwell had attempted some Bible translation during the past five years on the field, but had encountered so many difficulties in the language that he determined to take the course here at Wycliffe so that he would be better prepared to continue translating God's Word for his people when he returns this fall.

As we are receiving training, including reports from the various fields mentioned, we are becoming more and more impatient to be about our Father's business. We must constantly remind ourselves, however, that it is His work and that He will thrust us forth in His own time. We cannot go in our own strength, but we "will go in the strength of the Lord God."

Won't you pray with us, as we leave here the end of next month for deputation work, that the Lord may be pleased to burden hearts with the great need of dark Africa for the "light of the gospel of the glory of Christ" that we might be sent forth as bearers of that light. And so, until you hear from us again,

The Lord bless you — real good!
The Spainhowers

Jeanette's Comment: We Got Our Kicks on Route 66

Before we left Norman, Oklahoma, Dad planned our route and carefully marked up the map for his navigator—Mom. We had taken Route 66 (which stretched 1,000 miles from Chicago to Los Angeles) from St. Louis to Oklahoma City—and another route south to Norman. We were going to take Route 66 all the way from Oklahoma, through the Texas panhandle, New Mexico, and Arizona to California. Dad drove every mile of the way.

Along with our luggage and a few other items we'd need right away in California, we had an icebox to carry perishables, plus a little two-burner Coleman stove. We also carried the toaster Mom had used in the dorm in Oklahoma. We had cereal and toast for breakfast in our motel room, sandwiches for lunch on the road, and Mom managed to cook something good on that two-burner Coleman or in the tiny kitchenette of a motel every evening. By making our own meals, we saved enough money so that we could stay in a motel each evening. We didn't have room to carry camping equipment, and Dad thought it was more important to have hot baths and nice beds to sleep in. There were a lot of family-owned motels back in 1952—decent, clean places that didn't cost very much.

I don't remember anything about traveling through the rest of Oklahoma or the Texas panhandle. Dad didn't take any photos of them—and I think he just wanted to make good time through them. Dad loved what he called red-rock desert, but that didn't come until New Mexico. So we just pushed on. Marian and I rode in the back of the station wagon on a couple of mattresses, so we could play with our dolls or read or even sleep as the miles passed.

But Dad had great plans for things to see in Arizona, a state filled with innumerable marvels of God's creation. I don't know how many days it took us to cross that state, but we saw some wonderful sights! Too bad I wasn't old enough to enjoy them as much as I would today, but they did burn an indelible impression on my young mind even then.

Petrified Forest National Park and The Painted Desert

Shortly after crossing the border into Arizona, we came to the beginning of the "badlands" that stretched all the way across eastern Arizona to the Grand Canyon. The Painted Desert was the first stop we made. Some of the Painted Desert has been a part of the Petrified Forest National Park since 1962. The rest is home to the Navajo Nation.

We didn't leave the highway to get further back into the badlands, but we could see the colorful stratified layers in the rock formations right from the highway. We stopped at every scenic overlook. Dad was fascinated by everything he saw.

We took a little winding road marked "Petrified Forest" just down the highway from the overlooks for the Painted Desert. At a couple of places we stopped, Marian and I picked up some small pieces of petrified wood. The little road finally wound around to a Park Ranger station.

A smiling ranger asked us what we thought of the Petrified Forest—and Dad was effusive in his praise. Then the ranger asked if we'd picked up any petrified wood, and being good Christians, we acknowledged that we had. Regretfully, the ranger told us that we couldn't keep the wood—and added that if everyone who visited the area took a piece of wood, there would soon be nothing left.

So we turned over our petrified wood. The ranger smiled and said that there was a gift shop just ahead where we could purchase some polished pieces of petrified wood, which were very pretty.

Of course, Marian and I had been fussing to stop at all of the wonderful-looking gift shops all along Route 66—but we rarely did since both time and money were tight. This time, however, Mom and Dad stopped, and Marian and I rushed in to see if they had any polished petrified wood. The three- or four-inch polished pieces did look much prettier—and they only cost 25 cents—so Dad bought one each. (I imagine the Park Ranger turned in the pieces that we'd picked up, and they were polished for future tourists.)

The Wigwam Motel

After our day's adventures, Dad decided we would stay in Holbrook, Arizona, overnight. As we were looking for a motel, Marian and I immediately saw the fascinating Wigwam Motel, right on Route 66. Dad checked out the price, but said it was not in our budget. We finally ended up staying in a cheap little motel across the highway—but it had a kitchenette where Mom could cook supper. To this day, I've wished that I could have stayed in that motel.

Today, this Wigwam Motel has been authentically restored, even to the original hickory furniture. The only modern features are a window air conditioner and cable TV. There are no telephones or Internet access. By the way, the Pixar film Cars parodied the motel as the "Cozy Cone Motel."

Sunset Crater Volcano National Monument

As we were coming to Flagstaff, Arizona, Dad pointed out on the map that he had marked a side trip up to Sunset Crater on Highway 89. So off we went for our first adventure of the day.

Geologists believe that the volcanic eruption occurred around 1085 A.D., leaving a couple of lava flows like the one Mom, Marian, and I are sitting by. There used to be a hiking trail up to the crater, but tourists were doing so much damage that the National Park Service had to close that trail. A shorter trail at the base remains and skirts the lava flow.

Sunset Crater

Posing on the Lava Flow

Wupatki National Monument

As we were getting ready to go back down Highway 89 to Route 66 near Flagstaff, Dad saw a little sign that said "Wupatki Indian Ruins" pointing in the opposite direction. There was nothing on the map that indicated anything, but Dad decided to "head back into the wilds" to find the ruins.

The paved highway quickly changed to a winding dirt road. Just about the time we were ready to turn around, we saw it—the massive ruins of a pueblo, as red as the sandstone from which it was formed.

What a wonderful afternoon we spent—climbing around the ruins, eating a tailgate lunch, and generally having a great time! Not one other person was anywhere to be seen.

About mid-afternoon, Dad said we ought to be on our way, so we followed a sign that said it would take us back to Route 66. We wound around that narrow dirt trail for a couple of hours. Finally, just as it was beginning to get dark, the little dirt road ended up at a ranger station.

A tall park ranger came running out, and Dad rolled down his window. "Where did you come from?" the ranger demanded. When Dad explained our day to him, the ranger nervously wiped his face. "Do you realize that you could have had a flat tire or gotten hurt, and we never would have known to go and find you! Now, maybe they'll listen to me and take down that sign!"

Wupatki Indian Ruins

Usually, people would check in at the ranger station first before driving back to the ruins. In 1966, the Wupatki ruins finally became a National Monument and access became more highly regulated. But we had free access and a wonderful afternoon's adventure in 1952!

The Grand Canyon

We arrived at the Grand Canyon about mid-afternoon the next day. Dad secured a cabin for us, then off we drove to see what we could before dark.

Dad was absolutely in awe. Mom was in mortal terror that one of us girls would fall off the edge. To allow for unobstructed views, the overlooks only had metal rails to indicate where the edge of the cliff was. I was a lot like Dad and loved to look out—and down—to this huge expanse of rock formations and see the Colorado River gleaming in the distance.

Mom felt a whole lot more comfortable when we headed back to the cabin where she, again, had a kitchenette for cooking supper. It got cold overnight, so Dad built a fire in the big black wood stove—much like the one that had been in our little garage house in East St. Louis.

After breakfast in the morning, we repacked the Green Hornet. In the meadow across the road was a herd of deer, so Marian and I wandered over there. We got really close to one deer, who didn't move off with the rest of them. I quickly pulled some grass and held my hand out to it. Then Dad called sharply and told us to come back. A ranger had just pulled up and told him not to let us get any closer. The deer was pawing at us, and if she had suddenly struck, her sharp hoof could have torn my hand off. Lesson #1 in respecting wildlife!

After stopping at Yavapai Point, the highest elevation in the mountains around Grand Canyon, we began our journey once again.

Hoover Dam

We had one more stop that day—Hoover Dam on Lake Mead. It was overwhelming! I don't think we had the time to take a tour, but we did drive around the dam. We just stood in awe of this majestic dam. I saw a

TV documentary in 2010 about its construction and was awed once more by the audacity of those who could actually build the dam in the middle of nowhere—from the visionaries to the engineers, but most of all, the average workers who, during the depth of the Great Depression, were willing to put their lives on the line to build a dam in order to support their families.

The Power Plant

End of the Trip

We arrived in Baldwin Park, California, on August 27, 1952, grateful that the Lord had brought us safely to a resting place. Although the next prayer letter says that the little garage house waiting for us was filthy when we arrived, it still was good to stop traveling. We'd had a great trip from Oklahoma, but it was time to get down to the hard work of living—and preparing to go out to Africa.

427 North Vineland
Baldwin Park, California
August 28, 1952

Dear Brother and Sister Wright:

Greetings in our Savior's name. We arrived here yesterday morning and praise the Lord for a safe and enjoyable trip. A small house was ready and waiting for us when we arrived, praise His name. We have a wonderful Savior! The details are in the enclosed prayer letter, so will not duplicate the story here even though we want to shout His praises from the house tops.

Since the drinking folk who had occupied the house before us had moved out just the evening before we arrived, the house was still in a pretty filthy condition due to their drunken brawls, and we spent all day yesterday cleaning up the broken beer bottles and disinfecting the place in general. Today we continued the cleanup, and I have prepared the enclosed prayer letter so that the dear folk back home might rejoice with us at the goodness of the Lord.

Our finances are very close at the moment, but we have written to the Mission for additional funds, and praise the Lord, because of the faithful ones at Edgemont, there are funds there credited to our account. We know the Lord will raise up other stewards out here to help take part of the burden off Edgemont.

Pray with us very definitely for the guidance of the Lord as I set out to make the first contacts. We certainly want the Lord to go before and prepare the way — then we know our efforts will be blessed.

In case you are wondering where Baldwin Park is, it is about 15 miles from Los Angeles, but you never know where one city ends and another begins. They are all strung together right on into Los Angeles.

Will write more at length as we get settled. Love to all,

Rejoicing in Him,

Les, Gertie and the girls

"THE DARK CONTINENT

AFRICA

Berean Mission, Inc.
3536 Russell Blvd.
St. Louis, Missouri

Prayer Letter   * * * * *   September 1952

Dear Christian friends:

"We know that all things work together for good to them that love God, to them who are the called according to His purpose" (Romans 8:28).

    We know, because our God is continually demonstrating His faithfulness! Having finished the course in Bible Translation at the Summer Institute of Linguistics, we loaded up our trunk and foot lockers at Norman, Oklahoma and shipped them to Los Angeles, California—will call. Then, early Friday morning, we pointed the nose of our Plymouth Suburban westward and started rolling, not knowing where the Lord would finally bring us to a halt. But the Lord knew, "and He led (us) forth by the right way, that (we) might go to a city of habitation" (Psalm 107:7). And He has given us a place of habitation.

    Just a day or two before leaving Wycliffe, we were having fellowship with a dear Christian couple who live here in California. They said they knew of a small, furnished house which rented very reasonable and that they would write the owner airmail to hold it for us if it should happen to be vacant. There wasn't time to receive a reply before we left Norman, but they gave us the owner's address. When we arrived in California we looked up the owner of this little house at once and found that the Lord had gone before and made the crooked places straight. The little house was vacated the day before we arrived!

    It seems the owner had rented the place to a couple last July. To his chagrin, he found out afterward that the man was not a steady worker but was a very steady drinker. During the six weeks they were in the house, it was just one long, continuous drinking brawl. Needless to say, the owner and his wife were very happy to finally get them out of their house on Tuesday afternoon—and we drove up Wednesday morning. We were traveling right in the Lord's own time because had we arrived before Wednesday, the other folk would have still been in the house, and had we arrived later, the owner would have been gone—he left the same evening we arrived for two week's vacation in the mountains. It is good to know that our times are in the Lord's hands.

    The little place we have rented is on the back of the owner's property and is furnished (after a fashion). It was originally a two-car garage which has been improved for living. The Lord trained us for three and half years (during Bible School days) in the art of living in a garage, and so we thank the Lord for it and believe we can fix it up comfortably. Our new address is: 3427 North Vineland, Baldwin Park, California. We would rejoice to hear from each of you.

    On our way here we spent a day at the Grand Canyon and were enthralled with its beauty. We had not imagined anything quite so grand and majestic. It is simply beyond description. We took several color slides, however, and trust they will turn out good. We also have a few interesting slides taken at Camp Wycliffe this summer, and some day when the Lord brings us back to Edgemont, we can take all of you with us on this trip via the colored slide route.

As we traveled, Gertie did all the cooking on a little gas-burning camp stove. We would find a shady spot off the highway (and they are mighty few and far between in the desert) and set up camp long enough to eat our meals. Gertie dished up some fine meals, too, in spite of being limited to two burners on which to cook. It was quite a saving over eating in restaurants, and the meals were far superior—natch!

Jeanette and Marian were regular little soldiers on the trip, never once complaining. In fact, they were having such a good time watching the world go by as we traveled along that they were rather disappointed when we told them this was the end of the line. We laid some of our suitcases flat in the luggage compartment of the Suburban and then placed two light mattresses on top of them, making a soft bed for the girls. Here they could stretch out and sleep if they chose, or sit up and play with their dolls, or watch out the window and marvel at God's handiwork as we traveled along through the desert or into the mountains.

We have each come to realize to a fuller measure that "the earth is the Lord's, and the fulness thereof; the world, and they that dwell therein." Only an infinite God could have created the infinite varieties of color and shape which spread out before us for miles in majestic contours of beauty at the Grand Canyon and the Painted Desert. Even the barren desert wastelands are made up of countless grains of sand—and yet each grain is numbered of God. The God of creation has become the God of salvation, and now we can say with David, "I am poor and needy, yet the Lord thinketh upon me." To realize that the Creator of heaven and earth "thinketh upon me"! It's good to belong to the Lord, isn't it?

Now that He has brought us to this place, won't you pray with us that the Lord will open an effectual door of service for us. Pray that we may be faithful witnesses of Jesus Christ as we go about on deputation work, and that the Lord will make us a blessing to all with whom we come in contact. Pray for precious souls—that we might be privileged to lead some to the Savior. Pray, too, that we might reach the hearts of Christians and that the Holy Spirit will cause many to "lift up their eyes, and look on the fields; for they are white already to harvest." Pray that the Lord will raise up faithful stewards who will "stay by the stuff" that we might be thrust forth to Africa in His own time.

God bless you, each one, and may the Lord be magnified in your lives and in ours.

In His love,

The Spainhowers

3427 North Vineland
Baldwin Park, California
September 7, 1952

Dear Ones in Christ:

"Bless the Lord, O my soul: and all that is within me, bless his holy name" (Psalm 103).

This is our second Lord's Day in California, and how we do miss you and all the dear folk at Edgemont. We always loved it at Edgemont, but we didn't realize how much we loved you all until we were taken from you. "I thank my God upon every remembrance of you, always in every prayer of mine for you all making request with joy, for your fellowship in the gospel from the first day until now" (Philippians 1:3-5).

As missionary candidates we have not been too graciously received by many of the independent pastors whom we have contacted. We were becoming somewhat discouraged when the Lord took pity on us and led us to two gracious men of God who were willing to extend the right hand of fellowship in spite of the fact that we were missionary candidates. One of the brothers was kind enough to let me speak at prayer meeting last Wednesday night, and it was a real blessing to fellowship with the saints in prayer. The group was very small, and so the pastor had all present to come to the front around the pulpit after I had finished speaking, and we all got on our knees before the Lord and prayed around the circle, children and all. It was so sweet to hear Jeanette and Marian, as well as other small children lead aloud in prayer.

The other brother who has been so nice is Reverend James O. Henry, pastor of Calvary Baptist Church (Ind.), Monrovia, California. We introduced ourselves to him last Friday afternoon at his study, and he was so kind as to ask us to come back to their Sunday School picnic that night in a local park. We enjoyed ourselves very much and met many of their folk. Today we worshipped with them in their morning service, and tonight brother Henry has asked me to bring my trumpet and play for them. He has also given me Sunday night, November 30, to present our missionary challenge and show the colored slides of Africa. This was the first missionary night open in their fall program, and we praise the Lord for this opening. Pray with us that He will open many other doors of service. We desire to spend and be spent for Him.

The Lord has been teaching us some lessons in trusting Him, too. The cost of traveling, sleeping in motels, etc. was more costly than we had anticipated when we left Norman, Oklahoma. By the time we reached California, we were just about broke. At any rate, we were badly bent. But praise the Lord, because of the faithfulness of the dear folk at Edgemont, we had money credited to our account at the Mission, and so we sent home airmail for additional funds. Of course, the Labor Day weekend came at just this time and prolonged the exchange of letters. We finally reached the point where I had one dollar bill in my wallet and a few odd cents in my pocket. But we had all been asking the Lord to bring in our needs, and so Jeanette went to the mail box on this day, confident that our Lord would supply. In the mail was the letter from the Mission, and also a money order from Gertrude's mother. Jeanette came running in with the letters shouting, "I knew the Lord would answer our prayers!"

Our freight which we shipped from Norman, Oklahoma hasn't arrived yet, and so we are still sleeping on two borrowed sheets, and have two light ¾ size blankets which were in the car. You ought to see my three girlies (that includes mamma, too) crawling into bed at night with sweaters, robes and what-have-you on to keep warm. The fellow at the freight office says they don't even bother tracing shipments until they are at least a month on the way. So won't you pray our freight in before we freeze to death in sunny California. Strangely enough, we are having a heat wave—but I assure you, it is in the daytime only.

A couple of the pastors have suggested that we endeavor to reach the small rural churches about 100 or 200 miles north of this area as they never see a missionary. But we are at a loss as to how to go about it. We don't know where the interested churches are, or who pastors them; and to drive around at random would take a week or two weeks with the terrific expense of staying in hotels or motels. After we have exhausted all possible contacts in this metropolitan area, I believe I shall head up that way by myself, and plan on sleeping in the car at night—but then I'll have the expense of eating out. I could take our camping stove along, but I'd only die of ptomaine poisoning because I can't cook. Pray much for us that I might find those prepared hearts to whom the Lord has sent us. Pray, too, that the Lord might open to us a "prophets chamber" if it be His will, because the rent we are paying here ($42.50 a month), though very reasonable for a furnished house, is much more than we can afford to pay. Besides that's the Lord's money and shouldn't have to be spent in rent anyway. The Lord knows, though, and I'm confident He will lead us on. Ebenezer! "Hitherto hath the Lord helped us."

Jeanette has started her accordion lessons at long last. She has been playing her little heart out on the accordion from the hymnal—but it was zeal without knowledge, and she could only do so much. Ruthie Herin, bless her heart, has offered to provide for Jeanette's lessons, and so we enrolled her with Frank Ricchio here in Los Angeles. He is an Italian and very highly recommended to us as an accordion teacher. Best of all, we found out, after talking to him, that he is a Christian and formerly taught at the Pacific Bible College as an extra service. Jeanette is so interested, and we know the Lord can use her accordion in Africa. Perhaps Jeanette will be able to teach Marian when she gets a little older.

Must close now. Remember us to all. We think of you often and meet you daily at the throne of grace.

Yours in His never-failing love,

Les, Gertie and the girls

3427 North Vineland
Baldwin Park, California
September 15, 1952

Dear Brother and Sister Wright:

"Oh give thanks unto the Lord, for He is good: for His mercy endureth for ever" (Psalm 107:1).

We are certainly rejoicing and praising the Lord tonight for He is good! Again and again, He continually manifests His faithfulness towards us in multiplied blessings and answered prayers. His most recent answer to prayer is so marvelous that we must relay the news on to you and the folk at home that you might all rejoice with us, and that together we might praise and magnify the name of the Lord.

By the end of last week we were becoming rather discouraged in our attempts to find churches that would be interested in the work of Berean Mission, and had several pastors to advise us to go into the northern part of California because there were so many missions and missionaries in the Los Angeles area. Feeling that the Lord might be so leading us, we drove to Sacramento last Wednesday and contacted a Reverend Richard Foster, pastor of the Sacramento Bible Church. Brother Foster, it so happens, knows you quite well, Brother Wright; and is also acquainted with Brother Reuben Lindquist and Brother Roger Andrus. It was just like old home week as we fellowshipped together.

I believe the Lord used Reverend Foster as a means of turning us back to the Los Angeles area, as he pointed out how very few independent, fundamental churches there are in all of northern California and suggested that there were a great number of such churches in southern California, although it would take some time to obtain openings inasmuch as their missionary programs were usually full for several months in advance, but to keep making contacts and wait on the Lord. So, we felt that the Lord had answered the question in our mind and we returned to Los Angeles the next day.

Calvary Baptist Church, Monrovia, California – Parsonage is at the end of the church on the left.

The final answer from the Lord came late this evening when Reverend James O. Henry of Calvary Baptist Church in Monrovia, where we have been attending since we arrived in California, dropped by the house to ask if we would consider moving into the church parsonage, rent free and all utilities paid for as long as we are here in California. Would we consider it? Praise the Lord! It was all in His plan for us when He led us out here. And now we are waiting to see what other great things He has in store for us.

This parsonage is a four-room house adjoining the church and has a gas stove and refrigerator. It was the desire of the board of the church that someone live in the house after the pastor moves into the new parsonage, and so Brother Henry suggested that they make it a "prophets chamber" for missionaries and recommended we be permitted to so occupy it. Isn't the Lord good?

We have only one problem now, and that is how to furnish it; but I'm sure that the Lord who provided it will also furnish it sufficiently well to accommodate us.

The folks at Calvary Baptist have been so friendly to us. They remind us so much of the folks at Edgemont in the way they have received us into their fellowship and made us to feel at home. We praise the Lord for them.

"The Lord hath done great things for us, whereof we are glad."

Always rejoicing in Him,

Les, Gertie, and the girls

Keep praying and the Lord will do even greater things!

Marian's Comment: California

For some reason I really don't recall living a short time in the Kellogg's garage house in Baldwin Park, California, after we left Norman, Oklahoma. However, I do remember a little about moving into the former church parsonage offered to us by Calvary Baptist Church in Monrovia.

The inside of the parsonage is rather vague in my mind but what I really remember the most is the wonderful front porch. I played many an hour on that porch entertaining myself with my dolls, reading, or whatever struck my fancy.

Calvary Baptist was a friendly church, and I was especially fond of Pastor and Mrs. James Henry. As I recall, Pastor Henry had a great sense of humor and liked to tease us girls. Mrs. Henry was very gracious, and I absolutely loved her southern accent.

I never knew the struggles Dad and Mom were going through financially as well as their discouragement when pastors were not interested in us presenting our work in their churches. Through the eyes of a younger child, I didn't understand the faith in the Lord it took on the part of our parents for them to leave behind everything they knew, along with the security of our family and church friends, to set out where we didn't know anyone and didn't know what kind of reception we would receive. As far as I was concerned, as long as I had my parents, my sister, and my dolls, I was content and didn't have a care in the world. Little did I know!

The thing I remember most about our first trip to California was my first day of second grade. Jeanette and I actually started a week or so late because of the temporary move to California. I had to ride a different school bus than Jeanette did. This was rather traumatic because I had never ridden a school bus before.

On my first day I was picked up right in front of the parsonage and arrived at school with no problem. After school my teacher took us to the various buses, and I found a seat by the window towards the middle of the bus. As I was looking out the window, I saw us drive right past the parsonage. I didn't get frightened because I just assumed the bus driver knew where I lived and would take me home. So I sat there and didn't say a word.

After I had ridden for what seemed like a very long time, I suddenly realized I was the only kid left on the bus. The bus driver saw me in his rearview mirror, stopped the bus, and walked back to me. Thankfully, this very kind bus driver sat down beside me and asked if I knew where I lived. I didn't, of course, but Mom had written my address on a piece of paper that I had in my lunch box. I showed him the paper. The man graciously drove all the way back to the parsonage where Mom was anxiously waiting for me by the side of the road. As I stepped off the bus, he told Mom and me that he wanted me to sit right behind him every day because he wanted to make sure I got home, and mine would always be the first stop he would make. And that's what I did. For as long as we were in Monrovia, I sat directly behind the bus driver and he happily deposited me at the parsonage each afternoon.

To be truthful, I don't remember another thing about that school year. I don't remember my teacher and I also don't remember any particular friends at school. I just remember that first bus ride and the very kind driver who took good care of me.

Jeanette's 11th birthday celebrated in the parsonage on November 14, 1952

Jeanette's Comment

When Pastor Henry announced on a Sunday morning that furniture was needed for the parsonage—now a missionary house--the response was immediate. Within two or three days, everything a family could use in the house was donated. And best of all? An upright piano was placed in the living room because it would be used for an adult Sunday School room on Sunday mornings. So I had both a piano and my accordion to practice!

Of course, that meant that Mom spent every Saturday making sure the whole house was spotless, even though only the living room (and bathroom) were used. It was a different era, and we had no worry about people being in our house when we weren't there.

Now, Mom was one who got up and got dressed before she awakened anyone else. One month, the leader of the women's group at Calvary Baptist came up with the brilliant idea that they would round up all the women from the group for a "Come As You Are" breakfast meeting. So after the time when kids would be off to school, the two or three women who were duly appointed went around and picked up all the others. Turns out that Mom was the only one fully dressed, her hair in order, etc. The others were all in nightclothes with curlers in their hair—quite in disarray. They kept trying to get Mom to say who had told her in advance about the meeting. I don't think they ever believed that Mom never stayed in her nightclothes but always was the first one up and dressed in the morning.

After our family had to go back to East St. Louis in December, the little parsonage at Calvary Baptist Church was often filled with missionary families home on furlough. The church was very mission-minded, and the Lord blessed them abundantly for their care of His servants.

Marian's Comment: Family Time

There were times when Dad and Mom needed to get away from the pressures and uncertainties of deputation meetings. When Jeanette and I had a day off school, we would frequently drive into the mountains near Los Angeles and enjoy the beauty of God's creation together as a family. Or Dad would take us to deserted places on the beach, so we could search for shells and let the cold water wash over our bare feet. We always looked forward to these times together—just the four us—laughing, singing, giggling, and delighted for the chance to get away for a few hours.

We found this beautiful, cool spring on one of the many excursions Dad took us on in the majestic mountains of California.

We loved going to the beach. Coming from the Midwest with no beaches, it was the most beautiful sight we had ever seen.

Dad was fascinated with the San Diego harbor and the awesome sight of our American navy vessels docked there.

You've probably noticed by now that Dad almost always took the pictures so he is rarely included. Mom wasn't too steady with the camera!

November 2, 1952

Dear Brother and Sister Wright:

Thought it time I got busy and wrote for a change. My! Things are really popping around here. Very little from the missionary aspect but our precious Lord is granting us many opportunities to serve Him.

The young people of the church here in Monrovia are planning a mountain retreat the weekend following Thanksgiving. Les and I have been asked to bring the messages at the conference. We are thrilled with this wonderful opportunity to challenge young hearts to a closer walk with the living Christ.

A flourishing young people's work is carried on here, but they are having the same difficulty we had back home. They've had an influx of worldlings since the church has grown, and the spiritual welfare of the group is much on the heart of the church. The Lord laid on their hearts the idea of this retreat in order to inspire the group to dedication and consecrated living. The conference begins the 28th. Join with us in praying God will give us wisdom as we prepare messages and that His Spirit will have perfect freedom in the hearts of each one.

We surely praise the Lord for the generous gift sent by Mr. and Mrs. Mueller. Please have it placed in our personal account at the mission. We have had to draw heavily upon the mission. Due to being shorthanded at the office, they have been unable to send us an accounting of our funds so we don't know how we stand financially. It really hurts us to have to spend so much just "living" but the Lord knows where all our passage and equipment, etc. is coming from, and I'm so glad to leave it in His mighty hands.

Friday evening we were invited to Suzanne Springer's family's' home for dinner and a pleasant evening of fellowship. Mr. Murchison has asked Les to speak over the Union Rescue Mission Broadcast in the near future. It will be Les' first experience in speaking over the air. He will have 10 or 11 minutes. Did you write out fully, and time the radio messages you gave over "Song in the Night," Brother Wright? Les was wondering what was the best method.

We had a rough time at our last Good News Club. Had about 50 children, which was wonderful, but about seven Junior High boys also came with the sole purpose of busting the meeting wide open. With the obvious aid of Satan, they succeeded. Les dealt with them patiently but to no avail. He finally had to toss them out, and there the Lord was definitely with him as several of the boys were huge and made about two of him. We attempted to go on with the meeting for the sake of the younger ones, but the trouble makers got pretty tough—tearing the screens, screaming, etc. Les left the meeting with me and went outside to deal with them. Jeanette and our high school helper, Pat, went into the back room to pray and I attempted to tell the story. But they broke a couple of windows, then climbed into the attic and stomped on the ceiling until it broke. I've told a lot of flannelgraph stories but it was the first time I ever literally brought the house down.

They expended their energy on the roof and hightailed it away. Then we could dismiss the little ones without fear of them getting hurt. Les was really in the danger spot outside if the boys had turned on him, but all they used were words and that didn't hurt him.

They tried to break into the back room where Jeanette and Pat were praying, but the Lord didn't permit it. Jeanette said our Pat (who is so much like Ruthie) prayed—and cried—with a big stick in her hands. She was all set to fight a rear guard action.

Of course, we know that when work is being done for the Lord, Satan fights. So we cannot help but rejoice that Satan considers our work so vital for Jesus Christ he feels he must attack it. We definitely expect the victory, and souls saved at our next meeting.

Mom teaching the flannelgraph Bible story. *Dad playing his trumpet for the kids.*

We really rejoice in the way Edgemont Bible Church is growing. Where did you put the 435 you had in Sunday School? We are surely praying for the missionary conference. We have our first meeting to show our slides and represent Berean Mission the same day the conference begins at Edgemont, November 9th. We are trusting the Lord to accomplish great things for us both.

Must close now and write a thank you to the Muellers.

Much love in Christ,

Gertie

P.S. After the radio broadcast, Les is also to bring a short devotional to the staff of the mission. Then in the afternoon preach to the destitute ones who stumble into the mission. It will surely be a full day.

Jeanette's Comment: A Mountain Retreat

It was a tradition at Calvary Baptist Church to take the teens on a retreat at Thanksgiving break—Friday through Sunday morning—at the Forest Homes conference grounds in the San Bernardino Mountains about two hours away from Monrovia. During the Sunday evening service, then, the teens would give testimonies about what happened at the retreat.

Pastor Henry asked Dad if he and Mom would be the speakers for the retreat—and Marian and I could tag along. He gave Dad and Mom the theme for the retreat and asked them to formulate their presentations around that theme. The idea was to let the kids have a lot of fun and just a bit of serious thinking during devotionals scattered throughout the day.

What Mom's letter doesn't say is how she and Dad agonized over those presentations. I remember Dad saying that the Lord just wasn't giving him anything that would fit the theme. What he felt led to speak about was the teens seriously committing their lives to Christ—but that wasn't a fun topic.

At first, Pastor Henry demurred, saying that they didn't want to get too serious, but finally, after sitting with his head buried in his hands, he looked up at Dad and said, "Who am I to fight against God? Say what you need to say."

This was a wonderful excursion! Now, we Spainhowers were quite prepared for a trip up into the snowy mountains—we were used to snow in the winter and had our heavy coats and boots with us. But many of the teens from the church had only seen the snow on the mountains from a distance—they'd never actually been up in it. They got more and more excited the higher the bus drove up into the mountains. At any stop, some of the younger boys would get out and roll in the snow!

I remember that there were huge fireplaces in the cabins and conference rooms. Since Marian and I were underage, we stayed with Mom and Dad in their cabin instead of one of the big dormitory cabins. There must have been some kind of steady heat or else the water pipes in the bathroom would have burst. There was heat in the bathroom complexes for the dorms and for the kitchen areas, but it was supplemented by the fireplaces. I vaguely recall Dad getting up in the middle of the night to add logs to the fire.

On Friday night, the teens were kind of restless while Dad spoke—and he feared that perhaps he may have made a mistake in broaching such a serious topic. Mom gave the devotional on Saturday morning right after breakfast, then the teens had a break time before Dad spoke again about 11:00. Again, they seemed very restless. But they had the whole afternoon to be outside. Board games were set up in the dining area for those who really weren't into getting so cold.

After supper, Dad spoke again—and this time, the teens were quieter. As Dad closed, he gave a salvation invitation, and two teenage boys came forward to receive Christ as their Savior and Lord.

Sunday morning was bright and clear. After breakfast, everyone gathered in the conference room for Dad's last message. That's when he spoke very convincingly about the need for Christian teens to be willing to turn their lives over completely to Christ, to let Him rule and reign in their thoughts and lives, to be willing to do what He wanted them to do. At the invitation, a large number of the kids came forward to dedicate themselves to the Lord.

Sunday evening at church, Pastor Henry asked for testimonies from the teens. One after another jumped up to say what had happened to them at the retreat. Even the two newly saved teens got up to tell people that they'd been saved. Tears streamed down the faces of the parents and others who listened to their teens talking. Pastor Henry let them speak as long as they wanted to. Then instead of preaching a sermon, he called them forward in a dedication service—and asked their parents to come and stand with them.

Now, I know that people often come forward during a time of high emotion—and then forget all about it as they go on with their lives. But there was a core group of those young people who were very serious. All of them went on to Bible College. Several of them went out to the mission field or into pastoral service.

One couple, in particular, stand out in my mind—and I don't remember the boy's name. The girl was Pat, who'd helped in Good News Club. She was one of the sweetest girls I'd ever known. They were seniors in high school and going steady. They went to different Bible colleges but became engaged about midway through their courses of study. The young man was studying to become a pastor; Pat was taking a music course, which meant five years of college.

When we returned to Calvary Baptist Church in Monrovia before our second term on the field, we attended their wedding on Valentine's Day in 1958. They had remained faithful to the Lord and to each other—and had waited five long years before they could marry. Part of their marriage ceremony was to dedicate themselves to full-time service for the Lord—together. It was the most beautiful, spirit-filled wedding I think I'd ever attended.

2502 Peck Road
Monrovia, California
December 5, 1952

Dear Brother and Sister Wright:

"Great is the Lord, and greatly to be praised; and His greatness is unsearchable" (Psalm 145:3).

Gertrude and I want to thank you, and each one of the dear folk at Edgemont, in our Saviour's precious name, for your Thanksgiving offering of $33.60, which was forwarded to us. We know this was your thank offering unto the Lord, and we received it as from Him.

How we praise the Lord for the faithfulness of those at Edgemont! We know you have continually held us up in prayer, else we had become discouraged long before now. And it has been your gifts alone which have sustained us here, because the offerings we have received from our deputation meetings would barely provide food for our table for a week.

Nevertheless, the Lord has been with us and has blessed in other ways: in the salvation of two precious high-school-age young people, and in the consecration of many young lives to do the will of God. Our own hearts and lives have been enlarged and deepened through the experiences of walking by faith, and we have been drawn closer to our blessed Lord and Saviour Jesus Christ.

We are leaving early tomorrow morning for the San Diego area, and wherever the Lord may lead us from there. Whatever meetings the Lord may be pleased to open for us on this trip, for the near future, will probably be our last in California. After much prayer, we have concluded that the Lord has very graciously starved us out and that He wants us elsewhere. We anticipate leaving California by the end of February and continuing our deputation work in the Midwest, with Edgemont as our base of operations.

We covet your continued prayer support as we seek the Lord's guidance and His final "seal of approval" upon our lives as His emissaries to the Belgian Congo.

Yours in His never-failing grace,

Leslie and Gertrude Spainhower

P.S. Your gift arrived just in time to meet the expenses of our deputation trip into Southern California.

Jeanette's comment: Grade School in California

I was in sixth grade when we were in Monrovia, California. Three things stand out in my memory, although I don't even remember the name of the school or my teacher. I don't know if I was supposed to ride a school bus or not, but I rarely did. I really hated all the noise and commotion on the bus.

One thing I noted was how little discipline there was in my classroom—or maybe it was just that my teacher simply couldn't control the class. One day she asked Emil, a boy who sat at the front of the row where my desk was, to pass around the geography books. These were hefty books, well over an inch thick. The books were stacked on top of a bookcase behind my desk. Emil picked up about six of them and literally dropped all of them on my head, crushing my face against the desk, and shouted, "Here! Pass these on up!" The teacher's response was, "Now, Emil, was that a nice thing to do?" She never even checked to see if I was all right.

But then, there was another boy with the nicest smile who sat in the next row, several desks ahead of mine. He hurried back and picked up the books from the floor and distributed them to everyone in my row. I didn't know his name at the time, but we came face to face another time at a classroom spelling bee. The boy and I were the last two standing. "Mosquito," the teacher said. The boy went first—and he misspelled it. I spelled it correctly, so I got whatever the little prize was for that day. But just wait! There will be more about that boy, almost five years later.

The third thing I remember was being in the choir for the Christmas program at the school. In 1952, the Bible story of Christ's birth was not only appropriate but almost a requirement for any Christmas program—even in California. I so wanted to be an angel—they got to wear beautiful costumes and pose around the manger. But, of course, only the teachers' absolute favorites got that position. I was chosen, however, to sing in the choir. I remember that at the last practice I was there, we got to see the dress rehearsal of the play with the people in the tableau. The teachers had threatened the choir with mayhem if we turned around to see the stage during the performance, so they let us turn around to see everything during this rehearsal when we weren't actually singing. I was really excited about the play and knew Dad, Mom, and Marian would enjoy it.

That afternoon we received the call that Grandpa Spainhower was dying, and we needed to hurry back to East St. Louis. My feelings were really mixed! I was so disappointed that I couldn't be in that play—but then, we were going back to Grandma and Grandpa Wilson's. That made all the difference!

Dad with his father, Lloyd E. Spainhower, in 1950

"THE DARK CONTINENT"

AFRICA

Berean Mission, Inc.
3536 Russell Blvd.
St. Louis, Missouri

Prayer Letter 　　　　　　　　　　　* * * * *　　　　　　　　　　　February 1953

Dear Christian friends:

> *"Shall I lift up mine eyes unto the hills? From whence cometh my help? My help cometh from the Lord, which made heaven and earth" (Psalm 121:1-2).*
> *"My soul, wait thou only upon God; for my expectation is from Him" (Psalm 62:5).*

These precious verses from God's Word express in a very real way our feelings and attitude at this critical time in our lives as missionaries. Critical for us because we walk by faith, not by sight, and it is so easy for unbelief and discouragement to lay hold upon one during a time of waiting, but certainly not critical for our God because He knows the end from the beginning, and He will do all His pleasure.

We praise the Lord for bringing us safely home from California in time to be at the bedside of my father during his last hours. Though we miss him, yet we sorrow not as those who have no hope. Dad accepted the Lord Jesus Christ as his Savior about two years ago, and it is comforting to know that he is with His Lord now in glory. Oh, what it means to the soul on the brink of eternity to know that he is safe and secure in Christ, and that life is really just beginning—eternal life! Knowing this, how much greater should be the burden of each one of us for those in the regions beyond who have never yet heard of our wonderful Savior—countless millions who are "without Christ, having no hope, and without God in the world"—countless millions condemned to starvation for want of the Bread of Life.

In the few weeks since our return from California, the question on nearly everyone's lips has been, "When are you leaving for Africa?" We have simply replied, "We hope to leave this summer, the Lord willing." But, you know, the Lord is willing for He has called us, and His command is, "Go ye—!" And we, too, are willing, for we have heard His call and have given our lives. It isn't that we must have more preparation, for we have been instructed in the Word of God at the Midwest Bible and Missionary Institute and have been trained in the science of linguistics by the Wycliffe Bible Translators. The Lord has enabled us and prepared us for the work which He has for us to do. Yes, the Lord is willing for us to go, and we are ready. Then what are we waiting for???

We are simply waiting on the Lord to send us forth! We are waiting for His gracious provision of all our needs. Folk are so often amazed when they discover what it costs to send a family of missionaries to the field. The average Christian does not realize what a tremendous undertaking it is. Jesus said, "The Harvest truly is great, but the labourers are few: pray ye therefore the Lord of the harvest, that he would send forth labourers into His harvest" (Luke 10:2). Friends, it is prayer that moves the mighty hand of God! If you would like to see us on the mission field, "pray ye therefore—that He would send forth."

Before we can leave for the Belgian Congo, we must have approximately $3,500 for passage. This staggering figure does not cover the cost of making the trip in a few short days by airplane;

neither does it entitle us to the luxurious accommodations of an ocean liner; but it is the average cost of traveling on a freighter and includes the cost of transporting our equipment and all of our household goods inland to the station. If we are to take the Plymouth Suburban, which the Lord has so graciously provided, it will cost an additional $600 to transport it to the field. We do thank the Lord for the $50 received for this passage fund from the Stanton Community Church in Stanton, California.

We are thankful, too, for the many items of equipment already supplied by the dear folk of Edgemont Bible Church in East St. Louis, Illinois. However, before we will be ready to go to Africa, we will need about $800 more for equipment, clothing, etc. Remember, we will be gone for a term of five years, and we are endeavoring to take nearly all that we will need for that period of time. Also, there are several large items of equipment necessary for setting up housekeeping in the Congo. For example: a gasoline refrigerator, a wood-burning range, a gasoline-powered washing machine, etc. Or, are you one of those individuals who think that missionaries ought to go native? Do you drink lukewarm, room-temperature water in the heat of the summer, or go entirely without meat and perishables, and throw away all leftovers from meals because you have no means of refrigeration? Do you cook over an open fire in your back yard for lack of a stove? Do you beat your clothes on a rock by the bank of a river because you consider a washing machine a luxury? If you can honestly answer "yes" to the above questions, then you may eliminate about $500 from the amount needed for equipment as you make this a matter for prayer.

Regarding the matter of monthly support in the field, we praise the Lord for the many units already pledged. We are, however, still lacking about 50 units. A unit of support is $2.50 per month for a period of one term (five years) on the field.

We believe the Lord has called us to serve Him in Africa, and we also believe that He is going to meet our needs. Will you pray with us that the Lord will provide and send us forth by this summer, if it is His good pleasure to do so? "Pray ye therefore — that He would send forth." In the meantime, we are proceeding on faith in the construction of packing boxes and crates, making ready for later shipment to the Congo of those items of equipment already on hand, as well as those that may be provided.

During these next few months we will be pursuing an intensive study of French, which is the official language of the colonial government in the Congo. Please pray with us that we may be given grace to quickly grasp the rudiments of the language. How we thank the Lord for Mrs. Adeline Burroughs, a St. Louis public school teacher, who is giving sacrificially of her time to give us this instruction.

Now that you are acquainted with our needs, will you pray with us that the Lord will provide?

Yours in His never-failing grace,

The Spainhowers

Our Goal: "To give light to them that sit in darkness and in the shadow of death."

Jeanette's Comment: Readjustment

What a relief to be back with Grandpa and Grandma Wilson again! Of course, Dad and Mom were immediately involved in taking care of Grandpa Spainhower and were gone much of the time—and then came the funeral. Despite losing Grandpa Spainhower, Christmas was a joyous time for all of us because we were back together again.

Grandpa and Grandma Wilson had cheerfully made arrangements for us to live in the basement once again. The concrete block basement was divided into four sections by use rather than actual walls: Grandpa's workshop (he created beautiful craft items as a hobby), the "furnace room," a large kitchen area that was also strung with clotheslines, and a good-sized "bedroom." A huge coal furnace was the main centerpiece of the basement—and the coal bin was blocked off with a wall and a rough door. There was a gas water heater, too—and not every house had one of those! It was a fairly new-fangled contraption and didn't always run consistently—usually right when we needed hot water the most!

This basement wasn't as deep in the ground as most basements—the windows all around were about half the size of standard windows today and could be opened inward and hooked to the open rafters in the ceiling. There were both storm windows and screens for the basement windows that Grandpa had to take down/put up with each change of the season. In a bad storm, water would sometimes leak around those windows.

Usually, Grandpa Wilson slept downstairs because he worked for the railroad at night and slept during the day—and there was just too much commotion upstairs. To get to the only bathroom in the old house, you had to go through the back bedroom. The front bedroom was next to the living room and separated only by heavy curtains. Grandpa moved to the front bedroom while we were there—and all of us learned to go in and out the back door and be as quiet as possible while Grandpa was sleeping. Fortunately, Grandpa was able to sleep better during the day when we girls were at school. Usually Grandma and Mom fed us lunch down in the eating area of the basement so it would be quieter for Grandpa. (I could only practice my accordion after Grandpa got up.)

We girls had a double bed in the basement back in what was Grandpa's workshop. His tools had been carefully tucked here and there out of the way. But we sort of had to scoot around the table saw to get to bed. Mom and Dad used Grandpa's bed in the "bedroom" area. That room was blocked off from ours by a quilt hanging from the rafters. Dad just set up a table in their bedroom where he could study and write, and they could practice their French.

There was a "summer" kitchen area in the basement with pots, pans, dishes in a cupboard, a table and chairs—and a "jelly closet" under the staircase. Since Grandma was the only one at home in the evening, we ate together. In cold weather, Mom and Grandma cooked upstairs in a very tiny kitchen—especially when they had to hang the laundry in the eating area of the basement. In warm weather, they cooked in the basement where it was cooler—and they could hang the clothes outside. (At that time, Grandma still had a wringer washing machine—and dryers hadn't been invented yet!) It didn't make any difference to Marian and me because we'd lived in such small quarters for years.

Jeanette and friends

But while Mom and Dad—and our supporters—were concerned about our actually getting on the road to Africa, I was feeling overwhelmed in another area: fractions and decimals. Not only had my classroom in Monrovia been in a constant uproar because the teacher was unable to control the students, but we hadn't progressed far enough in math to be doing fractions and decimals like they were at Edgemont School in East St. Louis. Although I was so glad to be back with the friends that I'd gone to school with the five previous years, Dad spent many an hour with me those first few weeks helping me catch up to the rest of my friends. Cranky old Miss Hughes actually commended him for getting me on track with everyone else. Little did I know that I would never again attend school with the rest of my friends because Marian and I would fall behind a year of school during the year we were in France.

"THE DARK CONTINENT"

AFRICA

Berean Mission, Inc.
3536 Russell Blvd.
St. Louis, Missouri

Prayer Letter　　　　　　　　　　* * * * *　　　　　　　　　　April 1953

Dear Ones in Christ:

"Faithful is He that calleth you, who also will do it" (I Thessalonians 5:24).

During the past two months our hearts have been made to realize as never before the truth of this precious verse as we have witnessed the faithfulness of our God, accomplishing His purposes in our lives. He has called us "to give light to them that sit in darkness and in the shadow of death," and we know that He will also do it.

Since writing to you last February, the Lord has undertaken in a mighty way toward sending us forth to the Belgian Congo. He has burdened precious hearts to share in our support in Africa, and we now need only twenty-five more units of monthly support to complete our full quota. Many items of equipment have already been supplied by the Lord's people, including a bicycle apiece for Jeanette and Marian. The Lord is good!

We have been working feverishly for the past few weeks with saw and hammer, making cases and crates for exporting our equipment to Africa. One warm, sunny day last week, I went out into the back yard to make a crate for two double-bed springs—and it was no small package! Shortly after lunch my work was stopped by the voice of a little man informing me that he had come to help me. I looked to see who this volunteer was, and behold a four-year-old apprentice, his arms loaded with miniature tools from his Play-time Carpenters Kit. Well, my little helper and I went to work, and the sawdust flew. But it seems that mothers of little men just don't understand, and so it was that a tired little carpenter's helper was taken home for a nap, protesting every step of the way.

At the present time we have thirteen cases of equipment packed and ready to be banded with strap-iron and stenciled:

LESLIE SPAINHOWER
BEREAN AFRICAN MISSIONARY SOCIETY
SHABUNDA, PAR KINDU
CONGO BELGE, AFRIQUE

We are rejoicing in the fact that, after prayerful consideration, the Board of Berean Mission has set July 1 as a tentative date for our sailing. The Lord placed His seal of approval upon this action by sending in, through His stewards, more than $900 towards our passage fund and remaining equipment. How we praise Him for His faithfulness! Pray with us that the balance of $3,600 still needed to send us to the Congo will soon be supplied. *"Faithful is He that calleth you, who also will do it."*

We want to thank each one of you again, in our Saviour's dear name, for your faithfulness to Him and to us—for the part each of you have had in sending us forth, and most of all for your prayers in our behalf. *"Cease not to cry unto the Lord our God for us."*

In the Saviour's Name,

The Spainhowers

Jeanette's Comment: Of Saws and Shots and Sailing Dates

What a difference two months makes! In February, my parents were really concerned because we still lacked support as well as equipment and passage money. By April, everyone knew that we were actually on our way.

Once that tentative sailing date of July 1 was established, life went into high gear. We had dishes to pack, a treadle sewing machine, all the stuff churches had given us, toys, books—and until it was packed in a crate, it stayed in the basement, which made living space even more crowded. Once a crate was made, packed, stenciled, and banded, it went into Grandma's garage. Now, that garage wasn't very sturdy and actually collapsed after all the crates were taken out of it and shipped. But it certainly was a lifesaver for us while we were packing!

Dad used good lumber to make the crates because they would be turned into storage cabinets in the Congo or the wood used for other purposes. A complete manifest had to be made of everything in a crate, down to the tiniest hair ribbon—and listed as new or used. A crate could be opened by customs officials anywhere along the line, and if anything was amiss, it could be impounded—or even the whole shipment. Dad was extremely careful—and all of our crates arrived safely.

The field director of Berean Mission in the Congo told the home office that, if we preferred, we could buy a kerosene refrigerator and a wood-burning stove from some missionaries returning home on furlough. That's what we did, so we didn't have to ship those heavy pieces out to the Congo.

High on the list of what had to happen before we could leave were all the shots we needed to take. Now, Marian and I didn't find that idea appealing at all. But our being able to get into another country—and even more important, back into the USA—demanded certain inoculations. Our own physician, Dr. Santanello, could give most of them to us, but we had to go way out in St. Louis someplace to a military installation to get the yellow fever shots.

Some of the shots really knocked us out—fevers, nausea, etc. And the tetanus shots—three of them over time—meant that we couldn't even lift the injected arm for a couple of days. Dad kept right on building crates—working the stiffness out of his arms, he said.

In between shots and crate building, Mom and Dad still had to go on deputation meetings here in the Midwest. Once people realized that we were actually about to head overseas, more churches opened their doors to us. If the meetings didn't interfere with school, Marian and I went with them. Otherwise, we just happily stayed with Grandpa and Grandma Wilson.

But then, I became very ill—a high fever, extreme weakness—then spots! They were so close together that you could hardly have put a pin between them! The doctor said that I had chickenpox. But Mom reminded him that both of us girls had come down with chickenpox a couple of years earlier. He decided that we must have had light cases, so it didn't immunize us from getting it again. But I was not allowed in school for a whole month. Now, I studied at home and turned in my papers (after all, the teacher had had chickenpox as a child, so she wouldn't be infected). Marian came down with a light case of it, too, but she was able to return to school in about a week.

For years, we thought it was just a second, more severe round of chickenpox. But a doctor told me as an adult when I mentioned it that, more likely, I had cowpox (the basis of the smallpox inoculation) from an improperly sterilized needle when I received my smallpox vaccination. Marian got a light case because her needle was not as contaminated as mine. In the 1950s, every needle was sterilized and used many times—nothing was disposable. Apparently, someone slipped up at Dr. Santanello's office!

"THE DARK CONTINENT"

AFRICA

Berean Mission, Inc.
3536 Russell Blvd.
St. Louis, Missouri

Prayer Letter   * * * * *   July 1953

Dear Friends in Christ:

"Commit thy way unto the Lord; trust also in Him; and He shall bring it to pass" (Psalm 37:5).

How many times in the past the Lord has fulfilled this verse in our lives. How often we have simply committed, trusted, waited on the Lord — and then, in His own time and in His own way, He has brought it to pass. Great is His faithfulness!

And now, once again, the Lord has brought it to pass. For quite some time we have been asking the Lord where He would have us to study French before proceeding on to the Congo. As you may know, French is the official language of the Belgian Congo, and we must learn to speak it. We are very thankful to Mrs. Adeline Burroughs, a St. Louis Public School teacher, who has so graciously given of her time to teach us French grammar. However, we must have more conversational French before we can take the Colonial Course, offered by the Belgian Government, and which is required of all missionaries to the Belgian Congo.

But where to study French? After much prayer, we wrote one letter of inquiry in hopes of establishing a contact in southern France. We committed the matter to the Lord; trusted; waited — and He brought it to pass. Last week we received a reply to our inquiry from Monsieur A. Lejeune of "Le Phare" (The Lighthouse) in Marseille, France, in which he says, in part, "we can offer you to stay in our Mission Home as long time as you want." How we praise the Lord for this open door, particularly in view of the high cost of living in war-torn Europe.

Application has already been made for our passports, and as soon as arrangements can be made for our visas and passage, we will be on our way. The Lord willing, we anticipate sailing some time in August. We will proceed first to Marseille, France, where we will study French for about ten months. Then, we will drive the length of France and into Belgium, where we will take the Colonial Course during July and August of 1954. If it please the Lord, we will then sail from Belgium about September 1954 for the Belgian Congo and the work the Lord has called us to do.

It has been so long a time since we first heard the Lord's call to Africa, but He has been in all of our moments. And it still seems so long before we will actually reach our tribe, particularly when we realize that every day many of them are perishing — going out into eternity without Christ and without hope — never having heard of Him! How we long to be with our tribe even now; but our times are in the Lord's hands — He knows best. We must again commit; trust; wait — *"and He shall bring it to pass."*

We do praise the Lord for the way He has burdened precious hearts to supply our needs and send us forth. At the present writing we need only five more units of monthly support (or a total of $12.50 per month) to complete our quota. God is able!

Through His children, God has already supplied $2,400 toward our passage and equipment. We thank the Lord for His faithfulness in meeting the need, and we are grateful to each one of you for the part you have had in this respect. We are now in the process of buying and packing the last of our equipment before sailing. In addition to the many items of equipment and clothing which you have already given to us, we spent nearly $500 last week in the purchase of a great variety of goods—everything from bobbie pins, sewing machine belts and needles, iodine (ouch!), to a supply of stationary, drugs, shoes, and more lumber for crating.

Did you ever try to anticipate the size of your children's feet, in graduating sizes, for the next five years? If you were going 1500 miles into the dark interior of densest Africa, where callused soles are the only shoes available, how many pair of shoes would you take for your growing, active children, and what sizes? We have purchased nearly $80 worth of shoes for the whole family, and that is not a five-year supply by any means. It will still be necessary to have shoes mailed to us for the children at a later date.

Did you ever try to estimate how much toothpaste you would use in five years, or the amount of shaving creme, or just how many razor blades would be dulled by your beard in five years' time? Ladies, how many bobbie pins will you use in the next five years, and how many hair barrettes and pony tail bands will mother's little girls need? Do you have enough thread to darn a five-year supply of socks (and just how many socks is that)? How many airmail envelopes will you need to keep in touch with the folk back in the U.S.A., and above all, how many safety plugs will you need for your pressure cooker when it comes to tenderizing monkey meat??????

I'm so glad we can look to the Lord for wisdom in all of the little problems as well as the big ones. His grace is sufficient always, and in all ways. Isn't it good to know that "He careth for you"?

At the present writing, God has supplied just one-half of the amount needed to send us to our tribe in Africa. But that which He has already supplied is sufficient to take us to France and Belgium for a year for the study of French and to take the required Colonial Course. We walk with the Lord one step at a time, and so we feel that by faith we should take this step with Him and proceed to Marseille, France, trusting Him to supply the need in the meanwhile for sending us on to the Congo.

As we prepare to leave Belgium for the Congo a year from now, we will need nearly $1,000 for our passage. At that time we will also ship all of our equipment, which we are now crating, from the United States to Shabunda, Kivu District, Congo Belge, Afrique, at a cost of approximately $1,500. This means that we will need nearly $2,500 to send us on to the Congo about a year from now.

Where is that amount of money coming from? Where did the initial $2,400 come from? *"My God shall supply all your need according to His riches in glory by Christ Jesus"* (Philippians 4:19). Once again we are going to commit; and trust; and wait—"and He shall bring it to pass." Won't you pray with us toward this end, and share with us in the blessing of the Lord as He, in faithfulness, hears and answers prayer.

In His Glorious Service,

The Spainhowers

Jeanette's Comment

When Mom and Dad were shopping and packing, they had no idea that I would grow a little more than six inches in six months to my present height while we were in France—and then never grow a bit taller. I couldn't walk across an open floor without stumbling and falling. The landlady of our apartment building was afraid I had some terrible illness—but I simply had grown so fast that I couldn't coordinate my body.

By the time we arrived in Congo, I could not have worn one thing they had so carefully chosen and packed for me. In fact, I was relegated to wearing anything that halfway fit me from "mission barrels," old clothes that churches shipped out to the mission station that might be used for the Africans. Mom did what she could to make them fit better—but our equipment didn't arrive on the station for several more months, so her treadle sewing machine wasn't there to help. I was so humiliated! I really didn't want to put my face outside the house!

Before we had even left France, Mom had alerted Grandma about my predicament. Grandma Wilson—and other ladies at Edgemont Bible Church—started sewing, and after a few miserable months, a big box arrived with my name on it. Socks, shoes, underclothes, and beautiful skirts and blouses! My poor, bruised self-esteem shot off the charts!

Later, Mom could sew for us on her treadle sewing machine—and Grandma, dear Grandma, would always send out at Christmas a couple of beautiful outfits she'd made.

Part Three

Off to France
1953

"In all thy ways acknowledge him, and he shall direct thy paths."
Proverbs 3:6

New York City, N. Y.
Friday, August 14, 1953

Dear Brother and Sister Wright:

"In all thy ways acknowledge Him, and He shall direct thy paths" (Proverbs 3:6).

Received your two letters yesterday and today, also two from Gertrude's mother. Was so good to hear from you before we sail. Also received letter and package of Berean Mission pamphlets from Ronald Stevens. We handed one of the pamphlets to Mr. Percy of S.I.M. and again greeted him for you and expressed both your appreciation and ours for his kindness.

As I am writing this letter, you are probably rolling on your way toward North Platte, Nebraska, and the Missions Conference. We will be remembering you in prayer as you travel, and also ask the Lord's blessing upon the Conference in every respect. Greet Mr. and Mrs. C. Reuben Lindquist for us. Sorry we could not have seen them before we left. However, we did get to extend our congratulations to Mr. Lindquist via long-distance telephone the night of our farewell at Edgemont.

Had word from Brother Kelly this morning that the VOLTA will not sail today, as scheduled, but will sail tomorrow (Saturday, August 15). Sailing hour is set at 11:00 A.M., but Mr. Kelly said we would actually leave the pier at about 2:00 P.M. in the afternoon.

We also found out that we shall have the pleasure of a Mediterranean Cruise aboard the S.S. VOLTA. It came to our attention while at the pier yesterday that they were loading about thirty to forty unboxed automobiles (all used cars), and that they were being carded for various destinations, such as, Casablanca, Lisbon, Tangiers, Trinidad, and some port in Italy that I cannot recall just now, as well as some for Marseille, France. So Mr. Kelly informed me this morning that Marseille will be the last port, and that we shall have the pleasure of a 19-day cruise, putting in at all these ports before we reach Marseille. I suppose the average traveler would be vexed with the delay, but we are eagerly anticipating setting foot on African soil before we ever reach France, not to mention Portugal, Tunisia, Libya, Italy.

Hoisting the automobiles onto the S. S. Volta and down into the hull.

Since our sailing date will be August 15, that means we will probably not dock in Marseille, France until about September 3. If it is possible for us to get mail out at any of these other ports, we shall do so. But if we are not allowed this privilege, then we will not be able to mail anything until after September 3. According to the newspapers, the strikes have everything tied-up, including the mails, so if we are unable to get word through for quite some time, don't be alarmed. The Lord knows all about it, and He will prepare the way before us! If we are unable to get word out for a while, it will also be impossible to get funds to us from the Mission. We will investigate all means, and resort to cablegram only in case of dire necessity. Only we are confident the Lord will not permit necessity to become dire. From this point of view, I believe that American Express Company Travelers Cheques will be the best medium of exchange. The office in St. Louis merely forwards word to their office in Marseille, and we pick up the actual cheques there. However, will investigate all means with Monsieur Lejeune. The only difficulty will be *how* to let the Mission know if mails are not being handled. Also *how* to get communication in!

Give our best regards to all at Edgemont Bible Church and at the Conference, and may the Lord grant you all a blessed time. Greet Leo and Irene for us. We will be preparing a "Log" of our journeyings (or should I say sailings), although we may be delayed in getting it to you. The Lord bless you.

With love in Christ Jesus,

Les, Gertie, and the girls

S.S. VOLTA
Somewhere in the Atlantic
Saturday, August 22, 1953

Dear Ones in Christ:

"The beloved of the Lord shall dwell in safety by Him" (Deuteronomy 33:12).

Greetings in His Precious Name! He has certainly made us to "dwell in safety" way out here in the Atlantic. This is our seventh day out, and the Lord has given us seven perfectly calm days. It is as though He has stilled the winds and the waves until we are passed. All of the passengers have commented about the calm ocean, saying that it is unusually calm even for the month of August.

We have been averaging between 15 and 16 knots per hour, which isn't bad for a freighter. From 1:00 A.M. Sunday morning, when we left the pier in New York, until noon yesterday (Friday), we have come 1,980 miles across the trackless deep. At the present moment we are probably some 2,300 miles from the United States. That means that we are more than 3,300 miles from Edgemont, and we miss you all very much.

The official word has it that we are to dock at Lisbon, Portugal, next Monday (day after tomorrow), so we are writing this letter in hopes that we will be able to mail it from there. Armed with the "Linguapix" tourist's picture dictionary, and $1.00 worth of "escudos" (Portugese money), we shall invade Lisbon in search of their Post Office, and hope that we will be able to get this epistle off to you. We are hoping, too, that we can obtain some good pictures in the various ports along the way. The first stop will be Lisbon, Portugal; then Casablanca, French Morocco; the Tangiers, Spanish Morocco; through the Straits of Gibraltar to Oran, Algeria; then to Algiers, Algeria. I am not certain as yet whether we are to go on to Tunis, Tunisia, or not; but at any rate the final port will be Marseille, France.

We are writing a daily "Log" of our journey but will not mail it until it is completed at the end of the voyage. We were unable to locate onionskin paper in New York City (in our immediate neighborhood) so have written the Log on this heavier paper. Now that the reams are piling up, it is beginning to dawn on us that it is going to be expensive to send back airmail.

There are six other passengers aboard, making ten of us in all. All of the other passengers, as well as the Captain and two officers who take meals with us, speak French. And they speak French all the time! The only time they will speak English is when they talk to us or to a Mrs. Lee, who is the only other American aboard. So we are becoming acclimated to the French already.

Madame Rongier is giving Jeanette a special French lesson each day, at which time Marian sits in on the lesson to gather what she is able. Gertrude and I are reviewing "notre lecons de grammaire" as fast as we can, as well as picking up a word here and there from the other passengers. We have a great task before us in France in learning the French language, and we certainly covet your prayers in this respect during these months of study. Madame Rongier assures us that we will be speaking French to a certain extent within three months; but it seems so difficult as we view it now. Pray that God will enable us, won't you?

Even the menus on the ship are in French. Consequently, each meal is a big surprise. The other day the menu said we were having "Haricots verts sautee" and it turned out to be string beans. It takes about an hour to an hour and a half to eat a meal the way they serve it in courses. We'll all be five by fives when we waddle off the boat. Will hastily close.

With Christian love,
The Seafarin' Spainhowers

Tunis, North Africa
August 30, 1953

Dear Brother and Sister Wright:

Greetings from North Africa in our Savior's dear Name! Arrived here in Tunis about 7:00 o'clock this evening, but since Jeanette and Marian are always ready for bed about 9:00 o'clock, we are going to wait until tomorrow before going into the city. We will endeavor to mail this letter to you at that time; but one never knows whether one can make oneself understood sufficiently well to exchange money and buy stamps, or not. So far, it has been quite difficult.

At Casablanca, they used Moroccan francs; at Tangiers (an international city) they would accept any currency and short-change you in all of them; in Oran and Algiers, they used Algerian francs and would not accept Moroccan francs. All in all we have had quite a time mailing our letters since the various Post Offices will only sell stamps for the proper franc of the country. It is really quite silly since all of the cities (except Tangiers) are French colonies. Oh well, it has been good experience.

Today is Sunday, and we had our worship service this morning as we cruised along the coast of North Africa. Another young missionary family boarded the S. S. VOLTA at Casablanca, with the Gospel Missionary Union and headed for a year's study of French in Switzerland before returning to Casablanca to do work among the Arabs near that city. The Yoder family joined us for worship, and we all sang hymns while Jeanette played her accordion. We had our devotions from Ephesians 1:1-14, and then a season of prayer. It was so good to know that the Lord was with us here in the middle of the Mediterranean Sea, not only indwelling us by His Holy Spirit, but also in our midst in a special way because we were gathered together in His name—"*For where two or three are gathered together in my name, there am I in the midst of them*" (Matthew 18:20).

The VOLTA will be unloading and reloading cargo all day tomorrow, so we will probably not sail until about 4:00 o'clock in the afternoon or later. Then our next port will be Marseille, France. We should arrive there the morning of September 2; but I understand we will unload part of our cargo at one certain industrial pier (which will take about 5 hours) before moving on to the pier where we will actually debark. So it will probably be late in the afternoon before we are on our way to the mission home. In fact, if we have trouble getting through customs, I think we will just spend the night sleeping on a bale on the pier, and then call Mr. Lejeune the next day. What a job we have trying to make ourselves understood. The Lord grant when we leave France that we will be able to talk French as we make our way into the French-speaking Congo.

We have had quite an enjoyable time sight-seeing in these various ports. We have seen so many Arabs in their native dress by this time that the children are going around the ship all dressed up in their nightrobes, with a veil over their faces, and their dollies slung on their backs. All of the ports we have touched thus far have been very modern—not at all like you would expect in Africa. The buildings are tall, and the cities are spread out all over the waterfront. The cranes and warehouses and other dock facilities are modern and quite extensive. You would think you were in a large American port.

I have really been taking many pictures (colored), and I just hope they turn out good. Haven't been able to use the tape recorder though, because the current aboard the ship is 230-250 volts D.C. I am keeping a daily "Log" of our trip and will mail it from Marseille when the trip is complete.

Love to you all in Christ,

Les, Gertie, Jeanette and Marian

SPAINHOWER'S TRAVELOG
August 8 - September 2, 1953

SATURDAY, August 8

Today marked our departure from family and friends and the beginning of our missionary journeys. The good-byes were not easy, but we were conscious of the fact that we were not going alone, for the Lord is with us whithersoever we go. His command is, "*Go ye!*", but His promise is, "*Lo, I am with you alway, even unto the end of the world.*"

After we had prayer together with Pastor and Mrs. Wright, we said final "good-byes" to them and to Gertrude's mother and father and were on our way. We stopped at Ray Service for gas, and Brother Ray decided to put in a new battery to begin our trip. Soon we were rolling again and left East St. Louis about 8:30 A.M. with the nose of our Plymouth Suburban pointed east toward New York City, our port of embarkation.

It was a beautiful morning for traveling; sunny and cool; but with each passing hour, it became steadily more cloudy and threatening. By afternoon the rains came, and they continued coming for several hours. Consequently, traffic was slowed and we could not make the time we had anticipated. As a result we did not make it to Columbus, Ohio, but stopped at a motel about 40 miles west of Columbus.

August 8 (Jeanette's comment)

The "Green Hornet," as Dad called the Plymouth Suburban, was packed to the gills. The luggage that we would not need until we reached New York was packed in the middle seat of the Suburban. In the back was a layer of luggage that we would use on this part of the trip—including my precious accordion. On top of this luggage were a couple of thin mattresses Grandma had made. That's where Marian and I rode with our dolls, Ruthie and Eileen, a few other books and toys, and a couple of pillows. It was a great way to travel—even if we only saw where we had been instead of where we were going!

It was really hard to leave our grandparents. We'd lived in the basement of their house off and on for a couple of years—between our deputation trips. Their house had always been home base for us.

I know the import now of leaving family and friends for five years—the usual term for missionaries with Berean Mission—but it didn't sink in for Marian and me like it did for the adults. I was just anxious to get on the road. Let the adventure begin!

August 8 (Marian's Comment)

Saying goodbye to Grandma and Grandpa Wilson as we began our journey to New York City on Saturday, August 8, 1953 was very difficult. At the age of eight, I can remember suddenly feeling very sad and wanting to cling to my grandparents as long as I could. I think that morning is when I really realized for the first time that we were going to be gone for a long time. Everyone was crying. Even my dear Grandpa's eyes were red!

On a side note—it is a good thing God doesn't allow us to know what the future holds. As I hugged and kissed my Grandpa goodbye that morning, little did I know that the Lord would take him Home to be with Him while we were in Africa, and I would never see him again on this earth. He will always hold a very special place in my heart. I loved him dearly!

SUNDAY, August 9

Got off to an early start this morning hoping to reach Harrisburg, Pennsylvania, in time to attend church tonight. We started looking for a little church along the way about 10:30 A.M. where we could perhaps slip into a rear pew in our traveling clothes but could find none. Besides it started pouring down rain again, in such torrents that we could not make it from the car to a church door without being drenched. What a miserable day! Highway travel is very hazardous in this kind of weather due to poor visibility and slick roads, but we must press on.

Just a few miles before we reached the Pennsylvania Turnpike, we made a wrong turn because the beating rain afforded such poor visibility. We hadn't traveled very far before realizing our mistake, so we chose a solid-looking bit of shoulder where we could make a U-turn, and started back in the return direction. Almost immediately we heard the sickening "flomp, flomp, flomp" of a flat tire, the very first one since the car was new. As we found out later, we had picked up an old rusty nail when we made our U-turn on the shoulder.

What a time for a flat tire—in the midst of the worst downpour I have ever driven in. And you know where the bumper jack and tire tools were! Yes, right where they have always been since the car was new, underneath the back seat—and the back seat was loaded from the floor up with luggage. And the spare tire, you know where it was don't you?—underneath the balance of our luggage and mattresses where the kiddies ride in the luggage compartment of the Suburban. So-o-o-o, the children and Mama sat in the front seat while Papa unloaded every piece of luggage we had out into the rain (except the guns, camera, and mattresses), in order to get to the bumper jack and tire tools and to the spare tire.

Thirty miserable minutes later, four miserable missionaries (one of them soaked to the hide) made their miserable way through a most miserable downpour toward New York. But the Lord was gracious, for His grace always abounds in the midst of affliction, and we were soon all happy again, singing our way through the gloom of the storm. We turned on the automobile heater, and I dried out in a remarkably short time.

However, we were so slowed down by the rain that we did not get into Harrisburg until about 8:30 P.M.—so we again missed church. We were not only tired; we were simply "washed-out"! We secured a motel, bathed, and had our own family devotions, asking the Lord for better weather as we approached New York.

August 9 (Jeanette's comment)

I don't remember much of this first day's drive — until the flat tire. We couldn't really see out the windows because it was raining so hard. Dad unloaded that middle seat and we girls climbed across from the luggage compartment to the front seat where Mom was holding the gun bag and the camera. The accordion was put in the middle seat as well. The mattresses were light enough to work around to get out the tire — but the tools had been under the middle seat — so Dad got them out first before moving everything in the luggage compartment.

The main thing I remember is Mom telling us to be very quiet — so Marian and I whispered.

When the tire was changed, Dad put the luggage compartment to rights. Mom warned us again to be *very* quiet as we climbed back over the middle seat to the luggage compartment.

Dad repacked the middle seat area, turned the heater up to blazing, and off we went. Marian and I didn't say another word until Mom started singing and motioning for us to join her. Miserable but merry!

MONDAY, August 10

As we awoke this morning, we heard the "mews" of little kittens outside the door of our motel. We opened the door, and in popped two of the cutest little kittens. So Jeanette and Marian had the pleasure of being awakened by two kitties pouncing on them (with just a little encouragement from us). They were simply delighted, and we had great difficulty in getting them dressed and ready to travel. It was two reluctant girlies who bid farewell to two well-petted kitties and continued on to New York.

As we neared New York City, the traffic became terrific: more cars, wider thoroughfares, faster speeds. We crossed from New Jersey into New York's Manhattan Island via the Holland Tunnel. It was quite exciting. First we were flying along the Pulaski Skyway, which is an elevated roadway eight lanes wide; then we dipped down to the street-level toll gates, and as fast as the toll collector could grab fifty cents out of my hand, we were plunged into the Holland Tunnel and under the great Hudson River. Signs at the tunnel entrance warned motorists to keep thirty feet apart and be alert to stop at a moment's notice; however, the cars went through at a rapid clip, almost bumper to bumper, and honking at one another to move faster. A huge oil truck practically pushed us through. We accidentally entered the truck lane instead of the passenger car lane. We didn't mind though; we felt like a row boat being escorted to sea between two battleships.

We emerged out of the Tunnel into a huge "square" of traffic. The New York police keep a cordon of officers posted right at the exit of the tunnel to intercept bewildered tourists as they come shooting out into the bright sunshine wondering where in the world they are, and if not, where they ought to be. Naturally, we were intercepted and guided into a nice, quiet, neutral zone, and assured by a kindly-looking, soft-spoken, past middle-aged policeman that all was well, just be calm, and incidentally, where would we like to go.

Armed with directions right from the policeman's mouth we proceeded this way and that until we became so hemmed in by huge transport trucks on all sides that all we could do was just follow the crowd. We caught a glimpse, through the skyscrapers, every now and then of the elevated roadway we were supposed to be on, but could never figure out how the cars got up there. Besides the trucks had us very comfortably surrounded — we knew no one could hit us!

Finally, Gertie squealed, "There's 74th Street!" We made a screeching turn into a one-way street (we were thankful to be going the right one-way) and drove only one block further, rolling up in front of the Sudan Interior Mission Home at 164 West 74th Street at about 2:30 P.M. Praise the Lord for watching over our "entering in" to New York City. We know He will preserve our "going out" as well, for we have committed all our ways to Him.

At the Sudan Interior Mission Home we were accommodated in two lovely rooms and bath. Most of the afternoon was spent in unpacking the things we would be needing during our few days in New York City, and in walking around the immediate neighborhood to locate restaurants, etc.

August 10 (Jeanette's comment)

I don't remember the kittens nor the rest of the trip to New York. I just remember Mom occasionally turning to us and putting a finger against her lips. After the miserable experience the day before, Marian and I knew that this was a very stressful time—and it's always better to stay quiet then.

Having two rooms at the Sudan Interior Mission Home meant Marian and I could spread out a little more. We really couldn't sit upright on the mattresses in the luggage compartment of the station wagon because of the layer of luggage underneath them.

TUESDAY, August 11

A whole day in New York with nothing to do but see the city! After breakfast we walked to the famous Central Park which was only three blocks from the Mission Home. It was refreshing to walk in the midst of natural vegetation in the very center of Manhattan Island. You could look up at massive skyscrapers in all directions; but here in Central Park everything was green and fresh. Jeanette and Marian enjoyed watching the squirrels scamper about.

From where we stood in Central Park we could see the Empire State Building towering 102 stories above street level, with its new TV tower pointing heavenward an additional 20 stories in height. By unanimous vote the Spainhowers decided to stroll over to the Empire State Building and see it first hand.

We crossed through the Park and came out on famous 5th Avenue and were amazed to note that we had already walked from West 74th Street to East 59th Street. We continued walking down 5th Avenue, looking in all the store windows and ogling at the tall buildings all around us. We had intended to walk until the children became tired and then ride a bus the rest of the way, but we became so interested in the things around about us that we walked all the way to 34th Street and the Empire State Building. Then came the let-down; we all had to sit down and rest a while before going on. We were certainly glad we didn't have to walk up 86 flights of stairs to the Observatory. Instead, we stepped into an elevator and were whisked 1,000 feet heavenward in 60 smooth seconds.

Out of that elevator and into another which took us another 50 feet higher to the 86th floor Observatory. We could have taken a third elevator to the 102nd floor Tower Room, but the waiting line was too long, so we contented ourselves with all that could be seen from the Observatory.

On this particular day, visibility was posted as 25 miles in all directions. We could easily look across the Hudson River into New Jersey; to the south was the skyscrapers of lower Manhattan, and beyond them Brooklyn; to the east, the East River and the Queens; to the north, Central Park and beyond to the Bronx. It was quite a thrill to look out over the area in which some 15,000,000 souls dwell; one out of every 10 persons in the United States. It caused one to reflect on the fact that so few of them know the Lord Jesus Christ as their personal Saviour. How true it is that we need not go to the ends of the earth to find precious souls in need of Christ—there are plenty of them right in America! But they at least have the Word of God at their disposal; the light of the gospel shines round about them; it is only the hardness of their hearts, their unyielding wills that veils their eyes that they cannot see the light. But God has called us to go to those who have not the light; who are bound up in paganism; who are condemned to eternal starvation for want of the Bread of Life; and by His grace may we be enabled to give them His precious, life-giving Word, the Bible.

August 11 (Jeanette's comment)

I don't know if this was the day, but I vividly remember going to the famous Automat for lunch. The Automat was even featured in a few movies of the 30s and 40s. The Automat was a special treat--one of the first vending machine-operated restaurants.

Now in the 21st Century this is no longer a phenomenon—we can buy things from vending machines all the time. But in the 1950s, this was fresh food that was replaced from the onsite kitchen as items were purchased. Of course, Mom and Dad had to restrain our tendency to want everything because it was so much fun putting the coins in the slot to get our food!

I only vaguely recall going up in the Empire State Building—but I do remember running from side to side to see everything. The wall around the observation deck was too high for Marian to look over, so I don't think it made much of an impression on her.

WEDNESDAY, August 12

This morning, after breakfast, we inquired if there was someone at the Mission Home who could give us our final injection of tetanus toxoid. We were informed that one of their registered nurses, Miss Jackson, would be able to give us the shot and one of their doctors could sign the international record. So once again the Spainhowers all lined up for the needle, and soon it was all over except for a sore muscle. In conversation we found out that Miss Jackson was sailing Friday (the same day as we) for Nigeria, West Africa. This will be her first term, too.

Today we delivered the automobile to the pier for loading aboard ship. It was another hair-raising drive, as we had anticipated. Somehow we found our way through the maze of roads in Central Park and proceeded due east across Manhattan and wound up in a parking lot at the dead-end of a street. The attendant was very pleasant about the whole thing. He said this was a rather famous spot—most tourists wind up there at one time or another as they endeavor to get onto the Franklin D. Roosevelt Drive, which is just what we were trying to do. He directed us just one block further north to the proper street, and a few minutes later we were being pushed along the F.D.R. Drive by a mob of fanatic motorists, each trying to get someplace before the other fellow. We gave them all the slip at the foot of Market Street, however, as we eased out of line and turned into Pier No. 29.

Then for the first time we caught sight of the S.S. VOLTA alongside of the pier. It was the first time any of us had ever been close to a large vessel of any kind, and it seemed tremendous to us. We delivered our car to the proper authorities and watched as they took chalk and scribbled data all over our windshield and rear window. We also watched with fear as they were loading other automobiles into the ship. One fellow would get inside to steer while another pushed the car with a tractor of some sort. They would go flying down the pier, make a sharp turn, and stop right on the water's edge. Then four men would place four cables around the wheels of the car, and it would be hoisted about two stories into the air, over the side of the ship, and lowered into the hold. There must be at least fifty automobiles in the hold of the VOLTA. Somewhere down in the midst of them all is our little Plymouth Suburban.

As we left the pier, we walked through the bowery of New York to Broadway, that is, we thought it was Broadway; actually it was *East* Broadway. We let about four buses go by waiting for a Broadway—7th Avenue bus, which never came—naturally, we were on the wrong Broadway. Finally, in desperation we took the next bus that came along. The driver told us where to transfer, and we ended up about ten blocks from the Mission Home, which wasn't bad at all.

After lunch, we visited the Museum of Natural History, which was only five blocks from the Mission Home. We were looking around through the Museum, enjoying ourselves thoroughly and waiting for time for a showing in the Hayden Planetarium, when we noticed that Marian was not feeling too well. Finally she asked to go back to the Mission Home, which was most unusual. We took her temperature when we had her "home" again and found that she had 102 degrees. We figured that it was too much excitement and too much walking, so to bed went Marian for the rest of the day.

August 12 (Marian's comment)

My impression of New York City was that it was crowded and noisy. I wasn't overly thrilled to be there and was even less thrilled when my adventurous parents had us walking and walking and walking to see as much of New York City as we possibly could. My whining expression was "Oh, my aching feet!" This eight year old really wasn't too interested in Dad taking pictures from the Empire State Building. My starting to run a fever wasn't any fun either. I can remember being scared that they wouldn't let me get on the ship with my family because of my fever. Well, at least that cut out more sightseeing! HA!

August 12 (Jeanette's comment)

I think Marian's illness was actually one result of those tetanus shots. They were really rough! The first one (back in Illinois) put everyone but Dad into bed with fevers. Also the injection site became very red and inflamed, and we simply couldn't raise the arm because the muscle hurt so much. Fever or pain aside, Dad worked it all out by building crates to ship our belongings to Congo after that first shot. I think we had to have three of those shots, but Marian was the only one who got sick this last time.

I don't remember anything about seeing the S.S. Volta the first time. But I often watched the crew loading or unloading cargo at other times.

The big dinosaur skeleton in the Museum of Natural History stands out in my memory — but that's about it. We'd done so much walking over the prior two days that I was just as happy to stay quiet at the Mission Home!

THURSDAY, August 13

We remained in our rooms all day today, except when we went out for meals. Marian's temperature was normal this morning, but went up to 101 degrees later in the morning. We called Mr. Kelly regarding the sailing hour of the VOLTA, and he confirmed that it would be 4:00 P.M. Friday, as scheduled. So this evening we spent in re-packing all the toys and things we had unpacked on Monday so that we would be ready to embark Friday. Brother Kelly has kindly offered to pick us up with our truck-load of hand luggage and take us to the pier. Praise the Lord for this Christian business man. He has been most helpful.

FRIDAY, August 14

Received word from Mr. Kelly this morning that there would be a delay in sailing, and that the new hour was fixed at 11:00 A.M. Saturday morning. Not only that, but it is another of those miserable rainy days, and here we sit with our bags packed! Purchased a newspaper at the supper hour, and find that a hurricane is due to pass about 100 miles east of New York City tonight. Had we sailed at 4:00 P.M. as scheduled, each passing hour would carry us closer and closer into the heart of that hurricane. Certainly the Lord is "keeping" (guarding) our "going out." Praise His name!

SATURDAY, August 15

Repacked again — today is the day! After breakfast we started dragging out 15 pieces of hand-luggage down to the lobby. When we leave France, we are going to have another trunk, and about a dozen less pieces of hand luggage. Oh well, live and learn!

You don't telephone for a cab in New York. You just stand out on a corner and hail one down — which I did. He took one look at all of our hand luggage and groaned. He was a decent sort of a chap, though, and soon his bulging cab was honking its way to the pier. Mr. Kelly was unable to accommodate us on Saturday morning due to previous commitments, and so we did not get to meet him personally. The cab driver pulled up to the pier, stopped, opened his door, and the Spainhowers and their 15 pieces of luggage came tumbling out. Next the cabbie's hand was extended toward me (as though to say farewell), but instead he said, "That will be five

dollars, Mack!" After I recovered from that shock, we watched them load all of our gear onto a hydraulic hoist and drive it to a loading spot. I don't know whether there was a subtle insinuation in the use of the hydraulic lift or not.

Then, one of the rough-looking dock hands showed us to the gang-plank. As it was quite steep, he turned and held out his hands to carry Marian. She misunderstood him, and handed him her dolly to carry aboard. He grinned and took the dolly, but he also scooped her up—and she was the first aboard ship. Jeanette, then Gertie, and finally me, made our way up the gang-plank and found ourselves in a new world.

We spent the rest of the day watching the men load automobiles, bales, sacks, wood cases; even about a dozen huge caterpillar tractors bound for Oran; a tremendous wood case containing a self-propelled combine, and a huge road grader both going to Casablanca.

First we heard that we would not sail until 6:00 P.M., then someone said it would be 9:00 P.M. The dockmen were working feverishly trying to get everything loaded, and the sailors aboard ship were battening down the hatches just as soon as that particular hold was filled. It was really most interesting, and we didn't mind the delay at all. Little Marian became too sleepy to "stick it out" though, and so Gertie put her to bed at about 10:00 P.M. Jeanette and Mama and Daddy watched until the last hatch was covered, and they were tying down the big road grader on deck. It was too large to put in the hold. Midnight came, and Saturday was past, and still we were at Pier 19, East River, New York City, N.Y.

August 15 (Jeanette's comment)

Although disappointed at each delay, Marian was well over her fever and everything before we left for the Volta. I was so excited to be actually boarding the ship!

At first, we were a bit concerned because Marian and my cabin was down the hall and around the corner from Mom and Dad's. But I think we had the two best cabins—both on the main level. Mom and Dad's cabin was on the left just as we entered the main floor from the deck. It had two single beds, separated by a small chest, plus a "dressing table" with drawers—that Dad claimed for his typewriter and other office items. There was a washstand next to the dresser. This cabin had two sets of windows—one over the chest and the other over one of the beds. They were actual windows because the deck surrounded the passenger area.

Next to Dad and Mom's cabin was the dining room, then the lounge—or as the ship called it, the Smoking Lounge. The hallway went on out to the deck on the opposite side, but it also turned to the right. The first door on the right was the bathroom for all of the passengers—twelve maximum. And next to the bathroom was Marian and my cabin. At that point, about six steps led down to four additional cabins.

I think Marian and my cabin may have been even larger than Mom and Dad's, although we didn't have the dressing table and only one double window. A chest was between our beds. At the far end of the room was our washstand and some drawers in the wall beside it.

There was room to put the trunk with all the gifts from church in our room. We kept our unpacked suitcases under the bed. My accordion case went at the foot of my bed. Eventually, the steward brought in a chair, so I wouldn't have to sit on the bed to practice.

Considering the miniscule cabins we later had on the passenger liner from Marseille to Mombasa, Kenya, the cabins on the freighter were really terrific!

SUNDAY, August 16

Here it is just past midnight, Sunday morning. Two tug boats have now pulled up alongside the VOLTA; but even they turned off all their lights, and the crewmen are napping. One tug is the DORIS MORAN, and the other is the EUGENE MORAN. Don't know whether it is man and wife, or brother and sister! It is now exactly 1:00 A.M. and little Jeanette is still with us, wide awake. We intend to see "the Lady" (Statue of Liberty) if we have to stay up all night.

But at exactly 1:00 A.M. the VOLTA's steam whistle gave an ear-splitting "hoot," which was answered in turn by DORIS and then EUGENE. The two of them began pushing and tugging around on us, and the first thing you know we had been backed out of the pier and were right beneath the Manhattan Bridge in the middle of East River. DORIS signaling, when finally there was another deafening "hoot" from the VOLTA's steam whistle, and we started to move slowly forward. DORIS and EUGENE both cut away from us at once, and DORIS ran ahead as a pilot.

Everything was inky-black except for the myriad of lights ashore on either side of us. All of the other passengers except one are French and so they had gone to bed. I suppose leaving the United States didn't mean so much to them. However, Mrs. Lee, an American, and the three of us stood on deck watching the lights slip by. Marian, of course, was sound asleep. Even the loud blasts of the whistle had not awakened her.

We passed Ellis Island in the dark and never knew it, but soon we saw the lighted torch of "the Lady." All the rest of the statue was in darkness, however; even the flood lights were turned off. After all, who would be up at 1:30 A.M. Sunday morning to view the Statue of Liberty! Three, yes four, departing Americans, of course! We finally passed through "The Narrows" and into the Lower Bay. The lights ashore could hardly be seen now, and so at 2:00 A.M. three sleepy people made their way to bed, Mrs. Lee having retired about a half hour earlier.

Later Sunday morning, at 7:00 A.M., in fact, we awoke to find ourselves out to sea. We looked out one side of the ship, and there was nothing but water; out the other side of the ship, the same thing; to the bow and to the stern, still only water and lots of it. It is a very calm ocean, for which we praise the Lord, as all of us are just a bit "woozy," but not sick. We each had a seasickness pill before breakfast and slept most of the morning. We each had another seasickness pill before lunch, and slept most of the afternoon. So we are not taking anymore pills unless the weather gets rough, because we would like to stay awake and enjoy the trip.

We had a delicious supper aboard ship Saturday night, and so we went to "la salle a mangé" (eating/dining room) with high expectations for breakfast Sunday morning. We found the usual French bread and butter on the table, and also some jelly, and hot tea. We sampled a bit of everything and waited for the first course, which we felt quite certain would be "oeufs" (eggs, in English). The maître d'hotel (head waiter) looked in on us a couple of times, but no food was forthcoming. Finally, we ate a few more crusts of bread and departed. We found out later that the French just simply do not eat more than bread and jelly for breakfast.

But they certainly make up for the lack of breakfast at their other meals. They bring in course after course of food, and we Spainhowers with our "petit" appetites are simply being stuffed and gorged with most delicious foods. The waiters don't even allow us to serve ourselves—they serve the portions for us, and they are exceedingly generous. We asked one of the French passengers (who also speaks English) to explain to the maître d'hotel that our girls eat very small portions; but to no avail. They still give them more than I can eat. I guess they want them to grow.

Noticed a little map and chart of the Atlantic Ocean on the wall with some pertinent data relative to our course. At noon today, we were 144 miles from New York City. It will be interesting to follow this chart as we make our way across the vast Atlantic.

This evening all of the passengers assembled in the "Smoking Room" to sip their wine and chatter. One of the ship's officers (all dressed in a formal white uniform) is dancing with a Mademoiselle Champagne to the music of a phonograph. So we retired to the children's room and played one of the games given to them by the Junior Young People of Edgemont. Then we had our family devotions, and early to bed. That is, we thought it was early to bed until we were informed that we must set our watches ahead by 40 minutes each night. We lose that much time out of each 24 hours while crossing the Atlantic in an easterly direction.

August 16 (Jeanette's comment)

How excited I was to stay up and watch us depart from New York! It was absolutely fascinating—all the busyness in storing the cargo, the bright lights on the Volta, the busy little tugboats.

Mom ran down the corridors to check on Marian whenever the Volta's whistle blasted—but Marian could sleep through just about anything.

Mrs. Lee, the other American, was crippled and had to use crutches. She also was one of those American tourists—*obnoxious* is the word—who thought the fact that she was an American and could throw dollar bills around, she could do whatever she liked and deserved special treatment. In the post-World War II economy, most European countries had not yet fully recovered in 1953. Having such blatant behavior from some Americans did not endear us to most Europeans. It took a while for them to realize our family was different.

Mrs. Lee smoked like the proverbial smokestack! She was also very irreligious. In later conversations, she was quite incensed to discover I couldn't name all the USA presidents (and neither could she!), but I could recite the books of the Bible, many Scriptures, and play Christian music. She lumped all of that aside as worthless trivia—but she really couldn't say why it was important to be able to recite the names of all the presidents.

I think we were woozy from a lack of sleep that first Sunday. But Dr. Santanello, our doctor, had firmly instructed us to take the seasickness pills before each meal. I was so tired that I'm sure it did double duty on me!

We quickly learned to love the French breakfasts. Actually, more than just crusts of bread and jelly, it was hot croissants or fresh, hot bread with real butter (not margarine!) with wonderful *confitures*—jams and jellies.

When we were in France, Mom would go out every morning to get the hot bread and hurry home for breakfast. The only time in her life that Mom put on some extra pounds was that year in France. I guess it was a good thing she had a few extra pounds because she certainly lost it fast enough in her first bout with malaria when we reached the Congo!

The food on board ship was always fresh and bountiful—but I didn't appreciate it as much as I would today!

One funny experience: I'll never forget the look on the maître d's face the night he proudly fixed "Filet Americaine" right at our table—ground beef, raw egg, diced onion, special herbs and spices. He was ready to serve it with a flourish when Dad said, "It's not cooked!" The maître d' was askance! Did Americans actually cook it? Mom said, "These Americans do" — so he took Mom back to the little galley where she fried four hamburgers to eat on chunks of French bread. The French ate it raw!

August 16 (Marian's comment)

When we saw the S.S. Volta for the first time, I remember thinking that it must be the largest ship in the world. Of course, if I knew then about Royal Caribbean cruise lines like I know now, I probably would have refused to set foot on that freighter!! As it turned out, though, we had a lot of fun on the Volta. Naturally, I slept through our departure from the dock in New York. By 10:00 PM I was quite ready for a good night's sleep. I didn't even awaken at 1:00 AM to the extremely loud blowing of the ship's horn numerous times as we were leaving good ol' USA. Dad, Mom and Jeanette were up watching everything while I slept peacefully.

MONDAY, August 17

This is our second day at sea and there is still nothing but water and more water from horizon to horizon. We sailed another 380 miles from noon Sunday until noon today, so we are now 524 miles from New York City. The ocean is just a little bit rougher today, and we had a slight thunderstorm this afternoon with just a bit of rain. We seem to have our "sea legs" now, but we won't say for sure until we have had some rough weather.

We had our first "abandon ship drill" at 5:00 P.M. this afternoon, and the girls found it quite thrilling. We didn't actually abandon ship, but we did have to get into our life preservers and dash out on deck to the proper station. You should have seen Jeanette and Marian in their "enfant" -size life preservers! We could have put both of them into one preserver, but regulations don't permit it.

While waiting at our stations during boat drill, we saw some small birds flying low over the waters, and everyone was amazed because they said that birds never follow a ship more than one day's distance from land. But the maître d'hotel told us later that birds will follow a ship all the way across the Atlantic, resting on the ship. He said, however, that the birds we saw were a type of swallow that could actually rest upon the waters, and that they would be with us all the way to Europe. Gertie was the first of us to spot a flying fish today, and since then we have seen quite a few of them. Other than these few flying fish which we have seen, you would never know that there was a living thing beneath the waters of the ocean.

August 17 (Jeanette's comment)

What was to become standard on all of our trips occurred for the first time today — everybody saw flying fish, but I saw NOTHING!

Later, driving through East Africa, the rest of the family saw lions or giraffes—but I saw NOTHING.

Marian was a good monkey spotter in Congo—she would often point out monkeys even before the African who traveled with us. But I saw NOTHING.

Unfortunately, the inability to see wildlife from a moving vehicle continues to plague me to this day!!

TUESDAY, August 18

Since noon yesterday we have come another 372 miles, and are now 896 miles out in the Atlantic Ocean. We are certainly impressed by the almost infinite amount of water. We are reminded of Jehovah's questioning of Job, saying, *"Who shut up the sea with doors, when it broke forth, as if it had issued out of the womb? When I made the cloud the garment thereof, and thick darkness a swaddling band for it, and broke up for it my decreed place, and set bars and doors, and said, Hitherto shalt thou come, but no further; and here shall thy proud waves be stayed? Hast thou entered into the springs of the sea? Or hast thou walked in the search of the depth?"* (Job 38:8-11,16) Only the God of creation, who gathered together the waters unto one place that the dry land might appear, can answer such infinite questions.

We are having quite a time with our French-speaking fellow passengers. Madame Rongier is tutoring Jeanette in French, using our grammar book. Marian is listening in on the lessons and learning a few words. Gertrude and I are reviewing "notre lecons de grammaire" (our grammar lessons) like mad, as well as learning a word here and there from "les passagers" (the passengers). Even the menus for our meals are in French. We are having more fun anticipating the dishes before we are served.

This evening we had a "Little Concert" in the "Smoking Room." While the French passengers sat around sipping their wine, Jeanette played hymns on her accordion. We are rather like fish out of water around these people because they are always sipping wine. They asked to have Jeanette play for them, and we thought it would be a good testimony. Jeanette sang "I'm Glad I'm a Christian" for them, and we trust the Lord enabled them to understand sufficient of the words to get the message.

The captain and officers of the ship speak hardly any English, and so we have been able to say little or nothing to them. We had hoped to obtain their permission to take pictures in the engine room, but they do not understand sufficient English to make our request known to them, plus the fact that they are quite aloof. From what we have been able to understand from the other French passengers, they all think that Americans are rather crude and uncultured in general, and perhaps that is one reason why they remain so aloof.

We are not permitted all over the ship's deck—just one deck area in the center of the vessel is set apart for "les passagers." We had also hoped to get some tape recordings aboard ship; but the current is all 230-250 volt D.C., and the recorder will only work on 110 volt, 60 cycle, A.C.

August 18 (Marian's comment)

Eating on board ship was really fun—plus the food was delicious! Jeanette and I were the only children on board ship. One evening at dinner I noticed that the Captain had dropped a black olive on the floor. As the ship would rock back and forth on the waves, the olive would roll from his table to our table and back again. I started smiling at him and laughing quietly. Surprisingly, he did the same. The two of us couldn't talk to one another since he knew very little English and I didn't know any French, but we could share the amusement together. I remember him nodding his head to me. From then on he would smile and nod his head whenever he saw me.

Of course, at times things I thought were very amusing ended up not being particularly funny to my older sister. The French always served a delicious soup before the main course of our dinner. One night they served a broth with several fish eyes literally floating on top of the broth. Jeanette immediately was grossed out and refused to even eat the broth only. Naturally, since I was younger and more mischievous, I would put one fish eye in my mouth at a time, lean over to Jeanette, and crunch it so she could hear it. As luck would have it, she got sick at the very idea of fish eyes, and Mom and Dad failed to see the humor in my antics, so that ended that!

August 18 (Jeanette's comment)

Besides Mrs. Lee, the other American, there were four French passengers that left from New York:

- Mme Campi—an older woman with beautiful white hair. She always wore six starched petticoats under her lovely dresses.
- Mlle Champagne—a lovely, vivacious younger woman who shared a cabin with Mrs. Lee. She had gorgeous formals, and whenever the ship was in port during an evening, she went dancing with the Chief Engineer (who was a gorgeous rogue!).
- M and Mme Rongier—a middle-aged couple. The husband had very little to do with us. Mme Rongier tried to stuff some French grammar down my gullet—a lesson almost every day.

Mrs. Lee and the French passengers all sat at a long table with the captain and other officers. Our family had a table to ourselves. I think they were afraid Marian and I would be problematic—and later told our parents how pleased they were with our behavior.

Every day I spent time practicing my accordion. Although I'd had piano lessons for four years and could read music and knew quite a bit of music theory, I'd only had 10 lessons on the accordion, concentrating on the bass and moving the bellows. I had music books, however, and continued learning on my own.

Along with practicing every day (and having French lessons), I enjoyed the gifts that the Junior Department from our home church had sent for Marian and me. We opened one each day of the trip.

But the French may not have been totally wrong about our being "uncultured." You should have seen the look on Mme Rongier's face when she found Marian and me bathing our dolls in the bidet in the bathroom. We'd never seen a bidet before and thought it was a good place for bathing dolls.

(Marian and I only discovered what a bidet was when we went to see the first Crocodile Dundee movie. People in the theater actually turned around and stared at our hooting with laughter and nearly falling out of our seats! It *was* funny—but not to that extent for everyone else. They probably thought we were drunk!)

We had plenty of room to wander on the deck outside the cabins—and we never went to the top deck unless one of our parents was along. Again, the French were amazed that we behaved ourselves. They'd always heard how undisciplined American children were. They just didn't know our folks!

WEDNESDAY, August 19

This is our fourth day at sea, and according to the chart we are now some 1,260 miles from New York City. Whoever it was that said, "It is a small world after all," must never have sailed the ocean. It is now about 3:00 o'clock Wednesday afternoon, so I would estimate that we are just about in the very center of the Atlantic Ocean between New York and Lisbon, Portugal, our first stop. We are supposed to arrive there next Sunday, I understand.

We have been enjoying very much the "boat messages" written by all of our dear friends at Edgemont and handed to us the night of our farewell service. They have been a source of blessing and comfort out here in the middle of the Atlantic. Jeanette and Marian have been having a picnic with all the toys and games given to them by the Junior Young People. Mama and Papa have been enjoying them, too. So far as Jeanette and Marian are concerned every day is Christmas with one or two more presents to open.

August 19 (Marian's comment)

Before we left home, the young people at Edgemont Bible Church gave Jeanette and me wrapped presents for every day we would be on board the S.S. Volta. What a wonderful thing for them to do! Each morning we chose a gift to open and what fun that was! They gave us games, toys, and even a blow up map of the world where we started marking our ocean journey to France. It meant so much to two little missionary girls in the middle of the ocean with no other children to play with and no place to go. We have never forgotten their thoughtfulness.

August 19 (Jeanette's comment)

By this morning, Josef the steward told Dad and Mom that there was no need to get us girls up so early for breakfast. He would bring breakfast to our cabin about 8:00 — and so we usually had breakfast in bed while Josef was cleaning other cabins. After we'd dressed, we'd go over to Dad and Mom's cabin while Josef cleaned ours. Buy the time we got back, our cabin was spotless — and our dolls were resting peacefully against clean pillowcases. Let's admit it up front: Josef spoiled us outrageously!

THURSDAY, August 20

Our fifth day out, and the ocean is still as calm as a lake. The Lord has certainly undertaken for us in that respect. None of us have been the least bit sea-sick, although at the moment my stomach is very uneasy. It is because I ate four big sardines at noon today, and I think they are swimming around in my stomach right now. We are now 1,622 miles from New York City, or approximately 2,700 miles from Edgemont. (I won't say "home," because from now on "home" is where the Lord places us).

Things are quite damp now. The paper on which I am writing is so damp that it practically "slushes" with each stroke of the keys. Gertie washed out some of our clothing and hung them up in the room to dry, but they just simply don't dry. Gives us just a little idea of what it will be like in the tropics. Noticed one of the young officers and men checking over all of the screen doors and window screens today. We were wondering if some of the Mediterranean ports will be full of insects and flies and mosquitoes. You can't ask any of the crew without the usual reply, "Je ne parle pas angalis." ("I do not speak English.") We are also getting a little idea of how difficult it is going to be in Marseille as we endeavor to learn French. But God is able! And we know that what He has bid us do, He will also enable us to do it.

August 20 (Jeanette's comment)

The extreme dampness was not only affecting clothes-drying, but I'd awaken every morning with such pain in my chest whenever I drew a breath—pleurisy. If it were warm, Mom would have me sit up on the top deck in the sunshine until it baked the pleurisy out of my chest.

FRIDAY, August 21

We have come another 358 miles since noon yesterday, and so we are now 1,980 miles from the United States. The official word has it that we will arrive in port at Lisbon, Portugal next Monday morning (instead of Sunday, as rumored). Nine days to cross the Atlantic isn't bad time at all for a freighter. Our top speed was 16.3 knots per hour from noon Sunday until noon Monday; and our slowest was 15.4 knots from noon yesterday until today. It has been quite cool today. The maître d'hotel said it is because we are leaving the warm Gulf Stream which continues on in a more northerly direction toward the British Isles. At that we are now at latitude 45.5 North, which is on a level with Boston, Massachusetts. We are forming an arc across the Ocean instead of a straight line. We are now dropping down (southward) toward Lisbon, Portugal, which is on a level with Baltimore, Maryland.

We are rather looking forward to walking around some of these strange ports in faraway lands—just so it doesn't cost us! There is such a "rook-the-tourist" attitude that we are almost afraid to venture off the boat as missionaries. Nevertheless, we will have our little camera in hand, and the Spainhowers will invade a half a dozen countries before we get to Marseille. Which reminds me, I sure hope Brother Lejeune is able to find out when we are due to arrive in Marseille and meet us at the pier in order to help us through customs. But that, too, we can commit to the Lord and wait on Him.

Everybody on the ship is endeavoring to teach us French now. Even the maître d'hotel and the steward. Jeanette is having a regular lesson every day from Madame Rongier, and Marian is "sitting in" to absorb as much as possible. Gertie and I are still reviewing our grammar, and straining to use a few words now and then as opportunity presents.

SATURDAY, August 22

This "Log" is becoming rather voluminous, so believe it wise to type on both sides of the paper in order to save on postage. We thought of it at the last moment in New York, and then couldn't find a place to buy the lightweight onionskin paper. So this will have to do.

We have been on the ocean almost a week, and still nothing but water, water, water, everywhere. At noon today we had come 2,337 miles from the U.S.A., and I understand we have approximately 600 miles yet to go before we reach Lisbon. One of the children from Edgemont's Junior Young People gave Jeanette and Marian a large rubber beach ball printed as a globe map of the world. We have been plotting our course across the Atlantic Ocean in ink on this rubber globe so that Jeanette and Marian can see where we are from day to day.

Just as I was writing today's entry, we

heard the blast of our ship's whistle, and rushed out on deck in time to see our sister ship headed for New York with the words "FABRE LINE" in great letters on her side. I dashed back into our cabin for my little Argus C-3 camera and back out again for a picture, but the other ship was so far passed by that time that I'm afraid the name of the "Line" will not be visible. However, we should at least have a picture of a ship in the middle of the ocean.

Gertrude is busy at the present moment doing another family washing in our two lavatories. It's marvelous that size washing she can do in two face basins. The greatest difficulty is getting things dry after they are washed; and also in finding space to hang them. I practically need a chart to get through our cabin now without getting splashed in the face with little wet "unmentionables" hanging here and there.

SUNDAY, August 23

Today is the second Lord's Day we have spent aboard the S. S. VOLTA. Last Sunday, if you will recall, we remained up until 2:00 A.M. (Sunday morning), and consequently we were tired, and a bit woozy, too, as we became acclimated to the rolling of the ship. But today, we are all feeling fine. It is quite cold and windy outside, but we are comfortable and content inside — praising the Lord for His goodness! After all, "*This is the day which the Lord hath made; we will rejoice and be glad in it*" (Psalm 118:24).

We had Sunday School in our cabin this morning. Jeanette played a few hymns and choruses on her accordion and we all sang. We had prayer together, and then Gertrude taught us our Sunday School lesson. We would all like very much to be back in the second pew at Edgemont this morning, but we are so thankful that our infinite Lord is with us here in the Atlantic as well as with you all there at Edgemont.

We are now nearing the Old World. We have about 200 miles more to Lisbon, and I understand we are to dock about 6:00 A.M. tomorrow morning (Monday). At noon today we had come 2,701 miles from America. We saw another ship on the horizon this morning and trained our binoculars on it until it disappeared from view. We are quite satisfied now that Columbus was wrong after all; for the earth really is flat! We know, because the boat we were watching through the binoculars sailed too near the edge of the world and fell off over the horizon. We saw it with our own eyes! The only thing we cannot figure out is what keeps the ocean from flowing over the edge, too! The maître d'hotel told us that visibility with the naked eye is about fifteen miles to the horizon from the ship's deck. That perhaps explains why we have only seen two ships all the way across the Atlantic. One would have to pass within fifteen miles of another ship in order to see it, and the Atlantic is terrifically big.

It is just about tea time — 4:30 P.M., and the Spainhowers are seriously considering having four Coca Colas. We have to give it consideration, you see, because they cost extra, and we don't want to have to pawn Jeanette's accordion in order to get off the boat at Marseille. This is Sunday and if we were back in Edgemont we would have a Coke, and besides we are getting tired of their old tea — so four Cokes it will be. Are you convinced?

August 23 (Jeanette's comment)

We Spainhowers had Cokes all over the world. On board ship, they cost a lot — so we only had them once or twice.

Crossing East Africa on our way to Congo, we found Cokes in tiny stores in remote villages, but only indulged a couple of times.

I don't think we had Cokes much during our first term, except when we'd get to Bukavu—maybe twice a year.

When we got to Congo for the second term, Marian and I lived in the mission school dorm. All of us kids would occasionally walk down to Bomboli, a little native store about a mile from Katanti. Imagine our surprise one day to find two cases of Coke there. Eldon Green and I were the only ones with enough money to buy both cases (because we gave piano and accordion lessons). We sold the individual bottles at cost. (The dorm parents wouldn't allow us to make a profit!) But it was amazing how nice the other kids were to us until the Cokes were gone.

Also during the second term, Dad bought a seltzer bottle and Coke syrup, so we could have a Coke every Sunday afternoon when we were at home on Kamulila.

Cokes were just one of those things that made life a little more like home.

MONDAY, August 24

Land Ho-o-o-o! Land at last! At about 4:30 o'clock this morning we suddenly quit bouncing around in our bunks. Things became so calm so suddenly that it woke us up. The reason? We had our first rough weather late Sunday night and all through the night until we entered the bay at Lisbon. The waters of the bay were just as placid as the lake, and as we entered the bay from the rough ocean it was like getting back on smooth concrete highway after taking a rough detour. The change was so sudden that it awakened us immediately. Gertie and I sat straight up in bed at the same moment, and it was really pleasant not to be rolling about. Praise the Lord, none of us became seasick in spite of the rough sea.

It took us from 4:30 A.M. until about 6:30 A.M. to navigate the channel to the point where we dropped anchor to wait for the Health Officer and Customs Officials. They came alongside in a little launch at exactly 7:00 A.M., and by 9:00 A.M. the VOLTA was snugged against the slip, two of her hatches opened, and they were already unloading a part of her cargo. Additional cargo was to be placed in the hold, and we were scheduled to sail at 5:00 P.M.

So, about 9:00 o'clock, Gertie, Jeanette, Marian, and I made our way down the gangplank and onto our first solid ground in over eight full days. As we walked about on the slip we were still listing with the boat—purely psychological! One of the passengers of the VOLTA was debarking at Lisbon, and several friends had met him with their automobiles, and as he saw us walking toward the central part of Lisbon, they stopped and gave us a ride right to the Post Office. After we were in the Post Office, we found out that we could not purchase stamps with American money, so we set out to find a bank where we could exchange our money for Portuguese "escudos". We exchanged two American dollars for 56 escudos and 60 centavos. The stamps for four airmail letters to the United States was 27 escudos (or 94 cents), and with the balance of our escudos we set out to see the town.

Unfortunately we did not know the names of the famous old landmarks, nor could we speak Portuguese, so all we could do was to walk around and see what we could see. There are the palaces of two former kings, several monasteries, and other points of interest in this old city, also an old Moorish fort that dates back to the Middle Ages; but we did not know how to inquire about them or locate them. In fact, when we took a taxi back to the ship, I just pointed out the way to the driver; tapped him on the shoulder and pointed where to stop; read the charges on his meter, and handed him all of our remaining escudos, which amounted to 6 escudos and 53 centavos (the actual fare was a little more than 4 escudos). Oh yes, we bought some English candy along the way that accounted for the balance of our escudos.

Lisbon, like Rome, is built on seven hills, and as the ship was sailing in the bay we could see the brightly-colored buildings stretched out all along the bay and rising up to the heights of the hills. It was very beautiful in the early morning sunshine. Close behind us as we sailed in the bay came the luxury liner VERA CRUZ. It anchored just behind us, and was very shortly nuzzled into the slip by two adept tug boats. Though it was quite early in the morning, we attempted several pictures of the VERA CRUZ, and also of Lisbon, and we certainly hope that they turn out well.

We were all very fascinated as we walked the narrow streets of Lisbon to see quite a number of peasant women walking along in colorful garb with huge baskets of fish balanced on their heads. There were quite a number of automobiles in the city, but at least half of them were taxis, and everyone rode them freely because the fares for short distances were quite reasonable. Most all of the cars were small; on the order of our American "Austin;" although most of these were English makes. We stopped in one shop to buy a bar of soap, and we asked for it by merely going through the motions of washing our fac-

es. One clerk looked puzzled, but another caught on immediately and set before us three strange makes of soap from which to make our selection. We chose a bar and had her write the amount on it in escudos. We could not understand their spoken numbers, but written they were the same as ours. The bar of soap cost 5$50, which is their way of writing 5 escudos and 50 centavos (which is 18 cents our money. The name of the soap is "Alfazema" — perfumed, too.

We returned to the boat about 3:00 o'clock in the afternoon, completely walked out and worn out. We all flopped and rested for a while, and then Gertie did another family washing in the face basins while the children and I watched the final loading of the ship. At exactly 7:00 P.M. there was a blast of the whistle, and the S. S. VOLTA slipped silently from the pier and out into the bay with two little tugboats just pushin' and pullin' and shovin' around on us. By 8:30 P.M. we were out of the bay and into the Atlantic Ocean again and headed for Casablanca, French Morocco. I understand we are to arrive there sometime tomorrow night (that will be Tuesday night). First, our feet have touched European soil, and now within 24 hours or so, we shall be on African soil, the Lord willing.

August 24 (Jeanette's comment)

It was exciting to see land again after so many days with only water to see. Remember — I never saw a flying fish!!

Marian and I didn't get up until later, of course, but off we headed to explore—on foot, of course!

The one thing I remember seeing in shop windows was intricate gold filigree items—everything from small items like jewelry to a large, square-masted ship. We never even bothered checking the prices. No missionary could—or should—afford gold filigree.

After we returned to the Volta, Marian and I noticed that our suitcases had been moved around under our beds. When we told Dad about it, he came to investigate. Not only were our suitcases under the bed but several small crates as well. We closed the door, and Dad pulled them out.

There were two or three crates pushed to the back at the head of each bed. Under my bed were two cases of Portuguese port wine—called Tears of Jesus. Marian had crates with various parts and pieces of a small wringer washing machine.

Apparently, the Health and Customs officials didn't thoroughly search the cabins of passengers—especially those with dollies on the bed. A room filled with little girl toys wouldn't be so suspect. So the captain (as Dad found out later) had his purchases stowed under our beds where nothing but a cursory glance was given to our cabin.

Dad just put everything back in place, fronted by our suitcases, and told us not to worry—just leave everything as it was. But our cabin always passed inspection on each of our stops until we reached Marseille. By then, the crates had magically disappeared.

TUESDAY, August 25

Neglected to mention in yesterday's entry that the total mileage from New York to Lisbon was 2,955 miles, and we completed the trip in 191 ½ hours (deducting 6 hours for the difference in time). That would make us about 4,000 miles from Edgemont, or about 1/6 of the way around the world.

We left Lisbon at 7:00 P.M. yesterday, and arrived in the harbor at Casablanca, French Morocco, North Africa at 5:00 o'clock this evening. It was about half an hour after we dropped anchor before the Health Officer and Pilot came aboard, and after much delay and going and coming of small motor launches, we finally were shoved against our wharf at about 8:30 tonight. It was 320 miles from Lisbon to Casablanca.

We were issued our police permits to go ashore about 9:00 P.M., but it was too late to take the children at that hour, so we shall just wait until tomorrow to see the city. And, believe me, it is a city. Like other port cities, it is spread out along the shore, but Casablanca also has great depth. There are many very tall buildings, too. Many of them looked to be between 20 and 30 stories high. There seem to be many factories as well, and large oil storage tanks. What I am describing is only that which can be seen from the ship—tomorrow we will actually see the city.

The dock facilities at Casablanca are the most modern that I have seen in our limited journeys. Huge concrete docks covered with rails for railroad cars, and dozens of huge overhead cranes that roll back and forth along the dock on special rails. There are any number of freighters in port now, two of which are being loaded at the present moment (and it is now 11:45 P.M.). We have been watching from our top deck. There is one large passenger liner in port now; and while we were anchored in the harbor, we saw another liner leaving Casablanca for Dakar, West Africa. Our captain fairly blew the whistle off the VOLTA in saluting this large passenger liner, and we wondered why because he had never saluted any other. We found out that this particular liner was owned and operated by FABRE LINES, which is the operator of the VOLTA.

WEDNESDAY, August 26

We were up about 7:00 o'clock this morning, had breakfast, and by 9:30 A.M. were on our way into Casablanca on foot. Our first objective was to find a money exchanger where we could obtain a few Moroccan Francs, and then to the Post Office to mail two airmail letters. We walked and walked and walked, and finally after several attempts to question people found a fellow who understood what the airmail envelope was and pointed us this way and that—and sure enough, there was the Post Office. They would not accept our American money (we didn't think they would, but tried anyway), so what to do. We walked and walked some more, but no money exchangers, so we returned to the ship. Of course we were enjoying the sights of the city all of the time, but we were not getting our letters mailed.

After lunch, Madame Campi offered us a ride into the city, as an acquaintance of hers was calling for her at the pier with his automobile. In the meantime, we had obtained some Moroccan Francs from the First Mate of the ship, and so we asked to be taken to the Post Office. Madame Campi had about five post cards to mail, so we offered to mail them for her. We entered the Post Office, walked up to one of the girls behind a counter, and spread out our mail before her. She started tearing first one kind of stamp and then another, and eventually shoved a stack of odd-looking philatelic specimens toward us. I handed her a 1,000 franc note (worth about $2.75), and she shoved back a handful of smaller franc notes. Then I made motion to her as to which kind of stamps went on what letters, and she was kind enough to lay them all out for us in proper amounts on each piece of mail.

With the rest of our francs we set out to find Jeanette and Marian each a native character doll. We wandered up and down the streets, but could find no curios of any nature. We came to a huge department store on the edge of one of the main "squares" and so we roamed around through it and found it just the same as Famous-Barr in St. Louis. You must remember, of course, that Casablanca is a large, modern metropolis with skyscrapers and all.

Finally we found our way into the area of Arab shops that we had been seeking, but their character dolls were too expensive. However, we found some small ornamented leather purses for 200 francs apiece (about 50 cents each), which we purchased for the girls. I neglected to mention that they were so tired from the walk of the morning, that they remained on ship while we went out in the afternoon.

When we returned to the VOLTA, we were amazed to see the ship sitting about eight to ten feet higher than when we left. The gangplank was at almost a 45 degree angle, and it was not the type with individual steps, but more of a flat walkway. There were only two ways to get aboard ship; one was the gangplank, and the other was to hang on to the big hook and be hoisted aboard. We thought it more becoming of a gentleman, and especially of a gentlewoman, to crawl up the gangplank than to be hanging in mid-air on a hook. And that is just about what we had to do, too—crawl up the thing on our hands and knees (almost).

We were very pleased to learn that another missionary family had boarded the VOLTA at Casablanca just before our return. Reverend Maynard Yoder and his wife and 16-month-old daughter will be fellow-passengers until we reach Marseille. In fact, they are to spend the night at "Le Phare" with us. They are a very lovely young couple going out as missionaries to the Arabs in the region of Casablanca. They are on their way to Switzerland to study French and had stopped off at Casablanca on the way in order to visit the other missionaries in the field first. We shall be quite thankful for their fellowship during the rest of the trip.

At 8:00 P.M. we again went through the process of being "tugged" out into the open harbor, and by 9:00 o'clock were well out to sea again. Another day, another port, another country, another continent!

THURSDAY, August 27

We set our alarm for 6:00 A.M. this morning, knowing that we were to arrive in Tangiers early. When we arose and looked out the window, we were already within sight of land, and could barely get dressed and on deck in time to see us dock at 6:30 A.M. We had come only 164 miles from Casablanca in about ten and one half hours.

Tangiers is an international city, but is situated in Spanish Moroccan territory. On one side of the VOLTA is North Africa, and just a few miles away we can dimly see the coast of Spain from the other side of the ship. It is very fascinating to know that you are looking from one continent to another; from Africa to Europe in one easy glance! We are now very close to the Straits of Gibraltar, and should be there within an hour or two after leaving Tangiers.

We went with Madame Campi and Mrs. Lee in a taxi tour of the city this morning, and saw many wonderful sights, foremost of which was the Palace of the Sultan of the 8th or 9th century. It has been turned into a museum, housing many exhibits of 8th or 9th century guns, jewelry, rugs, etc.

We walked through the Casbah, Arab section of the city, and looked in many of their tiny shops, and one-room homes. The only thing I did not like was their manner of doing business—grabbing you by the elbow and pleading, haggling, scheming to get you to buy something, and then pronouncing a curse on you if you pass by without making a purchase.

We came to one place where there was a "snake charmer," and so we must have our first experience in seeing this famous performance. The old Arab pulled two snakes, about three feet long each, out of a heavy canvass bag and proceeded to handle them most adroitly. He wrapped them about his neck, and let them bite him on the wrist, and even on the tongue. It was really quite interesting. After he had put the snakes back into their little bag, he showed me the bites on his wrist bleeding. Then he took a handful of dried seaweed (or something similar) and wiped some of his blood off on a part of it, which he then folded into the center of the handful of weeds. He made a few "magic" gestures and then put the stuff to his mouth and blew on it. Soon we could see a few wisps of smoke, then more and more, until finally the handful of weeds were on fire. It was a neat trick, and together with the snake act, was well worth the 100 francs (29 cents) Madame gave him.

Back to the VOLTA again for lunch and a rest and make ready to sail again. I shall never cease to

marvel at the big cranes hoisting tons of material out of the ship's hold—everything from flour in sacks to automobiles, bales, crates, boxes, barrels, drums, International Harvester tractors, a self-propelled combine, and a giant road grader. I mentioned earlier that we must have at least 40-50 automobiles on board. The official count was 98, including our Plymouth Suburban.

At 4:00 P.M. we sailed out of Tangiers, very fascinated by the fact that we could see Europe (the coast of Spain) on the one side and North Africa on the other. By 5:00 P.M. the Rock of Gibraltar was in view, and about 5:45 P.M. we were within one half mile of the Rock. The Chief Steward had told us we would stay close to the coast of Africa, and he doubted that I could get a picture of Gibraltar because of the haze. However, the Captain headed the VOLTA right for Gibraltar and passed the Rock at the closest legal limits. I took several pictures in hopes that some would be good and remarked to the Chief Steward that we would have to thank the Captain for giving us this wonderful treat. Then it dawned on me why the Captain was so accommodating! He had just purchased a new camera in New York on this trip, as he was showing it to me a few evenings before. When I see him at supper tonight, I shall thank him for his kindness and then ask him if he had obtained some good pictures, too.

We are now on our way to Oran, Algeria, which is some 260 miles from Tangiers. The Lord willing, we should be there about 9:00 A.M. tomorrow. Until then, goodnight, and the Lord bless you.

FRIDAY, August 28

Arrived in Oran, Algeria at 8:30 A.M. this morning. It is uncanny the way they are able to bring us into port right at breakfast time, and depart right at supper time. One feels a little conspicuous craning his neck around to see out the three small front windows; and then when you think you do see something exciting, it is most embarrassing to leave the table to go on deck to view it. Nevertheless, we are getting the most out of our trip and not missing anything, at the expense of a little embarrassment.

In order to get into the city area of Oran this morning, we had to walk up a long drive cut in the side of a hill and about ten blocks long. By the time we made it up the incline and into the city both our time and energy were about spent (not to mention the fact that we had no money to spend), so we turned around and came back to the ship for lunch. Oran is just another big industrial harbor city, and the only thing of real interest is the old Santa Cruz fortress on the heights overlooking the harbor. It can only be reached by a road that winds its way up and around the hill to the fortress at the top, and it is much too far to walk. We feel that we should not be spending the Lord's money for taxi fares, so we contented ourselves with taking a picture of the old landmark.

We unloaded the huge road grader here at Oran, as well as much other cargo. At each port, we unload what seems to be a tremendous amount of lading, but we take on about as much again, so I don't think we are really making any progress. We sail this evening for Algiers, and we have been told that it is a city well worth seeing.

SATURDAY, August 29

We knew that we were scheduled to arrive in Algiers early this morning, but the Spainhowers are tired, so we all slept until 7:00 A.M. We hurried and dressed and got out on deck in time to see the VOLTA slowly ease into the pier at Algiers. We then had breakfast and waited for permission to leave the ship.

About 8:30 A.M., together with the Yoders (the other missionary family aboard), we set out for the city which is quite a long ways from the docks. Since Brother Yoder was carrying his 16 month old daughter, we felt that we had better take a taxi into town. He had two 100-franc notes in Algerian francs which we estimated would be enough for the taxi fare. We both wanted to go to a bank in Algiers in order to have a little money converted to purchase soap and some candy; and I wanted to obtain some French francs of small denomination to take care of taxi fares and small tips in Marseille when we dock Wednesday.

So Brother Yoder (who speaks about as much French as we do) told the driver, "La Banque, s'il vous plait." ("The bank, please"). The driver seemed to understand where we wanted to go, but was protesting about something. At any rate, he started driving toward town, and before long pulled up in front of "La Grande Banque." He pointed to the bars across the doors and said in thick English, "Iss clowzed." Then he started off down another street, and soon stopped in front of the Cook's Travel Agency, and pointed across the street to the Post Office (as I was holding airmail letters in my hand). The meter on the taxi read exactly 200 francs, which was just the amount of Algerian francs that Brother Yoder had.

We went into the Cook's Travel Agency to have our money exchanged, but they informed us they were not a bank and could not do it, and that it was so unfortunate that all the banks are closed on Saturday. We tried to buy several small items, such as post cards and chewing gum in order to cash a 1,000 franc Moroccan note that Brother Yoder had, but to no avail; they simply would have nothing to do with the Moroccan francs. Finally, we went into the Post Office, and I handed our four letters across the counter (fearfully, for I had no Algerian money), and let the fellow weigh them and give us the proper amount of stamps, which amount to 320 francs (or about 85 cents). Then I handed him an American dollar and Brother Yoder's 1,000 Moroccan franc note, but "no sale." Just as I was about to give the clerk back his stamps, a man standing next to me said something to the clerk in French, and the clerk told us in very broken English that the man wanted to know how much the stamps were and had offered to pay for them in the proper money and take my American dollar. It meant that he would be about 80 francs (15-18 cents) to the good, and it was certainly worth that much for the accommodation and to get our letters mailed. So we accepted his offer and thanked him kindly.

Then we were faced with the problem of getting back to the VOLTA. We still had no Algerian money—only my American dollars and some large denomination French francs, and Brother Yoder's 1,000 Moroccan francs. There we were with enough money to buy a taxi but couldn't ride in one. So we started out walking to the ship. Brother Yoder sighted another taxi and hailed him down. He showed the driver his 1,000 Moroccan franc note and asked in pigeon French if he would accept it as fare. He agreed and back to the VOLTA we sped. We got out of the taxi at the ship's side, and Brother Yoder handed the driver the 1,000 franc note—he shrugged his shoulders, and said thickly, "No change." The fare was only 140 francs, but he was hoping to get the whole 1,000 francs, knowing that we had no change either. So I ran up the gangplank and borrowed 200 francs real quick like from the steward, dashed back down and paid the disgusted driver, and we were safe in the confines of the VOLTA once again.

In every North African city we have been in so far, the natives will do anything (including slitting your throat) for a few francs. They grab you by the arm and try to force you to buy their wares; they try to cheat you at every turn; and go off in a frenzy, talking to themselves, if you are able to hang onto your pocket book.

We are scheduled to sail at 4:30 o'clock this afternoon for Tunis. Tunis is about 380 miles further east along the North African coast, and we should be there about 5:00 or 6:00 P.M. tomorrow (Sunday) evening. Tunis will be our last port before Marseille, and we are glad. We are getting anxious to be there and settle down to business. This cruising around the Mediterranean is all right for folk of means, but it is not for the missionary who has no money to spend. We are very thankful, however, for what we have seen, and most of all, for the privilege of setting foot on African soil a year before we had expected to. We are so anxious to be about our Father's business.

SUNDAY, August 30

Today is a beautiful, sunny day as we cruise along the coast of North Africa. The shore is about two miles away and perfectly visible. The coast is rugged and hilly and has a deep bluish and purple coast—very beautiful. The Mediterranean is quite blue, too, and Madame Rongier said that in France they refer to it as "The Blue Sea."

We had our worship service this morning with the Yoder family and really enjoyed the fellowship of other Christians at worship for the first time in over three weeks. Jeanette played her accordion while we all sang, and we had our meditation in Ephesians 1:1-14 followed by a season of prayer. Again it was good to know that the Lord was with us, not only as indwelling us by His Holy Spirit, but also in our midst in a special way because we were gathered together in His name—*"For where two or three are gathered together in my name, there am I in the midst of them"* (Matthew 18:20).

We arrived in the bay at Tunis about 5:30 this evening but had to drop anchor and wait quite a while for a pilot to take us on into the harbor and pier. They were short handed since it was Sunday, and it was about 7:00 P.M. before we reached the pier. Tomorrow we shall once again try to make it to a bank for the purpose of changing a larger denomination note into smaller denomination French francs in order that we will have small change handy when we reach Marseille.

MONDAY, August 31

We have learned that the banks and stores (all businesses for that matter) in these North African cities do not open until 10:00 o'clock in the morning, and many of the shops close from 12:00 noon until 3:00 o'clock in the afternoon; then they open again from 3:00 until 5:00 P.M. Actually they only have a four-hour working day. The same is true of the dock hands that load and unload the ships. They sit in the shade of the warehouse buildings from 12:00 noon until 3:00 P.M. when they commence work again.

Knowing that we could not get into the bank or Post Office until 10:00 A.M., we waited on ship this morning until about 9:30 before going into Tunis. Thank the Lord, it was only a short distance from the pier into the heart of the city, and it was not long before we had located a bank. I had a little note all typed up which read as follows: "Donnez-moi, s'il vous plait, des billets en francs francaise" and then a listing of the denominations desired. The note reads in English, "Give me, if you please, some notes in French francs", and then the listing of the desired denominations. I handed the note to the bank teller with a 10,000 franc note (worth about $25.00) as I desired to have it changed into smaller denominations. The teller read my note and then said in perfect English, "Do you speak English?" I was almost disappointed because I thought it was clever to have this note made out in advance and to get along in French. However, it was a pleasure to talk to someone in English, and he saw to it that I had plenty of small notes as I desired. Then we had a small amount exchanged into Tunisian francs in order to mail some airmail letters and get "des bonbons" (some candy) for us kids. Brother Yoder desired to exchange his 1,000 Moroccan francs note for French francs but found that he would have to go to a different bank. He had no end of trouble making the exchange but was finally able to do so, at a cost of 40 francs in fee.

Next we found the Post Office and, for once, did not have a bit of trouble in purchasing stamps because we had the proper Tunisian francs with which to pay for them. We then walked around until we found a clean-looking candy and pastry shop where we spent the rest of our Tunisian francs for "des bonbons," and walked back to the VOLTA. All of these North African port cities are about the same; the only amazing thing about them is the tall buildings and how modern they

are. Otherwise they are just large and very filthy cities. Of course, the old, native Arab sections are antiquated, but they are so tourist conscious that you take both your life and your pocketbook in your hands to walk through them.

In the late afternoon, we began the tremendous task of packing again. Gertrude began packing dresses that will not be needed for the next two days, and I started in on the children's toys. The Junior Young People at Edgemont gave Jeanette and Marian so many presents to open on the board that it is all I can do to pack them in a large fiber suitcase. The children have enjoyed all of the games and toys so very much, for the trip has been quite long—two and one half weeks.

We departed Tunis at 3:30 P.M. and sailed along the African coast in a westerly direction (retracing our former course) all the rest of the evening. Just before supper I could still see the African coast, and even after we had eaten and put the children to bed we saw a lighthouse blinking on the African side.

August 25-31 (Jeanette's comment)

There wasn't too much that distinguished one North African port from another—lots of noisy people I couldn't understand, the cranking and grinding of port machinery, dust, heat—and Arab women with their faces veiled.

Since we were always given to playing dress-up, Marian and I came up with our own version—thanks to headscarves, handkerchiefs, and our bathrobes. Mme Rongier warned Mom and Dad, however, not to let us play in sight of the crew members or dockhands, who might take offense.

I vaguely recall seeing the Palace of the Sultan, as well as the snake charmer, but that is about all that really stands out about those North African ports.

Seeing the Rock of Gibraltar, however, was fascinating to me because I'd seen its facsimile on Prudential Insurance papers that both my parents and grandparents had. And I was seeing it in real life!

I do not remember the Yoder family at all, which is kind of surprising since we were together so much after they came on board. All of us Americans (except for Mrs. Lee) sat at one table.

By the way, the crates under our beds disappeared while we were ashore in Tunis. That was the last stop where Health and Customs officials would come on board. What they did to smuggle them ashore when we reached Marseilles, I have no idea.

Jeanette's additional comment

This letter gives a better description of what I actually thought about the North African ports! (And it also shows a propensity for dramatic writing.)

August 28, 1953

Dear Junior Young People,

How are all of you? I hope you are as well and as happy as we are. We have stopped at many ports along the way, so I think I'll tell you about our experiences. We've even been to Africa. We thought we would go right to Marseille, but we were in Africa before we were in France. I guess we'd better start with our experiences.

We were supposed to leave New York at about 9:00 P.M. in the evening. Really we started at 1:00 A.M. Sunday morning. Marian had gone to bed about 11:00, but Mommy, Daddy, and I stayed up. Finally we went to bed for a little while. Soon we heard a blast of our ship's horn and we were on our way. Up we jumped out of bed and out to the deck. Mrs. Lee, Mommy, Daddy, and I were up until 2:30 Sunday morning. Then we all went to bed. Now that we're on the ocean there's nothing to tell about except seeing water, water, water, as far as you can see. Now for the first port.

Lisbon, Portugal

"Come on, Daddy," I said. "We have our permits to go ashore so let's get going." We saw women with baskets of fish on their heads running to and fro without holding onto them. We went into a post office to get some stamps for our letters. We didn't know where to change our money or how to get the stamps. A man came along and helped us. Then we walked and walked and got lost. We just kept walking till we found we were just about a mile from our ship. We took a taxi then. Now the next port.

Casablanca (North Africa)

A thrill ran through us as we stepped off the gang-plank to the African soil. Today we saw more interesting kinds of people. The Mohammedan women wore heavy clothes with veils across their noses and mouths. You could only see their eyes. There was nothing else interesting about Casablanca.

Tangiers

Yesterday we were in Tangiers. We saw the same kind of people, but we saw more things. We went on a sight-seeing tour with Madame Compi and Mrs. Lee. We saw the latest sultan or king's palace. It was beautiful. We went up into the mountains to a place called "The Caves." We got a young boy to take us through the caves. We went through them on and on till we could see some light. We turned around the bend and there was a hole. A great big hole, so big that we could see the ocean through it.

Some ladies were fishing there and we took their pictures. They were angry with us and jibbered and jabbered something in their language.

Oran, Algeria

Today we visited Oran and we saw nothing but people. So no more about Oran.

I forgot to tell you that in Casablanca we picked up a missionary family—Mr. and Mrs. Maynard Yoder and their 16 month-old daughter, Karen Sue.

In the Tangiers we went through a native market place. Oh the stink!

I'd better advise you not to write until you hear from us again.

I'd better close now as it's just about tea time.

Yours in Christ,

Jeanette

P.S. We have had a wonderful time opening our presents every day. We enjoy them very much.

TUESDAY, September 1

This is our 16th day out of New York City, and we are somewhere in the middle of the Mediterranean

Sea, between North Africa and France. We can see why the French people call the Mediterranean "The Blue Sea," because it is the richest, most inviting blue imaginable. It gives you the feeling that you would like to plunge in and have a swim—but I think we will wait until we are a little closer to shore. We are to arrive in Marseille very early tomorrow morning, and we are quite excited, of course. We rather dread the thought of customs tomorrow; but we know the Lord is with us and will see us through. Really, I suppose we should feel sorry for the customs officials. They have to get us through one way or another.

Today we are packing in earnest, leaving out just enough clothing to get us to the Mission Home tomorrow. I am sure we didn't get all of this stuff out of our suitcases; but it will have to go back into them. It will be good to see the Plymouth Suburban come swinging out of the hold and down over the side of the VOLTA to the dock below. I don't know how or when we get it, but we will soon find out.

September 1 (Jeanette's comment)

Dad was an expert packer—but even he was muttering at trying to fit all the new toys and things into our luggage. It seems as if somehow they'd dramatically expanded after being unwrapped. As anxious as Marian and I were, you would have thought we'd never see them again. It was another one of those days when Mom often put her finger up to her lips.

WEDNESDAY, September 2

We retired early last night, knowing that we would be docking in Marseille early in the morning, and we wanted to be up and dressed for a good start. All went well until about midnight when we were awakened by the blast of our ship's whistle. Of course, we thought we were pulling into Marseille, and so we jumped up immediately to look out the window. But everything was black to the front. Just as we started to climb back into our bunks there was another mighty blast of our whistle. About two minutes later, another long blast. So we went to the deck to see what it was all about, and the moment we stepped out onto the lighted deck we knew—the fog was so thick we could hardly see the railing. Back to bed we went, and for the next two hours or so we lay in our bunks listening to the blast of the whistle every minute or so. That is their way of navigating during a fog, sounding the whistle every minute or so as a warning to other ships.

Finally, about 2:00 A.M., the whistle stopped its incessant blasting, and we dozed off to sleep only to be awakened about an hour later by the sound of hammering and clanging of chains, and the groan of machinery. It was the crew making ready for unloading in Marseille, their home port. The quicker they would get the ship unloaded and cleaned up, the quicker they would get to see wives and children, or perhaps sweethearts and friends, which they had not seen for about 45 days. That was the reason for their 3:00 A.M. start.

So, we buried our heads under the sheet and tried to get a little more sleep. About this time there was a terrific clatter against the wall of our cabin, and the dragging of a chain. They were locking up the deck chairs just outside our cabin. This went on intermittently until they were all chained again. In the meantime, we had actually docked, and now the crew were singing and whistling about their chores, making no attempt to be quiet. They began scrubbing the decks above us and just outside of our cabin, and sleep was futile. We lay there and rested until about 5:30 A.M. and then dressed for the big day ahead of us.

Breakfast was at 7:00 A.M. (the usual French bread, jelly and tea), and about 8:00 A.M. the officials came aboard to examine our passports, etc. After they left the ship, the agency that conducts your baggage through customs came aboard and tagged all of our bags and began hauling them off the ship and into the adjoining warehouse where the customs officials had set up a table. We were the last to get our bags off the ship and spread out before the customs officer. He was in a "cranky" mood because there was only one porter carrying all the luggage for all passengers, and it had taken so much time.

He made us open about three of our suitcases, and all seemed to be well until he came to the guns. He grabbed them right then and there to be held in customs because we did not have any permit from America to carry a gun, or any papers on the guns. The rifle was given to us by Mr. Martin, and the Colt automatic pistol by Mr. Gerhardt. Next he grabbed the tape recorder and set it aside, and then our typewriter. All of the other passengers had left by that time and only the representative from the baggage agency could speak a little English. He made us understand that the customs officer was holding the guns, tape recorder, and typewriter for duty, and the rest of our luggage (that is, hand luggage) had passed customs. The pieces that had passed were delivered to "Le Phare" (the place where we are staying temporarily), and we took a taxi there.

We were certainly glad to pull up in front of the building with the sign printed over the small show window containing Bibles and tracts (in French). The sign reads, "FOYER CHRETIEN—LE PHARE" which means "THE CHRISTIAN HOME—THE LIGHTHOUSE". And it certainly has been a Christian home for us. No one at the home speaks a word of English except an adopted daughter who speaks a little, just enough that we can make ourselves generally understood but not enough to help us with the technicalities of taking care of the customs, locating an apartment, etc. "Le Phare" is more or less of a rescue mission, and Monsieur Lejeune does much work in the hospitals, prisons, etc., as well as the service held in "Le Phare" on Sunday. None of the drinkers are kept at the home, however, and although we only have one large room for the four of us, yet we are making out all right until we can locate a small efficiency apartment (if that is possible).

There was another family of American missionaries staying here when we arrived, Rev. and Mrs. John Fitzstevens, with the Mission Evangelique in Indo China, and they were of great assistance to us as interpreters; but they sailed today (Saturday) for Indo China, and now we are left with hardly any way of making ourselves understood. It will probably be good for our French, but it is awfully hard on our nerves.

Our troubles really started on Wednesday when we attempted to get delivery of our automobile. Monsieur Lejeune went to do the talking in French, and Mr. Fitzstevens went to be interpreter to me. Somehow the car was "blocked" in customs and we could not get it without paying 56% of its value in deposit, to be refunded when we left the country. This was to make sure we did not sell the car in France. It wouldn't do us any good to sell it in France anyway, because you can only take 10,000 francs out of the country in French currency (about $28 in American money). We finally ran up against a brick wall, so to speak. There just simply was not any way we could get the car. I was just about in the mood to ship it home again, and have it sold, which would have been a terrific loss due to the cost of shipping ($325 each way). By this time, the Lord had us completely at the end of ourselves, and although we had been praying for His guidance all along, now all we could do was commit it entirely to the Lord—we were perfectly helpless, not even able to know what was going on because we did not understand French.

When we retired Wednesday night, and again Thursday night, we were so distraught that we could have cried; but we committed all of our burdens to the Lord and tried to leave them there. Thursday we had gone to the American Consul (who left the room without even speaking to us), but an assistant in his office was very kind. We were registered and told how to handle an extended stay beyond the 3-months tourist limit, but we will be unable to do what is required until we can find someone who speaks both English and French to go with us.

At any rate, the assistant in the Consul's office told us to go to the American Express Company and they would handle all the details of customs for us—for a fee. So Friday morning we went to the American Express Office, and praise the Lord, they spoke English. They were French, but they spoke good old, solid English! So to make a long, tedious, nerve-wracking story short, they were able to get the car through customs and into France (or all of free Europe) for one year without any deposit or customs. I did have to join the Touring Club of France, however, in order to get the car in (at a cost of around 6,000 francs, or $17). Their representative was also able to get my typewriter out of customs, without paying any deposit; but the tape recorder and guns are locked up until we leave the country or else pay. It seems like every time we turn around they charge a fee for something else: nearly 5,500 francs ($15) just to unload the car from the ship, fee to the baggage agency, touring club, etc., etc. All in all we have spent 30,000 francs ($85) thus far in merely gaining admittance into France. I guess if it was my own money, saved up for a vacation in Europe, I wouldn't mind; but each dollar is the Lord's and at the sacrifice of some faithful steward at home, and we do mind!

The main task before us at the present moment is to find someone who can speak both English and French in order that we can obtain a residential permit for a year, and to locate an apartment. This morning (Saturday) we dashed over the city of Aix to see what we could find before the Fitzstevens sailed this afternoon. Aix is so much nicer than Marseille that we are fairly groaning to find an apartment there. It is a university town and is so clean and fairly new, whereas Marseille is very old and very dirty. The children have no place to play outdoors at all where we are. It is just like being locked up in a house for them. But at the present we can do nothing because we cannot ask a question or understand an answer—it is a terrible predicament in that respect; but will probably be very good for our French. One thing we know, Romans 8:28 is in the French Bible as well as our English version, *"And we know that all things work together for good to them that love God, to them who are the called according to His purpose."* We are claiming this precious promise in our present predicament and trying to wait patiently for God to work things out for us.

And here we shall have to leave you, dear friends, and bring our "Travelog" to a close. We will continue to keep you informed of how the Lord leads and undertakes for us through the medium of our Prayer Letter and by personal letter as we have time. Mail will have to be by regular post instead of airmail from us as the cost of airmail is too much for any quantity of letters. We miss you all very much, but can say with the Apostle Paul, *"I thank my God upon every remembrance of you, always in every prayer of mine for you all making request with joy, for your fellowship in the gospel from the first day until now"* (Philippians 1:3-5).

September 2 (Jeanette's comment)

I did hear the foghorn at first—but Mom ran down the hall to tell me what was going on. I'd read about foghorns, so I wasn't alarmed. Marian never awakened—and I quickly fell back to sleep until Mom came and got us up in the morning. We were already docked.

I can only imagine how "cranky" that poor customs official was when he saw our motley assortment of bags and bundles! But he made one huge mistake—he tried to hold my accordion for duty, along with the car, guns, typewriter, and tape recorder. Mom said the tears welled up in my eyes, and I started sobbing and sobbing. The message got through, however, and the accordion was released with the rest of the hand luggage that had passed customs and was taken on to Le Phare.

I remember very little about Le Phare except that everyone ate at one long table. A number of the young men there had been in the French Foreign Legion. Apparently, they had led rather dissipated lives before being saved.

We were in a very large room—but with all our baggage, it quickly filled up. There was a balcony overlooking an atrium-courtyard but not big enough to play on—and we weren't allowed in the courtyard. Mom and Dad made sure we took a lot of walks (of course!) just to get us out of the room for a little fresh air and exercise.

I also remember going to Aix-en-Provence and looking at an apartment. It was like the top floor of a fortress—massively thick walls, tiny windows, no central heating—just fireplaces. I loved it!

Fortunately, our folks weren't in a sentimental mood. There was only one entrance into the building. The door opened onto the staircase leading to the upstairs apartment and, to the left, was the door leading to the downstairs apartment. Neither apartment had an inside door that locked.

I look at Dad's accounting of all the money spent just to enter France. Today, it would be an even more incredible amount. But for missionaries in 1953, it was already pretty incredible.

Part Four

Marseille, France
1953-1954

*"Blessed be the Lord, who daily loadeth us with benefits,
even the God of our salvation."*
Proverbs 3:6

Marseille, France in 1953

Marseille is the oldest city in France. The Greeks set up a port there in 600 B.C. and called it *Massalia*. In its long history, Marseille has been a prize for any invading army—from the Romans, following the Greeks, to the Nazis in World War II.

The city is situated in southeastern France along the Mediterranean, one end of the Cote d'Azur or the Riviera. It usually has mild, humid or rainy winters and warm, sometimes hot summers. The main drawback is the Mistral, a bitter, harsh wind that sweeps down the Rhône River valley into Marseille, primarily in the winter and spring.

One of the primary attractions of Marseille is Le Vieux Port (the Old Port). Over the centuries, it was expanded and strengthened. Two forts were built on either side of its entrance in the 1700s. The main boulevard of Marseille, La Cannebière, stretches from Le Vieux Port through the heart of the city. Today, Le Vieux Port is a huge marina for pleasure boats and surrounded by entertainment venues, a popular place for tourists.

In 1940, both the German and Italian forces bombed Marseille, then the Germans occupied the city from November 1942 until August 1944. The Germans mined the Vieux Port to make sure no Allied submarines could use it. They destroyed much of the "old town" around it because the French Resistance hid out in the narrow streets and jammed-together houses and constantly escaped from them. The Germans finally evacuated the citizens from this area and captured many Resistance fighters. Then, they carefully removed metal pipes or anything else they could use in manufacturing their weapons, blew up the area, and bulldozed it to the bare ground.

Le Vieux Port looking up at Notre Dame de la Garde

As ships had become larger over the centuries, Marseille had also built a more modern commercial port—but the Nazis took it over and built submarine pens there. Consequently, the Allies bombed and destroyed the commercial port during the war. But their pinpoint bombing didn't touch Le Vieux Port and other important buildings like the basilica of Notre Dame de la Garde that is situated on a high hill overlooking the city.

Looking at Le Vieux Port from Notre Dame de la Garde

The people of Marseille suffered tremendously under the Nazi regime. Our landlady, Mlle Junod, told us that the convent at the end of street where our apartment was located had been taken over by the Gestapo—all those little rooms for the nuns became cells for prisoners—and the Germans sent anyone whom they wanted tortured to that location. Mlle Junod said that the cries of those poor victims echoed up and down the street, especially at night.

The Spainhower family invaded Marseille, France, in September 1953, just seven years after the end of World War II. All Berean missionaries to the Belgian Congo were required to spend a year in Brussels, Belgium, first to learn French, the colonial language of the Congo. But since Dad got excruciating eczema in cold climates, he couldn't go there. Someone suggested that we go to Marseille—on the Riviera where it was relatively warm all winter—to learn French. We found out later that going to Marseille to learn French was about the same as sending a foreigner to Mississippi to learn how to speak good English. The Provençal dialect had a distinctly different sound to it than either Parisian or Belgian French.

The first plan was that we would go to Marseille and then go up to Brussels to take some colonial exams in the summer before heading on to Congo. Well, that plan had to be eliminated because Europe suffered one of the coldest winters and springs in decades. We actually got about six inches of snow in the winter—the first snow in about 30 years—and the cold weather lasted off and on into the spring and summer, with increased incidences of the Mistral on top of it all. Dad couldn't go farther north to Belgium because of the climate, so we finally just went straight to Congo after almost a year in France.

Marseille was undergoing extensive rebuilding and restoration when we arrived. The governments of East/West Germany and Italy had to pay massive reparations to compensate civilians killed, injured, or left homeless or destitute as a result of the war. The United States, under the Marshall Plan, rebuilt the commercial port and helped with much of the reconstruction of the area.

Yet quite often, we could see "America Go Home!!" painted on various walls or signs. We quickly discovered that Marseille was a socialist and communist stronghold. It started almost immediately after the war and continued until the mid-1990s. Fortunately, Dad with his dark hair and moustache looked French and Mom with her reddish-blond hair and rosy cheeks looked like an Englishwoman, so we rarely ran into any problems with anti-American feelings. Jeanette was the only one who faced it every day at school—her teacher was proudly communist and took great delight in spouting anti-Americanisms at every turn.

Our sojourn in France gave us our first taste of learning to adapt to a different culture. We've often looked back with great fondness over that year. Mom and Dad faced difficulties that we girls couldn't understand, of course, but during that year, our family grew even closer together. It's where we learned the lesson that we could live anywhere and call it home—because our family was together.

"Le Phare"
133, rue Ferrari,
Marseille, France
September 5, 1953

Dear Brother Wright:

Greetings in our Saviour's Name! Just a hurried note to transmit our Travelog to you and the folks at Edgemont. I have been typing for the last two hours in an effort to finish it, and want to get it mailed out to you, to the Mission, and to the folks in California as soon as possible. We made three copies for that very purpose.

Our typewriter was held in customs until yesterday afternoon, and for a while it looked like we would not get it until we left France, or else pay a deposit on it, and they set the deposit at a little more than 50% of the value. But the Lord intervened, and now we have it duty-free. However, the lovely tape-recorder is locked up in customs, together with the rifle and revolver, and there they must stay until we leave France, or else pay a big deposit on the recorder to get it (the guns I cannot get without papers on them and a permit).

We have had a most miserable time trying to do anything at all because we cannot make ourselves understood in French, and cannot understand any replies we might get. But we know that the Lord will send us the help that we need in His own time; and we trust for grace to learn the language ourselves in a few months time. Right now it seems impossible, but with Him all things are possible, and we are His.

Will not try to prepare our Prayer Letter until things settle down and, if possible, we can give our permanent address in it. The Lejeune's are not willing for us to stay indefinitely but are willing to lodge us until we can find something else. All of this we must commit to Him who is able, our lovely Lord Jesus. I don't think we could face it all without Him—truly He giveth us strength as our day.

I must close now and mail the other copies of our Travelog also. We are missing you and all at Edgemont very much, and praying for you. It is comforting to know that we meet at the Throne of Grace.

With much Christian love to all,

Les and Gertie
Jeanette and Marian

Marian's Comment: France

When we arrived in France, I was 8 years old. I remember being delighted that we were finally leaving the S.S. Volta for dry land but I was apprehensive about being in a foreign country where I couldn't understand what anyone was saying. I never felt afraid, though, because Dad and Mom always made us feel at home wherever we were, which made me feel secure. But I wished we could go back to Grandpa and Grandma's. I was really homesick for them. I rather imagine Mom, Dad and Jeanette were, too, but they didn't say so.

I do not remember much about our stay at "Le Phare," but I do remember the apartment we finally found to rent. The outside of the building looked rather drab, and spray painted on the concrete wall opposite our building were the words "America go home!" This had happened when a couple of American servicemen had stayed a short time in one of the apartments. But as long as I had my family and my toys, I was fine.

However, when we moved to the basement apartment in the same building after a while, I thought I had died and gone to heaven for sure! Not only did we have a large porch with tall windows all the way across on one side, but if we walked up some concrete steps, there was a small, private garden that belonged to our landlady, Mademoiselle Junod. She told Mom and Dad that Jeanette and I could play in her private garden anytime we wanted to. She was a very kind lady and had already seen that Jeanette and I were well behaved, so she opened up this marvelous place for us. I spent many an hour playing on the porch and in the garden.

Whenever we received packages from Grandma, she would use newspaper comics for stuffing. How I did enjoy reading them on the porch with my doll beside me!

Jeanette and I were enrolled for a while at a French Catholic School because there was no room for us in the small public school. You can't imagine how badly I did NOT want to go there. We not only didn't know a soul, but school had already started a week or so prior to us enrolling, and no one spoke English! Talk about having a king-sized stomach ache our first morning!! Jeanette will write about her own experience but for myself, I can say it was a challenge, to say the least. I was put into a class taught by a heavy-set, very pleasant nun, dressed in her long, black, Catholic attire with only her face and hands showing. It was rather intriguing to watch her walk with her long, black skirt swishing from side to side. I had to stand in the front of the room while she introduced me to the class. I could understand enough to know she introduced me as an American girl, which brought cold, unfriendly stares from all the kids. Didn't quite feel the love!

The room was long and narrow, and the desks were made for two. She put me with another girl close to the back of the room where there was an empty seat. The boys were on one side and girls on the other. I don't remember anything about the girl I sat next to other than her surprising me by actually using some semblance of sign language to help me know what I was supposed to do. When it was time for recess, we all went outside. For this girl who enjoyed recess more than anything in America, I dreaded it there. At first some of the girls gathered around me because I was an American "novelty," but I quickly realized we couldn't communicate much. So when they laughed with each other, I felt they were laughing at me. That was my first experience at feeling "lost" and like everyone was making fun of me. At that moment, if I could have, I would have run all the way home and never returned. At that age I didn't understand that this is a universal feeling, and people sometimes laugh when they can't communicate because they are embarrassed. It doesn't mean they are laughing at you. Anyway, it was a tough beginning, but it wasn't long before a couple of the girls befriended me and, we would play around a little without actually knowing what was being said. If they didn't play with me, quite often I would just stay close to my teacher if she was outside.

One of the things that ostracized me from the other kids is when my teacher would call on different ones to stand up and read aloud from their French reader. So many couldn't seem to read but for some reason I could read our simple French reader, even though I didn't have any idea what the words meant. So she would call on me when someone faltered in their reading and then yell at them because the American girl, who didn't know French, could read French when they couldn't. Oh my! That didn't help me to win friends and influence people!

None of the students in the class had paper or pencils. We brought writing slates and slate pencils with us in our school bags, which were like briefcases. The slate material itself was a stony substance, 7x10 inches, which was encased in a wooden frame. We would write down what she wanted on our slates with slate pencils, which were made of soft slate, or of soapstone. Then my teacher would walk up and down the narrow rows looking at our answers. They were easily erased for the next answer.

Upon enrollment, our parents made sure the school knew we were not Catholic, and it was agreed that we would not participate in the Catholic rituals. However, when my class went to mass or to confession, I had to go along and sit in the back. I can still remember how strange that all seemed to me. The room was dark except for the altar area. They did a lot of kneeling, crossing themselves, and reciting prayers with beads. At times a few would cry as they individually went forward for confession. At home I began crossing myself and trying to recite one of their repetitive prayers in French to my parents. Needless to say, they were not amused! Then when my sister came down with a bad bronchial infection, they knew she couldn't continue in the unheated school and didn't want to send me by myself. PRAISE THE LORD!! So that ended our Catholic school days! Hurrah!

Mom and Dad gave us school work to do at home for the rest of the school year. They had brought arithmetic, reading, and spelling books for me to do. Then Dad started teaching Jeanette how to type. They kept us pretty busy but as a result of not being formally in school for any length of time that year, we lost credit for the year. It sure was a relief to be able to stay at home with Mom and Dad everyday instead of going to back to school. We didn't miss it at all.

One of the main streets we often drove on towards the Mediterranean Sea was called Le Prado. At the far end of the street was a very tall statue of David from the Bible. The interesting thing about this statue was that he was totally naked—and very muscular. As we would pass by, Dad and Mom would tell us to hide our eyes. We did... but I *never* could quite make my fingers come together completely. Guess that was the beginning of my sex education classes!!

Mom and Dad would take us to the shore every now and then. It was a short distance from our apartment. This gave them a needed break from studying French all the time, and we could all get out of the apartment for a while. We would sit on the rocks, walk on the beach, hunt for seashells, and watch for ships. These were always delightful times that we will always treasure.

Dad taking our picture with our Brownie camera while Mom photographed us with Dad's.

Our beautiful Mom

    I've mentioned just a few things that I recall from our year in France but Jeanette will have more to tell since she was older and remembers more. One thing I would like to say is that our parents were truly gifts from God. No matter where we lived, no matter what our circumstances, when the four of us were together, we had a home filled with love and laughter. Our family days are treasured memories I will always hold dear!

41, rue Daumier
Marseille, France
October 4, 1953

Dear Brother and Sister Wright:

"Blessed be the Lord, who daily loadeth us with benefits--". And truly, day by day, blessing upon blessing has come from Him! After we had moved into our apartment, we immediately began looking for a school where Jeanette and Marian could attend and learn French. Unlike our public school systems in America, here one must begin early to gain entrance in one of the many public or private schools for one's children. Some mothers began as early as last June in an effort to get their children enrolled for this fall. There are so few public schools that they soon fill their quota, and then more than one-half the children must be enrolled in the private schools, most of which are Catholic. And then, some of the children just simply are unable to attend for lack of facilities. The condition is deplorable.

But, praise the Lord for undertaking for us. The children are finally enrolled in a school, even though it is a Catholic school. It is understood, of course, that we are Protestant missionaries and that our children will not have to participate in Mass, etc. Our landlady, Mademoiselle Junod, telephoned the Directrice of this Catholic school, which Directrice was formerly one of her dear teacher's years ago. And thus the Lord used an old friendship in order to gain entrance for Jeanette and Marian into a school whose quota was already filled. The name of their school is "Cours Notre Dame de France." We just trust that the Lord will make the girls a blessing to their little classmates, some of whom are Protestants, too. Several of the teachers speak a little English, so that makes the path a bit easier for the girls. At any rate, they will learn French much faster than we. Pray for them, and for us, in this difficult matter of living daily among those with whom we cannot converse; and that we may soon learn to speak the language. After all, that is our purpose in being here!

We are praising the Lord, too, for a competent French tutor right here in our own apartment building. Madame Quinche is the wife of a personnel man with the Nestle Co. (Chocolate, Nescafe, etc.) and has one of the larger apartments in our building. For many years she taught both English and French in Switzerland, and she has consented to teach us until the end of December when they will return to Switzerland. We have already had our first lesson with her and feel that she is most competent, and definitely an answer to prayer. The Lord has provided the tutor; now pray for grace and enablement with the language. Pray, too, for wisdom in handling our finances, as the costs are rapidly mounting as our living becomes more organized. First, rent of the apartment is expensive (in war-torn France); then the car must be placed in a public garage, which is costly (it would not be safe on the streets of Marseille because of the Communists here—they would slash the tires and write "U.S. GO HOME" in acid on the car body, we have been warned); then, the cost of the girls' tuition in the Catholic School $20 per month); the cost of our French lessons; and finally, the cost of foodstuffs, which is perhaps higher for us in that we cannot ask questions and shop in general, but must get along with much sign language, and probably do not always make the best "buys." The Lord is certainly our Help in all of this.

By the way, the European Christian Mission has a work here in Marseille, which we have mentioned to you before. The American pastor, Reverend Phelps, whom we met while still at "Le Phare," is the founder of the work locally. They are the ones who conduct the street meetings Rev. Phelps and his wife have just returned to America on furlough, and we gave them the name and address of Edgemont and your name, and they promised to call on you when and if they get in the St. Louis area. Their co-workers, Rev. and Mrs. Howarth (English), have been very nice to us—helped us get the tape recorder out of customs, etc. Brother Howarth has asked me to preach at their indoor meeting next Sunday afternoon (through an interpreter, of course), and Gertrude gave a testimony at today's meeting via the same method. They are a dear Christian couple, with their little daughter, Margaret. We are glad, too, for the opportunities of service afforded through their work. Jeanette and I will be playing our instruments at their street meetings throughout the winter months, Lord willing. And God grant before we leave that I can preach to them in French, without an interpreter.

We have also made the acquaintance of another American woman, Miss Jerry Gaffner, of Greenville, Illinois. She is with the European Evangelistic Crusade and will be spending the winter here in Marseille. In fact, she lives just one block from us! She had telephoned Brother Howarth at his home regarding the possibilities of service during her winter here in Marseille with their group, and so he asked me to contact her at the home where she is staying since it was so close to us. The only trouble was that he did not get her name, or the name of the family with whom she lives— only the street address. So, I set out to find Mademoiselle "X", at 63, rue Daumier. There were only eight apartments in the building, so I started by knocking on the first door and working my way up. I would first tell the one who answered the door, "Je ne parle pas la Francais" ("I do not speak French"); and then ask them in "pidgeon" French and sign language if they knew of an American missionary visiting here. Finally, at the 7th apartment, top floor, an elderly, motherly French woman answered the door, and by the time I got as far as "missionarie Americaine"—I heard a squeal, and Miss Gaffner came running to the door to meet me. Needless to say, it was good to find out her name after all that door-knocking.

I see my space is up, so must close for this time. Greet all the brethren for us, and the "sistern," too.

With Christian love to you both, and to all,

Les, Gertie, Jeanette and Marian

Jeanette's Comment: Schooling in France

Even though I was ready for 7th grade in American schools, the administration at the Catholic school thought it would be better for me to stay in elementary school since I spoke no French. So they put me in 5th grade—with a teacher who spoke some English. I don't remember her name; all my classmates simply called her *Mademoiselle*.

The teacher was beautiful, and all the girls loved her, but she was also a Communist and didn't hide her disdain for me and for America. She didn't interfere with my education, but if I made a mistake, she was quick to say, "That's just like an American!" or other snide remarks. Even though I tried very hard to learn French, she told me over and over that I would never speak in French. And she was right. I could read and write good French—I even majored in French in college—but I never felt comfortable speaking it.

But when it came to certain subjects, I could outperform the French students in my class. I already knew the math well—I'd taken it two years earlier—and Mademoiselle sometimes had me help some of the other students. I was really good at memorizing the conjugation of verbs. I'd always ace those tests—and I could even stand and recite them in class. That's when Mademoiselle would shame the French students who weren't trying hard enough. I was even good at *dictée*. We were given a paragraph that we were to practice writing at home. Mademoiselle would then read it aloud in class the next day, and we were to write it. Our landlady, Mlle Junod, often read the paragraph to me to help me hear it with a correct accent. Again, Mademoiselle would be furious with the French students who hadn't done any studying because they let an "ignorant" American who didn't speak the language get the highest grade in the class.

I really didn't have any friends among my classmates—I was a couple of years older than they were. But the older girls gathered around me every recess or lunch period. They already spoke fairly good English and wanted to practice their English with me. I often helped them with their English lessons. When they asked me where I lived in America, I told them in a small town near St. Louis, Missouri, thinking they would have heard of that city—but they just shook their heads. Finally, I told them that I actually lived in East St. Louis, Illinois. Then they got downright excited! They'd heard about all the gangsters in East St. Louis—and were really disappointed that I hadn't met any personally.

There were two primary reasons why Dad and Mom took us out of the school after two or three months—besides the money. One was that, even though we Protestant girls (and there were a few others) were not supposed to be taken to mass or confession, Marian's teacher often had her go along and sit in the chapel with the others. When Mom and Dad realized that she could say all the prayers—and knew when to kneel and cross herself—they figured Marian didn't need that kind of education!

The other factor was that the school was unheated, as were so many buildings in France at that time. As the weather grew increasingly colder—and Marian and I were without heavy winter clothes because this was supposed to be the Riviera!—we could no longer cope with the weather. I came down with bronchitis, and Mom knew from past experience that could easily lead to pneumonia.

Now, Marian and I weren't terribly disappointed not to be attending school. Someone sent books for Marian, so Mom could keep her on track with reading, math, and spelling until she would enter the mission school in the Congo. They weren't worried about my math or reading skills—in fact, I read constantly. Grandma Wilson was hard put to keep me in books.

What I got was a high-school level book for typing—and Dad got busy teaching me how to type with the "touch" method, not looking at the keys. Sometimes, as I progressed, he'd even hold a piece of cardboard over my hands as I typed on a test. He insisted that I maintain a constant speed—even on the number keys. He was a tough taskmaster, but I learned how to type well.

Then, the typing led to other activities. I wrote all kinds of stories on the typewriter—and Mom would always carefully read them, not only looking at the typing skills but also at grammar and spelling and even content. So even though I wasn't working out of textbooks, I got continuing education in writing as well.

Marian and I often played school with our dolls. Since I was the oldest, I taught school—and Mom sometimes had me work with Marian to reinforce what she'd been learning that day. I guess it's not surprising that I ended up teaching college English for several years and then ended my working life with a writing and editing career.

Marian and I both "lost" a year of school when we were in France. There were times when I kind of regretted it while I was in high school, but not in the long run—and certainly not while we were in France. Our education expanded far beyond books and typewriters. We visited museums—the free ones—and other important buildings in Marseille. We spent hours at Le Corniche, the rocky seaside—and even played in some of the pillboxes that had housed German artillery. Dad took us up into the mountains. We drove through little villages and bought produce at the local markets. And we walked miles around Marseille when the weather was nice.

Yes, we may not have studied many schoolbooks that year in France, but we certainly had a good education, one that I'll never forget.

41, rue Daumier
Marseille, France
October 15, 1953

Dear Brother and Sister Wright:

Greetings in the name of our blessed Lord! We are writing to you from the land of rain. It has rained intermittently almost every day for the past three weeks. Even the Marseille newspapers have carried articles on the great amount of rain lately—at least we were told the articles were in the paper; we could not read them, of course. For it all, the house temperature has remained about 70 degrees, except for about two or three chilly days, which forced us to buy 50 kilograms of coal and 29 kilograms of kindling. 50 kilograms of coal is 100 pounds, and sells at the price of $55 per ton. Imagine it! Everyone tells us it is warm here in Marseille all winter long, except for the few cold days now and then, but we find it a bit damp and chilly even now. All of the homes and buildings we have been in thus far have tiny little stoves for heating, so it must not get very cold. Our heating stove has a fire box that measures 5 inches by 8 inches, so you can imagine how much fire can be built in it. And, at $55 per ton, you *KNOW* how much fire is going to be built in it!

Yesterday we received the colored slides taken of our trip from New York to Marseille, and we praise the Lord for good results—most of them are very clear and colorful. We are beginning the process of culling out the less pertinent slides, arranging them in order, marking them, and making ready for the tape recording. It will no doubt take several days to finish the tape, and then we will *airmail* both the tape and the slides to you. We trust that the tape and slides will be a blessing to all, and even though they are more of a travelog than missionary slides, yet may they glorify the name of our lovely Lord Jesus.

Jeanette and Marian are well into the routine of French school by now—six days a week. They have Thursday and Saturday afternoons off, so it is the same number of class hours per week as at home. They have made only a very little progress in French as yet, but everyone says that it takes at least three or four months to begin to "get hold of it." Gertie and I wonder if we ever will learn to speak French. But we have the Lord as our Helper, and if it is His will that we speak French, we know that He will bless our efforts toward that end and enable us. We certainly covet your prayers in this respect—it is so difficult. Our tutor, Madame Quinche is returning with her husband to Switzerland for a "fortnight," and so that will give us the respite from "home work" needed to prepare the slides and recording—although she did give us a nice, big assignment just so we would not forget our French while she was gone.

The enclosed Travelers Cheque represents a part of our tithe, which has been accumulating since we left the States, and we would like to invest it in the most fruitful ministry we know of, the Lord's work at Edgemont Bible Church! Will you please place it in the next Joash Offering for us. How we would like to be there and "march" down front and drop it in ourselves, but the Lord has other "marching" orders for us, and His will is best and sweetest. We are praying for you always, each day, and thanking God upon every remembrance of you.

Sincerely yours in Christ Jesus,

Les, Gertie and the girlies

"THE DARK CONTINENT"

AFRICA

Berean Mission, Inc.
3536 Russell Blvd.
St. Louis, Missouri

Prayer Letter * * * * * October 1953

"Call upon Me in the day of trouble: I will deliver thee, and thou shalt glorify me" (Psalm 50:15).
"God is our refuge and strength, a very present help in trouble" (Psalm 46:1).

Dear Christian Friends:

How good it is to know that you are praying for us, and how thankful we are that we, too, can commune with Heaven and find comfort and help and deliverance in the time of trouble. Since arriving in Marseille, France we have not ceased to call upon the Lord, spreading out our troubles before Him, much as Hezekiah did of old, and He has delivered us out of them one at a time. If you have ever had the experience of entering into a foreign land and passing through customs, unable to speak the language, then you know the troubles of which I speak.

For the benefit of those of you who have not had opportunity to read our detailed Travelog, we'll mention here that we sailed from Pier 29, East River, New York City at 1:00 A.M. Sunday morning, August 16, aboard the French freighter, S. S. VOLTA. 2,955 miles later we docked at Lisbon, Portugal, having crossed the Atlantic Ocean in eight extremely calm days, for which we thank the Lord. None of us were the least bit seasick. The S.S. VOLTA carried cargo for various North African ports, and so we sailed from Lisbon to Casablanca, Tangiers, Oran, Algiers, Tunis, and thence to Marseille, France, a total of sixteen days upon the water and a distance of some 4,750 miles.

At Marseille, our pleasant voyage ended and our troubles began! On the morning of September 2, as we debarked from the S. S. VOLTA, we ran right smack into a disgruntled customs official the very first thing. There was one porter to carry the baggage of all twelve passengers off the boat and to the waiting customs officer. Unfortunately, we were the last passengers to arrive before this impatient individual, and he was really fuming. As a consequence, by the time we had passed through customs, we were minus our much-needed typewriter, our beloved tape recorder, and the two guns which we are carrying as hand-luggage all the way to Africa. We could readily understand how they might think we were going to start a revolution with the artillery; but they had no right to keep our typewriter and tape recorder—nevertheless, they did! So, we called upon the Lord, and told Him all about our troubles, and He delivered our typewriter and tape recorder to us a few days later. It is evidently His good will that the guns remain in customs until we leave France for the Congo.

Next we found that our Plymouth Suburban (which the Lord has provided for the Congo) was "blocked" in customs until we paid 56% of its value in deposit as a guarantee that we would not sell the car during our sojourn in France. We were absolutely dumbfounded and of a mind to ship the car back to America to be sold, but—we called upon the Lord, and spread out our trouble before Him, and He delivered our car to us, duty-free. Praise His Name.

Our next problem was that of locating a furnished apartment in war-torn Marseille. Due to the housing shortage, furnished apartments are almost unobtainable and terrifically expensive. Again, we called upon the Lord, and looked, and looked, and looked, and waited. We were extremely handicapped in that we could not speak French and had to arrange for someone who could speak both French and English to go with us to interpret. After the Lord had taught us a lesson in patience and had us in the place of full dependence upon Him, then He delivered us out of our trouble. Praise His name, our new address is:

        41, rue Daumier
        Marseille, France

We have a nice, walnut-stained letter box in the entrance way just waiting to receive your letter, so won't you please write? We would rejoice to hear from each one of you, and we promise to reply.

Our apartment consists of a very large dining room with a double bed in one corner, a massive table in the center, and other items of furniture sufficient for living. The children have a bedroom to themselves which is large enough for a playroom, too. "La cuisine" (the kitchen) is very small with a two-burner electric plate, sink, cabinet, and water filter, but is adequate; and there is a nice hall with an ice box (rare in France) and a huge wardrobe closet. We have a nice bathroom, except there is no bathtub or shower. Instead, the French use these silly bidets and lots of perfume. However, the apartment is very clean and in a nice neighborhood (which is rare in Marseille). All in all, we are happy with it and praising the Lord for it.

In our dining room/bedroom we have a massive wardrobe closet that is over 250 years old, complete with the original lock and key. It is about ten feet tall and five feet wide, with beautiful metal filigree work on the doors. The key to the lock is six inches long and weighs nearly a pound. The library table on which my typewriter is now setting is also over 250 years old, and if you look real close you can see a lot of termite holes all through it. I get to feeling like Methuselah around all of these antiques!

We have been having quite a time doing our shopping via French plus sign language. At times it is mostly sign language, but we are making some progress in our French, too. We have been concentrating upon the ordinal numerals and the names of the articles we have need of. Before going to the market, Gertie looks up the French names of those items we hope to buy, and then we go and try out our halting French on the poor, unsuspecting sales people. So far we have been successful in eating regularly.

We have been attending services at "Le Phare" (The Lighthouse) thus far, which are conducted all in French, of course, including the singing. Also, the European Gospel Mission conducts a street meeting and an indoor service (in French) late Sunday afternoon, and we have attended these services too. Jeanette has played her accordion for them, and I am to play the trumpet in the future. It is so good to be able to have this part in serving the Lord, even though we cannot speak French. They have asked me to speak to them through an interpreter, and we will prayerfully do so as the Lord leads.

"Call upon Me in the day of trouble: I will deliver thee; and thou shalt glorify Me. – Whoso offereth praise glorifieth Me" (Psalm 50:15, 23). And so we continually praise the Lord for His many deliverances that His worthy name might be glorified.

        In His glad service,

        The Spainhowers

41, rue Daumier
Marseille, France
December 1, 1953

Dear Brother and Sister Wright:

"Praise the name of the Lord your God, that hath dealt wondrously with you."

Among many other things we are praising the Lord for bringing in the tape recordings of your special meetings with Darrel Handel. We received them about 9:00 o'clock last night. They were delivered while we were out yesterday afternoon and were accepted by our landlady, who then went out for the evening. We returned and had supper, did the dishes, and then about 9:00 PM she came home and gave us the packages that had arrived: the one containing the tape recordings, and the other from one of Gertrude's mother's neighbors. They are simply wonderful! We haven't had the time to play them all through as yet; but what we have listened to have been a rich blessing. We shall probably hear them over and over again until we can recite Darrel's message by heart. All so very, very good. Incidentally, they had been opened by the customs officials at Paris, who probably thought they contained some secret information for a spy ring regarding some diabolical plot for the overthrow of the government of France. We only hope that they had a recorder and listened to the wonderful gospel messages recorded on them. Maybe that's why it took six weeks to get them! We only had to pay 153 francs duty, which amounts to only 44 cents. Praise the Lord! Now we shall be anxiously awaiting the recordings of the Missions Conference but suppose they will also take six weeks or so.

We were glad to hear that the Lisles and Maxine will be sailing December 12, Lord willing, for Belgium. They will then be so near and yet so far away. We will have to make a trip to Paris sometime next July to obtain our visa for the Belgian Congo; perhaps we can go on into Belgium and see them at that time. And then again, they may already be on their way to the Congo by then if they are only going to stay six months in Belgium. We have heard from Brother Irving Lindquist that Helen Gow and Evelyn Nickerson will be coming home our way sometime in January, and we will get to see them if their ship puts in at Marseille. That will be a rich blessing, I'm sure.

Glad to know that you heard from Carl Blackburn. I am going to write him tomorrow asking for information concerning his trip inland through Kenya to Bukavu. When we visited with them on their way through Marseille last month, he said he would let me have the particulars regarding lay-overs, Mau-Mau danger, etc. We are seriously considering going in the same way, i.e., taking a Castle Line ship from Marseille to Mombasa, Kenya and then driving across Kenya to the Belgian Congo. It is time now for us to begin giving serious thought to the mass of detail involved in making such a trip.

By the way, *we must make our steamship reservations within a month or so*. In fact, we are already a little late in doing so. I was inquiring in a general sort of way the other day and found that the Tourist Class on the Union Castle Lines from here to Mombasa was already sold out completely for the months of June, July, August, and September. Imagine that! Just as soon as I can get the necessary information, as to deposit required, etc., I will airmail the Mission for the necessary amount to make our reservations while they can still be obtained. We could wait until after September of next year to sail except for two reasons: one, it would involve much red tape in getting our permit to remain in France one year extended, and most of all, it would risk another breakdown in my skin just prior to sailing into the tropics, which would not be good.

For your personal information, my skin began breaking out with eczema about the first of November as the weather became cooler. Now the weather is down to about 45 degrees at night and about 60 to 65 during the day, and I am covered from head to foot once again, although not as severely as the past two winters at home. However, December and January are the worst months here, and I greatly fear that I am going "under" with it again. It is a terrible ordeal, so please pray that God will give grace to bear it. Pray for sunny, warm days—that is the only thing that will help. We make a mad dash to the sea coast every sunny day that comes along, and I strip to the waist and lay on the rocks where I'm protected from the cold wind and sun my tender hide. So far it has been enough to hold it in check. Each time it gets some sun it improves; and then if we have a dismal, cloudy period, it gets much worse. So, pray much that the Lord will keep it within bounds, will you? If I ever do finally get to Africa, I don't think I'll ever leave that sunny land.

Will be meeting with you at the Throne of Grace each day. God bless you both and give you a blessed time at Christmas and at the Watch Night Service. This is probably the last word you will get from us before that time. Remember us to all.

Much love in Christ,

Les and Gertie
Jeanette and Marian

P.S. Yes, we have to pay duty on *all* packages. Some very nominal, others quite expensive. New clothing very high - foodstuffs, reasonable—tapes very nominal.

December 13, 1953

Dear Brother and Sister Wright:

Les decided it was my turn to jot a line to you. It's a pleasure to do so. We surely do miss you all, especially at this Christmas season, but our Saviour is truly all-sufficient and we are rejoicing in Him.

I can't begin to tell you what a blessing the tapes are to us. We have played them so much that we can practically recite Darrel's five messages by heart. We were really starved for such fellowship around God's Word. You know, the only message I've understood since coming to France was the one Les preached using an interpreter. It was a real good one, too, although he will think I shouldn't have said so. We are eagerly looking forward to the Mission Conference tapes, too. By the way, we would surely like to hear some messages by our mostest favorite preacher, a fellow by the name of Wright.

We have much for which to praise our precious Lord. We prayed so very much for Les' skin which was rapidly approaching the very critical stage. God answered our prayers and his skin is much improved. We are trusting the Lord to hold the eczema in check for the next couple of months, if it please Him.

December 23 we are to move into the basement apartment of this same building. That is also a real answer to prayer. That apartment faces out into a small garden, in which our dear landlady has said the children can play at all times. Also, there is a glassed-in porch all across the back of the apartment which faces the sun all day. The Marseille sun is warm but there is always a strong, quite cool wind. So the porch is the ideal answer, all the sun and no wind. Isn't the Lord good?

We felt led of the Lord to remove the children from school. It was a difficult decision because the children liked school. Jeanette's rather fragile constitution simply couldn't take the battle with French six days a week from 8:30 until 4:30 in unheated rooms. She came down with that old bronchial trouble she had four or five years ago. She lost considerable weight and had such a bad cough. So we knew she would have to remain at home, and we just couldn't see leaving Marian in that Catholic atmosphere as she is four years younger than Jeanette and more impressionable. Praise the Lord, they are good girls and keep themselves entertained right well.

We have so little time we can actually devote to them. We treasure every single minute to study French, and still it is not enough. Sometimes it is most discouraging but we have to remind ourselves that we are members in good standing in the K.L.U. Club. When we "look up," discouragements have a tendency to vanish.

Hope you enjoy the enclosed snapshots. Don't the girls look good in their French berets? I've been trying to get Les to wear one but I guess he is just bashful. He won't wear one.

Well, it's almost ten o'clock and I've written about eight letters and I'm just about "writ" out. Much of our love and much of our prayers are centered around you dear ones at Edgemont and the work there. God bless you.

Love,

Gertie

Jeanette's Comment: Basement Apartment

Moving to the basement was quite exciting! So much more room! Every main room opened onto that glassed-in porch. And the bathroom contained a shower—we could actually do more than take a spit-bath!

The front door opened into a large room—and all the other rooms opened off that entrance room. Since this was a very large room, Mom and Dad chose it for their bedroom. The landlady moved a bed into it, plus a big armoire.

After entering, a door on the left opened into what looked like a closet (which were totally non-existent in French apartments then). It contained the toilet—and only the toilet. The sink and shower were in another room completely across the entrance room on the other side.

The kitchen was straight ahead—and Mom rejoiced over that kitchen! Now, she could really cook. Along one wall was a four-burner stove with a small oven, plus a nice marble sink and an icebox. On the opposite wall was a china cabinet—with all the dishes and flatware included (all carefully counted and recorded)—plus a small table and four chairs. French doors opened onto the glassed-in porch.

This view shows the stove and part of the marble sink. That wooden "box" on the end was the icebox. Every day the iceman brought us a block of ice to put in the top compartment to keep our food cold. There was no freezer, of course, but it would keep a few left-overs, as well as milk and cheese. But that's why Mom had to shop every day for perishable items.

The middle door leading out of the entrance hall went into a smallish bedroom. The landlady, Mlle Junod, had the bed purchased for Marian and my bedroom upstairs moved down to that basement bedroom, plus a chest for clothes. It still left plenty of space for us to play. Again, French doors opened onto the porch.

The far right door entered into the living room. It was a very large room where the only source of heating for the entire apartment was located—a small stove connected to a beautiful fireplace. We had a daybed/sofa in there, a large table with several chairs, a large buffet, plus a desk for Dad. This room was large enough to have two French doors leading onto the porch.

And oh! That porch! Except for the coldest days, the sun kept it warm enough to enjoy. We girls played out there, read—squabbled, of course—but loved the freedom it gave to us.

Right above the glassed-in porch was a large deck that jutted out from Mlle Junod's apartment. She didn't have too much to look at, however. I guess during the war no one had time to take care of a garden. There were a few trees but almost everything else was overgrown with weeds. Flower beds lined the outside courtyard walls. A gravel path circled the entire garden, and in the middle was a large area that had at one time contained all kinds of flowers, including roses. Everything had just gone to weeds, however.

The whole apartment house was located directly by the sidewalk. You went up three steps from the sidewalk to the entrance hallway of the apartment—all up and down the street. There was no front lawn—just gray buildings built side by side along the sidewalk on each side of the street. Tiny wrought iron balconies jutted off the front windows, and some people put geraniums or other flowers on the balconies during warm weather.

The back areas were all divided into courtyards, each surrounded on three sides by a 10- to 12-foot wall. No one could get into the courtyard from the front except through an apartment. During

World War II, the Nazis insisted that the French top the walls with glass shards embedded in concrete, something that would deter any Resistance agent from trying to climb between the buildings. Behind the back wall was an alley—and each courtyard had a heavy iron door with a huge key that opened onto the alley. Dad had to park the Green Hornet in a garage a couple of blocks away because there was no parking allowed on the street. He could come and go via that iron door leading out of the courtyard.

Part of the good memories of France come from that wonderful apartment at 41 rue Daumier (named after Honoré Daumier, a French caricaturist and artist). It really felt like home to us, and we girls had plenty of room to enjoy ourselves.

"THE DARK CONTINENT"

AFRICA

Berean Mission, Inc.
3536 Russell Blvd.
St. Louis, Missouri

Prayer Letter * * * * * December 1953

"For unto us a Child is born, unto us a Son is given" (Isaiah 9:6).
"And thou shalt call His name JESUS: for He shall save His people from their sins" (Matthew 1:21).

Dear Christian friends:

At this Christmas Season as we think upon the Wonderful One about whom these verses speak, we readily say with the Apostle Paul, "Thanks be unto God for His unspeakable Gift." God gave His only begotten Son to be the Savior of all who would trust in Him; and His name was to be called JESUS (Jeshua, Savior)! As we contemplate the supernatural, virgin birth of this divine Savior, we are reminded of the many prophecies concerning His coming into the world. One of these prophecies is Isaiah 62:11, "Behold, thy *Salvation* (Jeshua, Savior, JESUS) cometh; behold, *His* reward is with *Him*, and *his* work before *Him*." God would have us to see that SALVATION is not a thing or an event, but a Person, the Lord Jesus Christ! How good it is to know this Wonderful Person and trust Him as your Savior.

Since writing to you last October, we have been having quite a time getting settled in a strange country and becoming accustomed to a different manner of life. We entered France on September 2 with the privilege of remaining in the country for only three months, as any other tourist, intending to ask the local authorities for permission to stay one year for the purpose of studying the French language. Upon inquiry we found that we must have a "carte de Sejour de Residence Temporaire" in order to remain in the country longer than three months. We at once placed application for this permit and have been busy ever since supplying the requisite identification, credentials, photographs, references, etc. And now, two months and six visits later, we have at last secured a temporary receipt which will permit us to remain until the first week in February, when our Carte de Sejour will be issued, we hope.

You should see Gertie and me heading out each day to do the marketing. It is really a two-man job! One doesn't merely go to the nearest supermarket and buy all the foodstuffs needed for a day or two. No, not in France! First, we must go to the Boucherie (Butcher Shop) to buy our meat. If you think meat is expensive in America, we pay 828 francs per kilo (about $1.30 a pound) here in France. The cost of living is terrifically high, and I understand that the average wage is low.

Oh yes, we want some boiled ham for lunch, but we cannot buy it at the Boucherie—you see, they do not handle lunch meats—instead we must go to the Charcuterie (Pork-butcher's Shop). And, of course, if one desires fish, it must be purchased at the Poissonerie (Fish Market). We must be careful how we ask for fish because in French "poisson" is fish, and "poison" is poison.

Having purchased our meat, we must now get along to the Alimentation (General Food Store) where we buy our staples, fruits, and vegetables. The French canned goods are not good at all—even the French seldom buy them; they just sit on the shelves. The few, rare items of American canned goods are priced completely out of reason. For example, a small can of Libby's sliced pineapple is priced at $1.35. Consequently, we have little use for a can opener here in France. How we long for a good can of peas, or asparagus, or pork and beans, or some ketchup for our meat; or best of all, a good old can of American popcorn.

But our shopping isn't done yet; we need some bread, but we cannot buy it at the little Alimentation. Who ever heard of buying bread in a grocery store? Ridiculous! No, we must now go to the Boulangerie (Bakery) in order to buy bread. While there we must use much will-power because the counters are loaded with delicious dainties; but they are much too expensive for the missionaries' diet. The flour here in France is coarse, and the baking powder is no good; what Gertie needs is some good old American cake-mix.

Then, to complete our shopping for the day, we must go to the Crèmerie in order to buy milk, butter, confiture (preserves), cheese, and formerly eggs. We were paying just a little over $1.00 per dozen for eggs,

but they have now jumped to $2.36 per dozen (some jump), and so eggs are no longer in our diet. You can see that shopping in France is not a simple matter, but a long, drawnout, everyday procession to the Crèmerie, the Boucherie, the Boulangerie, the Charcuterie, and the Alimentation. There are also the large, open-air markets where one can buy fresh fruits and vegetables; but we have been warned not to do our marketing there until we have a better command of the French language, lest we be "chiseled" out of our precious francs.

Volailles et Gibiers (poultry and game)

Drogurie (household sundries)

Jeanette and Marian are now attending a French school and enjoying it very much. We were unsuccessful in our attempts to enroll them in the "Lycees" (State-supported schools), and so had to send them to a private school. More than one-half the children of France attend private schools because the government simply does not provide sufficient facilities. Both Jeanette and Marian are doing their "devoir" (homework) in French now. Sometimes it takes all four of us to translate the assignments and figure out what is to be done. We have even had our landlady, Mademoiselle Junod, helping us "kids" with our homework. The cost of tuition, like everything else in France, is quite high, and we may not be able to keep the children in school for the full year that we are here. We must pay 22,000 francs ($62.85) every three months for their tuition, and that is considerable.

One day as Jeanette and Marian were walking to school, one of these tiny French automobiles pulled over to the curbing and a uniformed gentleman leaped out of the car in front of them and asked where they were going. When they recovered from their shock, they recognized standing before them none other than the Captain of the S. S. VOLTA, the faithful ship that brought us from New York to Marseille. While driving the children to school, he told them that the VOLTA was leaving that Friday on its return trip to New York and asked if they would be his guests and go back with him. Of course, they were torn between two loves, but they are good little missionaries.

Gertrude and I are working hard on our French and are slowly making a little progress. We are beginning to understand just a bit of what is constantly being said round about us—a word here and there—enough sometimes to catch the gist of the conversation; but at other times it is still just a lot of peculiar, unintelligible chatter. We need your prayers—particularly for *time* and enablement.

Life here in France seems to be entirely consumed with living, and it is so difficult to find the hours needed for study. The pace of life is not so fast in the Old World as it is in the New; but neither do they have many of the modern conveniences, and that is all the more reason why one's day

is spent, with much lost motion, in accomplishing little. We have learned to consider the long hours of shopping as part of learning French, however, for there we have our best opportunities of speaking and understanding the language. It is necessary, if one would eat!

God has brought us together with a very competent French tutor; the wife of an officer of The Nestle Company. Madame Quinche has taught both French and English for many years in Switzerland and North Africa, and so we just praise the Lord for leading us to her. We thought it more than mere coincidence that Madame Quinche was living on the third floor of our same apartment building! Surely, the Lord leads in marvelous ways, doesn't He? Pray much that we might learn the language, for our time to remain in France is so short.

When we first moved into our apartment, there was only one double bed, and so we borrowed a bed for the children from "Le Phare," until the landlady could secure another one for us. Now our landlady is a lover of French antiques, though she herself is Swiss. And so recently she bought a bed for the girls that satisfied her yen for antiquity. It is a Provincial "litoche" of Louis XIII era, which means that the bedstead is over 300 years old. Jeanette and Marian are the tenth generation of the children to sleep in this rather plain, unimposing bed.

Jeanette is still playing her accordion each Sunday afternoon at the street meeting conducted along the Vieux Port in downtown Marseille. When she opens the case and starts to put on the accordion, the people begin to gather round; and when she starts playing, they literally throng

our tight little circle. We have a tremendous crowd around us in no time at all. Then, two or three of the French pastors each bring a short gospel message, with Jeanette playing her accordion in between each message. Last of all, Rev. Howarth (English) makes an offer of free French New Testaments to any who will sign the pledge in the flyleaf to read it through. Each Sunday he has given away two or three New Testaments to interested individuals. We just pray that God will use His Word to bring those dear souls to our Lord and Saviour Jesus Christ. Some weeks ago we had the privilege of preaching by means of an interpreter at their indoor meeting, which follows the street meeting. It is a difficult way to preach, and one that is distracting both the speaker and to the congregation, but God always honors His Word.

As each of you dear ones keep the Christmas Season in America, we will be keeping it here in the land of the Noël (French for "Christmas"). We will be thinking of you and missing you, but God gives grace. We would like to take this opportunity of wishing each of you a Blessed Christmas and a Joyous New Year in the Lord.

The Lord bless thee and keep thee,

The Spainhowers

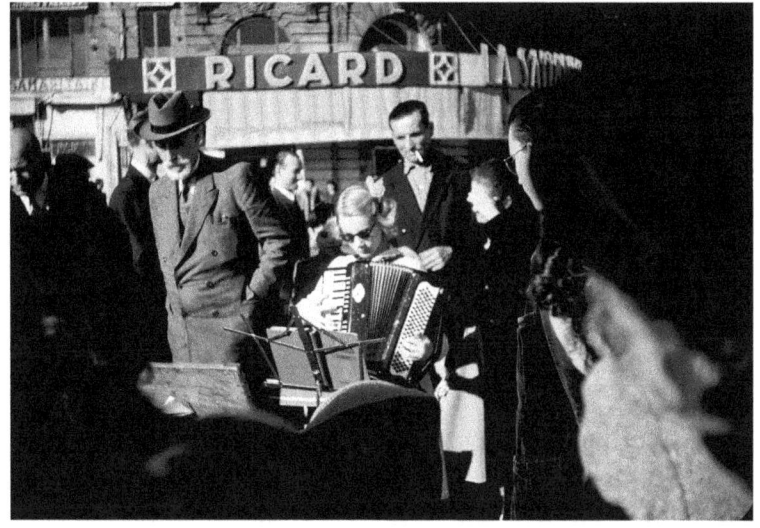

41, rue Daumier
Marseille, France
December 31, 1953

Berean Mission, Inc.
3536 Russell Boulevard
St. Louis 4, Missouri

Dear Ones:

Greetings in the name of our Wonderful Savior! We trust that you have all had a fine Christmas Holiday and that the blessings of the season will continue with you throughout the New Year. We have enjoyed a wonderful Christmas here in France, and can certainly say that the blessing of the Lord has been our portion. The more we cast ourselves upon Him, the nearer and dearer He becomes to us.

Perhaps the greatest blessing of this Christmas was received in conducting two worship services aboard the heavy cruiser U.S.S. MACON (CA-132) on December 20 and 27. The MACON, together with another light cruiser, a destroyer, and two mine-layers, was docked at Marseille for the Christmas Season. Chaplain Wallace of the MACON contacted us through the American Consulate and asked if we would take these two Protestant Worship Services, since there was no Protestant Chaplain in this particular group of ships. There were more than 1300 men and officers aboard the MACON alone, and I have no idea how many men aboard all five ships, and no Protestant Chaplain to minister to their spiritual needs!

We certainly had two wonderful services. Jeanette played her accordion and furnished all the music from the prelude to the postlude and special music as well. The sailors really enjoyed this little blonde missionary playing for them - and, in turn, they really sang for us. There were a good number of Christian lads at the services, which were held in one of the mess rooms, and they all entered into the spirit of the service. They were so captivated by Jeanette and Marian that they gave each of them a pretty French character doll for Christmas.

The Holy Spirit dealt with willing hearts there within the steel walls of the MACON's mess room, and five precious young souls accepted the Lord Jesus Christ as their Savior. They stepped right out during the invitation and came to the front of the room before all their buddies to confess Christ as Savior, and then we dealt with them following the service, and they all meant business with the Lord. I feel certain that much of this "harvest" was due to the faithful, patient, sowing of the "seed" by one of their Training Officers, Lt. Roy Rodgers of Wheaton, Illinois, who has been working among the boys, speaking a word here and there for several months since leaving the U.S. I don't know why God chose to permit me to be the one to preach the message that reached their hearts and brought them finally to Christ, but praise the Lord for His faithfulness in honoring His Word! Perhaps He knew that we needed that encouragement along the way — that drink of sweet water in this dry wilderness of language study in a strange land.

We also attended a service aboard the U.S.S. MACON on Christmas Day, conducted by Rev. Howarth of the European Christian Mission. We went along for the fellowship of another service in good old English language, and also in order that Jeanette could again furnish the music on her accordion. Brother Howarth brought a fine message on the uniqueness of the birth of the Lord Jesus Christ, and one more sailor boy found Christ as His Savior. What a precious time we had. I shall ever be thankful to my God for the memory of those sweet moments aboard the U.S.S. MACON.

Well, I'd better get down to the business at hand before getting too tedious to you with much-speaking. I would like for you to send me two New York Bank Drafts, one for the amount of $350, and the other for the amount of $250, both of which to be deducted from our passage and equipment account. Please do not combine the amounts in one check as it will then be drawn for such a large amount that it would have to be returned to New York for verification.

The check for $350 will be used as *deposit* on engaging accommodations with the Union Castle Lines for transportation to Mombasa, Kenya. This amount will be payable at once in order to book the reservation, and the balance of the fare to be paid not later than 21 days prior to embarkation. The local agents have written to London for accommodations "Tourist Class" during the month of July. The total cost for the four of us will be about $750 to Mombasa, Kenya.

The check for $250 is for the purchase of some additional equipment for the Congo, the largest single item being a set of five new 6-ply tires for the Suburban. I had planned on driving in with my original tires on the car, but Brother Irving Lindquist wrote me as follows:

"Do you have 4- or 6-ply tires? 4-ply do not seem to last any time at all out here. I made the mistake of bringing an extra set of 4-ply tires with me from America, and they didn't do much more than 3,000 kilometers (about 1,860 miles), and they were supposed to be extra good tires."

Inasmuch as my tires have almost 25,000 miles on them at present, I consider it wise to buy the new 6-ply tires and tubes and realize as much as possible out of the sale of my present 4-ply tires. Believe it would be good to keep the old tubes as spares for the Congo. In addition to the tires and tubes, we must purchase our sun helmets, mosquito nets, a supply of Paludrine for malaria, another packing trunk, a water filter together with candles, tubing, spicket, etc., etc.

We trust that all is going well at the home base. Our best regards to you all. We remember you daily at the Throne of Grace.

Love in Christ,

Leslie J. Spainhower

P.S. Neglected to mention it will also cost about $250 to ship the car to Mombasa; but that cost will come later.

Jeanette's Comment: SS Macon

The American Consulate was located on the main street in downtown Marseille. I vividly remember the first time we were walking down the street and there, ahead of us, floated the Stars and Stripes. That little bit of Marseille was American! In fact, a few times, Marian and I were invited to play with the Consul's children while Mom talked with the wife.

We'd attended a Thanksgiving Day service at a little French Protestant church where we were the only Americans. The others were all British. I believe Rev. Howarth conducted that service. That's the first time I realized how good it was to hear God's Word preached in English while we were in a foreign country. As the service closed, everyone stood to sing a last song. From the introduction, I figured it was "My Country, 'Tis of Thee." Instead, the English started singing, "God Bless Our Gracious Queen." Mom just grinned, and we quietly sang our own national song.

I was really excited when Dad told us we were going to hold two services on an American ship, the U.S.S. Macon. Even a twelve-year-old missed not only family and friends but also all things American, especially church. I played my accordion at Le Vieux Port every Sunday afternoon—and then we immediately went to the service Rev. Howarth held in a nearby building. But I really didn't understand much of what was being said.

Now, we were going to actually hold services ourselves on board an American naval ship! It was a gray, ugly morning when Dad pulled the Green Hornet onto the pier beside an absolutely HUGE ship. The American flag was whipping in the wind. A good-looking officer hurried down the gangplank, followed by another sailor. The young sailor balanced my accordion case on his shoulder and headed back up the gangplank.

Lt. Roy Rodgers (who looked nothing like the cowboy!) greeted us and led us up the gangplank where we were piped aboard the ship. Then he led us up and down open stairs, even ladders, to get to the mess room where the service was to be held. But before Mom, Marian, and I started down any stairs, the sailor with my accordion case called out a warning to clear the area around the stairs because ladies were on board (in dresses, of course).

The mess room was jam-packed with sailors and a few officers. There was even a Christmas tree in one corner. The meeting was wonderful—and the young sailors crowded around to talk with us after the meeting. Lt. Rodgers took us on a brief tour of the ship. Looking back, my 12-year-old feelings about being one of three females on a big U.S. cruiser full of American guys were kind of silly. Too bad I was only 12. I'm sure Dad and Mom, however, considered it a great blessing!!

When we went back the next Sunday with Rev. Howarth, some of the sailors gave Marian and me French character dolls as Christmas presents to thank us for taking time out of our holiday to visit with them. I had to swallow hard at that one. That meant they looked at me as a little girl when I was sure I had appeared much older and more sophisticated than that!

41, rue Daumier
Marseille, France
December 31, 1953

Dear Brother and Sister Wright:

"The blessing of the Lord be upon you: we bless you in the Name of the Lord."

We received your long, newsy letter before Christmas, but just simply haven't had a moment to reply since then. We want to thank you for your lovely Christmas greetings and also for your nice gift of $5. It was so good of you to remember us in this way. We received all of the Christmas packages from Gertie's folks before Christmas — the last arriving Christmas Eve about 4:30 P.M. All in all, we praise the Lord for a blessed Christmas. We received many, many Christmas cards from the folk at Edgemont, and they meant so much to us at this time away from all our loved ones.

Dad's 37th birthday on December 23, 1953

We actually didn't have time to be "homesick" over the Holidays inasmuch as the Lord granted us the privilege of conducting two worship services aboard the heavy cruiser U.S.S. MACON (CA-132), which together with a light cruiser, a destroyer, and two mine-layers were tied up at a dock here in Marseille. I have told about it in the enclosed copy of my letter to Berean Mission, so won't repeat the story here, other than to say that the Lord certainly blessed our hearts through these services. We also attended two French Christmas Programs with all the little French children singing carols and saying their pieces (in French, of course) much as we do at home. Apart from the language, the greatest difference was that they use real, live candles on their Christmas trees instead of electric lights. The wick of each candle is connected by a strand or "cotton of fire," and at the climatic moment someone lights this cotton strand and the flame travels all over the tree lighting each candle as the fire travels along the cotton strand. It was really very beautiful.

I have sent you the enclosed copy of letter to Berean Mission in order that you might be apprised of the $600 we are withdrawing from our passage and equipment account, and the expenditure of same. As you will note in that letter, our total passage to Mombasa, Kenya will be about $750, plus about $350 for shipping the car. We will be paying a deposit of $350 when we engage accommodations (in a couple of weeks), and the balance of $750 should be paid sometime in May, and must be paid not later than 21 days prior to embarkation. As you will note, we have asked for accommodations sometime during the month of July.

In addition, we will need at least $150 to ship our trunks and large wood crate all the way to Bukavu in the Congo. We hope to ship these about two months before our departure from here (or about May). Also, we will need to order the Calvert Courses for Jeanette and Marian in May to be shipped direct to the Greens at Katanti Station. This will mean about another $200. Inasmuch as the

Greens are using the Calvert System and Bob Hendry favors it, too, we don't believe a change to the other system would be well. At least not until Bob Hendry is on the field and ready to make the changes himself. (I refer to the other system Enoch Sanford recommended).

We feel that all of our packing cases at Leo's home and at Mother Wilson's home should be shipped in March. At the same time (March), the Mission should order our Majestic wood-burning range; Servel kerosene refrigerator; and gasoline-powered washing machine at a total purchase cost of about $600. The cost of exporting all these items plus our packing cases at home will be approximately $700 to Shabunda, Congo Belge.

Then, upon arrival in the Congo late in July or early August we should have with us about $300 for the purpose of paying custom duty on all of our equipment shipped in. There is simply no way of estimating customs - it varies with the mood of the official, and the heat of the day. I feel we should also have with us about $500 for expenses of the automobile trip inland, incidentals, and funds to keep us going until regular monthly checks begin to arrive.

All of this might be summarized as follows to give a sort of time-table account of our needs as we undertake this last great leg of our journey to the Congo:

January	Deposit on Passage	$ 350
	Auto Tires & other equipment	$ 250
	TOTAL NEED IN JANUARY	$ 600
March	Refrig., Stove & Washing Machine	$ 600
	Cost of Exporting above together with 25 cases at home	$ 700
	TOTAL NEED IN MARCH	$1300
May	Balance of Passage	$ 400
	Cost of shipping car	$ 350
	Cost of shipping trunks & crate from Marseille to Bukavu	$ 150
	Cost of Calvert System for both Jeanette & Marian	$ 200
	TOTAL NEED IN MAY	$1100
June or early July	Estimated Duty on all items	$ 300
	Travel Expenses from Mombasa, Kenya to Mission Station & Funds incidental to setting up in Congo	$ 500
	TOTAL NEED IN JUNE/JULY	$ 800
	TOTAL ESTIMATED PASSAGE & EQUIPMENT NEED	$3800
	Total pass. & Equip. Reserves End of November 1953	$1464
	Total Field Reserves End of November 1953	$ 755
	TOTAL RESERVES (End of November, 1953)	$2219
	TOTAL ESTIMATED NEED BY JUNE	$1581

I hope all of this has not been too difficult or tedious to follow, but believe it will give you a good idea of the need as it may be staggered by months. It is "staggering" all right. Believe it might be well for me to include this summary in the next prayer letter with the thought that it might stimulate some action from the church at Monrovia, California, if it is the Lord's will that they take any action. I have never heard any more from them with respect to their inquiry as to our needs, nor respecting the tape and slides. But, of course, it is still early. The Lord knows.

Want to get this in the mail today, so will close for now. Will write you later about the tape recordings and other matters when can find a spare moment. French is progressing slowly — so very slowly. We sometimes wonder if we ever will be able to speak it — but again, the Lord is able.

Much love in Christ,

Les, Gertie and girls

P.S. Am sending a carbon copy of this letter to Brother Leo Williams so that he may have these figures before him. Trust that will be all right.

Jeanette's Comment: Christmas in France

The Christmas we spent in France is one of the best memories I have of any childhood Christmas. Even though we were far from home in a foreign land, it was very special. A trip to the mountains was just the start.

The Ste. Baume mountains were about an hour and a half from our apartment in Marseille. In pleasant weather, we often drove up into the mountains. It gave us girls a chance to run and play and Mom and Dad the opportunity just to relax.

We had a favorite spot where we generally ate a picnic lunch, surrounded by pine trees and other evergreens. As Christmas was approaching, Dad got the idea of going back up to the spot in the mountains and cutting evergreens to use as decorations. We asked two other Americans, Paul and Betty Semenchuk (missionaries to the displaced Russians in southern France), to go with us.

What a jolly time we had! We sang Christmas carols and talked about Christmases past. Snow covered everything in the mountains, but the roads were passable. It was absolutely gorgeous!

When we got to our favorite spot, we not only found lots of greens to use in Christmas decorations but even a bright holly bush. We cut armloads of God's bounty and put it in the back of the station wagon. Paul and Dad, however, decided to take it one step further—they each wanted a small Christmas tree. Both of our families lived in apartments, so we couldn't have big ones.

Well, the trees in our favorite spot were all too big—and the small ones weren't nicely formed. So we started on our way home. Suddenly, Paul shouted for us to stop. There were two beautiful trees, perfect for Christmas trees—about eight or nine feet tall. But the two intrepid lumberjacks weren't after the whole tree, just the tops. Dad and Paul climbed the trees and cut down just the tops, producing two Christmas trees about three feet tall, while we four females fretted as we watched them.

Stuffing the two little trees into the back of the station wagon, we drove back to Marseille. It was already dark by the time we got there, so we unloaded one of the little trees and some of the holly and evergreen branches at the Semenchuks' apartment.

When we got back to our apartment, Mlle. Junod came out of her apartment to see what was going on as we tramped up and down the stairs. She had the most horrified look on her face when we told her about our day's big adventure. She ran out to the car to help unload the greenery. "Hurry! Hurry!" she urged. "They mustn't see you!"

Turns out, it was illegal to cut greenery, much less top evergreen trees, in the mountains—they are all national parks. She wanted us to get our stuff inside before any of the neighbors saw us and called the police! We were duly repentant, but there was nothing we could do after the fact. But for awhile we grew nervous whenever someone knocked on the door!

So here we were with a little Christmas tree and a pile of evergreens—but no other decorations. Dad declared that we would go downtown the next day to buy a string of lights and a few ornaments. Mom said she had some other ideas for decorations, too. So Marian and I went to bed to dream of Christmas trees—and being thrown in jail for cutting them down!

While Dad was studying the next day, Mom helped Marian and me make a pile of small paper snowflakes that would grace our little tree. Then we made one of our rare excursions downtown (French traffic was awful!!) to one of the big department stores. We found a string of lights and bought several glass ornaments to intersperse with our snowflakes. All the while, the store's loudspeakers were blaring the

favorite pop song of the day, "Combien le chien dans la fenêtre?" [How much is that doggy in the window?] We recognized the song, even though the words were in French, because it had been so popular in the United States in the summer before we left.

We spent the evening decorating our little tree and putting greenery on the fireplace mantel and the top of the china cabinet, with sprigs of holly in a bowl on the table. Mom got out the Louis-the-something brass candlesticks she'd bought in an antiques store to stand at either end of the mantel. Mlle Junod came downstairs and thought everything looked very beautiful. She happily took the leftover greens upstairs to her apartment for a little holiday cheer.

The doll dresses and everything that Grandma and other relatives had sent to us, plus Mom and Dad's loving gifts, made this one of the best Christmases ever! In quiet moments, we still missed our loved ones back in the States—but we knew they were thinking about us and praying for us. So, in spirit, we were celebrating together.

Marian's Comment

As we were growing up, no matter where we were, as long as Mom, Dad, Jeanette and I were together, our lives were complete and full as far as I was concerned. Our home was filled with love, laughter, and the comfort and security of being together as a family. Having our first Christmas in a foreign country, far away from the rest of our family whom we loved and missed very much, made no difference. Mom and Dad saw to it that Jeanette and I had a very happy Christmas.

It also didn't hurt at all to have a fabulous Grandma (Wilson) who knew exactly what would make our Christmas in France very special indeed. Let me explain.

There were many people who attended Edgemont Bible Church, our home church in East St. Louis, Illinois, whom we all loved dearly. Two of those people were Ruth and Eileen Herin.

Ruth Herin was the oldest of the two sisters and played the organ at the church. Jeanette especially loved Ruth because she gave Jeanette piano and accordion lessons. Ruth was a very sweet, gracious lady.

Eileen Herin played the piano at the church and had a lovely soprano voice. She had the prettiest red, curly hair and had an infectious, bubbly laugh. She was quite free with her hugs, which drew me to her.

The Christmas before we left for France (1952), Grandma Wilson gave Jeanette and me lovely dolls. She made some beautiful dresses for those dolls out of some of the leftover material from which she had made Jeanette and me dresses. Naturally, Jeanette named her doll "Ruth," and I named mine "Eileen."

Well, for this Christmas in France, Grandma made our Ruth and Eileen dolls matching wedding dresses and mailed them to us along with garment bags to keep the dresses clean. What made this so wonderful is that after we left the States, Ruth became engaged to Charles Brazeal and Eileen to Ron Krestan. Both men were study-

ing for the ministry at Midwest Bible Institute where Dad had gone. They were planning a big double wedding at Edgemont Bible Church in the summer of 1954. Naturally, we were very delighted for them but sad that we weren't going to be there to share in their special day. You can imagine how many times Jeanette and I played out their wedding ceremony with our dolls that year.

For your information...on November 4, 1966, Ruth (Herin) Brazeal played the organ for my wedding! I was thrilled!

41, rue Daumier
Marseille, France
January 10, 1954

Dear Brother and Sister Wright:

    Received your letter of January 4 and so good to get all the news. In fact, Mrs. W., we think it is a good idea for you to spend your evenings when Mr. W. is away writing nice, newsy letters to us! We spoil real easy like! It is true that the mails have been delayed, particularly in their handling through Paris, but praise the Lord for bringing through the many, many cards and greetings from the dear folk at Edgemont, and all of the Christmas packages, too. We have not begun to receive the boxes of canned goods which you told us were on the way; but then it takes at least six weeks or more for a package to arrive. Please thank the Church Family in our Saviour's dear name for their goodness in showering us with so many canned goods as you speak of. We were really only "hankering" for a few cans as a sort of a *luxury*, and not for a pantry full and running over. The Lord has demonstrated again that if we will but give ourselves unto Him, that *"it shall be given unto you; good measure, pressed down, and shaken together, and running over, shall men give unto your bosom."* (We would like to return a portion of our accumulated tithe back to Edgemont, too, and so enclosed $30 to be placed in the Joash Offering for us. We want to see that new Christian Education Building of the Edgemont Bible Church when we return five years hence.)

    Thank you for sending us the calendar. We have not received it as yet but will surely be able to use it on the wall just over my desk. After all, we must check off these last six months carefully! So glad, too, that you thoughtfully enclosed the Blackburn's prayer letter telling of their trip inland, inasmuch as we will be going in the same route. Carl wrote me a long, detailed account of mileages between points, where to stay overnight, etc., also actual costs along the way. His report will be of great benefit to us as we follow in his "tire-prints" in about seven months from now.

    No time for more. Love from us all to you and to all.

The Lord bless thee!

Les, Gertie, Jeanette and Marian

P.S. We are having an extended period of extremely cold weather with strong winds. The Lord is still "holding the line" on my skin, praise His Name! It is bad, but not severe. Six more weeks should bring full relief!

41, rue Daumier
Marseille, France
January 28, 1954

Dear Brother and Sister Wright:

"Blessed be the Lord, who daily loadeth us with benefits, even the God of our salvation. Selah" (Psalm 68:19).

About three o'clock this afternoon the front door bell buzzed loud and long, completely disrupting my study of French. I pushed the button that releases the lock on the outside front door leading into the foyer; then I opened our apartment door to see who had the audacity to interrupt my study. By this time there was a deliveryman standing in the middle of the foyer and shouting "Spenoway," "Spenoway, paquet pour Spenoway!" (Spenoway is the French for Spainhower). Realizing it was packages from home, we almost mobbed the fellow before he could get our name on the dotted line and beat a hasty retreat.

It turned out to be four luscious packages, which we dragged into the apartment and pounced upon, tearing them open in record time. One package contained cake mixes from Edgemont; another contained Jellos and Puddings, also from Edgemont; still another was a delicious tin of candy from the Handels, (also of Edgemont); and the fourth package was Christmas gifts for all from Gertie's sister. Merry Christmas! Will you please thank all the dear folks who had a part in this, and Brother and Sister Martin especially for packaging them all up and sending them to us. Gertie is so thrilled to be able to bake a cake whenever she wants to, (and so are we, too).

The tapes of the November Missions Conference have not arrived as yet; but the *Douane* (Customs) are probably listening to them in Paris to make sure they do not contain secret information regarding the overthrow of the government or something equally as drastic. It is an excellent means of getting the gospel to the Douane officials! In this respect, I don't believe it would be wise to mail anymore tapes to us after March for fear they would not reach us in time. But please let us have at least one of you preaching, Brother Wright, before the end of March, one that we can take on into the Congo with us. Also, I don't believe it would be wise to mail any other packages, other than airmail, after the first or second week of April. After the middle of April, anything else should be mailed to Ikozi Station for us. (Packages, that is). Regular mail will reach us all right if mailed by the first week in June, and airmail (letters) not later than June 21 or 22. Of course that is a long way off yet!

It is good we can commit all of these things to the Lord and let Him work them out. We may be puzzled, even doubt at times, but "He doeth all things well."

Christian love to you both,

Les and Gertie

41, rue Daumier
Marseille, France
February 14, 1954

Dear Brother and Sister Wright:

"Let all those that put their trust in Thee rejoice: let them ever shout for joy, because Thou defendest them: let them also that love Thy name be joyful in Thee" (Psalm 5:11).

We are praising the Lord, together with you, for the wonderful Joash offering last month—over $1,200. How we would like to be there for the note-burning! But even more—how we would like to be there and see and help in the raising up of that new Education Building of Edgemont Bible Church. But then, we will see it when we return on furlough some years hence. And, I hope by that time that you are so crowded that facilities will again need to be expanded.

As you know, Helen Gow and Evelyn Nickerson left Ikozi Station late in December to start their long journey to you-ward. Carl Blackburn drove them to Usumbura on the northern tip of Lake Tanganyika, where they boarded a lake steamer which carried them to Kigona, the inland terminus of a railroad which crosses Tanganyika to the Indian Ocean Port of Dar es Salaam. At Dar es Salaam they boarded the WARWICK CASTLE on January 7 for their voyage north along the East Coast of Africa, through the Red Sea and the Suez Canal into the Mediterranean Sea, and thence to Marseille, France.

The WARWICK CASTLE was due to arrive in Marseille on January 31, but when we checked with the office here they said it would be at least February 1 or 2. Upon later inquiry, they advised us that the ship would not dock until February 5, and still later developments indicated it would arrive the 6th or 7th. So, we secured a "laisser passer" (allow to pass), which would permit us to enter the dock areas, on the 6th or 7th. However, the ship finally came in on Monday morning, February 8, and we had to "bluff" our way through the harbor police with an outdated "laisser passer." Most the delay enroute originated at Genoa, Italy where they experienced a "slowdown" strike among the dock workers.

We drove the "green Hornet" (our green Suburban) alongside the WARWICK CASTLE at Mole G, Poste 22, at 7:30 A.M. the morning of February 8. Not a soul was stirring except a handful of men who had just hoisted the gangplank into place, and they soon left. We were forbidden aboard the ship until the Health Officer had finished his business, and so we sat in the car and tried to keep warm. There was a damp, icy wind blowing, and it would simply cut through you. Finally, about 8:00 o'clock, we saw the little man with the briefcase come off the gangplank and disappear into the warehouse. We went aboard and found Helen and Evelyn just about ready to emerge from their cabin. How good it was to see them after, lo, these many years (at least four)! The Lord had given them calm seas and a good trip, and they were feeling rested.

The girls had made arrangements to disembark at Marseille with just one suitcase each, and let the rest of their baggage go on to England aboard the ship, and they will pick it up there later. By about 9:30 A.M. they were through the (ugh!) formalities of the douane (customs) and we were on our way to 41, rue Daumier. As we passed through the gates out of the dock area we were again stopped by the harbor police who wanted to know what we were trying to haul out of the place. The girls' luggage was properly marked by the douane so all was well, that is until one of the douane officers at the gate decided to get suspicious about the "Green Hornet." Since I did not have my Carnet de Passages en Douane with me, he was certain that we were attempting to steal an American car.

After much haggling and wrangling (in French, of course), he let us go after I promised faithfully to write 1,000 times: "I have been a bad boy for not carrying my Carnet in the glove compartment of the car where anyone at all could steal it easily."

We had a wonderful visit with Helen and Evelyn in spite of very inclement weather which kept us from showing them Marseille. The first day they were here, we had a minor "mistral," an icy blast of wind coming down the Rhone River Valley out of the Alps. We have no overcoats, or winter clothing of any kind with us (remember, it was supposed to be warm here, they said); however, we pulled the lapel of our suits high up around our necks and took the girls up on a hill overlooking Marseille, on which is situated Notre Dame de la Garde, a minor basilica of the Catholic Church. From this summit one can see the Mediterranean Sea, the harbor, and all of Marseille to the mountains that rim the city. The icy "mistral" was blowing so hard that we actually could not stand still against its pressure. We had to hold onto Marian to keep her from being blown down. We had wanted to take pictures of the girls up there with the city in the background, but it was impossible because of the wind.

The next day, the wind had stopped blowing, but it rained and drizzled all day long. Consequently, we ate and then sat around the table and talked until time to do the dishes and fix the next meal. Then we ate and talked and ate and talked, etc. It was a wonderful opportunity for us all to get well acquainted with two lovely girls who are real missionaries of our Lord Jesus Christ.

We surely hated to see Helen and Evelyn leave; but they wanted to spend a day or two in Brussels, Belgium, with the Crumleys, Lisles, and Maxine Gordon, who are studying there. It would have been a help to the girls and a welcome trip for us, too, if only we could have driven them to Brussels. But it is extremely cold to the north of us, and we deemed it unwise to expose my tender young hide to such temperatures. Believe me, it is bad enough here. Besides, we haven't a thing warm to wear—Gertie has only her light spring coat; I don't have any; and Jeanette and Marian have only their light jackets with them. Praise the Lord, winter is just about over, and then we will never, ever again have need of warm clothing. Anyway, we put Helen and Evelyn aboard a train on a through car to Brussels at 11:00 P.M. on the 9th, and they were due to arrive in Brussels about 2:00 P.M. on the 10th. From Brussels, Belgium, they will proceed to England where they are to sail on February 18 aboard the Queen Mary for America. I know all at Edgemont will be waiting to give them a Christian welcome home.

We now have final confirmation of our accommodations aboard the DUNNOTTAR CASTLE which sails from Marseille for Mombasa, Kenya, on July 1. Arrangements had to be handled through the Union Castle Lines' agent here in Marseille to the home office in England, and three different times they tried to give us rooms other than those which we requested but finally confirmed the right accommodations. We will be traveling Tourist Class, of course, but we wanted outside rooms for traveling in the tropics and wanted the children just across the hall from us, instead of a half-block down the hall. We also asked them for a 10% discount, as missionaries, which was granted. Together with some other small savings, our passage will now be only $650, instead of $750, plus about $350 for shipping the automobile. Praise the Lord!

Gertrude has just interrupted me by walking into the room from the kitchen bearing a luscious, home-made, Edgemont Special, cake mix, cake. How much we do appreciate those cake mixes and Jellos and canned goods. Oh yes, the box containing the canned goods arrived a few days after the other boxes, and our larder is now full, thanks to Edgemont. We did not have to pay duty on any of the boxes, only the minimum handling charge of about 40 cents per box. The tapes of the Missions Conference have not been received yet. I imagine the douane in Paris are holding them until they can audit them to make sure they are not subversive in any way. Let us pray that the Lord will use them to the salvation of some officials in the douane.

Have been in correspondence with the Chicago office of the Consulat General of Belgium concerning our Visa of Residence in the Belgian Congo. He wants us to handle with their Embassy in Paris, which means that all forms, regulations, etc. would be in French, and we have been endeavoring to handle with him, inasmuch as Mission Headquarters is within jurisdiction of Chicago Office. However, received letter from him yesterday morning stating that since we were residing outside his 15-State area of jurisdiction we would have to handle through Embassy at Paris. I don't know whether it would have been a different matter if the Mission had handled for us from the St. Louis Headquarters or not, but it doesn't matter. I am going down to the Consulate Office here in Marseille tomorrow morning to see if they will serve as intermediary for this consular service with their Embassy in Paris, where the Visa must actually be issued. Please remember this important detail in prayer, will you? This Visa must be issued not later than June 1, and not too much before that date, if we are to enter the Congo around August 1. The Visa must be in our Passport, together with In Transit Visas for Kenya and Uganda before the Union Castle Lines will issue final ticket—and final ticket must be purchased no later than 21 days before sailing date, or else we'd lose our reservations and deposit. Visa is only good for three months before entering Congo, else it expires. And so you can see that only the Lord can work it all out for us.

This must be getting tedious to you by now, so will bring it to a close. We meet with you daily at the Throne of Grace and are remembering you both and the work at Edgemont. Cleo Cruikshank has been sending the bulletin to us regularly, and it is such a blessing to follow the services in that manner. The Lord bless thee and keep thee.

Always rejoicing in Him,

Les, Gertie, Jeanette and Marian

Jeanette's Comment: Notre Dame de la Garde

Notre Dame de la Garde (Our Guardian Mother) is a Catholic basilica that stands on a high hill on the outskirts of Marseille at the south side of Le Vieux Port. It is a major local landmark and the

site of a popular annual pilgrimage on Assumption Day, August 15. The original church of the same name was built in 1214 and went through many phases. Notre Dame was even shared as a military fort for hundreds of years. The current basilica was consecrated on June 5, 1864.

Dad and Mom only mentioned Notre Dame in passing to Pastor and Mrs. Wright because many people who received our prayer letters in 1953 would not understand why we would visit a Catholic basilica—even just as tourists.

When we were in Marseille, this was the basilica of sailors—and models of ships from years past through the more modern eras hung from the ceiling in the nave. Sea captains would often go to the basilica to offer prayers before a voyage, the wives and sweethearts of fishermen to pray for their husbands' safety. The basilica was topped by a 27-ft. golden statue of the Madonna and Child that could be seen miles out to sea, gleaming in the sunlight.

That statue, dedicated on September 24, 1870, was made in four sections in order to get it up the hill and place it on top of the bell tower. It had a spiral staircase from the base to the head in the middle of the statue to be used for maintenance. It was made of copper to make it as light as possible, then gilded. It has been regilded many times, the latest time in 1989.

But the views were absolutely breath-taking. We could see the sprawling city of Marseille and the countryside and mountains beyond, as well as miles out to sea.

The basilica was surrounded by a walled broad square that could hold hundreds of people for special occasions. The great bell could be heard ringing throughout the entire city. (This is when we made sure we didn't go up to Notre Dame!)

During World War II, both the Germans and the Allies were careful not to bomb Notre Dame—but the Germans also closed access to the basilica when they discovered the Resistance was using its great height to send messages. By the end of World War II, the Germans had the square of Notre Dame surrounded with blockhouses. But when the Allies were ready to liberate Marseille, the orders were "no air raid, no large-scale use of artillery. This legendary rock will have to be attacked by infantrymen supported by armoured tanks."

Thanks to a French soldier from Marseille who knew of a secret passageway from one of the city's streets into Notre Dame, the French soldiers were able to gain access to the basilica, and the liberation of Marseille—and Notre Dame—took place on August 28, 1944.

Even though Notre Dame is considered a minor basilica, it seemed huge to us. It was composed of the lower church—built in earlier times over the original church—and the upper church added in the 1800s. The lower church, also called the crypt, is not very well-lit and doesn't have much decoration to it. The upper church is lighted by bay windows and decorated with multicolored marble and mosaics.

The original silver Madonna in the interior of the church was melted down for bullets during the French Revolution. Once Notre Dame was reopened after the French Revolution, a former ship's captain purchased an 18th-century statue called "Virgin of the bouquet" for the church. It's brightly painted, and the Madonna holds a bouquet of flowers.

A new silver Madonna was commissioned in 1829, and the "Virgin of the bouquet" was given to a monastery, but later returned to Notre Dame in 1979. Both of the Madonnas predated the current basilica. Now, the Madonna with the bouquet presides over the crypt and the silver Madonna over the upper church.

Basically, Notre Dame de la Garde was a working man's basilica that perfectly reflected the culture of the city.

The interior of the crypt area was dark with winding passageways. Always there were crucifixes, paintings, statues—of the dead Christ. One statue in particular that I remember represented Christ just taken from the cross and lying across a slab of marble. The basilica had to have the big toe on the left foot replaced a number of times because people would kiss that toe and wear away the plaster or whatever it was constructed of.

Mom and Dad used these visits to Notre Dame to show us girls why hope for eternity is only through the Lord Jesus Christ, not a stunning golden Madonna and Child, not through rows of glittering candles, not by kissing the relics of a saint or even the toe of a statue of the dead Jesus. These things only showed that Jesus was dead.

But the Jesus Christ we worship is alive and seated at the right hand of the Father.

Marseille, France
February 18, 1954

Dear Mr. and Mrs. Wright:

Greetings from "once again" sunny Marseille. The enclosed pictures will show you that sometimes the sun forgets to shine here. It has been quite cold here and is still quite brisk, yet there is a wee hint of spring in the air. Believe me, we Spainhowers are waiting to welcome "la belle printemps" (beautiful spring) with open arms.

We got a real thrill right up and down our spines when we read that our boxes were being picked up. I hope Mother's garage doesn't fall down when all the crates are removed. Leo and Irene will feel like they have an addition to their basement to get all our crates out.

We have a real "praise the Lord." We went to the Belgian Consulate of Marseille. The young fellow was most accommodating. When Les' French bogged down on the technical matters of the visa, the official suggested that we go to the American Consul and have them translate for us. We did just that, and as Les puts it, "Between both Consuls they managed to tie us up securely in red tape." The Belgian said we would probably be able to get the precious visa affixed in our passport by the middle of May. Keep praying.

The girls are fixing supper. Les and I are in here sort of holding our breath, hoping we will have some supper to eat. Bless their hearts, we'll eat it and tell them it's wonderful. Alka-Seltzer, here we come!

Tomorrow we are going to a doctor for our health certificate required for the visa. Mlle. Junod gave us the name of an English doctor here in Marseille. At least we won't have to contend in French for medical terms.

We are told, by the French to whom we speak, that we are making good progress but there is so much to learn and time is so short. We are resting fully in the Lord for His enablement. Will have the French *He* wants us to have when we leave.

Must close for now. Much love to you both and all the dear ones at Edgemont.

In Christ,

Les and Gertie
Jeanette and Marian

"THE DARK CONTINENT"

AFRICA

Berean Mission, Inc.
3536 Russell Blvd.
St. Louis, Missouri

Prayer Letter   * * * * *   February 1954

Dear Christian friends:

"The blessing of the Lord be upon you: we bless you in the name of the Lord."

By the time you receive your mimeographed copy of this letter in America, the Christmas season will be long past, but its blessings certainly not forgotten. Even though this was our first Christmas away from home, yet the Lord has made it one of the most blessed in our experience. We want to take this opportunity to thank all of you for your lovely cards and greetings and gifts which you sent to us. Truly our cup is full and running over. It is so good to know that we are in your hearts and minds.

Perhaps the greatest blessings of our Christmas were experiences on December 20 and 27 when we were privileged to conduct the Protestant Worship Services aboard the heavy cruiser U.S.S. MACON (CA-132) which, together with four other United States warships, was docked at Marseille, France during the holidays. The Catholic Chaplain of the MACON contacted us in a round-about way through the American Consulate in Marseille and requested that we conduct these services inasmuch as there was no Protestant Chaplain attached to this particular group of warships. There were more than 1300 men and officers aboard the MACON alone, and perhaps between 3,000 and 4,000 men aboard all five ships—and no Protestant Chaplain to minister to their spiritual needs! How we thank God for this wonderful opening to present the gospel to these many American sailors!

What a thrill it was on Sunday morning, December 20, as we drove along Woodrow Wilson Quai at the Port of Marseille to behold "Old Glory" proudly flying from the stern of those five American warships. We parked our Plymouth Suburban on the Quai alongside the U.S.S. MACON and started up the gangplank. We were met on the quarter deck by a tall, young officer with an erect military bearing who desired to know our business aboard the ship. We informed him that we were to conduct the Protestant Worship Service at 10:00 o'clock, and so he dispatched a man to carry Jeanette's accordion case and led us to the Mess Room where the service was to be held. We followed this sailor's fast-disappearing form through hatches, down ladders, along narrow corridors, and finally ended up in a large room with steel walls, floor and ceiling, in which had been arranged rows of benches for seating, and a steel pulpit. If I had been a pulpit-pounding preacher, I could have done serious damage to my fist.

The Lord gave us a most precious service that morning. The sailor lads soon began to file into the room until it was so full that there were nearly as many men standing as there were seated. Promptly at 10:00 A.M. the bugle call to worship came over the ship's loud-speaker system, and then Jeanette quietly began to play her accordion prelude. A hush came over all the room that was broken only by the responsive singing of a few of the beloved old Christmas Carols. The Holy Spirit dealt with willing hearts that morning within the steel walls of the MACON's mess room, and five precious sailor lads trusted the Lord Jesus Christ for their eternal salvation. They stepped right out during the invitation and came to the front of the room before all their buddies to confess Christ as Savior.

We feel that this "rich harvest" of souls was due for the most part to the faithful, patient sowing of the "seed" by one of the MACON's Training Officers, Lt. Roy H. Rodgers of Wheaton, Illinois. Lt. Rodgers, together with a faithful group of Christian lads, had been working among their shipmates, witnessing for Christ, speaking a word here and there, ever since the MACON left the United States. Why God should choose me to be the one to preach the message that He used to reach their hearts and bring them finally to Christ, I do not know; but praise the Lord for His faithfulness in honoring His Word! Perhaps He knew that we had need of encouragement along the way—that drink of sweet water in this dry wilderness of language study in a strange land.

We returned for another service aboard the MACON the following Sunday morning, and the Lord gave us another precious time around His Word. Jeanette played her accordion for both services, furnishing all the music from the prelude to the postlude and special music as well. Of course, she and Marian played and sang, "I'm Glad I'm a Christian," and Gertie faithfully prayed and kept the music lined up for Jeanette. The sailors were so captivated by our little blonde missionaries that they bought each of the girls a pretty French character doll for a Christmas present. We shall ever be thankful to God for the memory of those sweet moments aboard the U.S.S. MACON, which left Marseille the morning of December 28 and will be back in the United States sometime in February.

On our way home from the last service aboard the MACON, as we were driving along the docks, we passed the Fabre Line warehouse, and what do you suppose we saw? There at the dock alongside the warehouse was the S.S. VOLTA, the good ship that brought us from New York to Marseille, France. Do you remember in our last prayer letter we told you of Jeanette and Marian meeting the captain of the VOLTA, who invited them to make the return trip to New York with him? That was last November, and now the VOLTA has been to New York and back to Marseille again. Somehow when you have spent sixteen days aboard a ship, traveling some 4,756 miles, you feel a certain loyalty to it.

And now, dear prayer partners, we would like to place before you two definite needs that you might take to the Throne of Grace. The years have a way of slipping silently by—even in the life of a young maiden. And so it is that since last November 14, Jeanette has found herself to be 12 years of age. Under the Unit Plan of Support of the Berean Mission, Jeanette's monthly units of support should now be increased from ten units to fifteen units per month. As you know, a unit of support is $2.50 per month for a period of one term (five years) on the field. Perhaps you would like to have a part in supporting Jeanette in the Congo by supplying one of the five additional units needed.

The other need is one of those astronomical things that, in the natural, we even hesitate to place before you, but which, in the Spirit, we can commit to God *"who worketh all things after the counsel of His own will."* We are already endeavoring to secure reservations for our sailing to Mombasa, Kenya, during the month of July 1954, the Lord willing. From Mombasa we will drive inland some 1,500 miles across Kenya and Uganda into the Kivu Forest District of the Belgian Congo, where Berean Mission maintains its various stations. We will have need of at least another $1,500 for passage and travel expenses in connection with this final leg of our trip to Africa. As we look at this amount, it seems impossible, and it is to us; but our God delights in doing the impossible! Can we count on you to pray?

Your Missionaries to the Congo,

The Spainhowers

41, rue Daumier
Marseille, France
March 5, 1954

Dear Brother and Sister Wright:

Christian love and greetings to you from your "children" in France. Trust this will find you both in good health and rejoicing in the Lord.

As you will note from the enclosed prayer letter, we now have all papers filed with the Belgian Consulate here in Marseille for our Visa of Residence in the Congo, and we are looking to the Lord to undertake for us. The Consular official said that our Visa should be good for six months (before entering Congo) instead of three months. I hope he is right as that will give us more leeway as to when it is affixed in our Passport and when we arrive in the Congo. I don't think we will even have to make the trip to Paris to have it affixed. When full confirmation is received here, he merely sends our passport to Paris.

We wrote to the Crumleys, Lisles and Maxine in Belgium, using an address from a letter the Crumleys had written to Helen Gow while she was here, and we heard from both the Crumleys and Lisles day before yesterday. It seems that they, too, are all loaded down with French. As Lena puts it, "French today, tomorrow, and forever." They (the Lisles and Maxine) have booked passage for the 24th of August from Antwerp to Matadi, so they will be arriving in the station area about two months after we get there.

By the way, when you see Helen Gow or Evelyn Nickerson, will you please tell them that their mail has been pouring into our box the last couple of days. We now have 26 letters forwarded from Ikozi for them but addressed to us. I am afraid they are too "beaten up" and "moth-eared" to read-dress another time, so we will bundle them up in some fashion and send them to Helen at her home in Columbus, Indiana, and to Evelyn at the Mission Headquarters, per instructions from the girls. My "common sense" is still struggling to maintain its equilibrium as I contemplate what "reason" they had in forwarding all of the girls' mail to us here in Marseille. Not that we mind forwarding it to them, but it seems sort of silly doesn't it?

Yesterday, we received two large boxes of canned goods from Edgemont, mailed by Mr. Martin, and our pantry is simply overflowing with goodies. Our heartfelt thanks to everyone for their goodness to us. You can't imagine how good American canned goods taste in comparison with some of the stuff we buy over here; and then, some things are simply unobtainable. By the way, we have not received the tapes of the Missions Conference yet. Did you receive our tape-slides from California? I don't know whether we will bother sending it out there anymore. Have just begun working on a tape-slide arrangement of Marseille, which should be ready to forward to you next month, the Lord willing. Until then,

The Lord bless you both, real good!

Les, Gertie, and the girlies

"THE DARK CONTINENT"

AFRICA

Berean Mission, Inc.
3536 Russell Blvd.
St. Louis, Missouri

Prayer Letter   * * * * *   March 1954

"Let all those that put their trust in Thee rejoice: let them ever shout for joy, because Thou defendest them; let them also that love Thy name be joyful in Thee" (Psalm 5:11).

Dear Friends in Christ:

You will rejoice with us to know that all of the many papers necessary to obtain a Visa of Residence in the Belgian Congo have now been filed with the Belgian Consulate here in Marseille, and we are now awaiting its issuance. The young consular official was very friendly and helpful, for which we were most thankful, especially since all of this detail had to be handled in French. We sure had to supply the S-T-R-E-T-C-H to our strained French vocabulary.

Another cause for rejoicing and thanksgiving is that we now have accommodations aboard the DUNNOTTAR CASTLE, scheduled to sail from Marseille on July 1 for Mombasa, Kenya, East Africa. The "Green Hornet" (our Plymouth Suburban) will go right on the boat with us to Mombasa, from which port we will drive inland some 1,500 miles to the Kivu Forest District of the Belgian Congo. The Lord willing, we will arrive at our station in the Congo about August 1. In the meantime, we have just three more months in which to study French. It has been very difficult endeavoring to digest a new language in so short a session, so please pray that the Lord will enable us. His grace is sufficient!

The other day we received a letter from one of our missionaries in the Congo advising that this was the harvest season there and time to buy our year's supply of peanuts and rice, which is used as a substitute for potatoes which are not always available. He told us that the unpounded rice is stored in 55 gallon gasoline drums, containing about 100 pounds each, and that the natives pound it for them as they need it. The peanuts come in 60 pound sacks. Now the question was this—how many 100 pound drums of unpounded rice, and how many 60 pound sacks of peanuts did we want him to order for us? What quantity of such staples would you have ordered, dear reader? It's a good thing the Lord takes care of those who are unable to take care of themselves, isn't it? Such are the many problems which confront the new and, as yet, inexperienced missionary.

Early in February, we experienced some unusually severe winter weather here on the Mediterranean Coast of Southern France. So seldom does it ever dip below freezing in this area that much of the plumbing that has been added to these old buildings in more recent years is exposed on the roofs and outside walls. However, this was the coldest winter in many years, resulting in a number of broken pipes due to freezing. During the first week of February, we had a series of snow flurries, which is practically unheard of in Marseille. The few inches of snow almost paralyzed traffic because there were no means of clearing streets, no chains for cars, and simply no way of combating the ice at all. I even had to add four quarts of alcohol to my radiator to protect the car from freezing.

In the midst of this cold weather we were asked by a Russian-American couple, who are missionaries to the refugee Russians in this area, to help them in taking some food and coal to an elderly Russian man and his wife who live in the mountains that rim the city of Marseille. All went well on the mountain roads, which were not too slippery with ice and snow, until we turned off the main route onto a single-track road that wrapped itself around the mountain in a steep upgrade leading to this elderly couple's shack. We slipped and slid and became "stuck" a number of times, but just simply prayed our way through to the very top where they lived. God knew they had need of the provisions we were hauling! The man had formerly been an officer in the Czarist Army of Russia but is now old and sick and a penniless refugee. Brother Semenchuk had led both this man and his wife to the Lord a few months ago, and now in Christian love we were ministering to their temporal need. We gave them food and coal and a little money to help them through the hard winter. Brother Semenchuk read the Scriptures to them in Russian and prayed with them. They were so grateful that they cried like little children. Pray for these destitute, pitiful refugees, that God will undertake for them in their temporal need. How good it is to know that they are His children now, through faith, and can cast all their care on Him!

Gertrude and I are mighty busy these days. Not only are we students (of French), but we are professors, too. I am teaching Jeanette to typewrite, using the touch system. Her fingers are so agile from playing the accordion that she is finding typing fairly easy. Before long I'll have a secretary. A friend has sent some seventh grade books, so I'll soon be able to teach her other subjects. We brought Marian's third grade books with us, so Gertrude has something with which to work. She is teaching Marian reading and spelling, and the two of them have some fine tussles with arithmetic. The other day Marian completed a test of some 140 problems. With fear and trembling she turned it in to her mother. After mother graded her paper, we had a real season of rejoicing because she had missed only two problems. Gertrude is also teaching the girls to cook and to do other household chores. We enjoy this fellowship with our girls a great deal, but it takes much, much time. It means burning the midnight oil to get *our* studying done.

In our February prayer letter, we laid before you, as a matter of prayer, our need of at least $1,500 for passage and travel expenses in connection with the final leg of our journey to Africa. During that same month, shipment was begun from America of some 27 cases of equipment, weighing more than 5,000 pounds. There is a tremendous expense involved in this final, great effort to thrust forth a missionary family, with all of their equipment, into the battle lines in the remote regions beyond. Thus far, there has been very little response to this urgent need. If the Lord is burdening you to do something toward meeting this need, will you do it *now*—for *now* is the need!

Yours for the salvation of the lost,
The Spainhowers

41, rue Daumier
Marseille, France
March 24, 1954

Rev. C. Reuben Lindquist
Berean Mission, Inc.
3536 Russell Boulevard
St. Louis, Missouri

Dear Brother Lindquist:

Christian greetings from Marseille, France. The sun has passed the vernal equinox, and the weather is beginning to moderate a bit, for which we praise the Lord. We have not had what one would call a severe winter here, the temperature seldom dropping much below freezing, but there is a different, damp character to the cold that just goes through you, plus, of course, the Mistral. My hide is beginning to look like skin again, and I think that misery is at an end — I trust for the last time in my life.

We have been in correspondence with many on the field during these past few weeks and are mighty anxious to join them and enter into their labors in making our Savior known in the Congo. Brother Neil Vander Ploeg wrote to me, as Chairman of the Katanti Station, advising that the Executive Committee had voted us to begin our work there, and welcoming us "home." If all goes well, we should be arriving at Katanti about August 10 to 15, the Lord willing. All papers are filed for our Congo Visa, and we are just waiting on the Lord. In the next week or so we will be filing for "in transit" visas for Kenya and Uganda.

In anticipation of our coming trip into the Congo and setting up residence at Katanti, I have made up some estimates of our needs which it will probably be well to submit to you at this time for consideration, especially since, as yet, there are not sufficient funds to cover these expenses in our accounts.

We would like to have an American Express Money Order mailed to us (or direct to American Express Co., Marseille, France if that is more convenient for one reason or another) on or about May 10 to 15, for the sum of $1,500, plus our regular funds for the month of April which would be mailed at that time. I am outlining below, in detail, the distribution of this $1,500:

Passage to Mombasa, Kenya	$ 650.00
(less amount already advanced)	350.00
Balance of Passage to Mombasa, Kenya	$ 300.00
Cost of shipping car to Mombasa	$ 350.00
Cost of shipping two large trunks and one large packing case from Mombasa to Katanti (estimate)	100.00
Miscellaneous Expenses at Mombasa:	
Port, handling, and unloading car	50.00
Trip Insurance on Car	15.00
Board and Room (in Mombasa)	40.00
Rubber Boots and short-handled shovel	10.00
Vitamins and Paludrine	35.00
TOTAL	$ 150.00
Customs Bond for goods passing thru Kenya	100.00
Gas, oil, repairs, board and room and miscellaneous	

expenses of 1500-mile trip inland	300.00
Initial food supplies, staples, drum of gasoline, drum of kerosene, etc.	200.00
TOTAL EXPENSES (estimated)	$1500.00

The reason we request this amount to be transmitted through American Express Co. is so that there will be no difficulty in cashing that large sum. Otherwise, payment might be held up while they send all the way back to New York for verification of a Bank Draft. The amount for passage and shipping the car will be exchanged into French francs for payment at the agency here. The balance will be converted into American Express Travelers Cheques for disbursement along the way as needed.

We will be able to receive our regular salary and personal funds here up to and including check usually mailed the 10th to 15th of June, which is for May accounts. Then, I would suggest that the July check be held and that in August you transmit both the July and August amounts to the Congo in the customary manner, as we will have opened our account in the Congo by that time, the Lord willing.

In the estimate of expenses on the first page, you will note the item of $100 for "customs bond for goods passing thru Kenya." We will be charged the usual customs on all dutiable articles, such as musical instruments, tape recorder, camera, films, etc., which amount will be refunded as we cross the border into the Congo. Therefore, this $100 (estimated) will be refunded and can be used, together with $200 so designated for getting set-up in the Congo with initial food supplies, gas, kerosene, and the 1,001 miscellaneous things needed at that time.

We would also like permission to order from Leggett & Company in New York about $100.00 worth of foodstuffs to be shipped to us through Keating, and billed to our account at Berean Mission, St. Louis. This shipment will consist of jellos, ketchup, canned meats, popcorn, certain canned fruits, spry, brown sugar, corn syrup, and other items which were advised by those on the field. They have let us know what is available, and mainly what *isn't* available, in order that we can intelligently order.

Now, as former President Roosevelt used to say, "Let us look at the record":

Fund balance Reserve Account (end of February)	$1188.12
Fund balance Field Account (end of February)	746.66
TOTAL RESERVE ACCOUNTS (end of February)	$1934.78

List of Disbursements and proposed disbursements:

Refrigerator and Range	$ 504.90
Calvert Courses for girls (estimate)	200.00
Expense funds requested on first page	1500.00
TOTAL DISBURSEMENTS	$2204.90
Deficit in Accounts	270.12
Bill from Leggett & Co., N. Y. (less shipping)	100.00
Estimated cost of shipping all cases from St. Louis to Congo (station), plus duty, etc.	1,000.00
TOTAL ESTIMATED DEFICIT IN ACCOUNTS (based on February balances)	$1370.12

This total estimated deficit in accounts is, of course, based on the account balances as of the end of February and does not take into consideration those funds which the Lord will be sending in during the next few weeks. The estimates of traveling expenses in Africa were taken from Brother Blackburn's actual expenses and increased sufficiently to allow for our two girls, who are much older than Carl's little ones, and consequently will increase our expenses. I am satisfied that, barring the unforeseen, this estimate will not miss the mark $100 one way or the other.

The balance of our passage and shipping charges on the car should be paid about the first of June, and therefore I have requested the full $1500 at that time for simplicity of handling the whole transaction and to make doubly certain that we have the funds in hand before departing Marseille. For your convenience, it was my thought that you could forward it, together with our regular funds which will be going out about May 10 to 15, and we would be sure to have it before the first of June.

We enjoyed your little folder entitled "News from our house to your house," and think that your new home is lovely. We trust that you and your family will enjoy within it that "heap of livin' that makes a house a home," and that the Lord will bless you together. Extend our greetings to Georgina and Paul, and to all at the office and print shop.

                                                Sincerely yours in Christ,

                                                Leslie J. Spainhower
                                                for all the Spainhowers

cc: Rev. G. Joseph Wright
cc: Mr. Leo A. Williams

41, rue Daumier
Marseille, France
Wednesday, April 7, 1954

Dear Brother and Sister Wright:

Greetings, dear ones, in the precious name of our loving Savior. Received your nice, long, three-page letter on Monday, and it was so good to get all the news—the little things and the big things all rolled into one, chatty letter. It is always a pleasure to hear from you and learn what our family at Edgemont is doing, how plans for the new additions are developing, etc. We are so thankful to see that the Joash offerings are staying around the $600 per month figure. It indicates that God is working in the hearts of His people to provide for the needed facilities at Edgemont. Just think, the new buildings will probably be completed and well in use in the Lord's service before we get back to Edgemont. What a wonderful reunion that will be!

You will rejoice with us to know that our visa of residence for the Congo has been granted. The authority for its issuance is at the Belgian Embassy in Paris now! However, we must actually enter the Congo within three months of its affixation in our Passport, and so we will not mail in our Passport to Paris until about the end of May. That will give us until the end of August to make our trip to the Congo border, and still give us a month before sailing date to take care of the final payment of passage, etc. It is certainly a time-table matter. We have to show our visa in our passport in order to purchase tickets to cover our accommodations on boat, and these accommodations have to be taken up at least 21 days before sailing date. Then, the trip to the Congo border will take a good month, and that only leaves about another three or four weeks leeway to comply with their three-month expiration limit. Some unforeseen holdover could cause a lot of trouble. Well, praise the Lord, *nothing* is "unforeseen" to Him. Romans 8:28.

We are happy to be able to say that the second slide-tape set has been completed, and we mailed it to you yesterday, April 6. There are 63 colored slides and 50 minutes recorded on the tape at 7 ½ inches per second speed. We send it along with the prayer that God will use it to His glory.

By the way, enclosed with the roll of tape (inside the cardboard box) you will find folded up a very nice map of Africa for your missionary alcove. It is just the right size for the alcove and a very beautiful map of Africa. I have carefully marked on it the location of Berean Mission in the Congo and feel sure you will be pleased with it. Am also enclosing (with this letter) a very tiny map of Africa on which I have marked the route we will be taking to the Congo, Katanti Station, as a personal prayer reminder for you and Mrs. Wright.

Not much in the way of "news" to report. It's just the same thing every day—FRENCH!!! When we aren't studying it, we are out using it. As Lena Lisle put it: "It is French today, tomorrow, and forever." Sure hope there will be a little room left in our tiny brains for Kiswahili and Kikumu (or whatever we will be dealing with) when we get to the Congo. I had wanted to review some of my linguistics, too, since it has been so long ago but time simply won't permit it.

Gertrude and the children send along their greetings and love to you both. We are remembering you, and Edgemont, in prayer daily, and rejoice to see how the Lord is blessing.

With much love in Christ,

Les, Gertie, Jeanette and Marian

41, rue Daumier
Marseille, France
"Resurrection Day" April 18, 1954

Dear Brother and Sister Wright:

Loving greetings in the name of Jesus our Lord, "*who was delivered for our offenses, and was raised again for our justification.*" Last evening a handsome French youth clad in a dark blue uniform rang the bell of our apartment and handed Gertie a cablegram, which read as follows: "LOVING GREETINGS THIS GLORIOUS RESURRECTION SEASON. CHRIST LIVES—EDGEMONT FAMILY." How we thank you for your thoughtfulness in remembering us at this time.

Easter, away from Edgemont Bible Church, away from home, and away from anyone who speaks English, has been rather depressing to us. Our only English-speaking friends are away in England for a Bible Conference at this season, and so we have no one with whom to fellowship in the things of the Lord on this glorious Resurrection Day. Oh, yes, there are many French Christians here, but we cannot enjoy Christian fellowship with them because of the language barrier. Someone may say, "But haven't you been studying French for nearly eight months? Aren't you able to speak it by now?" Ah, if that were only true! But one does not learn a foreign language well enough to speak of spiritual things in only eight months' time. And so the language is still very much of a barrier.

We had been looking forward to the street meeting at the Vieux Port this afternoon, and Jeanette had worked hard on accordion renditions of "The Calvary Road," "Christ Arose," and "Allelulia," but it has turned out much too cold to go to the open-air meeting. We have been held to the apartment for the past three days by an icy-cold Mistral wind coming down out of the Alps to the north of us. So you see how very welcome was your Christian greetings this glorious Resurrection Season.

As I sit at the typewriter, Gertie at the table (with pen in hand), and the children on the couch (with paper dolls), we are all listening to Ruthie on the organ and Eileen singing, "It will Be Worth It All When We See Jesus," as we have them recorded on tape. As you may know, I have an hour of Ruthie and Eileen's wonderful music recorded on tape, and what a blessing it has been to us these past eight months.

Our landlady, Mademoiselle Junod, frequently spends the evening with us talking "petit négre." Literally "petit négre" means, "little negro," and it is the French term for the type of French spoken by the Negroes from the various French colonies in Africa. Mademoiselle's English is quite broken, and so is our French, so we both speak "petit négre." Last evening she was telling us that she was a Jesuit Catholic, but not "pure" Catholic. She said that her grandfather from Switzerland was a Calvinist, and that she had some definite "Calvinist blood" circulating in her veins. Between our bad French and her poor English we have a difficult time getting across spiritual truths, but do believe that the dear woman is saved through faith in Christ, be she Catholic or Calvinist.

By the way, Brother Wright, you will recall that in our February prayer letter we made it known that five more units were needed for Jeanette, inasmuch as she is now 12 years of age. We can praise the Lord that all five units have now been provided. How very faithful you have all been to the Lord and to us.

Am enclosing a couple of new cards for our prayer letter file, one of them also to be placed on the list of those to be advised by post card as to when our slide-tapes are shown. Also, enclosed is the master copy for our May prayer letter. Unless something happens worth writing about, I don't anticipate preparing another prayer letter until we start our voyage. Then, instead of writing a lengthy travelog as before, I believe we will select the highlights and write it up into our prayer letter, even if it makes a somewhat lengthier letter. Have changed the heading of the prayer letter, per enclosed master copy, in order to conserve on space, and also to simplify the cutting of the stencil. Do you like it?

Trust that it won't be too long after you receive this letter until you receive the new slide-tape of Marseille, and that it will prove to be a blessing.

With much love in Christ,

Les, Gertie, Jeanette, and Marian

41, rue Daumier
Marseille, France
May 14, 1954

Dear Brother and Sister Wright,

"But my God shall supply all your need according to His riches in glory by Christ Jesus" (Philippians 4:19).

Time and again God has fulfilled the promise of this verse in our lives as we have trusted Him to meet the need, whether spiritual or material. Yes, and many times when through lack of faith we were not completely trusting Him, yet He has done "exceeding abundantly" above that which we have thought possible. My, how slow we are to lay hold of the truth that "God is able!"

And now word has again reached us of God's provision for our outgoing to the Congo as His dear children have faithfully responded to the urging of the Holy Spirit to meet this need. We want to take this means of thanking you, personally, for your gift of $10 in our behalf and in behalf of the gospel of our Lord Jesus Christ. Truly, we are "labourers together with God" in His whitened harvest field.

The Lord willing, we expect to sail from Marseille, France on July 7 for Mombasa, Kenya, and thence by automobile to the Belgian Congo. We hope to arrive at our Katanti Station sometime early in August. Should the Lord lay us upon your heart during this time, please pray for His protection and direction throughout this long and difficult journey.

May we again express our gratitude for your faithfulness to us, and may God bless you abundantly.

Sincerely yours in Christ Jesus,

Les, Gertie, Jeanette, and Marian

P.S. Will you please express our thanks to the congregation for the many anonymous gifts recently given by dear ones at Edgemont toward our passage to the Congo.

41, rue Daumier
Marseille, France
May 28, 1954

Dear Ones in Christ:

It was so good to receive your long, newsy letter from French Village (U.S.A.), and to learn of all the happenings at Edgemont and among the church family. We have heard so much from Mrs. Wilson and others of the big wedding, and now your comments on it, too, that we feel that we were almost there. Mother Wilson sent us the large clipping from the newspaper and the girls certainly looked lovely in their wedding gowns. They had written us earlier about sending the tape recording of the service to us here in France, but we told them not to for fear that it wouldn't clear customs before we had left for Africa, and it might in that way be lost.

You will rejoice with us to know that our passport has been received back from the Belgian Embassy at Paris with proper visa for entrance into the Congo. Praise the Lord, who guards our going out and our coming in! We have applied for "in transit" visas through Kenya and Uganda, which will be issued here in Marseille as soon as authority is received from London. We have also asked them to include Tanganyika in this visa in the event that the Mau Mau situation should suddenly worsen to the point where travel through Kenya should be prohibited. In that event we could still travel by way of Tanganyika, although the Mau Mau disturbance has also reached into that area. We are not afraid because we know the Lord is leading us out; but neither are we foolhardy, as there is real danger throughout all East Africa at the present. We shall simply trust the Lord to open and close the doors of travel for us and to protect us in the way. We will certainly covet your prayers for our safety during this time. Things have worsened considerably since the Blackburns went through last November.

We are so happy that the slide-tape system is working out and that the Lord is blessing their use. We praise the Lord, too, for the offering received on "Spainhower Night" toward our final passage and equipment. We are asking the Lord to clear up the entire deficit of our outgoing and establishment in the Congo. We do not like to allude to financial needs in every prayer letter that we send out. Perhaps God will meet the need by the time we arrive in the Congo, and we can devote our letter to thanksgiving and praise.

We have received $1500 from the Mission for our travel expenses to the Congo and for food supplies, etc. when we arrive and begin to establish our household once again. We feel a little ill at ease with so much money in our possession. It makes one feel like closing all the window shutters, barring the doors, locking oneself up in the closet, and swallowing the key. But it is far more practical to take all normal and possible precautions and then simply commit it all to the Lord. After all, it is *His* money, anyway, and not ours! Don't know what we would do if we didn't have the Lord for our Keeper. Isn't He Wonderful!

Before it slips my mind I want to tell you that Gertrude ate her first snail the other day—and probably her last. One of the ladies in our apartment picked a couple pans full of the slimy little creatures from around the plants and along the walls of our landlady's garden and prepared them for supper. It is really a delicacy to the French. Knowing that Americans as a rule do not eat such things, she brought down four snails for us to taste them. However, Gertie was the only one of us with enough intestinal fortitude to attempt eating one of the slimy things. She popped the first one into her mouth, gave a couple of quick chews, and down it went without even a taste. After working up her courage a bit, she put another one into her mouth and began chewing it. This time she chewed it long enough to get the full benefit of the exotic flavor of the snail, and—up it came again! Her record: one down and three to go! But that is as far as her courage or intestinal fortitude would take her. Needless to say, the girls and I have no further fear of Mama preparing snails for us to eat.

We are expecting the Vander Ploegs through Marseille sometime around June 17. They have come out of the Congo by train through Tanganyika Territory, and then by the same navigation company to Marseille as we will use to Kenya. We have never met the Vander Ploegs and so are looking forward to their coming. It seems that most of our missionaries prefer this East Coast, round-a-bout way of coming to America to that of the long haul down the Congo River and across the Atlantic Ocean.

This letter will probably arrive while you are on your vacation but should be waiting for you upon your return. The Lord bless you both, strengthen and refresh you in both body and spirit during this little respite. We are praying for you, and the Lord's work at Edgemont.

With Christian love,

Les and Gertie
Jeanette and Marian

Berean Mission, Inc.	<u>A F R I C A</u>	THE SPAINHOWERS
3536 Russell Blvd.		41, rue Daumier
St. Louis, Missouri	The Dark Continent!	Marseille, France

Prayer Letter	* * * * *	May 1954

Praise the Lord, call upon His name, declare His doings among the people" (Isaiah 12:4).

    We have many reasons for which to praise the Lord: for His Self, for His salvation, His blessings, His watchcare, His keeping, His provision, for His every goodness to us who are not worthy of the least of His mercies. We praise Him, too, for you dear ones who pray and give that we might go to the "regions beyond" with the gospel of His savings grace. Thank you for your faithfulness to Him, and to us.

    But "cease not to cry unto the Lord our God for us" because the next few months will witness another great upheaval in our lives as we tear up "roots" here in Marseille, France, where we have been studying French for the past several months and face the complexities of becoming acclimated to still another climate, another language, and another people in the Belgian Congo, Africa. Yes, at last, *AFRICA* — the place toward which we have been looking, praying, planning, preparing and waiting for more than five years! How anxious we are to take up our little place in God's great missionary program in Africa.

    You who have been calling upon His name in intercession for us will rejoice and praise the Lord to know that our Visa of Residence in the Belgian Congo has been granted and, at present, is at the Belgian Embassy in Paris, France. The Lord willing, we will have it issued in our passport about the first of June, and trust to be ready to sail from Marseille, France, on July 7, aboard the DUNNOTAR CASTLE, for Mombasa, Kenya. In the event you would like to follow our voyage on a map and to give you some idea of the distances involved, we are outlining it for you. We sail from Marseille to Genoa, Italy, a distance of 201 nautical miles (a nautical mile is 6080 feet); from Genoa to Port Said, Egypt, 1,438 miles; then through the Suez Canal to the port of Suez, Egypt, a distance of 87 miles; from Suez to Port Sudan, 703 miles; from Port Sudan to Aden, 671 miles; from Aden to Mombasa, Kenya, 1,633 miles. From Marseille to Mombasa is a total of 4,733 nautical miles, and about a 15-day voyage, sometimes longer if the ship is detained at any of the ports along the way.

    Of course, the "Green Hornet" (our Plymouth Suburban) will be on the same ship with us and will be unloaded at Mombasa. From there, we will drive inland some 1,500 miles across Kenya and Uganda to our Katanti Station in the Belgian Congo. This phase of the trip should take about another two weeks, the Lord willing. We will be driving through a large natural game preserve in Kenya, so may have opportunity to photograph anything from turtle doves to tigers (maybe even elephants), depending on how near the road they venture at the moment we are driving through. We will also be driving right through dangerous Mau Mau territory around Nairobi and Kijabe, Kenya. A recent report indicated that these Mau Mau terrorists, who control some 90 percent of over one million Kikuyu tribesmen, have killed 930 Africans, 22 Europeans, and 21 Asians. We are trusting the Lord that future figures will not show 4 Americans. We will be traveling in the Lord's time, and in His will, so we can trust Him to take us safely through. He has work for us to do.

    At the moment of writing, there is a deficit of $850 in our passage fund. Please "call upon His name" with us, that the Lord will meet this need in time for our scheduled sailing, July 7, if it be His will. God grant that we may soon "declare His doings among the people" — the Balega people of the Belgian Congo.

                                                       Yours for souls in the Congo,
                                                       The Spainhowers

41, rue Daumier
Marselle, France
Sunday, June 13, 1954

Dear Loved Ones:

"The blessing of the Lord be upon you: we bless you in the name of the Lord."

It was so good to receive your letter from Bryan University and to know that you were having a time of rest and relaxation with your loved ones, the Allems. You mentioned that Bryan was Helen Gow's Alma Mater—I believe Dick Tevebaugh graduated from Bryan, too, didn't he?

It has given us much pleasure to be able to put back into the Lord's work at Edgemont just a small portion of what He has so abundantly provided for us through the dear ones there. We have conserved a part of our tithe, too, to be used in the African work after we are there and as the Lord leads us at that time. I know that needs there will be so great that there simply won't be enough to go around, but our Lord has a way of multiplying the gift and adding the blessing. Regarding our Africa home, it is really too early to give much thought to it. We had best wait until all the "smoke" of our outgoing to the Congo has cleared away and all expenses in that respect cared for before considering any further financial burden on the dear ones who have so faithfully stood by us. And besides, it is not yet settled whether we will be going into the Punia Territory or not, so it will be some time before we will be given a permanent assignment. We must make it a matter of prayer, however, for there are some problems with respect to missionary housing that must first be worked out and concerning which we need the Lord's guidance.

We are looking forward to meeting the Vander Ploegs when they come through Marseille on their way to London and home. As it stands at the moment, they are due in Marseille, next Sunday, the 20th, but then you can never count on the exact date until the ship pulls in. We have really enjoyed being Berean Mission's welcoming committee at this intermediate point. First it was the Blackburns, then Helen and Evelyn, and now the Vander Ploegs. And, last of all, on or about the 7th of July we will close up shop and set sail ourselves. We now have in our possession all visas necessary for the trip and all funds for passage and traveling expenses. Praise the Lord, who goes before and makes the rough places smooth! Yesterday, I finished packing the big wood packing case, and we already had one trunk completely packed. The remaining trunk is more than half packed, so all we have left, for the most part, is our hand luggage. Doesn't sound like much, but our "hand luggage" is considerable, believe me! Did you ever try getting into a taxicab with your wife and two children along with 16 pieces of hand luggage? It is rather expensive, too, because the porters charge per piece to load and unload your hand luggage on and off the ship. Our natives in the Congo have the right idea; all they travel with is a toothbrush!

Yes, there are just 26 more days before we sail! All four of us are quite excited. Jeanette and Marian sort of protested as they saw their toys disappearing into the big packing case. In fact, Marian even shed a couple of tears over her old rubber doll, which she calls "Susie," as I carefully wrapped it in a blanket and tucked it in the case. Susie is eight years old—Marian is only nine—and so the dollie is very, very dear. Her face has been about scrubbed off (Susie's) and the hands slightly chewed up, but wherever the Spainhowers go, Susie goes too. Oddly enough, there was an entirely different attitude when Jeanette and Marian saw the arithmetic books, the English books, spelling books, geography, etc. disappearing into the box. You should have heard the shouts of joy then. "School's out, school's out!" But they will be happy to start back to school again in the Congo with all of the other missionary children. We are so glad that, for a time at least, we will be on the same station with them during their orientation to the living conditions in the Congo.

By the way, it would be well if no one sent any more regular mail after the 19th of June, and no more airmail after the 1st of July. Our new address in the Congo will be:

>Rev. and Mrs. Leslie J. Spainhower
>Berean African Missionary Society, Inc.
>Station Katanti
>Shabunda par Kindu
>Congo Belge, Afrique

Regular mail to the Congo takes from two to three *months* — so use *airmail* except in rare instances when time element is no factor.

Airmail to the Congo will be 25 cents (minimum) instead of 15 cents as it was to France, and it will take about two weeks each way instead of one week (even five days most of the time). That means that our lines of communication will be extended, and our contact with each other "slowed down" as it were. Nevertheless, we shall endeavor to keep you well informed of the Lord's doings in our lives. It will just take longer to get word through. We are thinking of preparing a somewhat longer prayer letter highlighting our trip from Marseille to Mombasa, Kenya, to be mailed to you from Mombasa before we start the trip inland. And then, another prayer letter highlighting the trip inland to the Katanti Station, to be mailed from Katanti shortly after arrival there. If the prayer letter is a bit long, perhaps it can be mimeographed on both front and back of a sheet, and perhaps legal-sized sheets. You can decide when you receive the letter.

We are enclosing some final shots of Marseille, France and ourselves. The picture of the four of us was taken from atop a high hill overlooking the city, and the wind was blowing strong. That will explain our windblown expressions. Am also enclosing a new name for our mailing list. We do not know who this lady is, but she gave $50 toward our passage and equipment on Spainhower Night.

Now the Lord bless thee and keep thee, and if we should not be writing before we leave Marseille, we will let you hear from us along the way. We love you in the Lord, and will be meeting with you daily at the Throne of Grace.

>Lovingly in Christ,
>
>*Les and Gertie*

41, rue Daumier
Marseille, France
Saturday, July 3, 1954

Dear Ones in the Lord:

"Grace to you and peace from God our Father, and the Lord Jesus Christ. First, I thank my God through Jesus Christ for you all," for your faithfulness to Him and to us since the first day we came to Edgemont until now. You have been much in our thoughts and on our hearts as we have been preparing to leave France and push on to the Congo. The lines of communication are lengthening, and yet the bond of Christian love is growing ever closer and sweeter. Praise the Lord, by His everlasting grace we can meet thee instantly at the Throne of Grace, *"and truly our fellowship is with the Father, and with His Son Jesus Christ."*

We received your long, newsy letter this morning and also your letter-packet to Jeanette and Marian containing the aprons for them to embroider from D.V.B.S. Thank you for all. It is much appreciated, and the girls will have fun embroidering the aprons on the ship. Thank you, too, for the five dollars for "treats" on the boat. With each Coca Cola we drink and each candy bar we eat, we will think of "Pop and Mom" Wright and their goodness to us. We shall savor these "last" goodies, as I don't imagine there is much selection in the way of goodies in the heart of the Belgian Congo. We will not complain, however, for the goodness of the Lord is our everlasting portion.

We want to express our thanks to the D.V.B.S. for the aprons for Jeanette and Marian and also for their gift of $27.20 towards our passage to the Congo. Several have written to us concerning the wonderful D.V.B.S. had this year—good attendance and excellent attention and interest on the part of the students. We know there will be eternal benefits, too, in the hearts and lives of the children and young people who came. God always honors His Word. It will never return to Him void.

We are so thankful to hear that Mr. Knight has volunteered to present our slide-tapes at the churches that want a showing. We are really grateful to him for this as many churches still do not have the recording equipment. It will make for a "smoother" program, and also insure the safekeeping of the tape and slides. Please express our gratitude to him, and I'll be writing him personally, in time, to let him know how very much we do appreciate his interest. Rev. Henry, in Monrovia, California has volunteered to do the same thing out there, which should make for the widest possible circulation of the slide-tapes. May the Lord give us grace and wisdom in preparing them prayerfully, and may He use them as a missionary challenge in the churches, and as a challenge to service to young people.

Believe it or not, it is still rather cool here in Marseille—disgustingly cool! Several from home have written us of your 100 degree weather there, and how we have longed for some of it. We have had only one week of nice, balmy, warm, weather since last October—and that was last week. We thought that summer had finally come at last, only to have another of these dreadful "mistrals" begin, and it has been blowing a cold wind for the past seven days without a letup. We are certainly looking forward to some of that tropical heat. Human nature being what it is, after we had had a certain amount of the tropical heat we will probably long for some of that cool Marseille wind. Gertrude and the girls have made three different attempts to go swimming in the beautiful, blue Mediterranean Sea but have been "frozen out" each time. I tried it once, but as I still have just a slight amount of the skin eczema from this cold climate, it became much irritated from the cold salt water and I haven't risked it again since.

Monday, July 5, the transit company will pick up two trunks, one large wood case, one metal foot locker, and two large fiber suitcases for the hold of the ship. After that is all out of the way, then I must prepare the car for shipment by securing in the back end the roof luggage rack, jerry can, mattresses, spare tires; and endeavor to hide a few necessary tools, the hub caps and windshield wipers, so that they will not be stolen on the docks, etc. Then, on Tuesday we drive the "Green Hornet" down to the docks and (as the French say) "abandon" it there. Actually, it is turned over to the proper authorities and must be taken through customs, gasoline drained, battery cables removed, etc. And, if you are not careful, you will discover at the other end of the line that they not only removed the battery cables, but the "battery" as well. We have committed the car to the Lord who gave it to us, and He will see it safely through, if that be His will.

As mentioned before, we leave here on July 7, and should arrive at Mombasa, Kenya on July 23, the Lord willing. If we can get all cleared from the ship on Friday (23) and Saturday, then we will endeavor to start the trek inland early Monday morning (26). However, if ship is a day or two late, or we experience difficulties in clearing customs and conducting necessary business in Mombasa, it may be later in week before we can start inland. Don't like to take too much time in Mombasa because the hotel is very expensive. In fact, all hotels in the Congo are most expensive. We will endeavor to stay at the Church Missionary Society guest houses as much as possible on the way in. Unless forced to by adverse circumstances, we do not want to spend the night in the car on the road either, because of the food problem (and water), and also because of the Mau Mau bands which do their terrorist work after dark. "The Lord is (our) Helper, and (we) will not fear what man shall do unto (us)" — "He hath said, I will never leave thee nor forsake thee."

At any rate, dearly beloved, keep praying, and we know the Lord will keep us according to His promise — "The Lord shall preserve thee from all evil: He shall preserve thy soul. The Lord shall preserve thy going out and thy coming in from this time forth, and even for evermore." May He bless and keep each one of you at the "home base." We will write enroute.

Les, Gertie and the girlies

P.S. Started taking our preventive medicine for malaria today so that our systems will be well permeated before those pesky lil' mosquitoes begin their bitin'.

Part Five

Africa — First Term
1954-1956

*"The angel of the Lord encampeth round about them that fear him,
and delivereth them."*
Psalm 68:19

Travelog from Marseille, France to Katanti, Belgian Congo

Timeline for Dunnottar Castle from Marseille, France, to Mombasa, Kenya

Wednesday, July 7 — Board the Dunnottar Castle at 7:30 p.m.

Thursday, July 8 — Port stop in Genoa, Italy

Tuesday, July 13 — Port stop in Port Said, Egypt

Wednesday, July 14 — Enter the Suez Canal

Friday, July 16 — Storm in the Red Sea; Children's Fancy Dress and Tea

Sunday, July 18 — Port stop in Aden

Monday, July 19-20 — 36-hour storm in the Indian Ocean

Friday, July 23-25 — docked in Mombasa, Kenya, at 2:00; cleared customs by 3:00; stayed at the Pentecostal Mission through Sunday

Trip from Mombasa, Kenya to B.A.M.S. Katanti, Belgian Congo

Note: There is no specific information about daily travel across East Africa.

Monday, July 26 — Departed from Mombasa at 8:00 a.m.

Saturday, July 31 — Crossed the border of Uganda into the Belgian Congo; arrived in Bukavu at 9:30 p.m.

Monday, August 2-3 — Stayed with the Bothwell Family at Mushweshwe

Wednesday, August 4 — Arrived at B.A.M.S. Ikozi Station about 4:30 p.m.

Friday, August 6 — Arrived at B.A.M.S. Katanti

Berean Mission, Inc.	AFRICA	B.A.M.S. – Katanti
3536 Russell Blvd.		Shabunda par Kindu
St. Louis, Missouri	The Dark Continent!	Congo Belge, Afrique

Prayer Letter * * * * * August 1954

Dearly Beloved of the Lord Jesus:

"I will go in the strength of the Lord God" (Psalm 71:16).

It has seemed that the day of our departure for Africa would never come! And now that it has arrived, we suddenly feel so inadequate for the tasks and responsibilities that lie before us. It is only the realization that we "*go in the strength of the Lord God*" that sustains us. "*Hitherto hath the Lord helped us*" — and we know that He will lead us on.

Our ship, the DUNNOTTAR CASTLE, arrived in Marseille, France, late in the afternoon of July 7, and we were not able to embark until about 7:30 that evening. As soon as our hand luggage was all safely in the cabins, we made our way to the Dining Room for our first meal aboard ship. By this time we were utterly exhausted from all of the details of packing, customs, baggage handling, not to mention the endless waiting, and so we decided to go to bed early. The ship was scheduled to sail in the early hours of the morning, and we wanted to be on deck to watch as Marseille faded away in the distance, and to take some colored slides for our next travelog.

The good old Marseille "mistral" had been blowing for the past eight or nine days, and due to the lack of rain, there was considerable dust in the air. As a result my sinus passages, eyes, throat, and one ear became infected, and I spent the first three days aboard ship in bed, receiving six injections of penicillin as well as other medicines from the ship's doctor. Because of this illness, we were unable to obtain pictures of our departure. The day after we left Marseille, the ship put in at Genoa, Italy. We endeavored to go ashore and take some pictures for our travelog, but had only walked a few blocks from the ship when we had to turn back and go to bed again. The Lord has been gracious and strengthened me since that time. We know He had His purpose in it all, so we shan't complain; rather, let us praise His Holy Name.

After ten months in France, unable to understand most of what was being said round about us, we looked forward to an English-speaking environment once again. However, we have found life aboard the DUNNOTTAR CASTLE still somewhat like that of a foreign country. As Marian put it, "They all speak English, but they don't talk plain." We are jolly well progressing, howevah!

Our cabins are really quite small — in fact, both of them could easily be placed within the average garage and still leave ample room for the car. There is much more "elbow room" up on deck with the other 500 passengers. Jeanette and Marian are delighted to have English-speaking playmates once again, and their greatest fun is an afternoon plunge in the deck swimming pool.

From Genoa, the DUNNOTTAR CASTLE sailed along the western coast of Italy, passing through the Straits of Messina (between the Island of Sicily and the "toe" of Italy) and headed out across the Mediterranean Sea in a southeasterly direction. We passed so close beneath the Isle of Crete that its rock hills could be plainly seen. By late afternoon of Tuesday, July 13, we arrived at Port Said, Egypt. The ship pulled into the narrow Suez Channel where it was tied up for several hours awaiting entrance into the Canal. With a shout of delight, Gertrude called me to look at something. There, just outside our porthole, we beheld "Old Glory" proudly waving over the United States Consulate in Port Said, Egypt — not more than 200 feet from the ship.

As we emerged out on deck we noticed that nearly everyone was standing at the railing and looking over the side of the ship. We found ourselves a place at the railing and looked down to see about eight small boats alongside the DUNNOTTAR CASTLE, each one more heavily loaded than the other with lovely leather goods. These Egyptians are marvelous salesmen—they simply won't take "no" for an answer. They stand in their little craft looking up at the sea of faces hanging over the ship's railing above them, and shout, "Hey! Mr. Mac-Gregor! Here's a wee mite of bargain. Hey, you! Wanna buy a brief case?" And so on and on it goes. As soon as they find an interested party, they throw a line over the railing of the ship by means of which the desired article  may be pulled up for close inspection. If the article is purchased, the money is sent down in a small basket secured to the rope. There is no such thing as a set price. The original price asked is always about three times the value of the article, and then you "haggle" on down to the actual purchase price. The final cost of your purchase will depend entirely upon how good of a "haggler" you are. Not being very proficient in the art of "haggling," we did not attempt to buy anything. Besides, leather goods are no good in the Congo—they mildew overnight, and become stiff and brittle.

The reason for the several hours' delay at Port Said was to allow a convoy of ships enroute through the Suez Canal to pass out our end of the channel before our convoy of ships made its entrance. Finally, about one-thirty Wednesday morning, we were released from our mooring and slowly began the 14-hour trip through the Canal. About halfway through the Canal we emerged into Bitter Lake, the largest salt water lake in the world. There again we dropped anchor and waited a few hours in order to bypass another convoy of ships coming through in the opposite direction. The Canal is only about 100 yards wide and one has the feeling of being able to reach out and touch both banks. We saw many British military installations along the way and were quite thrilled to catch sight of a few camels from time to time.

Wednesday afternoon we emerged from the Suez Canal into the sweltering heat of the Gulf of Suez, and at some unknown moment during that afternoon, we passed directly over the place where almost 3,500 years ago *"Moses stretched out his hand over the sea; and the Lord caused the sea to go back by a strong east wind all that night, and made the sea dry land, and the waters were divided. And the children of Israel went into the midst of the sea upon the dry ground: and the waters were a wall unto them on their right hand, and on their left"* (Exodus 14:21-22). It was also a thrill late that evening to stand at the railing and gaze upon Mount Sinai as we slipped silently by, knowing it was here that *"He gave unto Moses, when He had made an end of communing with him upon Mount Sinai, two tables of testimony, tables of stone, written with the finger of God"* (Exodus 31:18).

The DUNNOTTAR CASTLE did not call at the port of Suez, nor at Port Sudan, for which we were very thankful because of the terrific heat. The temperature averaged about 104 degrees in the shade on the deck, and about 112 degrees in our cabins throughout the four-day trip through the length of the Red Sea. Needless to say, most of the passengers were sleeping on deck. The only difficulty was that at 2:00 A.M. the crew began hosing and swabbing the decks which forced everyone back into their hot, stuffy cabins.

We awoke Friday morning about half-way through the Red Sea to find the day quite hazy and windy. The Sea became increasingly rough until by mid-morning nearly everyone aboard was seasick. Little Marian was the first in our family to go under, closely followed by her most sympathetic mother. We gave them both some Dramamine and put them to bed. It didn't seem to bother Jeanette and me, so we stayed on deck to watch the tremendous waves. It was most fascinating. The ship would be riding on the very top of a large swell, and then the next moment would sink down into a hollow with much the same feeling as an elevator dropping. Then the waves would almost break over the railing on the deck, and with a tremendous heave we would find ourselves riding on the crest

again. It kept this up for about four hours—long enough that there were just a handful of us in the dining room for lunch. We found out from the Captain later that we had been riding on the fringe of a sandstorm which centered about 100 miles away in Arabia. In spite of the fact that the DUNNOTTAR CASTLE was some 50 miles off the Arabian coast, still the ship's decks and railings and chairs were covered with a thin deposit of very fine sand dust.

By that afternoon, most everyone was feeling better, and the Children's Fancy Dress and Tea was held as scheduled. There were 51 children aboard ship and at least 40 of them appeared in the Fancy Dress. The youngest contestant was eight months of age and her costume consisted of a necklace of safety pins and, of course, the usual diaper—she was depicting a "pin-up girl." Jeanette and Marian went as an organ grinder and monkey and won first prize in their class.

About 2:00 A.M., Sunday morning, July 18, the DUNNOTTAR CASTLE was tied up in the roadstead just off shore of the British Colony of Aden. Aden consists of two extinct volcanic craters forming rocky peninsulas, and stretching out to the north lies the vast Arabian Desert. Passengers were allowed ashore for only two hours Sunday morning as the vessel was scheduled to sail again by 10:00 A.M. Since there was really nothing to be seen ashore in that short time, we chose to remain aboard and watch the Arab "barkers" selling their wares from little boats drawn up alongside our ship. By 10:30 A.M. we were heading out across the Gulf of Aden toward the tip of Somalia. By 11:00 A.M. the next day, Monday, we had rounded the tip of Somalia and were headed down the east coast of Africa towards Mombasa, our port of debarkation.

The Captain announced Monday morning over the ship's communication system that we would run into a monsoon as we entered the Indian Ocean at approximately 11:00 A.M., and we did! The official record read, "Rough head sea, with heavy swell." The ship pitched and rolled. All port holes had to be closed as the waves were lashing against the ship. The monsoon lasted 36 hours, at the end of which time few of us cared whether we lasted or not. Gertie was quite seasick. For 24 hours no food would stay with her, and she spent most of that time in her bunk. Finally, the Dramamine began to win the battle. At the urging of Tony, our room steward, I helped Gertie up onto the deck, and the fresh air did the rest. The children and I were not sick, for which we praise the Lord, but we did experience a woozy, tired feeling. Needless to say, all on board rejoiced when the monsoon had spent itself, and the sea was calm again.

Now the word on everyone's lips was "Mombasa." In spite of the many problems ahead, we Spainhowers were jubilant at the thought of placing our feet on African soil. Though it would be several weeks before we would arrive at our inland destination, Katanti Station, in the very center of Africa, still we looked upon Mombasa as the stepping stone to the Congo. But again there was packing to do. I worked in one cabin, Gertie in the other, as there wasn't room enough for both of us, plus a suitcase in one cabin. Several times we were dumped unceremoniously into a suitcase when Jeanette or Marian would fling open the cabin door. Then, there was the never-ending job of trying to keep everything clean. Gertie was forever washing out a little dab of this or that, hoping they would dry in time to pack.

Our first look at the Mombasa, Kenya dock

Experienced travelers kept telling us, "It is impossible to obtain hotel accommodations in Mombasa. You should have made arrangements from Marseille." In our ignorance we had not made reservations. What to do? We simply committed the matter to our Travel Agent, our Blessed Lord, and left the details in His capable hands.

Friday morning, July 23 dawned clear and cool. Everyone was up early—excitement and confusion reigned. Nightclothes were flung into a suitcase—closet and drawers checked. Gertie and I looked at each other, nodded agreement, everything was ready to go. We hurried to the dining room for breakfast. Everyone was anticipating an early arrival in Mombasa. We were doomed for disappointment. The Captain announced that we would dock in Mombasa at approximately 1:00 P.M. Actually, it was nearer 2:00 P.M. before we docked, and after 3:00 P.M. before we

were cleared through the immigration authorities and hurried down the gangplank to the Baggage Shed and the inevitable customs officials.

It seemed that everyone had someone to meet them: a friend, a relative, or even an agency. We felt a bit like orphans. We reminded ourselves anew that we had Someone, too. Our blessed Lord was with us. Matters were in His hands. A native dressed in what looked to be his nightgown, a sport jacket and a bright red fez came up to me, produced proper credentials as a baggage agent, and asked to handle our baggage through customs, to which I readily agreed. Seating my three girls on a bench where they could watch all proceedings, the baggage handler and I began to snip away at the maze of red tape. Little by little we made our way through customs.

As Gertie and the girls were sitting on the bench, several people from the boat approached them and asked, "Where are you spending the night?" When she answered, "We don't know yet," they would shake their heads mournfully and go on. Gertie said they were Job's comforters. Finally, a tall, friendly-looking stranger approached. "Are you by any chance Mrs. Spainhower of Berean Mission?" he asked. Recovering from a shock of surprise, she replied in the affirmative. He stuck out his hand and said, "I'm Bud Sickler of the Pentecostal Mission in Mombasa. One of your missionaries, Carl Blackburn, wrote and asked me to meet you. You can stay at our place." We cannot put into words our thankfulness to our Lord Jesus Christ. He had surely "gone before and made the crooked places straight." Praise God, from Whom all blessings flow!! With Mr. Sickler's help, soon everything was cleared through customs. $100 in duty had to be paid, which duty is to be returned to us when we cross the border

into the Congo—but will probably be taken away from us again by the Congo customs before we proceed inland. By 6:15 P.M. we were on our way to the Sickler home, rejoicing in the Lord.

It is now Sunday morning. I have just finished packing the car ready for the long journey into the Congo. The Lord willing, we trust to leave early tomorrow morning. This afternoon we shall participate in a street meeting in downtown Mombasa. This evening I am to preach in Mr. Sickler's church, my first message from the Word of God on African soil. I'm thankful that the service will be in English.

Our next prayer letter will be written from Katanti. The long journey will then be over. We will be acclimating ourselves to the new way of life and to the new ministry God has for us in the Congo. Our prayer is that it will be fruitful and well-pleasing to our Blessed Lord. For the journey ahead we shall continue to lean upon Him, for we "go in the strength of the Lord God."

                              Yours in His Never-Failing Grace,

                              The Spainhowers

Jeanette's Comment: Aboard the Dunnottar Castle

Life aboard the Dunnottar Castle was quite different than it had been on the French freighter, the S.S. Volta. We'd had such big rooms on the Volta. The cabins on the Dunnottar Castle were about the size of a healthy closet—and there wasn't one of those! We were fortunate, however, to be on the outside, so each of our miniscule cabins had fresh air.

The other big change was that the steward really couldn't have cared less about us, unlike Joseph on the Volta. No breakfast in bed—nope, we went at the appointed time to the children's dining room. The adults certainly didn't want to be bothered with children! I could have dined with the adults since I was over 12, but Dad and Mom wanted me to stay with Marian.

Dining and Etiquette

What the Prayer Letter didn't say was that the time for children's dinner was past by the time our family got to the dining room at 7:30 the night we boarded. That meant that Marian and I had to eat with the adults. Unfortunately, there was no room at our parents' table, so Marian and I were seated with total strangers—impressive Brits who appeared quite alarmed when two American children were seated at their table.

Marian and I were terrified. There was such an array of silverware—I'd never seen so much. Marian whispered to me, "What're we gonna do?"

That's when I remembered reading something in a ladies magazine that had stated, "If you don't know which utensils to use in a formal setting, watch the person who seems to know the most about it, and do what she does."

I carefully observed all of the very important-looking people at the table and decided the lady at the head of the table—a very British Brit indeed!—was the one I'd watch. Whatever she picked up, I picked up—and punched Marian so she would choose the right one, too. We kept quiet unless someone spoke directly to us, and then we answered as politely as possible.

Later, the woman sought out Mom and told her how very pleased—and surprised—she was with our behavior. She said she hadn't expected us to be able to carry on a conversation, much less know how to use the formal silverware. Mom later asked me how we had managed that array of silverware and seemed amused that my voracious appetite for reading had paid off.

That was only the beginning of our dining adventures on the Dunnottar Castle. Starting with breakfast the next day, Marian and I were to dine at the children's sitting, in a smaller dining room and at a different time than the adults. Marian and I were seated at a smaller table with two other small children—all Americans, and children of missionaries. The mother sat with her children, but Marian and I were on our own.

We could tell that the steward was not a happy camper. He obviously didn't want to be dealing with roughneck Americans! But he soon changed his tune. We said, "Yes, sir" or "no, sir" when offered food, "please" and "thank you." We smiled at him and greeted him at each meal—and told him "goodbye" when we were finished.

But the British children in the rest of the room were absolute terrors! They screamed if the stewards tried to serve them something they didn't want. They even threw food at the stewards.

Finally, one morning, our steward had had enough food thrown at him and bad language screamed at him. He stood tall, squarely faced the nannies and governesses there with some of the children, and announced, "I'd far rather serve these Americans any day" (he nodded toward us and the missionary mother) "than deal with these uncivilized British brats!"

That spread around the ship pretty quickly and got back to our parents, both from some of the

Brits and the other missionary mother. (I don't remember their names, and the Prayer Letter doesn't mention them.) They commended us for behaving like good Christians—and good Americans.

In the meantime, Dad and Mom were having their own mealtime trials. The six Brits at their table constantly made derogatory comments about the United States. One day, Mom had had enough. She put down her fork, leaned forward slightly, smiled, and said, "Oh, you have to make allowances for us Americans. We're quite revolutionary, you know."

There was dead silence for a moment. Then they got it: Americans...the Revolutionary War. They erupted into laughter. "Jolly good" ..."Well said"...and there was no more nonsense after that. Their mealtimes were generally enjoyed by all. In fact, Mom and Dad's tablemates were the ones concerned that we didn't have hotel rooms in Mombasa. One man even brought us ice cold orange squash soft drinks while we waited for Dad to get our stuff through customs.

After a few days of kids running wild during adult meals—somehow the nannies or governesses always disappeared—the stewards in the lounge were getting desperate. Marian and I didn't join in the noisy rampages—and Mom and Dad would have skinned us alive if we'd acted like the British children. Since I barely had room to practice my accordion in our cabin, one evening I asked permission to play the piano in the lounge until the adults returned from dinner. The steward hesitantly unlocked the piano. Many of the kids stopped their mayhem and came to listen—and I would let none of them bang on the piano. One night, I did what was to come naturally the rest of my life—I started telling stories, the usual children's stories plus Bible stories. A lot of the kids sat quietly and made the noisy ones go out on the deck.

The adults finally returned and claimed their children. Just before I was ready to leave with Mom and Dad, the steward came with a nice, frosty bottle of orange squash held high on a tray and gave it to me with a flourish. "Thanks," was all he said. After that, I usually played the piano every night during adult dining and quite often either told stories or organized games—and I got lots of orange squashes to share with the family! (Maybe that's why I'm NOT fond of orange soda now!)

Angry Billows Roll

One of my favorite accordion solos was an old hymn called "My Anchor Holds" that talks about angry billows of trials and troubles rolling through our lives but that Jesus is the anchor that keeps us safe and secure. That was a nice song to play, but the words didn't mean much to this Midwestern girl—until I saw the ocean billows rolling for the first time in the Red Sea and crashing over the bow of the ship.

Even though it was kind of chilly, Dad and I stayed on deck—and the fresh air kept us from getting seasick. But this was just a four-hour rehearsal.

The 36-hour storm in the Indian Ocean was the prime production! I still loved to stand on deck where I could see the waves rolling under the ship. One moment the bow of the ship would be lifted high as a wave approached, only to come descending like a runaway elevator as the wave rolled away. Again, staying on deck despite the chill is what helped the most. A group of young nuns on their way to a Catholic mission in Africa also stayed on the deck—making periodic runs to the railings. When Dad would go below to check on Mom, they'd assure him that they would look out for Marian and me. Actually, I think we took care of them.

Dad and I were about the only ones who would appear at meals. Marian wasn't much interested in food—and the very thought of food would make Mom feel even worse! Even many of the crew were very sick in this storm! Needless to say, the food also wasn't very terrific during this time, but Dad and I kept it down.

I remember the very strange feeling I had, however. Even though I never threw up, I did feel woozy and extraordinarily tired. But being in the upper bunk of our tiny cabin didn't appeal to me at all. I hated to be there, even at night. Dad didn't want me up on deck after dark, however, so I just lay in my bunk. But it was nearly impossible to sleep while being tossed from one side of the bunk to the other.

Everyone appeared rather pale and wobbly when we all finally emerged from the storm into bright tropical sunshine 36 hours later. We had survived!

The Organ Grinder and the Monkey

The date for the Children's Fancy Dress and Tea had been set long before we even boarded the Dunnottar Castle. But when we heard about it, we immediately knew what we would do: I would be the organ grinder and play my accordion while Marian hopped around as the monkey. Truth be told, she wasn't thrilled with that idea—but since she couldn't play the accordion, she was cast for that role.

I was wearing my beret from school, and Mom painted a flaring moustache on my face. I can't remember precisely what either of us wore otherwise—although I think I wore one of Dad's suit coats with the sleeves rolled, maybe even one of his ties.

Everyone was quite excited—especially since the storm that morning hadn't lasted very long. Each individual—or group—was announced over a microphone and strolled around the broad deck area where the entertainment was taking place to better show off their costumes.

There were oohs and aahs as Marian and I started out. I played "O Sole Mio" as we promenaded around the onlookers. We were the only ones with a musical prop! And Marian felt a little better about her role because, as she hopped around the crowd, she actually got a few coins tossed into her outstretched cup—just enough for an orange squash.

The accordion—and Marian's pitiful begging eyes—did the trick, and we walked off with first prize for the best costume overall.

So what was our grand prize? The opportunity to dine in the adult dining room. Mom made sure we wore our best dresses and gave us all kinds of instructions about how to act. But since we had survived our first night on board, we figured we could handle just about anything.

Dad walked us to the dining room—but then he was supposed to leave. We two missionary kids (12 and 9) walked alone into the lovely dining room—and we were the only ones there. We were met by a steward who obviously wasn't thrilled to be serving a couple of kids, especially Americans.

We were seated at a table in the corner—just for the two of us—with a limited array of silverware. The steward began bringing out the various courses of the meal, all the while urging us to hurry because we had to be gone before the adults arrived. Fortunately, Marian and I didn't eat much. We hurried as fast as we could and were glad to escape lest we upset finicky adults who didn't want any children in sight. So much for the grand prize!

Berean Mission, Inc.	AFRICA	B.A.M.S. — Katanti
3536 Russell Blvd.		Shabunda par Kindu
St. Louis, Missouri	The Dark Continent!	Congo Belge, Afrique

Prayer Letter   * * * * *   September 1954

"The angel of the Lord encampeth round about them that fear Him, and delivereth them" (Psalm 34:7).

Dear Ones in the Homeland:

Christian greetings from the Congo. When last we wrote, we had arrived in Mombasa, Kenya. While there, it was my privilege to preach, in English, in a Pentecostal Gospel Hall. It was thrilling to hear the gospel hymns and choruses sung in English, Swahili, and in some Indian language. Those people really sang, and we had a blessed time in the Lord. Monday morning we were up early with last-minute preparations for our long journey to Nairobi, more than 300 miles of what would be considered rough, dirt roads in America. When we left Mombasa at exactly 8:00 A.M., the sun was shining brightly, and we were filled with anticipation for the journey ahead. The "Green Hornet" (our Plymouth Suburban) was loaded to capacity with more than 500 pounds of luggage, plus the four of us. Some load!

Now, about the roads in Africa!!! Some of them surprised us. They were smooth and well surfaced with a black top, but they were also decidedly in the minority. For the most part, they resembled the old-fashioned washboard. We jiggled and bounced over them for hours on end. If we drove too slow, we would hit every bump; and if we tried to go about 25 or 30 mph, we seemed to bounce over every other corrugation. We were singing choruses, and the girls would burst into giggles at the funny way our voices quivered as we were thoroughly shaken up over the "washboard." We now feel that our Plymouth has had a 1500-mile "shakedown cruise."

About 1:00 P.M., Monday afternoon, we pulled into a little place called Mtito Andei. There we were to eat lunch. Met a husky, young man in the washroom who was also trying to remove some of the red dust of the road before lunch. I noticed that he had a big revolver strapped to his hip and ready for service. Since we were in the heart of the Mau Mau territory, I asked him if that sort of equipment was necessary. He replied that nearly all European residents of that area were armed at all times. He then asked how far we were going and if we were armed. I told him we were traveling all the way to the Congo, and that I had guns but they were underneath the rear seat with 500 pounds of luggage resting on them. The Mau Mau situation in East Africa is so severe that there is a fine of $700 for each gun lost or stolen within the Colony — and we were not taking any chances. After all, our trust for safety wasn't in a couple of guns — our safekeeping was in the hands of Almighty God, who had called us out here.

After we had eaten, as we were buying gasoline, this same young fellow and his wife drove up to the pump. As they could speak Swahili, they kindly did all the talking for us which helped immensely. We were finished first, so we said goodbye and went on our way. About five miles down the road, we saw a transport truck stalled and two Africans in the road waving us down. So with a quick prayer for safety, we stopped beside them. We could only catch one word of what they said, "petrol." They were out of gas. I handed them my Jerry Can of extra gas (you never travel in Africa without one) and they were putting the gas in their tank when who should drive up but our husky friend and his wife. "Having trouble?" he asked. Upon explaining the situation to him, he immediately took over. He extracted from them the money for the gas (which I couldn't have done, not being able to speak to them) and sent them on their way. Then he scolded us mildly for stopping, and said, "Think I'll follow you for a while. We'll just keep together" — and so we did.

A short distance from Nairobi, our destination for the night, he stopped us at a little "hole-in-the-wall" shop and bought us a Pepsi-Cola (they have them even in Africa). Then he proceeded to give us a good lecture. "You're in the heart of Mau Mau territory," he said. "Stop for no one on the road. If a car is parked and you see no white man, don't stop, even if they try to wave you down. If several Africans block the road, unless you see a white man, drive right through them." We shook hands all around and again headed for Nairobi. We arrived about 7:30 that evening, found a reasonable (??) hotel and made ourselves comfortable for the night. The first leg of our journey was over. Praise the Lord for His watchcare.

As we had some shopping that needed to be done, we decided to stay in Nairobi an extra day. We were crossing the main street of this very modern city when whom should we meet in the safety lane but our guardian of yesterday and his wife. After a bit of conversation, we were shaking hands in parting when our "guardian" said, "Say, if you ever need a friend in Kenya, just call on me. Ask for Chief Inspector Angel of the Kenya Police. You won't need an address — just contact the police." We were trusting in Psalm 34:7 as our traveling verse, "The angel of the Lord encampeth round about them that fear him, and delivereth them," but we certainly had not expected a visible "angel" with a gun on his hip — but that is who the Lord sent: Chief Inspector *Angel* of the Kenya Police!

That night as we were preparing for bed we heard that which all travelers in Africa dread — rain! The roads become a quagmire after a rain, and we were so heavily loaded. The next morning, however, the sun was shining brightly, and so with thanksgiving unto our Lord, we began the second lap of our journey inland. We ran into deep mud just once. Another car was stuck, but the Lord pulled us through with no mishaps. And so went each day of the journey. God wondrously watched over us.

On Saturday, July 31, we crossed the border of Uganda into the Belgian Congo.

In a small border-town bank, I inquired as to the possibility of driving all the way from the border to Bukavu, our final bit of civilization before we headed into the forests and our mission station. The man assured me it was perfectly possible to make the trip as we were just 123 miles from Bukavu. When I asked how the roads were, he replied, "Comme ci, comme ça", which means "so-so," not too bad, not too good. After prayer, we decided to push on.

W-e-l-l, we made it — BUT! The man had neglected to tell us that it was winding, mountainous road all the way. Never have I seen such sharp curves, dips and steep inclines. It was really treacherous. Sometimes we hit stretches where the dust was four to six inches deep or more. Then the car would skid just as if it was in deep snow. Twice we turned particularly sharp curves and there facing us would be a steep incline. The Green Hornet would make a valiant attempt—cough, sputter and give up. Our load was too heavy for such a steep incline without a little run for it. Gertie would get out and direct me back down. I couldn't see out the rear window because the luggage was piled to the roof. Then we would try again. With six cylinders pulling for all they were worth, and the Lord pushing from behind, up we went. We finally pulled into Bukavu about 9:30 P.M., Saturday night, awfully dirty and exhausted. But, praise God, we were just 144 miles from Ikozi, one of our Berean Mission stations.

We stayed two days in Bukavu getting Congo insurance on the car, buying foodstuffs ahead for several weeks, etc. Canned goods cost terrific here—60 cents for a small can of peas. Yet we must depend upon canned goods because few vegetables can be grown in our area of the Congo. We do have native fruit which is very good. Some of the missionaries eat as much native foods as possible to try to stretch their food money a bit, but that is a questionable practice as far as health is concerned. We must reserve judgment on that until we are more experienced.

We left Bukavu on Monday afternoon, August 2, and stayed at a Conservative Baptist Mission Station with our good friends the Bothwell family for two more days. On Wednesday morning, August 4, we said goodbye to the Bothwells and headed for Ikozi, one of our Berean Mission Stations. The terrain between Bukavu and Ikozi was beautiful. We went through a bamboo forest high up in the mountains. Of course, the classic remark was made, "My, look at all the fishing poles." After we drove out of the bamboo forest, then the scenery was typical jungle. Underbrush was so thick that we had the illusion of driving along a red path with a green, impenetrable wall on either side.

About 4:30 P.M., we saw the sign "B.A.M.S.—Ikozi Station." We nosed the Plymouth into the narrow road and up the hill we went, honking our horn all the way. The Africans came running from all directions, yelling and jumping up and down. Many of them were calling, "Samba, Samba," which is their way of saying "hello." We pulled up in front of Mrs. Amie's house just as she and Miss Amanda Johnson came running out. As we were shaking hands with them, Carl Blackburn came running up the hill from his house. Last October 31, we had visited with Carl and his family in Marseille as their boat docked there en route to Africa. A large group of African Christians had gathered and began to sing "There's a Welcome Here" in their own tongue. The way they sang made us feel truly welcome, too. By this time, Miss Dorothy Reich, our mission dentist, and Barbara Blackburn had also come a-running. My such a commotion! We were then introduced to the African elders and teachers. We shook so many hands that we began to feel like celebrities.

That evening all the missionaries on Ikozi gathered at the Blackburn house for supper and fellowship. What a good talk-fest we did have! About nine o'clock as we were just finishing our meal, there was a knock on the door. An African stood there with a pleading look in his eyes. This was his story. His pregnant wife had walked to a village about 25 miles away. Something had happened. She was terribly ill. Please go get her or she will surely die. That plea could not be refused. Carl Blackburn and I went in his panel truck to get her. With us went the African male nurse, Jacque, an African midwife, and the husband. Although the village was only 25 miles away, it took us over two hours to drive it because of the narrow, winding road through the mountain forests. At one point we came to a river and had to wake up the ferry men to take us across. At another time, the headlights of our car picked up a large creature slinking across the road and into the forest. It was a huge leopard, startled by the lights of our truck.

Finally, we reached the village. The woman was terribly sick. She had miscarried and gangrene had set in. Jacque administered several injections, and we brought the woman back to Ikozi, arriving about 2:30 A.M. The suffering woman was made as comfortable as possible, and Carl and I fell into bed for about three hours sleep. Early the next day we would take her on to the nearest medical doctor. How desperately we do need a doctor and hospital on one of our stations. This same sort of emergency arises time and time again. Pray that our Berean Mission hospital may soon be erected and that Dr. Harry Zemmer, who is soon to be in Belgium with his family for a year's study of tropical diseases, will be enabled of the Lord as he undertakes the courses and that he may soon join us here in the field where the need is so great.

The next morning, we loaded the sick woman into my car, and Mrs. Amie, Jacque, and I started out for the nearest doctor, some 2 ½ hours drive from Ikozi—again over terrible, mountain roads. We arrived just as the doctor was driving home to have lunch. He examined the woman immediately, and said she had about a 50-50 chance to live. Life and death dwell close together in Africa. We left the woman there and arrived back at Ikozi late that afternoon after tending to other business along the way. Such was my introduction to missionary life. Within twenty-four hours of our arrival, after our 1500-mile trip inland, I drove or rode another ten hours, and had three hours sleep our first night on the station. Such is the life of a missionary if he would be used of God in reaching and helping precious souls in need of the Savior.

Marian also had a rather grueling introduction to missionary life. Dorothy Reich checked her teeth because Marian had developed a gumboil. She found one tooth very rotten, with poison draining into her system—so she pulled it. Marian was a brave little missionary and decided she liked Dorothy even if she did pull a tooth the first time Marian smiled at her.

Friday, August 6, we left Ikozi and headed for Katanti, which will be our mission station in Africa. Katanti is about a three-hour drive from Ikozi. We saw the sign, "B.A.M.S. - Station Katanti"

and turned in the driveway. First we passed a native village, the homes of the native workmen and schoolboys. Everyone came running out, waving, and calling, "Samba." They were expecting us. We wound up the little road and stopped in front of a brick house called "Jansen Hall." This is the dormitory for the missionary school children, and also the home of Ernest and Hallie Green and their four children. They came running out of the house to greet us. It was so good to see them. We had entertained them in our home in East St. Louis before they left for the Congo three years ago. Coming from the house next door were John and Phyllis Sanford and their three children. They took us across the road to "our home." It is made of sticks and mud and has a leaf roof, but it is home. The African women came to greet us first. They sang the welcome song and brought us a lovely bouquet of tropical flowers. Later the men came. We shook hands until we were almost "shaken out." Many said, "We have waited long for you. We are glad you are here." Believe me, we were glad too.

We have had one severe time of testing since our arrival. The very night we arrived at Katanti, Marian became quite ill with malaria and tonsillitis. Her temperature remained around 104 degrees for four days. Hallie Green, who is a nurse, did everything she could for her, and we waited upon the Lord. *"Wait on the Lord: be of good courage, and He shall strengthen thine heart: wait, I say, on the Lord"* (Psalm 27:14). God heard our prayers and has raised her up. She is still terribly thin and weak. Pray for her. Pray for Gertrude, Jeanette and me, too. These are days of adjustment for all of us, but we sing with the Psalmist, *"The Lord is my strength and my shield; my heart trusted in Him, and I am helped: therefore my heart greatly rejoiceth; and with my song will I praise Him"* (Psalm 28:7).

We want to remind you, dear ones, that we are now some 10,000 miles from you, and the lines of communication are greatly lengthened. *Airmail* letters require at least two weeks one way, and regular mail is useless, taking from two to three months to arrive. If it seems that we are not in as close touch with you as before, remember this vast space between us and the uncertainty of the mails here in the center of Africa. We shall do our best to keep you informed of the Lord's leading and blessing.

God bless you each one. We remember you daily in prayer.

Yours in His Never-failing Grace,

The Spainhowers

Jeanette's Comment: On to the Belgian Congo

Marian and I wondered at first why so little had been written about our journey across East Africa to the Congo. It's as if we were so anxious to get to the Congo once we debarked in Mombasa that we just hurried along. Dad didn't even take many photos.

Then we realized—we weren't supposed to get out of our cars, except at specified places because of the MauMau uprising. The Kikuyu tribe basically ruled the area from Mombasa until a good distance past Nairobi. They had started the fight for independence from Great Britain in Kenya—a revolution that within the next six years would spread like wildfire across all of Africa.

Killing white people was a basic tenet of this revolution. But Dad kept his two guns under the middle seat of the Green Hornet with piles of luggage and boxes on top of them. He had come to Africa to minister to the Africans and bring them the Good News about Jesus Christ—not to kill them, not even in defense of our own lives.

The story of Chief Inspector Angel has become a favorite of many people because it's one that I've related many times across the years in my own family's travels. Our travel verse, as Dad noted, was Psalm 34:7 that talks about the angel of the Lord watching over those that trust God and delivering them—and we had a big, brawny one packing a six-shooter to watch over us throughout the most dangerous part of our trip!

Our trip across East Africa was made with much prayer. Once we left Nairobi, we stayed on mission stations across the Kenya and Uganda. One of the other Berean missionaries, Carl Blackburn (noted in some of the previous prayer letters), had written to us in France, telling us where to write and ask for shelter. All mission stations had guest houses in those days or made arrangements to house traveling missionaries.

Since we were crossing savannah grasslands in Kenya, especially, Mom or Marian would call out occasionally when they saw animals out in the distance. Dad never stopped the car, but might slow down a bit to take a look himself. And me? I never saw a thing! I think I probably needed glasses, but it would be two more years before we got back to the States, and I finally got some.

I remember how thrilled we were to finally get to Bukavu. We stayed in a real hotel with all the hot water we wanted for baths—but we had to be careful not to drink the water coming out of the faucets. We were in the tropics, and amoebic dysentery was a nasty possibility unless the water was boiled thoroughly before drinking. Nonetheless, Bukavu in the 1950s was a wonderful oasis of civilization as a respite from jungle living.

Of course, in a civilized situation, bars were a fact of life. I was amazed to hear Dad ask someone at the bar in the hotel in which we were staying if he had any Johnny Walker whiskey bottles. What I didn't know was that these *empty* bottles were perfect for storing boiled and filtered water back on the mission station. Square in shape, many more would fit into the refrigerator than round containers. In addition to the whiskey bottles, Dad bought a filtration system that would help improve the flavor of the boiled water and take out any particles that remained. Thanks to Carl Blackburn for passing that bit of information to us ahead of time, so we could be prepared. To the 500 lbs. of luggage in the Green Hornet, we added about 20 square *empty* whiskey bottles.

After spending the two days on Musheshwe with the Bothwell family, we headed back into the true jungle—more properly called a *rain forest*, which doesn't really sound as dense as it was. All the way across East Africa and into Bukavu, it was primarily grasslands. There were trees and bushes, of course, but nothing like the thick jungle. In the jungle, the foliage varied between bushes and grasses all the way up to high-canopy trees. Everything grew so tightly compacted that if a person unaccustomed to the jungle were to wander five feet off a beaten path, that individual would become totally disoriented and unable to find the path again.

To complicate matters, all of the thick, green jungle wandered up and down mountainsides. Driving along the two ruts hacked out of the jungle called a road, you could tell the mountainside on one side—but you could not tell how deep the ravine was on the other side because the high-canopy trees came up past the road level. Often, it was hundreds of feet down to the valley below.

The roads across East Africa had been dusty corrugated roads (which turned to mud after rains), but they were usually two cars wide trailing across the grasslands. In the jungle, the roads were cut into the sides of the mountains—and there were only a few spots here and there where two vehicles could pass. On part of the road from Bukavu to the Berean mission station Ikozi, vehicles were to head toward Bukavu on Mondays, Wednesdays, and Fridays, and were open inland on Tuesdays, Thursdays, and Saturdays. You traveled at your own peril on Sundays. The terrain was supposed to be much more dangerous in that area—but I didn't see much difference anywhere else!

Bridges over the ravines or creeks were one-way only and rather precarious. If a bridge washed out, then you waited for several days until another one could be built. The Belgian government set up villages every few kilometers and paid workmen to keep the roads in decent repair. After the Belgians left the Congo, there was no more upkeep on the roads. Today, what is left of the original roads is no more than a small path running through the jungle, kept intact by people walking on it. Logs thrown across the ravines are the only bridges. The only motorized vehicles that can get through are small motorbikes.

The main difference we could see as we drew closer to the area where the four Berean Mission stations were located was the response of the Africans as we came near a village. (See Appendix B.) Everyone would run to the side of the road and wave ecstatically to greet us. What we didn't know was that the jungle drums were busy from village to village, pounding out the news that the new missionaries were coming.

B.A.M.S. Ikozi (Berean African Missionary Society) was the second station that Berean Mission established in the Balega tribal area some thirty years prior to our arrival. (See Appendix A.) Mrs. Beulah Amie and Miss Amanda Johnson were among the original missionaries, along with Irving Lindquist. The three missionary houses on Ikozi were built of kiln-dried brick with metal roofs—and Mrs. Amie had directly supervised the building of these houses several years before.

A large stone fireplace in Mrs. Amie/Miss Johnson's home immediately drew my attention. Chunks of purple quartz protruded from many of the large gray stones and sparkled either in the sunlight or firelight. I asked about them—and found out they were amethysts. Mrs. Amie had asked the workmen to bring in stones that sparkled—there was a lot of mica in that area. She nearly fainted when they brought in numerous stones with amethyst quartz sticking out of them. Since it was illegal for anyone but the Belgian government to sell minerals from the Congo, the missionaries couldn't profit from the amethysts, not even to give all of the money to the African church. So Mrs. Amie just put the stones around the fireplace where they twinkled and sparkled for all of us to enjoy.

What great joy when we finally headed out on the last leg of our journey from East St. Louis, Illinois, to B.A.M.S. Katanti. It had taken so many years since Dad and Mom had first committed themselves to become missionaries until we finally reached the place where we were to settle down and minister. Katanti was the first station established in the Balega tribe, followed by Ikozi, and then Kamulila (where we would serve during our second term), and finally, the hospital station, Katshungu. Later, Uku station would be established in a different tribal area for the Bakumu.

As we passed every village, the Africans were even more vocal and enthusiastic in their joy—and the drums kept beating out the news that we were coming. By the time we went honking up the hill on Katanti, we were all in a fever pitch of excitement—and discovered the mission Africans were just as excited as we were! They already knew we were coming!

The missionaries were the first to greet us, but except for the Africans working around the missionary homes, none of the other Africans came up the road. We could see them gathering in front of a large building closer to the African village (later, we discovered it was the church), but there they stayed.

Finally, we could hear the strains of "Onward, Christian Soldiers," and the schoolboys (most of them teenagers) came marching up the road, preceded by the African elders, followed by the women and younger children. Once again, we were greeted with "There's a Welcome Here"—and couldn't understand a single word. But the heartfelt greeting was quite obvious. We were home!

Katanti
Wednesday, August 11, 1954

Dearest Family and All:

Praise the Lord, we are writing from our home in Africa. We pulled into Ikozi on August 4, stayed two days and came to Katanti on Friday, the 6th. Needless to say, we've been in a terrific whirl trying to get settled as well as acclimated a bit. We haven't started eating in our house yet as Hallie Green is training the young men who will work for us.

Guess I had better back up to Bukavu and bring you up to date. Monday, August 1, Les was handling some of our affairs when a familiar voice hailed him. It was Bob Bothwell, Conservative Baptist missionary, who had attended Wycliffe with us. He insisted we sign out at the hotel and come to his mission — about ten miles from Bukavu. So we finished up the last bit of business, packed up and went to Mushweshwe. We spent a couple of days with Bob and Marie and their four children. We sure did a lot of talking to span the years since we had shared the same dining table at the Summer Institute of Linguistics.

Wednesday morning we drove to Ikozi. Pulled in about 2:00 P.M. It was sure a thrill to hear the Africans sing "There's a Welcome Here" in Kilega. They can sure sing. We shook so many hands that we began to feel like President Eisenhower. Finally, the crowd dispersed and we went to Carl and Barbara Blackburn's to wash up. Everyone gathered there for supper: Mrs. Amie, Amanda Johnson, Dorothy Reich, the Blackburns, and, of course, the Spainhowers. In the middle of dinner, who should drive up but Irving Lindquist. So we surprised him.

Right after dinner, an African came to the door with news that a woman was very, very ill in a village quite a distance from Ikozi. Would someone please go get her or she will surely die. So Carl Blackburn and Les started out with the African nurse, a fine Christian man with a good testimony for Christ. The woman was desperately ill. They brought her back to Ikozi, getting home about 2:30 in the morning. The next day Les and Mrs. Amie took the woman some distance away to the hospital. The doctor said that she had lost a baby and gangrene had set in. She had only a fifty-fifty chance of survival. Les really got a rugged introduction to missionary life.

Friday we left Ikozi for our station on Katanti. How happy we were to see Ernest and Hallie Green and their four children, and John and Phyllis Sanford and their three children, and to take our place with them in the Lord's service in this part of Africa.

Marian, bless her heart, is the first of us to succumb to the old malaria bug. She has been very sick, and the battle still isn't won. She has a high fever and all the aches that accompany malaria. Aunt Hallie, as she calls Mrs. Green, has already given her five shots and, Marian fears, there is more a-coming. Pray much for Marian. Pray that God will undertake for her and strengthen her little body, enable her to gain weight, so that she will be better able to fight off this fever.

Sunday Hallie stayed with Marian while Les, Jeanette and I went to church. Jeanette played her first accordion solo in our own African church, and Les preached his first sermon. Ernest Green translated for him. The church was full to overflowing. Of course, the church was mud with a leaf roof, and open places for ventilation, and believe me, when you get a crowd of Africans in a small room, you need ventilation. The seats were benches. Every place was filled and people sitting outside, others peeking in the window openings to see the new missionaries. Now I know how a goldfish feels. It was really a heart warming event.

Wish you could see our house. You would be surprised how nice a mud house can be. We were. Ernest and John had it all whitewashed for us and Hallie and Phylis put up clean curtains, scarves, etc. It is adequately furnished. Some furniture, especially in the living room, was woven by the natives. The dining room furniture was made by Albert Jansen while he and Mamie were still here. We are using Vander Ploeg's stove until ours arrives. We even have a bathtub—a 55 gallon gasoline drum, which has been cut in half, legs fashioned on it, and painted white. Of course, our knees sort of touch our chins but it's a bathtub nonetheless.

There are a few other occupants in the house that I sometimes find a bit disturbing. We have lots of spiders. They come in two sizes, big and bigger. The biggest roach I've seen was two inches long, but I'm told they come bigger, too. Of

Dad standing in front of the first house we stayed in when we arrived on Katanti.

course, ants are into everything and there are lots of mice. The worst thing is a scorpion. I've killed one in the house. There are lots more, and they are dangerous. Their sting isn't fatal but dreadfully painful. Does it all sound awful? Well, we have another occupant, our precious Lord, who, by His presence with us makes our mud house the best place in the world for us.

Pray much for us. There are difficult days of adjustment. Pray for real enablement in the language, for health and strength. We are so encouraged to receive all the letters when we arrived at Ikozi and even after coming to Katanti. I can't begin to tell you how good it made us feel.

Please share this letter with the Wrights and others as we don't have time between nursing Marian, trying to get settled, Les working on the station water pump, and on and on and on to catch up on our letter writing.

Much, much love to you all,

Les, Gertie, Jeanette and Marian

Marian's Comment: Katanti Arrival

We were all very excited to finally arrive at Katanti, our mission station and new home. We were eager to see the Greens and Sanfords, the other missionaries on that station. Our arrival in Africa had been a long time coming, and the traveling had seemed endless. We were all tired but happy.

Since the missionaries didn't have any family on the mission field, we children called the adults Aunt and Uncle. That was to help us feel like we were all family together. So the Greens became Uncle Ernie and Aunt Hallie. The Sanfords were Uncle John and Aunt Phyllis.

Berean Mission headquarters in St. Louis, Missouri, had four mission stations in the jungles of the Belgian Congo when we first arrived in the Congo: Katanti, Ikozi, Katshungu, and Kamulila. About a year later, Uku was started to minister to a different tribe. The dormitory and school for missionary children were located on the Katanti station.

To give you a feel for the layout of Katanti—as we drove up the hill on the one-lane dirt road past the Katanti African village, we first passed on the right the mud church where we all worshipped and mud school buildings for the Africans. Farther up the hill on the left was a small mud building which was the school for missionary children. By our second term in Africa, they had built a new school out of concrete blocks. A little past the school on the right was the mud house where the Sanfords lived. Next on the right was a brick, two-story building which was the dormitory for missionary children attending school on Katanti, headed by Ernie and Hallie Green. Past the dormitory on the left was a mud house belonging to the Parcel family. Then at the far end of the mission station on the left was a two-bedroom, mud guest house. There was one road to get to the mission station and the same road to leave. All about the length of two or three city blocks.

We arrived at Katanti in the afternoon and by late afternoon I wasn't feeling very well at all. My body started to ache, and all I wanted to do was to lie down on the bed. Mom thought I was just tired from all the traveling. But by evening I began running a high fever, and the body aches quickly became very intense. They were the worst I have ever experienced. The ache of malaria absolutely outdoes any aches I have ever experienced with the flu. My body hurt so badly, I could hardly stand the feel of my clothes on my body or to have anyone touch me. As if that wasn't bad enough, then came the chills. My body shook so hard from the inside out with chills that my teeth literally chattered. To add insult to injury, Aunt Hallie Green, who was a nurse, started giving me injections. I quickly felt like a human pin-cushion! I do believe those needles got larger every time she came to the house.

During the day, Dad would carry me into the living room and put me on the couch which was across from a fireplace. They would pile blankets on top of me and build a fire in the fireplace to try to stop the chills. (The Congo is not cold so everyone else must have been very hot with the fire going.) At times when the fever would break, I would be dripping from sweat. That would only last a short time and then the fever, chills, and aches would return again. I became very weak.

One evening I distinctly remember Dad coming into the living room. He picked me up and held me in his arms for a while as we sat on the couch together—just my Dad with his little girl. My fever was raging, and I was so weak I couldn't even speak. I remember just laying my head on the comfort of his shoulder, and Dad kissing me on my forehead. After a while he kissed me again, told me he loved me, and gently laid me back down on the couch.

What I didn't know until years later was that as Dad left the room, he called for my mother to come with him. They went into the bedroom together and closed the door. Then Dad told my mother that it was time for them to give me back to the Lord. Mom told me she was startled at first and wanted to protest, but Dad told her they needed to confirm with the Lord that they were still answering His call to the mission field. Even if the Lord wanted to take me Home to be with

Him, they would remain His faithful servants. So together they knelt beside their bed, with arms wrapped around each other and tears streaming down their faces, they each prayed to the Lord, confirming their commitment to serve Him in the jungles of Africa even if the Lord took me Home.

But God in His faithfulness and mercy did not take me Home to be with Him that night. Instead, He rewarded the commitment of my parents to His will, and that very night my fever broke and didn't return. Little by little my strength began to return and they had their little girl back again. However, if the Lord had taken me that night, my parents would have remained in Africa where the Lord had called them to go. Now that's faith!

I was plagued with malaria the entire time we were in Africa but never as severe as in those first weeks on the mission field.

Jeanette's Comment: What's in a Name?

Here in America, children are sometimes named for relatives and, on occasion, a family picks a name because it has special meaning. But usually, children get their names because the parents like the sound of the name or simply because it's popular at the time.

In the Balega tribe, however, children are given names that speak either to an event that was happening around their birth, to something the mother or father saw, or even to emphasize a traditional proverb. One of our houseboys, for example, was named *Ngabo* — which meant *shield* because there had been a shield standing in the corner of the room where he had been born. Another one was called *Kibekiangabo — a piece of a shield*. By the time we arrived in the Congo, Christian Balega were naming many of their children after Bible characters.

It was the custom among the Balega to observe newly arrived missionaries for a couple of weeks and then give them African names. About two or three weeks after we arrived on Katanti, the African elders told Uncle Ernie Green, the station chairman, that they were ready to bestow Balega names on our family. Aunt Hallie volunteered to stay with Marian, who still wasn't well, so Mom could go down to the church to receive her name.

Upon our arrival, Dad had spoken through an interpreter, telling the Africans how God had called him from a life of sin to salvation through Jesus Christ, how God had called him to full-time Christian service, and then, to missionary service in Africa, and then, specifically, to the Balega tribe. So they named him *Tata Wemaninua — the called one*. (The greatest respect shown among the Balega was to call a man *Tata, my father*, or a woman, *Mane or Mama, my mother*.)

We weren't sure at first about Mom's name: *Mane Utamusonga — the one you would not marry*. We thought it was because she was handicapped, and the Africans were not kind to handicapped people. But the elders explained it to us. They saw that Dad was very careful to hold onto her arm when they were walking, so she would not trip. They saw that he often would bring her a glass of water or take a heavy package from her. "No," they said, "you would not marry Mama because Tata takes good care of her." Interestingly, there is no word for love in Kilega, so these Africans had no other way to describe Dad's love for Mom — they just knew it was very special.

Marian was named after a Balega proverb that basically described a person who "looked forward to tomorrow but didn't know if he would live to see it": *Walanga Muaka — the one who will not live for a year*. Because she had been so very ill, the Africans didn't expect Marian to survive her first year in the Congo. Thankfully, they were wrong! God intervened — and that, too, helped the Africans see the mercy of our Heavenly Father.

I was named *Wanga Lukoba* — after a flower that grows tall, straight, and beautiful in the forest, according to the Africans. I preened about that for a while, but you can see in my comment about building a mud house how my pride bubble was so easily burst!

Katanti
August 12, 1954

Dearest Grandpa and Grandma,

Here we are at last at Katanti! We sure do thank the Lord for bringing us safely here. We didn't have even one flat tire. Praise the Lord for that. We hit rain and muddy roads for only a little time one morning. But we didn't mire down.

We arrived here Friday the 6th. I think that was the date. Anyway, we arrived on a Friday. About a mile off we saw a round sign that said, "Mission B.A.M.S. Katanti Station." Then about 8 blocks farther we saw another sign and turned in the little side road. We could see Katanti as soon as we turned off onto that road. It sure was thrilling to know that at last we arrived at the place where the Lord had called us. At first all we saw were some mud buildings which turned out to be the schoolrooms and the church. So we drove on farther down the road to the brick house. We pulled up and honked our horn and the Greens came running out. I could hardly recognize them. Eldon is so tall; David, well I didn't even remember what he looked like; Roger was only four or five when we saw them last so you can imagine what he looked like. Patty, the baby, isn't any more. She is three or four and quite a big girl. Aunt Hallie and Uncle Ernie hadn't changed much at all.

We sat down and talked just for about five minutes when the other couple with their children came up to see the new missionaries whom they were to work with. It turned out to be Mr. and Mrs. John Sanford, Danny, Joy and Skippy. Mr. and Mrs. Sanford are now Aunt Phyllis and Uncle John. Out here in Africa the children don't have their real Aunts and Uncles so the missionary men and women become Aunts and Uncles. I think that is rather nice.

As you probably know, we are living in a mud house. It's the biggest we have ever lived in and I like it more than any I've ever stayed in. I could like it more than that if it weren't for the bugs, snakes, rats and mice which live in the same house with us. At night you sure feel good to be underneath the mosquito netting. That means that nothing can sleep with you—like bugs and things. This morning we were trying to put up our own mosquito netting and when I stood up on a chair to unfasten the mission mosquito netting, I found out why we use the stuff. There was dirt and bugs (dead ones, of course) just littering the thing. As you may be sure I didn't want to take down that netting.

David, Roger, and I have killed two great big spiders. They would be as big as your fist. The

first one we killed may have been a bit bigger. As soon as we saw that first one, we grabbed a stick to squash it with. We knocked it down and killed it and to make sure the old thing was dead, I stepped on it. The other one we found on the floor of our club house.

For the time being we are taking turns eating at the Greens and the Sanfords. Maybe when our vegetables come from Bukavu we can start eating at our house.

I must close now.

Your granddaughter in Africa,

Jeanette

Marian's Comment: Katanti Housing

For our first term in the Congo, our family was stationed at Katanti. When we first arrived, we stayed in Parcels' house because they were home on furlough. Also, we had to wait several months for our household belongings to arrive at the station so we needed to borrow everything from others. It was the plan, though, that we would eventually live in the two-room guest house at the end of the station. However, there was no kitchen. So another two room house would be built next to it for a kitchen, dining room and living room combination.

Parcels' house was a large mud building with a leaf roof. The walls inside and out were white-washed so they looked clean and helped to brighten up the place. All of the windows were screened. With a porch all the way around the house and with the roof overhanging the porch, it stayed fairly cool inside. We had no electricity except for a generator that the mission would use for a couple hours every evening—if it worked. Other than that, we used kerosene lamps.

After a while we had to leave Parcels' house because of their return to the field. So the four of us lived in the two-room guest house until the second house was finished next to it. In one room of the guest house, we had two double beds with Mom's sewing machine in between (once our belongings arrived). The other room was an office, living room, dining room, and "catch all" room. Katindi had to cook outside on the porch since we didn't have a kitchen. We were all very thankful once the second house was completed!

Once we were able to move in, Katindi had an indoor kitchen, and we had a dining room/living room combination. Also, Jeanette and I finally had our own bedroom—and Mom and Dad had their privacy.

Now, you may be wondering if we had to use the forest as our bathroom or if we had that convenience in the house. Well, there was a smaller room between the two bedrooms for the bathroom. When the doors were open, we could walk straight through from one bedroom, through the bathroom, to the other bedroom (or earlier, to the general room). The sink was a small table with a wash basin on top. Hot water had to be brought in from the reservoir in the cooking stove to put in the basin for washing. Then we would empty the basin down the toilet.

We had a toilet?? Well…….it was a toilet framed in concrete that emptied into a septic tank. We had a "real" toilet seat with a lid on it. The toilet was flushed by pouring a bucket of water down into it so we had to always have buckets of water sitting beside the toilet for that purpose.

It was very important in the Congo to be extremely careful when walking around or sitting down. You always looked first. It was a good thing Jeanette had learned that practice quickly because one time she lifted the lid to the toilet and found a black mamba curled up under the seat! She nearly raised the leaf roof screaming for help!

Our bathtub was a big tin washtub. Water was heated over the laundry fire and carried into the house to pour into the washtub when we needed a full bath. Needless to say, we didn't bathe every night! We did have one rather humorous incident that happened, though. We had a guest speaker at one of our yearly conferences for missionaries held on Katanti. Dad got the bath all set up for him but unfortunately he was a very rotund gentleman. After he completed his bath, he realized he was stuck in the washtub and couldn't get out. He called Dad but Dad couldn't get him out by himself, so he had to call a couple of our African houseboys to assist him. I bet that was a hilarious sight to behold! Needless to say, Dad threatened us severely if we dared to laugh or tell anyone.

Marian's Comment: Why We Employed Houseboys

All missionary families had houseboys for two special reasons: 1) Missionary women were free to devote their time to missionary work, and 2) it enabled these young men to pay their way through school or Bible School or just take care of their families. Over the years we had some very special houseboys whom we grew to appreciate a great deal.

These are the houseboys we had by the time we moved to the guest house on Katanti during our first term. You can clearly see our two houses behind them. Two of them worked for us during the second term as well.

On the left in the picture is Mukenge. He did general housework for us. I learned to appreciate him greatly one day. I was prone to get athletes feet in Africa which frequently would get infected. I also would get little black chiggers that would burrow into my infected feet—usually around or between my toes. These had to be removed with a needle because left unattended, they would reproduce in a "sack," and I would have a mess. Mom usually dug them out—under my protests—but she had to be very careful not to break the reproduction sack while pulling them out. One day she kept digging and digging and just couldn't get them out. I was crying and begging her to stop when Mukenge came into the room and offered to help. Mom gave him the needle with a little uncertainty while I froze, thinking he was surely going to do me bodily harm! With one quick, totally painless movement with the needle, Mukenge had the chigger and sack removed. From then on, he was the one I went to when I spotted chiggers in my feet!! Mukenge only worked for us during our first term in the Congo. He went on to be a teacher in one of the villages.

The man second from the left was Ngabo. This young man was certainly one of my favorites. He cleaned our house and did other chores for Mom. He laughed a lot and was always very pleasant. One day I teased him by putting some ice cubes down his back. He acted like he was going to "die" as he tried to get them out. He jumped around and hollered. Dad scolded me for that and told me that Africans can pick up a very hot pan without any problems, but aren't used to the feel of ice since it never gets cold there, so this was a new sensation for him. I was forbidden to do that again. Frankly, I thought it was rather hilarious, and from then on Ngabo would laugh and shake his head at me as if to say "I've got your number, and I won't be fooled again!" Ngabo was still in school during our first term on Katanti, so he only worked in the house. During our second term on Kamulila he often traveled with Dad on evangelistic trips.

Katindi is the man second from the right who was our cook. He was actually from another tribe and, thankfully, spoke quite a bit of French which helped Mom tremendously as she instructed him concerning our meals. He was one of the kindest, most cooperative men we had working for us. I was so thrilled when his wife had their first baby girl and they named her "Maliana," which was their way of saying Marian. Katindi was a very good cook and very trustworthy. Mom depended on him a lot in helping her with our other houseboys. Katindi worked for us during both terms. He traveled with Dad in the first term but, because of his expanding family, he was the one who stayed to help Mom during the second term.

Jeanette and I remember the houseboy to the right of the picture, but cannot think of his name or what work he did for us. He tended to be rather surly, so he wasn't with us very long.

This is a picture of Jacque, our bedroom boy. I honestly think Mom and Dad hired him because he was cute and gave them his winning smile. All Jacque would do was earn a little money for his family by making our beds in the morning, and in the evening, folding back the covers as he tucked in the mosquito netting all around our bed to keep the night bugs and creeping things out of our beds while we slept. I don't think he was with us for very long but we enjoyed him while he was there.

Mom drastically cut back the number of young men we needed working in the house. She said there was no reason we couldn't make our own beds, just as we did in the United States, or serve ourselves at the table by passing the food family style!

Dad is standing by our "modern" plumbing system behind our house in this picture. We had four or five metal barrels in which we stored water for drinking, bathing, cooking, dishes, etc. All water for drinking or cooking had to be boiled, filtered, and put into bottles in the kitchen to be available when needed. We had a young man that kept these barrels full by going to the spring and bringing back two buckets full on either end of a pole that he carried across his shoulders. We marveled at how he could fill the buckets up almost to the top and rarely spill a drop on the steep path on his return.

Yes, this was our washer and dryer! However, Mom is only posing for the picture. Obviously, she would not have been able to scrub our clothes on the scrub board after heating the pans of water over an open fire in order to wash them. The houseboys were in charge of that task.

Here are two houseboys wringing the water out of linens so they could be hung on the line. The black pot was over a hot fire to make the water scalding hot. Our clothes and linens had to be made of good, hearty material or they never would have lasted. Notice how the dense forest was practically right outside our back door!

This was Ngabo doing our ironing. You may wonder how he could iron when we had no electricity. He used old, heavy flat irons made of cast iron, which were heated on a fire. Victorian housewives had used flat irons before electricity became widespread. We'd had to search in antique shops to find flat irons to take to the Congo with us. We had several so while one was being used, the others were getting hot. The handles were very hot so he had to wrap his hand in a heavy cloth to keep from getting burned. We tried an iron that used charcoal—but it actually spit tiny bits of charcoal that burned holes in our clothes. Eventually, we found an iron that used kerosene and had adjustable temperatures—which made Ngabo and our clothes very happy!

Katanti
Sunday, August 15, 1954

Dearest Family:

Received another letter today, also one from Frances and another from Mr. Wright. Sure good to get them. Think I'll start by answering your questions.

We didn't get a picture of the girls in their costumes on the ship as we didn't have any flash bulbs. There were quite a few babies on board, but only about six children about the age of our girls. We crossed the equator at night, about one or two A.M. so there were no ceremonies.

We didn't get a letter from Mr. Wright at Mombasa and am wondering if you received the one I wrote from Mombasa. Les wrote to Mr. Wright from Mombasa also. You mentioned a letter from Aden and then one from Nairobi. There should have been one from Mombasa, too.

Yes, we got a Pepsi along the way in Kenya but we bought one in Bukavu and it cost us sixty cents a piece. No more Pepsis until we go home at that price.

This is our second Sunday at Katanti. Les preached last Sunday. Mr. Green interpreted, and Jeanette played an accordion solo. I must tell you of God's blessing upon His Word. Les spoke on Psalm 121. He spoke of God's loving watch care over his children; of His ability to care for His children in any circumstances, and also that we can break fellowship with God by our sins. The next day, a native teacher who had been giving the mission much trouble because of his backslidden condition, came to Ernie Green, confessed his sins and asked Ernie to pray with him. Ernie said that the teacher really repented of his sins and rededicated himself to the Lord Jesus. We sure feel that this is our "first fruit" of a ministry in this place.

I'm the Sunday School teacher of the missionary children which suits me fine. You know how I love to teach Sunday School! Also, in the missionary children's school, I will teach a class in Beginner French (Ha! I'm just a beginner myself) and Les will teach Bible. The rest of the day, approximately 4 to 6 hours will be spent in studying Kilega. Sounds like a full schedule.

Six shots and dozens of pills later, Marian is beginning to feel O.K. again. She's awfully thin, and we watch how much of her strength she expends, but we surely praise God for her recovery.

We've stopped eating at the Sanford's and the Greens and settled down in our own home. Have four houseboys which is about four too many. Our cook is Katindi who speaks a fair amount of French which is helpful. He is partly trained. I prepare a menu and send Katindi to Hallie Green for instructions. Then I help him cook because I want him to cook *my* way. Our table sitter and assistant cook is Kibekiangabo—kick that one around for a while. We call him Kibe for short. Then we have Jacque, our bedroom boy. He is about eleven years old and cute as a button. I'll be hard put not to spoil him. Our wash and iron boy is Wasolela. They all go to school on the station and work part time to pay their way through. I gave them Sunday afternoon and evening off. What a relief it was to do my own cooking and fuss around my own kitchen! I will be grateful for them, though, when we begin our heavy schedule in September.

All the spiders and creeping things don't bother us nearly as much as they did the first day or so. We are most grateful for our mosquito nets over the bed, though. We don't have too many mosquitoes but the nets protect us from the other things.

Must close this letter. Have to watch the amount of postage now. Keep asking questions. Then I'll know what you are curious about and can tell you.

Lost and lots of love,
Gertie

Marian's Comment: Undesirable Intruders

Living in the jungles of the Belgian Congo, Africa, in a mud house with a roof made of leaves, was an invitation to many different critters that inhabited the area. Needless to say, we did not put out the "Welcome" mat, but they came anyway.

First, let's talk about snakes. The Africans told us that there were two kinds of black snakes and two kinds of green snakes that looked alike. One of each kind was very poisonous and one was not. The only way we could tell if they were poisonous or not was to look inside their mouths at their fangs. Well, no! Our motto: a good snake is a dead one! We were advised by the Africans to treat ALL black and green snakes as though they were poisonous.

The Black Mamba is one of the most deadly snakes found in Africa. On an average they grow to be 8 to 12 feet long, sometimes longer. Let me tell you a story....

One time during our first term in Africa, when we lived in the two-houses on Katanti, Mom, Jeanette, and I were sitting in the bedroom having our family devotions after lunch. Dad had been gone a couple days in the jungle holding evangelistic meetings. After we finished praying, I looked out the screen door and saw a long, black Mamba was stretched out on the rafter of our leaf roof that hung down over our porch. It was at least 8 feet long. Mom quickly told Jeanette to run and get our houseboys to help us. Without even thinking, Jeanette opened the door right where the Mamba was and actually ran under it to the other house where the houseboys were! Unfortunately, before our houseboys could reach us with their machetes, Mom and I watched as the Mamba hurled itself from the rafter into the forest, looking almost like spear flying through the air. It was a terrifyingly awesome sight! God really protected Jeanette because Mambas are known for being very aggressive and highly venomous. It could have easily hurled itself onto Jeanette, delivering many deadly strikes. We saw the Mamba one more time the very next day, slithering up a tree behind our house at the edge of the forest. It makes me shudder just thinking about it even after all these years!

How about a cobra story! One afternoon as Mom, Dad, and Jeanette were resting, I walked into Dad's study to get some paper from off his desk. When I turned around to go back out of the room, there in my pathway was a cobra, head up, looking right at me! I had to have walked right by it on my way in. I immediately started screaming for Dad, "Snake! Snake!"—and jumped on top of his desk. I knew Dad would come prepared for the kill. He did, and all was well again—except perhaps my nerves!

Congo also had many kinds of scorpions. Unfortunately, Mom was the one who had a bad run-in with a scorpion. As she was stepping up onto our porch, she put her hand around a pole to help give her balance. There was a scorpion on the other side. As her hand started to unknowingly cover the scorpion, it stung two of her fingers badly on her right hand. The pain was severe for quite a while and left her hand and arm paralyzed for several days. Our missionary nurse had to slightly cut Mom's fingers to release the poison as much as possible. As a child, Mom had polio, which resulted in her left arm being unusable. As a result of not being able to use either hand and arm after the scorpion sting, we had to dress her, bathe her, feed her, and help her with anything else she needed during that time. She said that was one of the most painful experiences of her life.

We also had black, poisonous centipedes with dozens of little legs, and some that looked the same, but were not poisonous. The fun part about any of them is that if you gave them a kick, they would roll up in a ball and stay that way until they thought the coast was clear. They were around a lot so I always had fun kicking them, trying to make their lives miserable!

Driver ants were one of our undesirable intruders. Colonies of driver ants can number up in the millions. Even animals would run away when driver ants were swarming. There were times when we had to quickly vacate our house for the night while driver ants took over. There was nothing we could do, but go to another missionary's house for the night. The ants were raiding for food to bring back to their nest. When we returned to our house the next morning, the ants were gone—and the house was critter-free for a few days.

They didn't sting to attack. Instead they used their large "pinchers" to create puncture wounds. Let me tell you—that quickly got our attention!

We had a few incidents with driver ants, but let me tell you one that I think you will find humorous.

Dad was out hunting with some of the African men, and they ran into millions of driver ants that had already broken ranks and were scattered over an area in the jungle. The guys didn't even know the ants were around until they were suddenly being bitten from head to foot.

Dad and the men ran on down the trail a little bit, stripped as fast as they could, and started pulling ants off each other. So there they all stood, in their "nothingness," when all of a sudden a group of African women carrying heavy baskets came down the trail. The women stopped and politely greeted each one, including Dad, who was about to pass out from embarrassment.

The men told the women how to bypass the driver ants, so they went down a different trail. Dad said he'd purposely avoided looking directly at the women because he didn't want to blush as he was shaking hands with them the next Sunday if he recognized any of them at church. As embarrassed as he was, Dad said the women didn't act as if anything was wrong at all. Our reserved father found this to be an excruciating experience, to say the least!

Here are just a few other critter intruders found in or near our home—praying mantis, Katydids, four-inch flying cockroaches, mosquitoes that carried malaria, all kinds of spiders along with a variety of tarantulas. The ugly, furry tarantulas in particular are why we always shook out our shoes before putting them on. Jeanette shook out a tarantula on more than one occasion.

These are horned beetles Dad captured, killed and preserved. Jeanette still has them preserved in a canister after all these years!

We also had huge palm tree spiders that crawled on the walls all the time. The good thing about them is that they ate mosquitoes! They were literally the biggest reason for using our mosquito nets at night.

It was because of all of these undesirable intruders, as well as the malaria-carrying mosquitoes, that we slept under mosquito nets at night. These nets were suspended from a frame above our beds. Around 5:00 PM every evening, we would pull our bedding back, check the bed for bugs or whatever else might be there, and then we would pull the net down and tuck it under the mattress around the bed. Critters always came out at night, so when we crawled into bed and slept through the night, we knew we were protected as long as we were under our mosquito nets.

The Congo had many different kinds of critters, both large and small. Some we knew about, but many we can probably thank the Lord we didn't know about!

Katanti
August 16, 1954

Dear Grandma and Grandpa:

    This letter will be poor writing because I am weak. I have been very sick for seven days. The first day we were here I got sick.
    I like it a lot out here. We have seen lots of spiders. We have not tasted monkey meat yet. We did have some wild pig.
    We had one rain and the wind blew some leaves off our roof but no water came in.
    In Bukavu we bought a kerosene lamp. It is very pretty.
    We have three houseboys. One is my age.
    Soon it will be Mommy's birthday (August 18).
    Well, don't know anything more.

                Love,

                Marian

B.A.M.S.—Station Katanti
Shabunda par Kindu
Congo Belge, Afrique
August 17, 1954

Dear Brother and Sister Wright:

Just a hurried note this time to let you know that we received your airmail letter of July 29, addressed to us here at Katanti and also want to forward to you our Prayer Letter, which is enclosed. Again, the Prayer Letter is long; but it brings us up-to-date and to our station.

We did not receive your letter sent in care of the steamship company at Mombasa, and by the time we received your airmail letter of July 29 (we received it on August 15), it was then too late to think about cabling our safe arrival at Katanti. The cable would go fast enough, but getting the message from here to a point where it could be telegraphed to the coast and then cabled, would take longer than some of the letters Gertie has already written to her mother and which Mother Wilson will no doubt share with you.

As I mentioned in my prayer letter, the lines of communication are tremendously long. You can't quite realize it at that end of the line—but out here, the last leg of the journey for any letter (airmail included) is a two-day trip on foot by a native runner from the closest Post Office in Shabunda.

We are going to have rough going for the next three or four months until our goods from America come up the Congo River to us. The folk here on the Station have been lovely about trying to scrape up sufficient dishes, silverware, kitchenware, food storage tins, etc., but at the best they hardly have sufficient for their own needs, without trying to supply us temporarily, too. We will not have a refrigerator until ours arrives either, which makes it difficult, too. Praise the Lord, all of these things are coming, but it will be 3 or 4 months before they get here at the best. All shipments are held up at the ocean port of Matadi until the missionary arrives at his station and is registered with the local authorities. That we did last week. Now word must be sent back to Matadi and then our goods will begin the slow trip up the river. In the meantime certain import licenses must be obtained from the Bank at Kindu, and we are waiting on them at the present time before sending all papers back to Matadi.

Our greatest need at the present time is sufficient funds in our Reserve Account at the Mission to pay all outgoing expenses which will be charged back to the Mission by Keating, etc. Also, we shall need an estimated $300 out here to pay for transport from Kindu to Katanti of all our goods, plus the heavy costs of establishing ourselves here. Foodstuffs are terrifically expensive and so much is needed to begin with because supplies are always two to four weeks distance from us, making it necessary to order for three or six months ahead, case lots being some cheaper than smaller order. We have some food coming from Leggetts in New York, which the Mission is deducting from our salary at the rate of $40 per month, but it will be about four months before it arrives too. If it is possible to send this amount ($300), it should be designated "Personal" so that it will come out in the next transmission from the Mission. If the Lord does not so provide, then we will wait upon Him and see how He works it out when the bills begin to arrive and the shipments start coming in. His promise is never to forsake us.

I see my "note" has reached the bottom of the paper so will close for this time. We are quite tired now, and the tasks before us are overwhelming, but the Lord is the strength of our lives. We are leaning upon Him. Our love to you both, and more news when we get settled and work out a living routine.

Love in Christ,

Les and Gertie

Katanti
Sunday, September 26, 1954

Dear Brother and Sister Wright:

Here it is the Lord's Day again and another week has slipped quietly and quickly by. We are kept so busy throughout the week that there is no opportunity for writing letters. But when Sunday comes, we lay aside all duties and responsibilities, except for the two African Church services, and write letters home. Since it takes so long for mail to get from here to there, we thought it best to start another prayer letter on its way to you. Notice that I have dated it "November," because you probably will not receive this epistle until past the middle of October, and need some time to mimeograph and mail it out.

We have been studying the Kilega language for about three weeks now, and it really calls for grace and grit to "knuckle down" to more language study. It seems that we have been studying and preparing for missionary service for such a long time: three years of Bible School; Summer Institute of Linguistics; about nine months of language study in France; and now we are faced with another year of studying the Kilega language before we can even begin to minister God's Word to these dear people. And, if we are to be sent to the new tribe at Punia with the Kennedys in about a year from now, that will mean starting all over again in another language. Don't know whether I could take that or not. God's promise is grace sufficient for the day, so we will just trust Him for it. It certainly calls for much, much grace to live each day out here. We constantly remind ourselves that *"He hath said, I will never leave thee nor forsake thee,"* and so we just keep looking up.

We have received word that the Lisles and Maxine Gordon have left Matadi with Brother Irving Lindquist last Wednesday (Sept. 22), so they should be arriving in about two more weeks. We will probably see them at Ikozi the last week in October when we have the Conference with Gavin Hamilton, if not before. Maxine is to live in the house with us at Katanti, and the Lisles will stay at Ikozi according to present arrangements.

Just as I was writing this letter, we received word from TRANSITCONGO that our two trunks and large wood case of household and personal effects from France are at the customs office in Ruhengeri on the Congo border, and there they are "stuck" until we produce certain papers (and the keys to the trunks). All of the papers were accompanying the shipment, but must have been lost enroute. Believe we may make the trip to get them out (about 300 miles one way). Haven't decided for sure as yet.

Will close for this time. The Lord bless you both, and all of the dear ones at Edgemont. How we long to be with you all.

With much love in Christ,

Les, Gertie, Jeanette and Marian

P.S. We have decided not to make the trip—too expensive!

Marian's Comment: The Balega

There are at least 3,000 tribes in Africa. Each tribe has its own language or dialect and culture. Hundreds of tribes are located in the Belgian Congo alone since it is one of the largest countries in Africa.

The African tribe we worked with while living in the Congo was called the Balega. Their tribal language was Kilega, the language Dad and Mom spent so much of their time trying to learn.

For the most part, they were a friendly people and warmly received us wherever we went. But they weren't always that way. In fact, the Balega in the 1870s were known as a tribe of terrible warriors—and cannibals. When Henry Morgan Stanley was hired by King Leopold II of Belgium to trace the course of the Congo River, Stanley wrote in his book, *Through the Dark Continent*, that he and his party purposely avoided going through the territory of the terrible "Warega" tribe. Jeanette read the book in 1966—and could tell from the maps and descriptions that he was talking about the Balega.

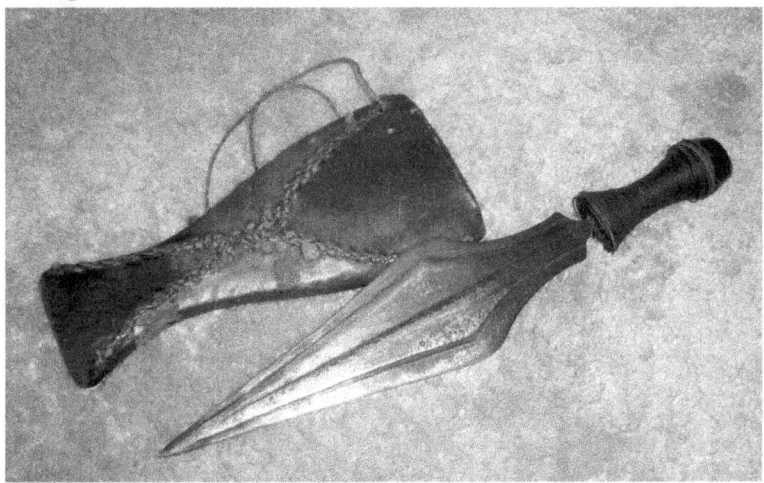

In the 19th century, the Balega had only knives and spears as weapons—but they were more than proficient with them. They were known for silently slipping up behind an enemy and quietly slitting that person's throat with a knife [like the one in the photo] before anyone even knew the Balega were nearby.

When we were in the Congo, we saw a very old woman who had actually eaten human flesh as a child. She told us that the Balega had a purpose in eating the warriors they killed—they believed they would gain the strength of the enemy warrior and, therefore, become even stronger.

Although the Belgian government that had ruled the Congo since 1908 had done much to curtail tribal warring and cannibalism, it was God's message of peace and love that turned the Balega into a peaceful tribe.

Berean Mission entered the tribe in 1938, establishing Musuku Station—later, Katanti—and in 1940, Ikozi was founded. (See Appendix A for the history of Berean Mission in the Belgian Congo.)

Most tribes had certain customs that would set them apart from other tribes. Often that included tribal markings or scarring. The marking of the Balega consisted of a thick scar that started in the middle of their forehead at the hairline and extended down to the tip of their nose. Sometimes they would start again under the lower lip and continue down under the chin. The woman in this photo also had her face cut with other markings. Both men and women often received other markings across the back or chest—like tattoos—to indicate special events or circumstances.

Once the markings were cut with a knife, soot from a fire was put into the open wounds. If they became infected, that would be all the better because the scars would be larger and deeper once they healed. These scars were worn with pride.

By the time we arrived in the Congo in 1954, many of the Christian Balega did not bear these scars. That was an old tribal custom, and when they received the Lord as Savior, they did not participate in this ritual or pass it on to their children.

When we would visit out in the villages, especially in our second term, Jeanette would wear nylon stockings. Back in the late 1950s, nylons had dark seams running down the back of the leg. The women and girls often poked and prodded Jeanette's legs to see if that were her tribal scar. Needless to say, she quit wearing nylons to the villages!

We passed this village one day as we were driving, and these boys looked arrogantly at us from the side of the road. They had just finished a pagan ritual where they were circumcised and had to live alone in the jungle for three months to prove their manhood. They now wore the beads to show that they had passed their time of testing. We prayed that their arrogance would some day be turned around into love for our blessed Lord and Savior.

This man was the head of a white-man-hating cult, but through God's saving grace, he came to know the Lord as his Savior during a time when Dad was holding evangelistic meetings in distant villages.

His headdress was made of beads. Those are leopard teeth around his neck. In order to wear them, he had to be the one who killed the leopard.

See that fancy spear he's carrying? After he came to know the Lord, he visited our mission station. This time he brought this spear and gave it to Tata Wemaninua — our Dad — in appreciation for Tata telling him about God's love.

Jeanette and I still have that spear!

As Dad would go on evangelistic trips to remote villages, he would often hunt monkeys and bring them to the villagers for meat.

Here is Lutete, one of the faithful church elders, holding a monkey Dad had shot for the villagers. There were more in the back of our truck. Everyone ate well that night!

Jeanette's Comment: Kilega, Language of the Balega

Kilega is the language of the Balega tribe. On the surface, it appears to be a very simple language. If you know the vowel sounds, you could sit down and read off a written sentence with no trouble at all, even though you don't know what the words mean.

Vowels

    A = ah (as in **ah**-choo)
    E = aye (as in b**ay**)
    I = ee (as in s**ee**)
    O = oh (the same as in English)
    U = oo (as in mar**oo**n)

Consonants

The Balega do not use all of the consonants that are in the English alphabet, but they do often combine consonants, especially **mb**, **nd**, and **ny**.

    Kasa**mb**ile (to gather)
    Muka**nd**a (the book)
    Nya (mother of)

When reading Kilega, pronounce every syllable. Here's the chorus of *Jesus Loves Me*. See if you can read it.

    E, anelama
    E, anelama
    E, anelama
    Mukanda wambula.

Simple, right?

Well, Kilega is a lot more complicated than those simple words. For one thing, it is a tonal language—it has two tones, a high and a low pitch. Two words with different meanings can be spelled the same, but you have to know the correct tone to use for each syllable. For example, if you said, "Samba" to someone—and you kept both tones even and low, you would be greeting them, telling them "Hello." However, if you said, "Sam'ba" and emphasized that first syllable, speaking it in a higher pitch, you would be telling the person, "Get sick!"

Few missionaries ever perfected the tonal qualities of Kilega—and, admittedly, it didn't matter in singing, for example, or in silent reading. There was no way in translating the Bible to put a marking in to delineate the few words with identical spelling that were distinguished by tone. But in speaking or reading aloud, tones could make a lot of difference. For example, "mikila'" meant "blood," but "miki'la" meant "tails." We had to be careful when talking about the blood of Christ to use the correct tones. The Balega laughed and said most of the missionaries spoke Kilega like four-year-olds who hadn't yet learned the tones.

Kilega kind of bundled itself into long words, depending on the verb tense, pronouns, etc. A simple version of a complicated way of bundling is the last word in the chorus of "Jesus Loves

Me" — *wambula*. Not only does it contain linked consonants, but it also puts the "me" in the middle of the verb — [The book] says me this.

So although we can easily read or sing Kilega without even knowing the language, learning to speak it properly is quite a different story.

Tones and Drum Messages

Their tonal language served the Balega well in communication — by drums. When we think about drums, we normally picture Africans dancing to the beat of drums — that's what we've seen in the movies. But the drums served a far more important task deep in the jungle. There are no telephones, no cell phones — no way to communicate with someone who is far away from you. That's where the drums come in — to send messages over a distance.

The Balega had two-tone drums — high and low tones — that matched the tones of their language. The calls they beat out on these drums meant something specific — just like Morse code.

Here is the code that they beat out to call people to come to church or any important meeting in the village. I've put the tonal marking in the words.

>Muvua yi'di' na' yidi'
>Muvua yi'di' na' yidi'
>Kukitondo ki'a mafundi'sio
>Kabulu ka'ku lu'uzi
>Kabulu ka'ku mo'se
>Ka'sambile kiziba ki'mozi
>Ta'kumuntu siga'la
>Ta'kumuntu siga'la

Here's the literal translation of this drum call:

>Come quickly with quickly
>Come quickly with quickly
>It's a matter of a meeting
>The frogs of the river
>The frogs of the pond
>Are all gathered together in one swamp
>Don't anyone stay away
>Don't anyone stay away

Aside from specific calls like the meeting call, the Balega could beat out other messages, too — like 9-1-1 calls.

The prayer letter dated Wednesday, December 21, 1955, mentions that Dad and an African evangelist from Katanti Station had gone to a distant village to minister. That's when Mom became deathly ill — and she needed to go to the doctor at the state post in Shabunda. But none of the other vehicles on Katanti Station were working at that time — only the Green Hornet — and Dad had taken it on his evangelistic trip.

Without telephones, there was no way to reach Dad and tell him to come back to Katanti. So the drums began beating — every few moments for the next couple of hours, the drummer on Katanti would beat out the message for Tata Wemaninua (Dad) to return to Katanti. The drummer in Bomboli, about two miles down the road, would respond to the message and then send it on to the next village. The message was sent to many villages until it finally reached the village where Dad was staying. He immediately packed up the Green Hornet and headed back to Katanti Station to take Mom to the doctor. And the drums again marked his progress back toward the mission station.

During our second term on Kamulila Station, drums played another important 9-1-1 role. Dad and an African elder had taken the mission truck, loaded with several pastors—new Bible School graduates--their families, and their *bintu* or belongings, and dropped them off at the villages where they were to set up churches and schools. The drums from Kamulila notified the villages that their pastors were coming. There was great rejoicing all along their route.

But Dad and the elder didn't make it back to Kamulila that evening. Finally, the next morning, other African elders came dashing up to our house to tell Mom that something had happened on the road. There had been an accident—a huge rock had fallen on the truck, and to use the Balega's expression, the truck "had died." Now, that message didn't say anything about how Dad was or the elder who had gone with him, nor even any of the pastors and families that had been in the truck.

So Mom, Helen Gow, Marian, and I headed out in Aunt Helen's car to the village that had sent the drum messages. What they discovered was that Dad had finished delivering all the pastors and their families to their villages, and he and the elder were on their way back to Kamulila when the body of the truck had struck a large boulder that had been jutting out over the road. When the top of the truck hit that boulder, it just slid onto the truck, pinning it solidly to the road--but both Dad and the elder had escaped unharmed.

For the full, exciting story of this adventure, see the September 1959 prayer letter.

The Balega drums are the only means of quick communication in the jungle—and these two stories show how effective they are because they're based on the tones of Kilega language.

Katanti
Tuesday, September 28, 1954

Dearest Ones:

"Rejoice in the Lord always: and again I say, Rejoice" (Philippians 4:4).

How we do praise God and are filled with rejoicing as we have received the good word contained in your letter of September 14. In fact, we are overwhelmed by such evidences of the Lord's good will toward us. We realize more than ever before that we are not forgotten out here in the middle of Africa—God is with us, and you dear ones are holding us up in intercession.

Words cannot express our gratitude to the dear ones at Edgemont for the way they have so abundantly provided for us in this special need. When we heard how the Lord had His stewards sitting in the pews with the full amount of money needed in an envelope with our name on it at the time you made the need known, we were reminded of Isaiah 65:24, *"And it shall come to pass, that before they call, I will answer; and while they are yet speaking, I will hear."*

Then when we heard that the folk at the church in Monrovia had also sent in a gift of $100 (when we had not even made known to them our need), we were again overwhelmed at God's goodness. As mentioned in my other letter enclosed (written earlier), our two trunks and large wood case from France are still in customs at the Congo border. When they are finally delivered here, and only the Lord knows when that will be, the customs duty plus transportation from Mombasa inland will probably be about $100. Then when our large shipment of household goods, equipment, and personal effects arrive here from the ocean port of Matadi, there is hardly any "guestimating" as to what the customs duty and transportation charges will be on them. But this we do know—God has already supplied the need, and how we praise Him for it. It makes us realize once again how our anxiety reflects our lack of faith—a lack of restful trust in the One who knows all of our needs and who tenderly cares for them, each one.

Our love to you all,

Les and Gertie

(Written for Edgemont's Missionary Conference)
BEREAN AFRICAN MISSIONARY SOCIETY
STATION KATANTI
Shabunda Par Kindu
Congo Belge, Afrique

October 14, 1954

Les and Gertie, missionaries of Jesus Christ by the will of God, to the saints which are at EDGEMONT, and to the faithful in Christ Jesus: Grace be to you and peace, from God our Father, and from the Lord Jesus Christ.

We would like to take opportunity on the occasion of your Fifth Annual World-Wide Missions Conference to present some of our first impressions of the work of the Lord in the Belgian Congo. *"First, I thank my God through Jesus Christ for you all"* (Romans 1:8). How sweet are the memories of the wonderful Christian fellowship we have enjoyed together with you at Edgemont. These rich memories are made all the more precious as we contrast them with the overwhelming spiritual and temporal needs round about us here in the Congo. And yet, we are not to dwell upon the pleasantries of the past but rather to be occupied with Him who called us out of darkness into His marvelous Light and who hath appointed us as heralds of that Light to this shadowed corner of the earth.

Since our arrival at Katanti Station last August 6, we have had opportunity to witness, to some extent, the work of Berean Mission among the Balega tribe here in the dense Kivu Forests of the Belgian Congo. The fruits of those labors are being manifested in the lives of countless African Christians who but a decade ago were worshipping all manner of evil spirits. Today they are "new creatures" in Christ and are taking their places in the indigenous African Church as evangelists, preachers, teachers, elders, as well as Christian laymen and women. We certainly praise God for His work of grace among this people, and for the way He has blessed the labors of those faithful missionaries who have come before us to bring them the light of the gospel of the glory of Christ.

As we have observed these dear African Christians here in the innermost regions of the Congo, we have been reminded of two precious portions from the Word of God. The first is found in Isaiah 45:22, *"Look unto Me, and be ye saved, all the ends of the earth: for I am God and there is none else."* And then, the counterpart to this verse we read in Psalm 34:5, *"They looked unto Him, and were lightened: and their faces were not ashamed."* Many, many, of these dear Balega people have looked unto Christ for salvation from this remote "end" of the earth. God has given them the enlightenment of His precious Word, and in Jesus Christ they have found the answer to their souls' deepest need. They have found salvation and eternal life in Christ, and their faces are no longer ashamed.

What a joy it has been here on the Mission Station to attend worship services, evangelistic services, and prayer meetings, all of which have been conducted by the African Christians themselves. And then to know that there are numerous African teacher-preachers situated in many of the heathen villages for miles around the Mission Station. These faithful men of God are serving their fellow tribesmen in a twofold manner: first, they conduct a school five days a week in which they teach reading, writing and arithmetic; and second, but of more importance, they conduct two Christian services daily in these same heathen villages. In this manner God is calling out a people from among the Balega for His name.

These Teacher-Preachers have been trained right here on Katanti Station. First, in the Primary School where they received five years of instruction in the three "R's", as well as daily Bible Classes. Then, in the Bible School, they received three years of intensive training in the Word of God. Rev. Neil Vander Ploeg is to be highly commended for pioneering the establishment of this Bible School nearly four years ago and also Rev. Ernest Green for his labors in more recent years, and who now has the full responsibility of this Bible School.

Then there are the faithful station elders. On Katanti Station they are eight men of God who are "blameless, the husband of one wife (which is foreign to the culture of these people), vigilant, sober, of good behavior, given to hospitality, apt to teach". These are the missionaries' "crown of rejoicing." These are the men upon whom the missionaries "lean" in their relationships and dealings with the people. These are faithful men of God who, together with the elders of the other Berean Mission stations, form the backbone of the indigenous church among the Balega Tribe of the Belgian Congo.

Another fruitful phase of the missionary program is the medical work. A dispensary in the charge of a registered nurse is maintained on each of our mission stations. Here medical attention is tenderly and patiently given to those sick in body, and at the same time, the "healing balm" of the Word of God is ministered to their sin-sick souls. There are special classes for expectant mothers, as well as "well-baby" clinic and classes in hygiene. At each of these classes God's wonderful message of salvation is clearly presented, and many of the Balega women are being reached for Christ. How we do praise the Lord for our first medical doctor, who is now in Belgium on his way to the field. With his arrival we shall be able to establish a hospital and much more effectively serve these needy people.

Perhaps from the foregoing you have received the impression that the missionary's job is nearly accomplished and that little remains to be done. Please let me hasten to say that although great strides have been made under the blessing of God, yet that which remains to be done in reaching "every creature" with the gospel is so tremendous as to stagger the imagination. There are still many, many villages in the more remote recesses of these thick forests whose inhabitants are as yet unreached with the gospel of Christ. And there are still multitudes upon whose ears the gospel has fallen, but whose hearts are "stony ground."

We need to send more and more African Teacher-Preachers into more and more of these heathen villages to reach the unreached for Christ, but there are not the funds to support them there. We need to train more and more Evangelists and Teacher-Preachers in our Primary and Bible Schools, but there are not enough missionaries to teach them, and there are not enough funds to equip and supply the present facilities, much less expand them. The present dispensaries are treating a tremendous number of patients each month, but oftentimes the missionaries dig down into their own pockets and give from their meager allowances to buy needed medicines and equipment—and still there is not enough!

Beloved, it would appear in this modern age of the "almighty dollar" that Satan is endeavoring to place an impenetrable "dollar barricade" around about his domain—the tremendous cost of world-wide missions. It is true that *"the weapons of our warfare are not carnal, but mighty through God to the pulling down of strong holds"* (II Corinthians 10:4), so let us not despair. God's great missionary offensive must never grind to a stalemate for lack of ammunition. God has provided the weapons, beloved, but we must supply the soldiers and the ammunition! May God awaken each of us to our personal responsibility to Him in this great fight of the faith, and may it never be a case of "too little, and too late."

Gertrude and Jeanette and Marian join me in thanking you dear ones at Edgemont for sending us forth as your missionary family and for the wonderful way in which you have provided for our passage and equipment and other needs. May God richly bless you at the "home base" for your part in sending forth the gospel to the ends of the earth. We shall be praying for you as you assemble for your Fifth Annual World-Wide Missions Conference, and may God perform great and wonderful things in your midst.

Much love in Christ Jesus to you all,

Les, Gertie, Jeanette and Marian
The Spainhowers

Marian's Comment: African Church Services

Going to the African church on any of our mission stations was always an adventure, to say the least. The church was made of mud and with a leaf roof, like our homes were. It had a dirt floor with two sections of long, backless benches for everyone to sit on, with a wide aisle in between. There were open doorways in the front and on either side, along with plenty of open windows to let the air and light inside. There were no framed doors or screens on the windows. For any rare after-dark meetings, the missionaries would bring their Coleman lanterns.

In the Balega culture, it was expected that the men and older boys would sit on one side of the church, while the women and smaller children would sit on the other side. If the church was over-crowded, the men and boys always were given the seats. That meant that some of the women would have to go outside and either stand at the windows or go to one of the African school buildings next to the church to get some desks to sit on. That's what the women in this picture are doing. They are sitting on top of the school desk with their feet on the attached bench.

During the service, an elder would walk up and down the aisle making sure no one was falling asleep and the mothers were keeping their children quiet. The elder carried a stick and would poke anyone who might be sleeping. If a baby was crying, the elder would go to the mother and sternly tell her to "put the child to the breast" to keep it quiet. Also, if a young child had to go to the bathroom, the mother would get up from her seat with the child, cross over other women, and hold the child out the window until the deed was done—provided, of course, no one was sitting on the outside at the window. In that case she would take the child outside, sometimes letting the child walk or crawl by itself, and then return. All of this was taking place as whoever was preaching carried on with his message as though there wasn't a disturbance anywhere in the church.

One of the fun things about attending the Katanti church when we were living in the dorm was that we had our own "band" for the song service. Jeanette and I, along with three other missionary kids played our accordions. Two of the boys plus Uncle Ernie Green played trumpets; one of the missionary men played a trombone, while another played a saxophone. Sometimes, the Africans changed the melody of a hymn to fit their particular "feel" for music. Of all those playing instruments, Jeanette was the only one who learned to play the melody the way the Africans sang the songs. The rest of us would sometimes have to stop playing while she played right along with them. The Africans sang praises to the Lord loudly and enthusiastically. Their singing was inspiring and uplifting!

The Africans dressed in their very best clothes to go to church—but we missionaries had to learn to keep a straight face when some of the men, in particular, walked into the church. One man we saw wore a pair of blue-striped flannel pajamas to church. Of course, he wasn't aware that these were pajamas because Africans didn't have such articles of clothing.

On another station, one of the missionaries told of a man who wore a one-piece suit of old-fashioned winter underwear with a back flap. Unfortunately, there were no longer any buttons to hold the flap in place, so his suit was rather airy!

One dear, very old Christian man on Katanti wore a heavy beaver coat (like they wore in the 1920s) over his loincloth every Sunday. It must have come in a mission barrel sent out by one of the churches years before, and that became the "best" he wore on Sunday—no matter if the temperature reached 120 degrees!

The preaching was mostly done by the African church elders and evangelists, who were taught in our mission Bible School. And could they ever preach! Time was not important. They preached until they were finished. Many of us missionary kids didn't know their language very well so we couldn't always follow along with the messages, but we could sure enjoy playing our instruments, singing, and watching what was going on around us.

The important thing was that there were many Balega believers who truly loved the Lord. Worshipping their Lord and Savior in church every Sunday was very important to them. What a blessing it was to hear them sing, "Yesu Klisto Muida Wetu!" (What a Friend We have in Jesus), and "E, Nelamo Yesu" (Oh, How I Love Jesus), just two of the hymns the missionaries had taught them over the years.

The Balega Christians recognized the difference in the songs and chants of their tribe and the "Jesus music," even though they may not have known the musical terms for it. Their tribal music was always in the minor key, filled with the hopelessness and despair of people without the knowledge of Jesus Christ. "Our tribal songs are sad," one old Christian man told Dad. "But the Jesus music is happy and makes me feel good!" That's why they cherished their Kilega hymnbooks and loved to sing about Jesus.

Berean Mission, Inc.	AFRICA	B.A.M.S. — Katanti
3536 Russell Blvd.		Shabunda par Kindu
St. Louis, Missouri	The Dark Continent!	Congo Belge, Afrique

| Prayer Letter | * * * * * | November 1954 |

"I will bless the Lord at all times: His praise shall continually be in my mouth" (Psalm 34:1).

Dear Friends in Christ Jesus:

Slowly but surely we are beginning to get settled here in the heart of Africa. Many and varied have been our experiences since arriving. *So* many and *so* varied that it is difficult to know what to share with you first.

Perhaps you would enjoy a description of our house. It is a comfortable house even if it is made of sticks and mud, with leaves for a roof. We have a living room, dining room, study, three bedrooms (one of which will be occupied soon by a single woman missionary) and, of course, a kitchen. The walls are mud, but nicely whitewashed. All of the windows are screened (except for the holes), and some even have glass in them. The ceilings are constructed of woven mats, which are supposed to protect our innocent heads from bugs and dirt that drop from the under-side of the leaf roof. I might add that they are *partially* successful. We cozily share our house with scorpions, roaches, spiders, beetles, and 57 other varieties of creeping things. Gertrude, Jeanette and Marian are getting so they don't even yell for me anymore—they just "squash 'em", as Marian says.

Most of our furniture was either woven by the Africans or made in the Mission carpenter shop. The furniture isn't new or soft, but it is well made and reasonably comfortable. All of our lovely household equipment, furnished by you dear friends, is securely tied in red tape at the port of entry to the Belgian Congo. At this writing, even the baggage, which we brought with us in the hold of the ship, hasn't made its way over the winding roads of the Congo to us. Will you pray earnestly with us that God will deliver these greatly needed things to us soon? He is able!

We have already experienced our second invasion. Invasion of what? Why "driver ants," of course. This morning at the awful hour of 5:50 A.M., Gertie arose to begin the day. She stuck her tender tootsies out from underneath the mosquito net and—zing! They nabbed her. Gertie's big toe was thoroughly gnawed upon. Naturally her reaction was such as to abruptly awaken Jeanette, Marian and me. "Quick, Henry, the flit!" Or, should I say, "Quick, Les, the D.D.T." With a steady hand and undaunted courage I began to give them the well-known DDT-foot. In about a half-hour, the ants that were left decided to call it quits and march in the other direction. And, so begins a day in the Congo!

Our language study has already begun. One might say that Kilega has its ups and downs since there are at least two tones in the language, and perhaps more. It is very important to pronounce the tone correctly. For example, the word *nkumbu* pronounced with a certain tone means "egg yolk"; whereas the same word pronounced with a different tone means "hat." It would cause much consternation if Gertrude told our cook to put his *hat* in the cake instead of the *egg yolks*.

We had an enjoyable assignment today. We were to go down and walk through the African village and say as many of our few words to them as we could possibly get out. Gertie and I really had fun. We would ask a simple question or make a most simple statement. The Africans would answer with a whole string of words, of which we understood absolutely nothing. We would smile, intelligently we hoped, and move on to the next place. We were followed by a group of about ten small, quite naked, African children, all full of giggles. At first they would really scatter if we turned toward them, but by the time we had finished our tour of the village they were our friends. Pray much for us as we study their language. Our ministry to this people of the Word of God will only be as effective as our ability to speak their language.

Last Saturday one of the missionary children came running to the study door. "Uncle Les", he called, "This guy (meaning an African) says that he saw some monkeys. Can we go shoot 'em?" So I grabbed my .22 pistol, which was given to me by a Christian friend, and we headed for the forest. There one of the African elders was waiting for me. We had only gone a short distance into the forest when they spotted the monkeys. I am happy to report that I downed one on the first shot. I am unhappy to report that I missed the next six shots! I console myself with the thought that the last six shots were too far away from the pistol. The next time I'm going to take my heavier rifle for the longer shots.

Now perhaps you are wondering, "What does a missionary need to go hunting for? I thought he was supposed to preach the gospel." That is true; but the only meat we get to eat here is what we shoot or what the Africans are able to trap. Yes, we missionaries eat the monkey meat. Monkey-burgers are right palatable when you haven't had meat for several weeks. And we share what we are able to shoot with our Africans, just as they share what they are able to trap with us. After all, they like meat too.

Mom, Jeanette and Marian entering the African church at Katanti

We are enjoying very much the Christian services conducted here on the mission station. Naturally, we cannot understand one word the speaker is saying, but we can enter into the song service; and we can somehow "sense" the Christian fellowship. Berean Mission has published a Kilega Hymnal which has been put into the hands of all those who can read and desire a copy. We cannot understand what we are singing, but we can sound out the words phonetically and, of course, the music is the same as our old, familiar hymns. It is quite a blessing to sing, Yesu Akunelama to the tune of "Jesus Loves Me." There are many African elders, teachers, and evangelists who preach at the various services; and then Brother Ernest Green, our senior missionary on this station, does some preaching and, of course, all of the teaching in the Bible School. It has been a real blessing to my heart to see so many African Christians who are capable of preaching the Word of God. We can certainly praise God for His work of grace among this people, as well as for those missionaries who have come before us during the past fifteen years to bring them the Word of God.

There is much, much more to tell, but we will save it for another letter. May we again ask you to *"cease not to cry unto the Lord our God for us"* (I Samuel 7:8). Prayer is being answered. Marian, who was so ill with malaria when last we wrote, is much improved, although still quite thin. Praise the Lord for undertaking for her. God is still on the Throne, and we meet you daily at the Throne of Grace.

                Forever in Him,

                Les, Gertie, Jeanette, and Marian
                The Spainhowers

Marian's Comment: The Great White Hunter

Anytime we would travel, I would always gaze up into the trees in the forest for monkeys. Frequently, I would see a band of monkeys and quietly let Dad know. He would very slowly, and as silently as possible, bring the car to a stop. Jeanette would hand Dad his .22 rifle as he was opening his door. Aim…FIRE! We always listened for the "thud" in the forest. That meant Dad's aim was right-on, and either we or some Africans would have good meat!

The Africans loved Tata Wemaninua (Dad) and his fine marksmanship because that meant good meat for the villagers. When Dad and the Africans who accompanied him would go hunting, they would return home with the back of our car loaded with monkeys. The missionaries would use only a few back legs, and all the rest would go to the Africans. Many times, Dad would stop at villages along the road as he headed home to give them fresh meat as well. Dad also provided the meat for special African conferences when hundreds of people would come. In all the years we served in the Congo, Dad killed 636 monkeys for food. Yes, he kept count.

By the way, you see the road I am standing on? That is our main, two-way "highway." The dirt road looked good at the time this picture was taken, but you should have seen it when it rained—or when there was a mudslide.

Katanti
Sunday, November 28, 1954

Dear Brother and Sister Wright:

It has been so long since we have written to you that we must simply take out the time and write now. I started this letter Sunday morning before church and it is now late Monday afternoon and we are still in the first paragraph. Just as we were concluding services Sunday morning, we heard a truck shift into low gear and come droning up the hill of our driveway past the church into the area of the missionary homes. The Africans were shouting "Bavua, bavua" ("they come, they come"), until we could hardly restore order in the church long enough for the new arrivals to knock off the dust of the road after their 2,000 mile trip inland from Matadi and make their appearance on the platform. Yes, it was a great homecoming for the George Kennedy family, whom we had been expecting for over a week. We certainly praise the Lord again for the safe arrival of another of our missionary families. We are just waiting for an opportunity to talk with George regarding his plans for our opening the new station at Punia. We know God will work it all out in His own time, even though the problems are many.

We were thrilled to receive word last week that our three trunks of personal effects which we had with us in France have finally arrived in Bukavu, some 225 miles from Katanti. We are asking the Lord to bring them in to us in the next couple of weeks. That will help greatly until our cases of equipment finally come in from Matadi. We are so thankful for the funds that came in from the dear ones there at Edgemont in response to our plea to cover the incidental costs of some of this shipping. Sometimes we become quite discouraged when we see how much it is costing the folk at Edgemont to keep us here in the battle line, and we wonder why the Lord doesn't spread some of the expenses around to other churches. But we know that He doeth all things well, and He has His purpose in laying the burden upon you dear ones at Edgemont. Please express again our gratitude to each one who has so faithfully stood by us in their prayers and in their gifts.

This may be the last opportunity I'll have to write before Christmas, and if so let me now wish you a very blessed Christmas. The Lord bless thee and keep thee.

With much love in Christ,

Les and Gertie

P. S. Am enclosing December's prayer letter. Gertie wrote most of it this time, bless her busy little heart.

Berean Mission, Inc.	AFRICA	B.A.M.S. — Katanti
3536 Russell Blvd.		Shabunda par Kindu
St. Louis, Missouri	The Dark Continent!	Congo Belge, Afrique

Prayer Letter　　　　　　　　　＊ ＊ ＊ ＊ ＊　　　　　　　　　December 1954

"Be careful for nothing; but in everything by prayer and supplication with thanksgiving let your requests be made known unto God" (Philippians 4:6).

Dear Friends in the Homeland:

A "prayer" letter should also be a "praise" letter, for as we commit everything to our Heavenly Father in prayer we are exhorted by the Word of God to make this committal "with thanksgiving". Back home in America, November is our month of Thanksgiving. How thankful we are for our heritage as Americans, for the wonderful country which God has given us. God forbid that we should sin against the Lord in ceasing to pray for our beloved country.

November was a month of thanksgiving for the Spainhowers, too. On November 14, Jeanette reached the ripe old age of thirteen. How we praise the Lord for our sweet daughters. What a joy and blessing Jeanette and Marian are to their mother and dad. Then, on November 24, Les and I celebrated our seventeenth wedding anniversary. When we were married, Les was still living in the darkness of unbelief, knowing not the Lord Jesus Christ as his Savior. I was a Christian, but so backslidden I could not point Les to the Savior. However, six years later the Holy Spirit wrought the miracle of redemption in Les' life, and he accepted Christ as His Savior. What a change He has made in our lives! He has filled our cup of joy full and running over. We rejoiced to celebrate our 17th wedding anniversary in the heart of Africa serving our lovely Lord Jesus.

Since writing you last, Marian has again suffered a severe attack of malaria, her fourth since our arrival in the Congo. Her little body seemed to be just wasting away. After much prayer we felt that the Lord would have us take her to the nearest Belgian doctor at Shabunda, about 50 miles from our mission station. The road was so slippery after hard rains that it took us three hours to drive the 50 miles. The doctor was very kind. He examined Marian thoroughly. He told us that had we waited much longer before coming, her condition would have been most grave. She has a serious vitamin deficiency. We had been giving her vitamins, but apparently they were not sufficient. The doctor gave Marian a real vitamin jolt. He gave her two vials of vitamin D, to be taken a week apart, each containing 600,000 units of vitamin D. He also gave her calcium to strengthen her bones as she has a curvature of the spine caused from weakness, and medicine to fortify the blood as malaria destroys the red corpuscles and causes anemia. She takes three kinds of medicine before breakfast, four at lunch, three at supper, and one vitamin at bedtime. We call her the "Vitamin Kid." She does seem to be picking up a bit now. Continue to pray much for her. The Lord is able!

All of our Berean missionaries, as well as several from other missions, assembled recently at our Ikozi Station for a Bible Conference with Rev. Gavin Hamilton, author, evangelist, and Bible teacher. Missionaries do become hungry to be taught the Word of God! Most of the time it is give, give, give of oneself, and little time for a refill. We all were delightfully refreshed during a time of real blessing.

The last night of the Conference I stepped in a hole and sprained my ankle. It was such a severe sprain that at first our nurses thought the ankle was broken. We do praise the Lord that there were no broken bones; however the tendons were torn. I am now able to hobble around with the aid of a crutch, but believe we will have to make the trip to Shabunda to see the doctor there for possible x-rays. Pray that the ankle will not be permanently weakened. We need good feet out here.

We have now been in Congo a little over four months. Our equipment and personal effects are still in a warehouse at the ocean port of Matadi, securely bound up in red tape. We have received notice that the storage charges since last May when the shipment arrived at Matadi have mounted to more than $150, and the bill will continue to mount until the cases are shipped inland to us. In addition to this bill there will be duty to pay and the cost of shipping inland. Pray that God will undertake and that our equipment will soon be shipped in to us without excessive charges. Our three trunks of personal effects which we shipped from Mombasa, Kenya when our boat docked there have now arrived at Bukavu, some 225 miles from us. We are eagerly awaiting their arrival at the station any week now. We have already received invoices for some $125 shipping charges on these three trunks. We do praise the Lord for the wonderful way in which He has been meeting these terrific expenses, and we are confident that He will continue to supply all our need.

Because of the high cost of gasoline (80 cents a gallon), as well as other difficulties of travel, trips are made only when absolutely necessary. As a result, there is a tendency to greatly overload our automobiles, and particularly so in the case of a station wagon such as ours. We have now reaped the results of such overloading. While in Bukavu last month it was necessary for us to install new coil springs in the front of our car; new heavy duty shock absorbers, front and back; and a new muffler (the old one had been scraped off on the high crown of the roads). The cost of this bit of work, plus new parts was $200. Compare that with what the same thing would cost you there in America, and you will have some idea of the high cost of living here in the heart of the Congo. We still need to install new rear springs, plus overload springs, and it will be necessary to put on new brake linings, too (the old ones are down to the rivets now). That will be at least another $200, or more. Well, if it costs so much to keep a car running what does a missionary need one for anyway? Our car happens to be the only one in running condition on Katanti Station (since Ernest Green's car died in the path). If there are to be any evangelistic trips made to the outlying villages, a car is necessary. I could go into monotonous detail as to the uses of a car when one is situated more than 225 miles from any semblance of civilization, but perhaps the most important is this: At the present time there are thirteen missionary children living on Katanti Station and attending the missionary children's school. In the event of an accident or sudden serious illness, our only contact with the closest medical doctor (50 miles away) is by automobile. We feel that an automobile is essential in the heart of Africa.

It is Christmas time at home. In our imaginations we can see the gay decorations, the happy faces, feel the aura of joyous anticipation. Families will be reunited. I'm sure all missionaries feel a tug of homesickness at Christmas. But one day we shall be gathered together around the Throne of Him who is the prince of Peace, and then shall all creation ring out the glad message, "Glory to God in the Highest, and on earth peace, good will toward men."

Yours in His glad service,

The Spainhowers

Dear Friends,

Permit me to add this word of information to this interesting letter from our dear Spainhowers. Word has been received through the shipping agency that the 29 cases of household and other equipment, shipped to Africa by Brother Spainhower for their use there, has been cleared by customs and released at Matadi for delivery to the mission station. The customs, shipping, and storage charges amount to over $950! Would you please ask the Lord to supply this need of theirs? We thought that you, their dear friends, would be interested in knowing about this very special need at this time.

Sincerely,

Rev. G. Joseph Wright
Pastor, Edgemont Bible Church

Marian's Comment: Sprained Ankle

In the preceding letter, Mom casually mentioned that on the last night of the missionaries' conference on Ikozi, she "stepped in a hole and sprained" her ankle. Well...that is not exactly what happened. Let me tell you the "real" story.

Every time we left the home where our family was staying during the conference, we had to cross a ditch. Due to polio as a child, Mom's balance was never good, so every time Mom attempted to cross the ditch, Dad always had to securely hold her right arm to make sure she didn't fall. I noticed this, and it bothered me that it was difficult for her to maneuver the ditch. So I decided to fix it! Good ol' Marian.

I looked around until I found a couple of small, narrow, wooden planks. I really don't know where they came from or what they had been used for, but in my young mind, I thought these planks would do the trick. I just knew Mom and Dad would be delighted, and this would solve the problem nicely. So I took the planks and laid them side-by-side across the ditch. Several times I walked across them to make sure they were securely in place. The ends of the planks dug into the sides of the ditch.

That night, after the evening conference meeting was over, we walked back to our lodging place. When we got to the ditch, I proudly showed Mom and Dad the two planks I had put there to make it easier for Mom. I had succeeded in surprising them which made me feel wonderful.

But my jubilance didn't last long. With Dad still holding her arm, Mom stepped on the side of one of the planks, instead of in the middle. Unfortunately, she was too close to the side and it tipped over, causing her to fall into the ditch and badly sprain her ankle. She was in horrible pain and doing everything she could not to cry in front of Jeanette and me. We ran for help. Dad and one of the other missionary men were able to get Mom into the house where several missionary nurses looked at it. I looked on in horror as I could see Mom's face contorting in pain as her ankle was carefully examined.

I began to sob. My guilt was overwhelming. I knew this never would have happened if I hadn't put those planks across the ditch! But you know, there is nothing more precious than a Mother's love. In the midst of Mom's pain, she saw the pain in my heart. She called me to her and wrapped me in her loving arms as she consoled me and assured me that this was not my fault. She told me my "bridge" was wonderful, but she just couldn't clearly see the bridge in the dark.

Mom suffered for quite a while with that sprain. Yes, I still felt guilty, but I wasn't demoralized—all because of a Mother's love that went beyond her own physical pain to the wounded heart of her little girl.

Mom, I love you and miss you!

Katanti
December 12, 1954

Dear Brother and Sister Wright:

"The blessing of the Lord be upon you: we bless you in the name of the Lord."

We have your two newsy letters, one written November 21, and the other on Thanksgiving Day. It is always so good to hear from you and to get all the news of things around Edgemont Bible Church. In fact, it is so good to hear from you that I get ashamed of myself for not writing you more often, but it seems that there is never a free moment. Gertrude has even written the last two prayer letters, bless her busy little heart.

We were really thrilled by your description of the Missionary Conference, and how we do wish we could have been there to fellowship with you. And then the gathering together on Thanksgiving Day. We were thinking of you and praying for you.

Marian is feeling much better, too, for which we praise the Lord. We are taking her to the doctor in Shabunda again next Tuesday for a check-up, and to have him look at Gertrude's ankle. She is able to walk now without the aid of her crutch, but the foot still gives her a good deal of trouble and pain. The ankle is full of knots and swells up each day.

The recent survey trip I made with Brother Irving Lindquist was not into the new Punia territory, but back into the forests near Mount Kibwe to survey a possible future site for a station in the event the new super-highway across Congo should ever be built. If the road ever materializes (which is doubtful) then both Ikozi and Kamulila would be isolated, and the site at Kibwe would be for their relocation along the new road. We have been anxious to go into the Punia area, but the opportunity has not presented itself as yet. George Kennedy is going up there for about two months in the near future; but we, of course, must continue with language study for some time to come. We are not doing too well as yet in speaking the language. We have been here four months now; but Ernie Green (our language teacher) was gone the first month we were here; then we were at Kamulila and Conference for a month. Then the many interruptions and comings and goings have taken away about another month; so we have actually had only about one month of language study.

At the present time we have just moved from the large mud house into the two room "guest house," in order to make place for the Parcel family who will be stationed at Katanti upon their return in a few days. The Kennedy family has moved into the brick dormitory with the Greens, Maxine Gordon, and all the missionary school children. Our two-room house is about the same size as the little garage we lived in on 85th Street—the main difference is that it is made of mud and has a leaf roof.

We are trusting the Lord to open up the Punia territory to us. As soon as the concession is granted, I imagine that George Kennedy will begin construction on his mud house, and we hope to do the same as soon after him as possible. You mentioned that the "thermometer" has been repainted and put up for "Spainhower's House." We certainly appreciate your kindness and interest in us, but we frankly feel that Edgemont is already doing more than their share. Housing is undoubtedly the greatest problem we have to face on the field at the present time. There is no extra or vacant house on any station, and we are already two houses "short" on Katanti, and have seven more families on their way to the Congo during the course of the next year. Up to the present time all houses have been built from the field general fund (with the exception of the Jansen brick home); but there simply is not the money to build nine or ten needed mud houses during the next year. It is simply going to be pitiful when everyone gets here. We are sitting in one another's laps on Katanti now. It is certainly a matter for much prayer.

The only house under construction now is at Kamulila for the Cross family. It takes from nine months to a year to build a mud house, and at least a year and a half to two years to build in brick. So you can see there will be no houses ready for the new missionaries now in Belgium. The situation is critical, and we need to keep it much before the Lord.

We are planning on building in mud at Punia when the time comes as brick is too costly and takes too much time. We would be coming home on furlough before we could get a brick house finished. It would be too difficult to attempt going up and building in brick to begin with, and if we build first in mud, then why reinvest in brick? At any rate it is probably still a little too far in the future to make definite plans. In fact, nothing out here is definite. It's a good thing we walk with the Lord one step at a time, and He knoweth the end from the beginning.

Any funds that the Lord may be pleased to send in through the faithful ones at Edgemont could certainly be used in the construction of our mud house at Punia, if the concession is granted and if we are eventually sent there. Labor is actually the least part of construction. The big expense is leaves for the roof, glass cloth and screening for the windows, hinges, and other hardware items, electrical fixtures and wiring, etc. We are praying about it, together with you, and we know the Lord's will be done.

We have finally received the flash bulbs and batteries to take some more slide pictures and hope to find the time to give some thought to it. We have about twenty slides or so taken on our way inland, and after we have this new roll developed will number the slides and write a little note as to what each one represents, and you can be our narrator. It may be a few weeks before we can take all the pictures, and then it takes about one month to send them to South Africa for development at Johannesburg, then about another two weeks to airmail them home. So you see it will be quite some time yet. Everything takes so much time out here, and so much more effort. Satan places every obstacle in the way, but God giveth more grace!

Could write reams more, but time will not permit. We want to thank you in advance for the Christmas box, which you mentioned is on the way, and for your faithfulness to us. We know it is as unto the Lord, and we are endeavoring to keep our eyes on Him and by His grace abide faithful to Him. We think of you all so often, and pray for you daily.

The Lord bless thee and keep thee,

Les, Gertie, Jeanette and Marian

Jeanette's Comment: Building a Mud House

The entire Spainhower household—white and black—really rejoiced when word went out that the time had come to build the second two-room house for us. It was so cramped living in just two rooms—and Katindi needed a real kitchen for cooking meals!!

It was our first experience at watching a mud house being built. First, a group of workmen cleared the necessary space—a big job in itself to get rid of all the vines and bushes and underbrush. Then they dug a shallow foundation—no basements in a mud house.

At the same time, another group of workmen spent time finding just the right trees of various sizes to cut—straight, tall—to form the main supports for the walls and roof. When the foundation was finished, they used a post-hole digger for setting the upright poles. In between the large poles were some just slightly smaller.

Openings were left for windows and doors. At the workshop, lumber was prepared for a framework for those openings and to make doors. Only screens would eventually cover the windows—no need for windows with the veranda protecting the house from rain--and except for a front and back door, this two-room house required no other doors.

After the framework was up, smaller branches were woven between the supporting poles to form a firm place for the mud to adhere. That took a long time. The walls were about a foot thick on the perimeter. The one inside wall that divided the kitchen from the main room didn't have to be as thick.

The next step was to put on the roof, which would extend at least six to eight feet beyond the walls, all around the house. The large veranda had two purposes: 1) to protect the outer walls from the daily driving rains, and 2) to keep the hot sun from beating into the house. Mud houses were always cooler than those of brick or concrete blocks!

But the roofing process brought a crushing blow to my life! I had been kind of proud of the name the Africans gave me: Wanga Lukoba. It was the name of a flower, they said, that grew tall and straight and beautiful in the forest. I thought, of course, that they had excellent taste.

But the workmen began bringing in from the forest sheaves of special leaves to use on the roof. One of the men was taller—and sturdier—than all the rest. His muscles rippled with every movement. He was a powerfully built man. I was coming down the path to our house as the workmen brought in the day's sheaves, and Uncle Leonard Parcel introduced me to them as a courtesy. I acknowledged all of them with a smile—and then he introduced that big man, "Wanga Lukoba meet Wanga Lukoba." We stared at each other for a moment, then laughed and shook hands. But my pride was destroyed!

After the roof was finished, it was time to mud the house. A big trough was dug just down the hillside from the house, the dirt left loose. The workmen poured water over the dirt and invited all the missionary kids to take off their shoes and socks and mush it around. What fun! — only I refused to do that. I just didn't muck about in mud!! More water or more dirt was added as needed to make the right consistency.

Marian sitting in the window as mud walls were drying.

Then the workmen would carry buckets of mud up to the house and start stuffing it between the poles and filling in the woven foundation of the walls. After that initial mudding was complete, it had to sit for several days for the mud to dry all the way through. When that was finished, then the workmen brought in some special mud from near the riverbank. It was much smoother in texture, and they smoothed it on the inside walls like plaster.

Again, we waited for the mud to dry. In the meantime, the workmen brought slate from the riverbed, fitted it together with concrete, and we had a beautiful, if rough, slate floor. Once the mud had dried, the house was white-washed, both inside and out.

You should have heard the shout go up when the house was pronounced finished! Even the houseboys were excited as the wood-burning stove was brought inside the new kitchen. No more cooking on the veranda! New workspace and places for the dishes went up—everything had to be set up with an eye toward keeping bugs and other things out of the food and off the dishes.

A nice big table and six chairs, made in the station workshop, were set at one end of the main room. We purchased a woven raffia sofa and easy chair, and Mom made pillows for added comfort. Altogether, we were extremely pleased! Now, we had a proper living space—even if it were spread between two little houses!

Jeanette's Comment: A Night on the Edge of the Jungle

The night noises on Katanti Station were always somewhat creepy. What kind of animal made that shriek in the jungle? A twig snapped…Could that mean a leopard outside our closed doors? A rustle in the leaf roof…Is our house filling up with driver ants?

But bathed in prayer—and tucked under our mosquito nets—we learned to sleep soundly.

The first night in our little two-room house, however, was different from any previous nights. The noises seemed much closer—and they were. Our little house was but a few short feet from the edge of the jungle.

A small comfort for me was the fact that all four of us slept in two double beds in one room. Mom and Dad were right there—just a whisper away.

We finally fell asleep—only to be startled awake by the most horrendous sounds we'd ever heard. Girls shrieking wildly….wicked men laughing with glee. It was horrible! The sound drew closer and closer to our little mud house on the edge of the jungle.

Dad quietly climbed out of bed and reached to the top of the cabinet for his rifle and pistol. He drew up a chair at the foot of the bed and sat there until the sounds moved deeper and deeper into the jungle, and quiet was restored.

The next morning, Dad hurried to talk with Ernie Green, the station chairman, to find out if we'd heard some sort of horrible ceremony taking place in the jungle—and to make sure that we were really safe living so close to the jungle. At first, Uncle Ernie didn't quite understand what we'd heard. Then he started laughing.

All that evil noise had been made by a troop of chimpanzees moving through the jungle. Something must have disturbed them—and that had set off all the ruckus.

Katanti
February 6, 1955

Dearest Brother and Sister Wright:

Just decided that it was time you received a letter written from the feminine angle. We are all well. Les had malaria about three weeks ago and it's hard to bounce back in the Congo. Hazel Leigh Parcel is "shooting" him full of vitamin B12, and he is beginning to feel stronger. Man-like he is protesting all the shots. Insists that if he does get any strength it will just leak out because he feels like a sieve.

Les and I made another trip to Kamulila. This time it was to drive the big truck in with a load of the Cross' crates which were picked up at Kindu. We took Maxine Gordon with us as she had never been to Kamulila Station. Les had gone to Kindu with John Sanford to pick up the crates. That was the first time he had ever driven a truck. The day after he returned from Kindu, we were told to go to Kamulila. We sure did a lot of praying along the way because the Kamulila road is the most treacherous road I think I have ever been on, and there is a lot of difference between driving a pleasure car and handling a truck. I think Les did just wonderful driving that monster but, of course, I think he is pretty wonderful anyway.

Bit by bit we are going through our crates. It is a difficult process because, as I mentioned in the prayer letter, we have no place to put things. It is wonderful though to use our lovely aluminum ware, linens, etc. Everything is so beautiful. It is almost like getting married all over again. So many of the things call back memories. Do you remember the night we put a lot of these things on exhibition in the church basement? Oftentimes we can call to mind just who gave us certain things and it makes us feel much closer to home.

Phyllis Sanford has a sewing class for the African school girls once a week. She has invited all the missionary girls to come also. They are having a lot of fun, and they will learn Kilega, too. Jeanette helps Maxine in a music class. I help in the music class, too, when I have time. Maxine wants the girls to sing harmony, the harmony that's written, not native harmony, but she doesn't sing harmony so that is how I can help.

How thankful we are for the prayerful interest of the folks at Edgemont. Les and I realize that these first few months of language study and adjustment will be among the most difficult we will have. The pressure is at times overwhelming. So many things to do and yet hours must be spent in language study, and we have no quiet place to study. Les straps his pistol on his waist for protection and heads into the forest to study. It's quiet there. I don't like the bugs, snakes and "things" of the forest, so I do the best I can in a house full of children and houseboys. Praise the Lord for His sustaining grace—and a sense of humor that He has given us. Someday we *will* speak to these dear Africans. Someday we *will* lead precious souls to Christ. All the struggle, pressure, inconvenience will be worth it all if our Lord says, "Well done," when we see Him face to face.

All our love,

Les, Gertie and Girls

Katanti
February 26, 1955

Dearest Loved Ones,

"I love the Lord – I will call upon Him as long as I live" (Psalm 116-1-2).

It was so-o-o-o good to receive your letter of February 1-12, and also your air letter sheet of the 14th. You asked that we let you know if they arrived at the same time - yes. Even though you pay 25 cents for the regular airmail rate, yet the 10-cent air letter sheets come through in the same mail bags. You can send two air letter sheets cheaper than one regular airmail envelope. Of course, when the airmail arrives at the airport in Kindu, that ends the efficient handling. It is then loaded onto a truck which hauls "airmail" to Shabunda twice a week. We send a runner on foot the fifty miles from Katanti to Shabunda (100-mile round trip) to expedite the "airmail," once a week. So, you see why it takes at least two weeks, and sometimes three weeks to close the gap between us.

We also received your lovely gift package of crackers, tuna, Jell-O, candy, vanilla, cake mixes, life savers, and puddings. Thank you so much for your thoughtfulness. It is appreciated. Jeanette baked the Devils Food Chocolate cake today, and it was delicious. We also received two packages from the Guild containing feed sacks and foodstuffs. All is appreciated so much. Gertie is writing to the ladies now to express our thanks.

We mailed about three boxes of colored slides to Mother Wilson this week and have asked her to let you know when she receives them. We have marked each slide and want you to feel free to use them at Edgemont (or elsewhere) as you may desire. Many of the slides are similar in subject matter, but you may be able to edit through them for a series that you may wish to show. Use them as much and as often as you wish. We would only ask that Mother Wilson get them back when you are finished with them.

Perhaps after we have finished with our language study (that grueling period, you know) we will have a little more time to get other slides for you. Pray for our language study that God will give us enablement; that He will open our ears and loose our tongues to hear and speak this language.

We are grateful for the funds given to our house fund. I wrote to both you and Leo about this last week, and know that you will prayerfully seek the Lord's leading. We personally feel that the prefabricated houses are impractical, much too expensive; and that we would like to build either in mud or brick as the Lord may provide. At any rate, it will be months off. We do not even have the concession yet, and George Kennedy will be building first. By the time we complete the building of our house, it will be time to come home. The Lord knows - we must look to Him, and wait upon Him!

We pray for you and Mrs. Wright and all the dear ones at Edgemont each day in our devotions.

Much love in Christ,

Les and Gertie

Praise the Lord! All of our goods are now received, except the small refrigerator repair parts kit.

BEREAN MISSION, INC.	A F R I C A	B.A.M.S. — Katanti
3536 Russell Blvd.		Shabunda par Kindu
St. Louis, Missouri	The Dark Continent!	Congo Belge, Afrique

Prayer Letter   * * * * *   March, 1955

"Serve the Lord with gladness; come before His presence with singing" Psalm 100:2.

Dearly Beloved in the Homeland:

Triple wedding - our houseboy Kibonge is on the left wearing one of Dad's ties.

Excitement reigns here at Katanti! Next Sunday there will be, not one, but three weddings, and one of the bridegrooms is Kibonge, our houseboy and a favorite with Jeanette and Marian. Naturally, it will be a great occasion. The church will be decorated with palm branches and flowers. We do not have the music for the traditional Wedding March, but Jeanette has been able to pick out enough by ear to at least get the three couples down the aisle; that is, if she doesn't get so excited that she forgets which buttons to push on her accordion. Jeanette and I have been helping to train the girls of the Mission to sing a hymn for the occasion. Yes, weddings are a happy time the world around.

The Balega men buy their wives. Where Christ is not known, wives are simply numbered among a man's possessions: so many goats; so many chickens; so many cows; so many wives. It thrills our hearts when a young man in our Mission school, who has found Christ as his Savior, brings in the girl he has purchased and places her in our girls' school. There she is taught of Christ and every effort is made to bring her to the Savior. They are also taught cleanliness, hygiene, and basic home nursing. We do not try to teach them the white woman's way of cooking for that would be foolishness; but we do endeavor to impress them with the necessity of cleanliness. We stress, of course, the Biblical teaching that every man should be the husband of one wife, which is sure a hard teaching for the African who believes in many wives, which results in more hands to labor in his garden and, therefore, *he* has more food and more time for hunting and fishing.

Rejoice with us! All of our crates of equipment have arrived safely at Katanti Station. I'm sure you can imagine the four Spainhowers with their heads and hands inside a crate saying, "Look at this! I have forgotten we even had that!" We are having difficulty unpacking because we have no place to put anything. The housing shortage has caught up with us. We had to move from the large mud house in which we were living into a small, two-room, ready-to-fall-in mud house. The Parcel family was transferred to Katanti, and since they have a larger family than we, it was naturally felt that it would be easier for us to "rough it" than for them. It is hoped that two more rooms can be built for us, but it takes time. So we open a crate, look at all the nice things, take out the essential things, and repack the crate to be stored in the carpenter shop until some future date when we may have more room.

Perhaps you are thinking, "Why don't they build more houses for their missionaries? What's the matter with that mission?" Dear friends, money just does not come in for houses for missionaries. Praise the Lord, money comes in for the support of the missionary; for a hospital; for other special projects from time to time; but almost no money comes in specifically designated for missionary housing in Africa. We Spainhowers are very grateful that a fund has been started in our home church for a house for us. Will you join us in praying that many hearts will be burdened for the tremendous need of missionary housing in Africa? We have seven new missionary families who will arrive on the field in the course of this year. How are we going to house them? Pray much.

Les and I feel that we are beginning to get ever so slight a "toehold" in this language. But there is still a long road ahead of us before we can handle the Word of God in an effective manner. Pray for us in this time of study. Each Sunday we go on an evangelistic trip with Miss Maxine Gordon, a senior missionary. We have services in three or four villages. Samasuli, one of our Katanti elders and a fine Christian, goes with us, too. He leads the singing, teaches Scripture verses, and preaches. He is a wonderful personal worker. Miss Gordon gives a flannelgraph lesson directed particularly to the children (but what adult can resist one). Jeanette plays her accordion. Les and I give brief testimonies in Kilega, and all of us sing lustily. The Africans are interested in our children, so they are delighted with Marian. They look upon Jeanette as a grown woman. After all, she is thirteen and that is a marriageable age out here. The Lord has been pleased to bless these meetings, and several souls have been saved. It is a thrilling experience to see a sin-sick soul seek salvation in our blessed Lord Jesus Christ. Pray for these newborn babes in Christ, and for these meetings.

I'm happy to report that Marian seems to be gaining strength. This past week she did have another attack of malaria, but it was the first she has had in about three months. Her fever did not go as high as before, and she seemed to have more strength to resist the malaria. Continue to remember her in your prayers. My injured foot is still black and blue and has some sore places, but it doesn't bother me too much. Praise the Lord! It could have been much worse.

We do want to thank all of you dear people who sent gifts, cards and letters during the Christmas Season. Our hearts were encouraged and blessed because *you* remembered us. Let us pray for each other as we "serve the Lord with gladness"—you in your corner of God's world, and we in ours.

Yours in His glad service,

The Spainhowers

Dear Friends of the Spainhowers:

I want to thank you in behalf of the Spainhowers for the fine response you gave to the special appeal for funds to defray the extra expense incurred in shipping their goods to the mission field. There is still a deficit in their account caused by this extra expense but we are confident that our God will supply in answer to prayer. Also, I suggest that we go along with the Spainhower's thought about missionary housing. There is now over $300 in this fund. Perhaps there are some of you who would like to dedicate some funds in memory of a loved one to this much needed missionary project.

Rev. G. Joseph Wright
Pastor, Edgemont Bible Church

Jeanette's Comment: A Purchased Possession

Balega men purchased their wives—and, usually, the entire clan had to pitch in to raise the bride price, especially since young women who had some schooling would bring a higher price. Goats, rice, lengths of cloth, as well as money—all of these things were part of the bride price. That's why young men in the mission Bible school often had problems getting a Christian girl for a wife—she would be too expensive.

I was 13 shortly after we arrived in the Congo—and that was marriageable age. On one of our Sunday trips out to a village, an old man carefully watched me play my accordion as everyone sang. He later told Dad that he ought to get a pretty good bride price for me. While I wasn't very strong, I could make music come out of that strange box. Dad said his first instinct was to belt the old man—but common sense told him that the man wasn't even a Christian. There was no use in even trying to talk to him about the difference in cultures and what the Bible said about marriage. Dad just patted him on the arm and went to talk with someone else.

Everyone was delighted with the triple wedding noted in this prayer letter. There had been Christian weddings on Katanti before, but this one was extra-special: Kibonge was getting married! I cannot imagine what these simple people thought of all the preparations for this wedding—the Wedding March, the flowers, even little flower girls. But Kibonge was special to us, and we wanted this triple wedding to be something that these young couples would always remember.

Finally, everything was ready. The rose bushes in missionary yards were stripped of their blossoms, as well as any other flower available. Each bride had a bouquet to carry. Dad went so far as to kick in a tie for Kibonge—and made sure there was plenty of rice and monkey meat for the big feast following the wedding.

Jeanette and Joy Parcel, with the brides and flower girls

The two little flower girls, daughters of village elders, had new dresses as well. In fact, they had matching panties for their dresses. But since the Africans wore no underclothing, the girls and their mothers didn't know what to do with the little lace-trimmed panties, and the flower girls arrived for the wedding wearing them as hats! This was one of those times when Mom had to threaten us girls with mayhem if we so much as smiled too much. You can tell from the smile on my face in this photo that I was about ready to burst into laughter at any moment.

The church was absolutely packed. Rumors had spread far and wide about the glories of this triple wedding—and not only had family members come to church, but so had as many people as possible from the surrounding villages.

After the regular service, Mom waved to me from the back of the church, so I started playing the Wedding March. It took a little urging before the two little flower girls came giggling and skipping up the aisle, merrily tossing flower blossoms everywhere. I'm not really sure what happened at the back of the church, but it seemed like a long time before the three couples finally came parading down the aisle. The girls kept their heads bowed, their eyes on the ground, holding gingerly to their intended's arm; the young men strode confidently down the aisle.

That was probably the only time those young women ever walked beside their husbands. The Balega women traditionally walked a couple of paces behind their husbands. How often we saw a family on the road—the man was striding along in front, carrying a spear. The woman was trudging behind him with a heavy basket on her back, a baby in her arms, perhaps a couple of other children holding onto her skirts. That's just the way it was.

That's the way it was—until Kitondo came along. He was Aunt Maxine Gordon's houseboy, He really was enthralled with Malia, a sturdy young woman—another of Mom's fence girls—and went to his father to make arrangements to purchase her. But Malia came at a high price because her father didn't want her to marry a Christian—and Kitondo's family really wasn't interested in helping him either. But Kitondo persevered, and they were finally married in the church as well. But that wasn't the end of the story.

When Malia became pregnant, she had trouble—and Aunt Hallie Green, who was the station nurse at the time, was afraid Malia would lose the baby. Aunt Hallie told Kitondo that Malia should not carry heavy loads and must rest often. Now, Kitondo had worked several years for missionary families, and he saw how differently the missionary men treated their wives. So he made Malia stay in the village—and he went out to cut wood and do the heavy work she would have done. The other men laughed at him when he trudged back into the village carrying the heavy basket on his back. They called him "Woman!" He was the laughingstock of the village. Again, Kitondo persisted. He told the others that this is what Jesus would want him to do.

Malia finally delivered a strong, healthy baby boy—and the laughing stopped.

Marian's Comment: Mud Hair

As Dad mentioned, for a while each Sunday we would go into villages away from Katanti with Aunt Maxine Gordon and one of the African elders named Samasuli, to hold evangelistic meetings. This was a good way to help Dad and Mom use the language by giving their testimonies during the meetings as best as they could in Kilega and talking to the people as they gathered around them. I must admit that I really wasn't very excited about going to these meetings. So many of the women would gather around me and want to touch my arms, my face, my blond hair, and my clothes.

The worst thing that happened to me was at one particular village where a woman was braiding the hair of another woman by putting her hands in mud and smearing the mud on the hair as she braided it into tiny, tight braids. When she saw me with my curly, blond hair, she came up to me and immediately started rubbing my hair excitedly with her muddy hands. My first reaction was to kick her and run, but I knew Mom and Dad would never stand for that. She talked excitedly to other women, and they all started touching my hair, too. I glared at Mom, hoping she would rescue me, but with a smile on her face, Mom quietly told me that it was all right, and she would wash the mud out of my hair when we returned to Katanti. The women motioned with their hands and laughed as they exclaimed to each other how different mine felt than theirs. I felt totally humiliated and couldn't see the humor in the situation at all. Then Mom slowly took my arm and moved me away from the crowd. I couldn't get into the car fast enough!

Katanti
March 23, 1955

Dear Brother and Sister Wright:

Greetings to you both in the Savior's dear name! We are now having our Fall weather way down here two degrees south of the equator. The only way you can really discern that it is Fall is because it is rice-harvesting time. Other than the rice fields on the hillsides, the forests are just as green and dense as ever. There are no Fall colors and no more than the usual amount of dead leaves on the floor of the forest, but it is Fall just the same.

The Katanti women leave early in the morning each day for their rice fields and return about noon or one o'clock with their baskets on their backs loaded with rice freshly harvested from the fields. Some of these baskets of rice weigh nearly one hundred pounds and these women carry them for four or five miles along the forest paths day after day. Of course, when they arrive home at one o'clock they must prepare their husbands' meal, take care of the children which have been running wild all morning during their absence, etc. The life of an African woman is not easy.

Just this afternoon Gertie and I made a rush trip to our sawyers village, some 15 miles from Katanti, to pick up the wife of one of our sawyers who had severely burned her chest, neck and one side of her face. She was in a pitiful condition with large, watery blisters and in much pain. We rushed her back to our dispensary where she was cared for.

About three weeks ago some Africans came to our dispensary bearing a sick road workman on a kipoi. The poor fellow had a hernia which had been strangulated for five days and Mrs. Parcel

did not think he would be able to live through the night without immediate attention. So we rushed him off to the State Hospital at Shabunda (50 miles away). The doctor took one look at him in the automobile and had him placed on the operating table immediately. He was under anesthetic by the time we left to return to Katanti.

Then, about a week later, the Africans came carrying in a man who had been gored by an elephant in the forest. The elephant had picked the man up and dashed him to the ground twice, and then thrust him through with his tusk. Brother George Kennedy dashed off to Shabunda with him about 5:00 o'clock in the morning. This man, too, was placed immediately on the operating table. We have not heard yet as to his condition, but it is very unlikely that he could live. One of our station elders dealt with the road workman just before we took him to the hospital, and he made a profession of faith in Christ. But the man mauled by the elephant was beyond dealing with by the time he arrived at the station.

We have been going out to village meetings each Sunday with Miss Maxine Gordon. Last Sunday I noticed a very elderly man with whitening hair (which is most unusual for these people) standing out on the edge of the crowd. He was trying hard to hear but wouldn't come closer to the speaker. He moved to first one place and then another but always kept his distance. The poor old soul had heathenism written all over his sagging features. My heart fairly ached for him knowing that he had lived out a hard, sinful life of fear in heathen darkness, and that he would soon be going out into outer darkness with Christ and without hope. During the service I prayed that the words of the native evangelist would find lodgment in his heart and that the Holy Spirit would bring enlightenment. God heard and answered that prayer because he sought out our native evangelist after the meeting and inquired further of this Savior he preached. We had the joy of seeing this dear old soul confess Christ as his Savior before we left the village. He will not grow much in grace because he is too steeped in heathenism, and because he has only the Word which we could leave with him verbally since the Kilega Bible is still not in print (and he couldn't read it if it was, although some younger, literate person could read it to him). Nevertheless, he is a firebrand plucked from the burning—he is saved, yet so as by fire. The dear old soul does not even have any conception of the glories that await him in heaven above when he shall see his Lord and Savior face to face. Won't it be a glorious day, Brother Wright?

Pray for us much, as we pray for you in your work there at Edgemont. God has blessed you much down through the years and given you much fruit at Edgemont, and we are so thankful for you both for what you have meant to us in our lives. We can appreciate more and more the many problems which confront you in a large church as Edgemont, and we pray for you daily. It is a long time off yet, but we are looking forward to the time when we can slip back into that second pew on your left and listen as you feed our hungry souls again. Well—that is three years hence, and there is a lot of work to be done before that day, and it is getting quite late. The rain is beating down outside (and inside, too). Oh yes, tell Brother Arney that the shells for the guns are now in Shabunda and we will get them on our next trip in. I didn't know until I read your letter that he had to get a Congressman to arrange clearance with the State Department, etc. I'll think of that each time I shoot down a monkey or a baboon.

Well, I must stop. We love you both in the Lord—may He bless you abundantly.

In Him,

Les, Gertie and the girlies

Marian's Comment: For Your Eating Pleasure

As you recall from Dad's hunting adventures, monkey meat was enjoyed by missionaries and Africans alike. But what else did we have to eat in the remote jungles of the Congo?

Since I just mentioned monkey meat, I'll start with our meat selections. Monkey meat tasted like strong beef and wasn't bad at all. Mom taught our cook how to make delicious spaghetti with ground monkey meat, which we ate frequently. One time new missionaries, who had just arrived in the Congo, were sharing their first meal with us. The lady asked Mom where on earth she was able to get such delicious beef. Without even thinking twice, Mom casually told her that was monkey meat. The lady almost gagged and didn't touch another bite. From what I understand, she never ate another piece of monkey meat while they were in Africa either, even though her husband enjoyed hunting!

Other meat available to us was wild pig. Sometimes an African would kill a wild pig and sell us a portion of the meat. It was usually tough but had a good flavor—more like roast beef than pork. We also ate chickens or, occasionally, fish that we could buy from the Africans. The Africans also ate fish, crocodile, and just about anything else they could kill. We tried crocodile once, but the meat didn't have much of a taste, and it cooked down to very small pieces.

One day an African brought us a duck. Where it came from, we never knew. Mom thought this would make a delicious Thanksgiving dinner. We had invited Aunt Maxine Gordon, one of our single missionary ladies, to join us. Our cook, Katindi, told Mom that we would never be able to eat the duck because it would be too tough. Mom assured Katindi that it would be just fine after it cooked in our pressure cooker for quite some time.

Well, it came time for our Thanksgiving dinner, and we all gathered at the table. Katindi brought in the rest of the food, but no duck. Mom asked him to bring the duck. Katindi brought the duck to us, stuck on the end of a cooking fork, not on a platter. He said, "Do you really want to eat this?" Mom assured him we did and asked him to please put it on the platter she had laid out for him. Well, Katindi did as Mom asked, but was muttering as he set the duck before her. That was not like him at all. He shook his head and exited into the kitchen.

We all watched as Mom tried to carve the duck. No success. Dad got up to help her, thinking she just wasn't doing it right. He couldn't cut into the duck either. By this time Aunt Maxine and all of us were laughing hysterically. Katindi was absolutely right. Ducks out there were way too tough for human consumption! We ended up eating a Thanksgiving meal of corned beef from a can!

A couple of times a year, some Africans from the southern plains would drive a herd of cattle down our roads up north to Stanleyville. These were long-horned, rangy cattle that really didn't like to be in the jungles at all (and couldn't survive there). The interesting thing about these small cattle drives were the white birds that flew with the herd. The birds ate the ticks off the cattle when they were at rest. The Balega called them "nkokonyangi"—the chicken that follows.

Once when we were on Katanti and once when we were on Kamulila, Dad bought one of the cows for the station. The first time, Dad shot it, and the Africans strung it up to drain the blood out of it—and that's as far as their expertise went. One old African man told them how to get the hide off the cow (and what to do with it). Then, one of the missionary women who had been raised on a farm sort of helped Dad and our houseboys figure out how to cut up the meat. The other missionaries paid for the meat they got—and whatever wasn't used was sent to the African elders to divide among the villagers. Such a bounty!!

During our second term, when Dad was supervising the butchering of a cow, he ended up with rickettsial fever. Those *nkokonyangi* didn't do a very good job of picking the ticks off that cow—and one of them got Dad. But what a treat to have real beef—tough as it was.

We could get American canned meats shipped in to us by Le Grand Transport out of Bukavu. We ate a lot of spam, corned beef, and sometimes tuna, if we could get it.

We had wonderful fruit in Africa. Here's Mom holding a juicy pineapple. We had pineapples in abundance and really enjoyed them.

We also had a lot of bananas. The stalk would be cut while the bananas were green. We would hang them on our porch and eat off the stalk as they started ripening. They were quite delicious.

A few times we saw banana trees completely pulled in half from a band of gorillas that had passed through that particular area. They would eat what they wanted and then rip the trees in half just for the sake of destruction.

My favorite fruit were papaya. They were like a soft melon but with the most juicy, sweet flavor. They tasted the best when the green outer rind started to turn yellow. You could cut them in half, take out the seeds, and eat them like a cantaloupe. Or they could be sliced. They could even be made into delicious jam. I tried buying a papaya here in the States one time, but it was just not the same as in the tropics.

Another fruit we enjoyed were guavas. The tough outer skin was round and green, which began to yellow as it ripened. The deep pink pulp was a little sour to the taste with small seeds in the middle. They slightly resembled a pomegranate. Some of the missionaries made jam out of them, but we didn't care for it.

We had a lot of avocados. I can say with certainty that I didn't like them in Africa at all. However, I have recently tasted some guacamole here in the States made with avocados that was actually quite good! I may have to change my opinion after all.

Missionaries could order things like potatoes, flour, sugar, condiments, and canned items from the closest city, Bukavu. These items would then be brought to us through Le Grand Transport. Those were usually old, rickety trucks! The enterprising drivers often made a little side currency by loading them with passengers—who always got sick. We never knew when the truck would arrive or in what condition the food would be in once we received it. We rarely ordered raw vegetables besides potatoes or yams in season. Getting fresh produce to us before it rotted—or was contaminated with other things—was a problem not worth hassling with.

The Africans' gardens and the surrounding jungle provided us with all the starch food our diets required.

We had an abundance of plantains, which are referred to as "cooking bananas." They look a lot like bananas, but are not nearly as sweet. Bananas are eaten raw, while plantains are to be cooked. They could be steamed, boiled, or fried. We preferred them sliced and fried, eaten along with our meals. They were quite good. Missionaries and Africans ate a lot of plantain.

The Africans ate what they called *bugadi* derived from the cassava root, also called manioc. They would grind the root into a paste and serve it with meat or other vegetables. It was considered the African's potatoes. The roots are poisonous so they soaked them in water for about three weeks before using it in any way. We didn't like bugadi because it had very little flavor. The Africans would scoop up a ball of it with their index and middle fingers, make an indentation in it with their thumb, and then scoop that into another food item. By the way, tapioca is made from processed cassava root.

One of the food items they dipped the bugadi into was called *sombe*. This was young, green leaves of the cassava root (manioc), which was high in Vitamins A and C, as well as iron and calcium. It looked a lot like boiled, chopped-up spinach. We had it occasionally at the dorm and at home, but it had a slightly bitter taste. Of course, if you doused it with a lot of vinegar, like Dad and Jeanette did, it was even more palatable—that's what they said anyway.

One of our main staples in Africa was rice. The kind of gardening the Africans did is now called "slash and burn." They would cut the trees down and burn some of the area. Then the women would plant rice in the midst of all the fallen trees. They would have to climb over and around the fallen trees both while they planted and as they harvested the rice. (The white "god" on a pole at the entrance to the garden was to put a hex on anyone who went into this garden to rob it. It was respected!)

These women are pounding rice to prepare for eating. We ate many a meal with rice. One of my favorites was rice for breakfast. We would put rice in a bowl and sprinkle it with sugar and cinnamon. Some added milk to it, but since we only had powdered milk, which I detested, I ate it with just the sugar and cinnamon.

The Balega grew their own peanuts. We ate a lot of boiled and roasted peanuts. Plus the African cook at the dorm knew how to make the best peanut butter you could ask for. When we were getting ready to go out to the Congo, one of the things on the list given to us of items we needed to take was a coffee grinder. Since neither Mom nor Dad drank that much coffee, they questioned the need for the grinder. Come to find out, it was used to make peanut butter. All it took were roasted peanuts, some peanut oil to moisten it, and a bit of salt. We've never tasted peanut butter as wonderful as that! Jeanette's downfall was eating lots of boiled peanuts. I loved spreading peanut butter on slices of bananas. Yummmm!

Palm nut trees were very prevalent in our area of the Congo. The palm fruit, or nuts, were cultivated for its oil, which could be used in cooking as well as to make soaps and candles. The palm nuts were reddish, about the size of a plum, and grew in large bunches high up in the tree. The

Africans would climb the trees with their machetes and cut down the bunches when ripe. Almost all of the African foods used this palm oil, which was high in saturated fats.

The African's hot peppers were called *pili pili*. They were fiery hot, oblong, red peppers that were put into a lot of the food. Most of the missionaries could handle no more than two or three in a whole dish. The Africans would throw in a handful of them. Aunt Lydia (one of our nurses) said she never saw an African with gallbladder problems, and she believed it was because they ate so much pili pili.

Dad and Jeanette's favorite meal in the African village was chicken cooked in palm oil and pili pili over rice. That was a special treat, of course, and the Africans in that village sacrificed to give that to us. That's why Dad always made sure to shoot monkeys when he was on evangelistic trips, as well as taking a good supply of rice and palm oil to leave in the village, so that the Africans didn't have to use up their supplies to feed him. Katindi cooked for him, but Dad shared the bounty with the African family he was staying with.

One of our teenage missionary boys had been out in the forest foraging around when he found some pili pili. He put them in his shirt pocket and forgot about them. When he got to wrestling around with one of the other boys later, the pili pili got squashed onto his chest. He ended up with severe blisters across his chest from those pili pili. Yes…..they were HOT!

Cutting and sucking the sweet sugar juice from sugar cane stalks was something I thoroughly enjoyed. It took the place of not being able to go to the store and buy sweet candy. One problem — it ruined my teeth and has caused me to have extensive dental work throughout my entire life.

Hopefully, this will give a little insight into some of the things we ate while we were in Africa. And just in case you're wondering — NO! We did not eat any kind of bugs — that we were aware of!!

April 13, 1955

Dear Brother and Sister Wright:

Today for the first time, Les and I understood most of what was said in the morning service. Ernie Green preached. It as so good to enjoy a message for a change. It is easier to understand a missionary, of course, than a Mulega.

Next week we are going to Ikozi. We will spend Easter with the Lisle family. Of course we are taking Ellen and Linda with us. Everett and Les are going hunting Saturday. Monkeys are way more plentiful at Ikozi than here.

In a round about way, news has reached us that at long last the government is checking into our request for a concession at Punia. So maybe before too many months Punia station will be a reality. Two of our Katanti elders have volunteered to go with us. We praise the Lord for this. We did not want to assign someone to Punia. Our desire was that they would be led of the Lord to offer to go.

Well, dear ones, I'm afraid this letter will be short because I'm loaded with a cold and all my thoughts are running out my nose. Enclosed is our prayer letter. We trust it will be a blessing to those who read it. Thank you so much for sending it out for us.

Much love in Christ. We'll write more next time.

Much love,

Gertie

BEREAN MISSION, INC. 3536 Russell Blvd. St. Louis, Missouri	**A F R I C A** The Dark Continent!	B.A.M.S. — Katanti Shabunda par Kindu Congo Belge, Afrique

Prayer Letter　　　　　　　　　　　　＊＊＊＊＊　　　　　　　　　　　　May 1955

"Behold, the Lord's hand is not shortened, that it cannot save; neither His ear heavy, that it cannot hear" (Isaiah 59:1).

Dear Co-Laborers in Christ:

We have been witnessing the wonderful moving of the Spirit of God in our Sunday meetings in the out villages. We cannot testify to great throngs being saved because we are not reaching great throngs of people. Instead we go into the villages, sit down with these people, and the wonderful way of salvation is quietly given to them by Miss Maxine Gordon, and by Samasuli, one of our African teacher-preachers. We Spainhowers can say very little as yet, but we can pray as the others teach. How thankful we are to have a car in which to go from village to village in this manner.

"Behold the Lord's hand is not shortened, that it cannot save...." At the conclusion of a recent meeting in the village of Nkenge, a tall, proud-looking man boldly spoke out, "I want this Jesus as my Savior!" An astonished murmur swept over the people. We missionaries, too, were astonished. This man had stood on the outskirts of the crowd gathered for the meeting and had rudely interrupted the teaching from time to time with a remark or a seemingly ill-timed question. The teaching, both by Miss Gordon and by Samasuli, had been on the second-coming of our Lord Jesus Christ. One point seemed to eat away in this man's soul, "How could this One called Jesus come to the village of Nkenge, Katanti, Ikozi, and all the villages all over the world at one time and call all His children to Him at one instant." Our hearts were thrilled as Samasuli replied that this One called Jesus is truly God, the only God, all powerful, all-seeing, ever-present.

The Lord performed a marvelous work of grace in the heart of this man. He is the chief of the village of Nkenge and was a leader in the Buami Cult. Those of this cult are devil worshippers and haters of the white man. They are more or less the Congo version of the East African Mau Mau. Sawasila, as he is called, is known to be the killer of many people. All in all, he is a most unsavory character. Nevertheless, *"Is anything too hard for the Lord — His hand is not shortened that it cannot save."* Sawasila trusted in Christ as his Savior and now has the sure hope of the believer that his Lord will one day return to the village of Nkenge to take him up to be with Him in glory.

Also in the service was the wife of Chief Sawasila. She was a "medicine woman," well versed in the art of black magic. With tears in her eyes she received Christ into her heart. She gave us her basket full of "gods and gadgets" which she used in her so-called "healings." "I have no use for them now," she said. Most of the Africans were afraid to touch the things, but Samasuli, our African Teacher, picked them up and said, "These are not gods. They cannot see nor hear." A young man, and an elderly man, and two young boys were also saved. Praise the Lord! Pray for these dear babes in Christ. They have no Bible to read. No teacher in their village. How difficult it is for them to grow in grace and in the knowledge of our Lord Jesus Christ. But they do have the Holy Spirit in their hearts, and He will teach them.

We bid the people of Nkenge goodbye and went on to a village in which our Mission maintains a teacher-preacher. There we were joyfully received by the many Christians in the village, and invited to dinner. We were fed great quantities of fluffy, white rice, chicken, and palm oil gravy. The chicken and gravy were cooked with African peppers called "pilipili." They scorch the stomach, but are really good. We figured that no amoebas could possibly exist in all that pepper, so we ate heartily. After dinner we had services in the chapel, and hearts were blessed through the Word of God. The people were gracious and friendly. One woman urged Les and I to come and live in the village with them. They would teach us Kilega. They would help us to speak.

About two weeks ago a young woman was carried into our dispensary. She had gone into the forest to deliver her first baby. She had much difficulty, finally delivered one baby, but—there was another one and she could not deliver it. Finally, about twelve hours later, relatives carried her to the mission. Mrs. Parcel, our nurse, ministered to her, but several hours later the young mother slipped into eternity leaving a tiny two pound bundle of humanity to fight for its life alone. Mrs. Parcel took the baby boy into her home to care for him until he is strong enough to be placed in an African home. As yet, the relatives have expressed no desire to have the baby. However, a Christian couple who are childless are anxious to give the tiny boy a home. In the meantime, Mrs. Parcel cares for the baby during the day, and we take turns having him at night. It's nice having a baby in the home again, even if he is quite black with kinky hair.

As most of you know, we have fallen behind with our correspondence. We write between five to fifteen letters a week, and still we haven't been able to acknowledge all of the gifts that have been sent in to us, as well as your many personal letters. We love you all so much and we are so grateful to you for your loving, prayerful interest in us. We thank you from the bottom of our hearts for your gifts and letters, and prayers. You are a great encouragement to us. Many times we are financially pressed and then your gift comes to us; the need is met. Often we are discouraged, then your letter comes, and the burden is lighter because you take us home with you for a little while. We don't know how to really express our deep gratitude to you all, but the Lord does. *"The Lord bless thee and keep thee; the Lord make His face shine upon thee, and be gracious unto thee; The Lord lift up His countenance upon thee, and give thee peace."*

In His precious Name,

Les, Gertrude, Jeanette, and Marian
The Spainhowers

Katanti
May 7, 1955

Dear Brother and Sister Wright:

Since Les wrote the prayer letter, I will write the letter to you all. I am not much of a typist but will try anyway. We really enjoyed your long, long letter. We just sit down and catch up on all the news.

I've practically worn out my sewing machine these days. Irene Williams sent me some material for a skirt but I wanted a dress so I combined it with some white material Mother had given me before we left home, trimmed it in red rickrack which the ladies in the Guild had given me, and made a lovely dress. George Kennedy said, "You look just like America in that dress." I don't know exactly what kind of a look that was but I gathered it was nice.

I've also been working on mosquito nets, making Jeanette some needed clothes, and the usual darning and patching. As if that wasn't enough sewing, I have also been given the native women's sewing class. They are making tablecloths out of a square of white muslin and they sew quilt blocks around the edge. They just love it. They really have so little of beauty in their lives. Incidentally, Mrs. Wright, I will need lots of quilt blocks to take to Punia if you would like to tell the Guild for me. We are so thrilled at the clothes the ladies made for Jeanette and Marian. They can hardly wait for the boxes to get here. The ladies are so good to us—but aren't you all.

Ruth and George Kennedy left for Uku today. We sort of hated to see them pull off without us. You want to pray much for them as it won't be easy to be the only white people for miles and miles, especially for Ruth.

I've been training the missionary children in a program to be presented before all the adults on Katanti next Friday—sort of a closing of school program. We have really been having a lot of fun. There is a lot of real talent among our missionary children. We are trying to get ready for the conference. You know that it will be held here at Katanti. I'm having to train a new cook as my very expert cook fell into sin and had to be discharged. I can just see myself during the conference getting up at five in the morning, baking cakes or pies and making special dishes for 16 people at every meal, before seeing to breakfast. Leonard Parcel is working real hard on the two-room addition to our two-room house to get it done by conference. In fact, it HAS to be done because the speaker and his family are supposed to stay with us and they would have to sleep on a packing crate on the porch if the house wasn't finished. Besides that, I've been teaching the new cook to cook on a kerosene stove, and he will have to learn to cook on the wood range for the conference. We are awfully busy and at times, awfully tired, but through it all our blessed Savior grows more precious with each passing day. We are glad to serve Him here in this place.

In Christ,

Les, Gertie and the girls

BEREAN MISSION, INC.	A F R I C A	B.A.M.S. – Katanti
3536 Russell Blvd.		Shabunda par Kindu
St. Louis, Missouri	The Dark Continent!	Congo Belge, Afrique

Prayer Letter　　　　　　　　　　* * * * *　　　　　　　　　　June 1955

"Fear the Lord, and serve Him in truth with all your heart: for consider how great things He hath done for you" (I Samuel 12:24).
"The Lord hath done great things for us; whereof we are glad" (Psalm 126:3).

Dear Christian Prayer Helpers:

As I finished typing the above greeting, I gazed up at the bare wall, pondering just how to begin this letter. A slight movement caught my eye, and the next moment I sat watching a good-sized scorpion make his way along the wall. One quick blow with a stick, a few quivers of his long tail, and I knew that the poisonous stinger on the tip of that tail would not have its opportunity to cause one of us hours and hours of intense pain. The houseboys wanted to make doubly certain, so they carried the scorpion on the end of a stick and put him in the fire. Thus the scorpion is finished, and my letter begun.

We have much for which to praise the Lord, many of His blessings to share with you. Last April 19, Brother George Kennedy and I set out for the Punia area on an evangelistic trip. That evening, we arrived at a small African village about one mile from the site of our proposed new mission station. The natives were glad to see us and welcomed us to their village. They were extra glad to welcome us when our houseboys unloaded several monkeys and a baboon which we had shot along the road on our way there. To them (and to us, too) that meant meat to eat. We had several expensive cans of meat with us in the event that our rifles failed to provide "fresh" meat. However, we kept most of the village supplied with meat during the week we were there, killing two more baboons and seven or eight more monkeys.

While the houseboys set up our camp cots and mosquito nets and prepared supper, Brother Kennedy and I walked to the site of our new UKU Station, named after the Uku River which flows nearby. It was the first time I had the privilege of viewing the new site, but there was not really anything to see except dense tropical rain forest. We walked in along a narrow path, but our view of the site was limited to about five feet in all directions by the thick maze of undergrowth everywhere. Above our heads the sky was hidden by the intertwining branches of the many trees. Being out in these tropical forests gives one the feeling of being buried in a living, green tomb.

Upon returning to the village, we were greeted by Yacobo (Jacob), the African preacher, and Bitondo, the teacher in that village. They showed us to our house in which everything was in readiness for supper and for the night. The menu: monkey legs cooked in palm oil; cooked rice with palm oil gravy; and "sombi," a green leaf which is much like spinach when properly prepared. We bowed our heads and thanked our Heavenly Father for this provision and for journey mercies of the day. Brother Kennedy told me that the house in which we were staying had been built by Yacobo with the help of the village natives nearly two years ago when they were first told that Berean Mission might locate a new station in their area. The house was built expressly for the use of the missionaries as they came and went until such time as the mission station could be started. They had also constructed a small church building, which is used during the week as a school building. There Bitondo teaches his school of some thirty Balega children. How we praise the Lord for the work that has already been established by these two faithful men of God.

George Kennedy at the Uku village house.

The next morning we drove some twenty miles into the State Post at Kasese to see if there were any new developments in regard to our request for this new mission site, which request had already been pending for nearly two years. Truly we can say with the Psalmist, *"The Lord hath done great things for us; whereof we are glad."* When we arrived at the State Post, we found that there had been a change of officials about two months ago. The new government official had "unearthed" our request for this concession and had already put it through the proper channels, securing the right for us to occupy a limited portion of the new site immediately. The final granting of the concession is now only a matter of governmental "red tape." How we praise the Lord for His undertaking after nearly two years of waiting for this permission to occupy. We felt like Joshua and Caleb ready to cross the Jordan into the promised land—ready to occupy for the Lord.

The next day we drove to two other villages in this territory where Berean Mission maintains Balega teacher-preachers. We told them the good news, and they immediately rounded up the larger school children and set off on foot for UKU Station, arriving the following day. These thirty or forty school boys, together with their teachers and many of the men of the village began to "hack" and cut down the thick underbrush covering an area 200 meters long by 100 meters in depth. During these days of mowing we were conducting services each morning and each evening in the village. Three men professed faith in the Lord Jesus Christ as their Savior, and several Christians came to confess sin and be restored to fellowship. After the mowing was finished, the teachers and their pupils returned to their respective villages, and the time came for George and me to return to Katanti Station with much good news to tell our fellow missionaries.

We had only been back at Katanti for a few days, however, when word reached us from a village nearby that Bitondo's wife was there and seriously ill. She had been at the State Hospital in Shabunda, but had left without release and was in a critical condition. It was thought best that we return to Uku to get Bitondo and take him to the village where his wife lay sick. Since Brother Kennedy was gone to our Ikozi Station at the time, it was decided that Gertrude and I should make the trip to Uku to bring back our teacher, Bitondo. It was a good five-hour drive over typical Congo roads. We arrived at the Uku River at 3:00 P.M. to find that a large truck had fallen off the ferryboats and was half in the water and half on the shore. So Gertrude and I had to cross the river in a little "dugout" canoe, which had been carved out of a tree trunk. An African with a pole about twenty feet long expertly navigated us across the swift river. On the other side, we had to walk about two miles in the hot afternoon sun to reach the village where Bitondo taught his school. We could have sent a message after him, but we wanted to greet the village folk once again, and I wanted them to meet Gertrude. None of the women of our mission had as yet been to Uku. The people were so delighted that they would have gladly carried us both back to the river on their shoulders. We found that in the week since Brother Kennedy and I had been there that Yacobo and the village people had built a kitchen onto the missionaries' house, as well as the very necessary little house situated at the end of the path out back. They had also begun to fell the big trees on the mission site. How very anxious these people are to have us come there.

Now we are once again back at Katanti. Tomorrow morning (May 7), Brother Kennedy and his family leave for Uku with sufficient of their belongings to occupy the little house in the village while they clear the land on Uku Station and build their house. After they are moved into their house on the mission site, then Gertrude and I will move up to the village and begin building our house on Uku Station. Pray with us that we may have the leading and the blessing of the Lord as we open this new mission station for His glory. In addition to our own houses, we must also build school buildings, a church building, and eventually a dispensary. There is a great need among these people for the gospel. Only a few evangelistic trips have been made in that area, so the masses are as yet unreached with the gospel. Pray that God will bless the opening of Uku Station with the salvation of many precious souls and to the calling out from among the Bakumu Tribe of a people for His name. There has been great interest shown on the part of the few native Christians in this area. Pray that God will bless them for their zeal and for their help to us in starting this new work, and that they might be built up in the faith.

This past week Gertrude and I have had the exciting experience of teaching "calcul" (arithmetic) in the African School. Gertrude taught the second grade, and I taught the fourth grade. Probably when you think of the second and fourth grades, you think of small children about Marian's size or smaller. Not so in the Congo. Some of our scholars were almost as tall as we were and between twelve and fifteen years of age. We had to sort of map out our class discussions in advance and hope that the children would not ask any questions for fear that we would not understand what they asked. Besides all that, it is necessary to teach the Belgian method of arithmetic which is entirely different from the American method. We enjoyed ourselves immensely—but we have our doubts as to how much arithmetic we imparted to our pupils.

Last Sunday afternoon, Brother Ernest Green and I, together with some of our missionary children, decided to have a meeting in the village of Kakwidobola, which is situated several miles from the mission. However, on our way there, as we passed the village of Masanga, we saw an enormous crowd of some 350 to 500 people in the center of the village. We wondered what was happening. Certainly this was a big palaver. We rejoiced to see that the one in charge was former Chief Songo, a long time friend of the mission who had been led to the Lord several years before by Brother Albert Jansen. There seemed to be about five villages involved in the discussions. We found out that this meeting was being held to investigate the death of a village woman. Here in the Congo no one simply dies of old age, sickness, disease, or accident. Oh no! Someone has to cause the death, either by poison or by casting a spell on the victim. So the palaver was to determine who was the guilty person. The African fears death, and an African Christian must grow in grace many years before he begins to realize that life and death are in the hands of God.

Brother Green approached Chief Songo and asked for permission to have a meeting. This permission was granted provided we did not make the meeting too long as they had much yet to investigate. Ernest and I played our trumpets while they sang. How these Africans do love music!

Then, Brother Green preached on the text, *"And it is appointed unto men once to die, but after this the judgment"* (Hebrews 9:27). The whole group listened attentively, and only eternity will reveal the lasting benefits of this meeting. God has promised that His Word will not return unto Him void.

Well, we have really had a lot to chat with you about, haven't we? The Lord has been good to us. Yes, truly, *"The Lord hath done great things for us; where of we are glad."* Daily we pray God's blessing upon each one of you who, under the Lord, make it possible for us to serve Him in this dark place. The Lord bless thee and keep thee.

In His Service,

Les, Gertrude, Jeanette, and Marian

Marian's Comment: Of Birds and Gila Monsters

The Africans loved to eat birds and other things—as evidenced below.

Two different hawks shot and killed by Dad. These Africans ate well that day!

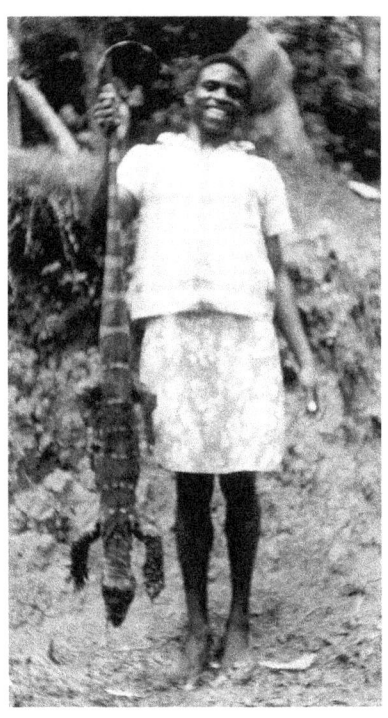

A beautiful bird for another delicious meal

Anyone for gila monster stew????

Dad always said that the most beautiful birds he saw in the jungle usually had the most terrible cries. He had no interest in shooting birds—but the hawks would steal the Africans' chickens, so he obliged them. The Africans ate the birds, but aside from the free-range chickens the Africans kept, we didn't eat any other birds.

Katanti Station
August 10, 1955

Dear Brother and Sister Wright and all the loved ones at Edgemont:

"Bless the Lord, all my soul: and all that is within me, bless His holy name. Bless the Lord, O my soul, and forget not all His benefits" (Psalm 103:1-2).

Greetings in His wonderful name! It was so good to receive your double (two envelope) letter and to learn all the news of home. Your letters came Sunday evening with our runner who left Shabunda Saturday morning. Today it is pouring down rain, and since all other activities have been brought to a halt, it is a good opportunity to let you all know what we have been doing.

The last week of July, Gertie and the girls and I drove into Bukavu (225 miles away) to replace a broken front coil spring and to have new rear springs put on the car. You will remember that last December we had new front coil springs and new heavy duty shock absorbers mounted. Well, the back end of the car felt a little "let down" about it all, so we had to "boost" her morale. Oh, how these mule trails can wreck a car in a hurry! We were also sort of expecting the Pearsons to arrive in Bukavu by airplane around the first or second of August, and we were going to bring them back to Katanti. They did not arrive, however, and we still do not have any definite word from them as to when they are coming. It certainly will be good to see George and Barbara again, and little Stewart. Of course, they have two new ones that we have not had the privilege of meeting yet. We have the Sanford's former house all ready for them to move into.

However, when the Hendrys arrive next October, they will have to crowd into the dormitory with the Greens and all the school children. How desperately we do need houses out here. Somehow we can't seem to get any building done on Katanti, that is, houses for missionaries. They are building a new dispensary now and are going to put up a concrete block school building for the missionary children. That will be all the work that our crew of workmen will be able to handle for the next year. Won't it be wonderful when we get home to glory, and there's a mansion waiting for us there!

We visited George and Ruth Kennedy at Uku last week. Their house is coming along well. They are about ready to put on the first coat of mud, and they should be ready to move into it in about five or six more months. I know they will be glad to move into their large mud house on the station site because they are now living in a small, two-room mud house right in the native village nearby. That is rugged! If we move to Uku, that is what we will have to do while building our mud house on the mission site. We are seeking the Lord's will in all of this. Somehow, we just don't seem to have the strength and will to tackle another language. We are just now beginning to speak a little Kilega—still not enough to really preach; and to think of going to Uku to another people and another language seems too much.

Joanne Kennedy, Jeanette, Charlene and Billy Kennedy, and Marian at Uku

Pray with us about this that the Lord's will may be done in our lives, as well as in the working of the Mission as a whole.

The Lord has already blessed the new work at Uku. There have been several souls saved, and a wonderful spirit of cooperation between the local Africans (even the unsaved ones) and the Balega from Katanti. The Balega families are having a difficult time obtaining sufficient food because they have no gardens, and it will be a year before the gardens they are now planting produce the food they will need to eat. In the meantime they must buy their food from the local natives, and we bring some up from the Balega territory, too. The Balega have their houses about half completed at Uku and will be able to move into them in another three months or so. They are building their kitchens now, extra big, so they can live in them until such time as they are able to construct their full houses. Of course, even their full houses are much smaller than the houses we build for ourselves, because they do not have near the possessions and fuss and bother that the missionaries have. Perhaps they are the wiser and happier.

Naturally, whenever we travel along these Congo roads, I always take my gun and shoot monkeys en route for meat. On the way back from Uku, the Africans had me stop the car to shoot a monkey. We walked back to where they had seen the monkey in the tree, and I beheld the largest monkey I had ever seen in my life sitting in a tree near the edge of the road and looking down at me. He didn't even move, much less run away. I took careful aim, pulled the trigger, and shot him right in the head. Instead of crashing to the ground, he caught the tree limb on which he was sitting and hung by one arm for a moment, then fell with a tremendous thump to the ground. The Africans looked at one another sort of dubiously and then cautiously made their way into the edge of the forest to the spot. They returned quite soon to inform me that what I had shot was a female gorilla, and that it was not killed. It had crashed on into the forest wounded in the face. The gun I shot it with was only a 22 rifle and not nearly powerful enough to kill a gorilla. I believe the 32-20 would have killed it, but I don't ordinarily carry it with me because it is so difficult and expensive to get shells for it from America. You know, Brother Chester Arney sent me 1,000 shells some time ago, and I'm trying to make those last a long time.

A few weeks ago, the Katanti elders and I went out to get some meat for the mission village. At the close of a very successful day, we returned to the station with one soul saved and thirty-one large, red monkeys. On the way home the elders witnessed to a native riding in the car with us. While we were waiting to cross the river on a boat, the elders dealt with the man concerning his need of accepting Christ as his Savior, and he did. These are simple people, and when they believe, they accept the Lord on simple faith. They have not as yet been exposed to education that tends to turn one away "from the simplicity that is in Christ."

We are all bracing ourselves for the beginning of "hostilities" here on Katanti Station next month. The African grade school, the Bible School, the missionary children's school all begin their new terms in September. Maxine Gordon has the African grade school, Ernie Green has the African Bible School, and Hallie Green has the missionary children's school. Gertie has the African girls work and will teach little Susie Parcel and Patty Green. I will be going out to all the villages in Katanti territory with our African evangelist and just living with the people. I am hoping that this constant living with the people will be the means of acquiring the language faster. It is one thing to desire to witness to a person who is not interested in hearing what you have to say (you often have that in America), but it is quite another thing out here to find yourself surrounded by those who desire to be taught the things of the Lord, and not to be able to adequately speak to them. Pray for us that the Lord will give us the language. It seems that we have been struggling with it for such a long time, without too much success.

We are rejoicing with you that you are now situated in the new parsonage. I know what a chore it was for you to pack up and make the move, and we are happy that you are now settled in and comfortable. Perhaps even going to the Berean Mission Annual Conference will be a rest after moving. Of course, by the time you receive this letter the conference will be a matter of the past, and you will be entering upon the fall and winter work at Edgemont Bible Church. How we do miss you all and wish we could be with you, but we have work for Him to do here. Pray for us. The problems sometimes are overwhelming.

We want to thank you all again for your faithfulness to us in prayer and in your giving. We note that the full amount is now in for our house, for which we praise the Lord! We do not know where or even when we may be able to build it, but it is consoling to know that the money is there for it. Pray much for the Lord's leading in this matter. There are many great problems in this connection. The Lord is able!

We noted from Leo and Irene's latest report that Edgemont's D.V.B.S. has placed $25 to Jeanette's account for a new accordion. We had no idea that such a fund was being started, but praise the Lord for it. She has progressed very much on the accordion and is sufficiently accomplished now for a full accordion like Ruthie and Eileen's. We had been asking the Lord for a full-size accordion for Jeanette, in order that Marian could have Jeanette's smaller accordion to practice on. It is uncanny how they both want to practice at the same time. We are certainly happy to see this fund started, and we know that if it is the will of the Lord for Jeanette to have a full-size accordion, He will provide.

The rain has stopped and it is beginning to clear a bit. Must close for now. Much love to you all in Christ Jesus.

Les, Gertie, Jeanette, and Marian

Marian's Comment: And We Complain About Our Work!

How often have we grumbled because we have to go grocery shopping? Or do our laundry? Or mow the lawn? Or as children, complained that there was nothing to do? It really takes living in another culture that has none of the luxuries we take for granted today to appreciate how blessed we truly are.

These women are returning from their rice gardens, carrying heavy loads of rice in their baskets. They've probably walked miles with their loads on their backs. Life is not easy for women in the jungle. They have no grocery stores. If they want to eat, they grow it or kill it.

Once they get back to their huts, there is more work. They have to thresh the rice to remove the rice grains from the stalk. That is accomplished by beating the rice in a wooden mortar with a pole, as the picture shows.

Once that is done, the rice is transferred to baskets where it will be tossed up and down gently to remove the hulls or chaff by allowing it to be blown away from the rice. Each day they pound only enough rice for that day's meals for their family since they have no way to keep it fresh.

These school boys are "mowing" the lawn in front of their school buildings! They are using machetes to chop away at the grass—and we were hoping they didn't chop a leg in the process. They didn't have to be concerned about mowing in a straight line!

They would quite often chant Balega songs while they worked.

The Africans had no indoor plumbing in their huts. Need water? Send the children to draw water from the nearby river or spring. Everyone had to do their part—from the smallest child on up. Look at the ages of these children and then try to carry a pan full of water on your head up a winding path to your home! Not an easy task but one that was done multiple times during the day.

Need to do the laundry? Perhaps you would like to join these women at the river as they wash their clothes and beat them against rocks.

See the men sitting on the planks? They are watching for crocodiles. We knew of several instances where a woman was snatched by a crocodile and disappeared forever.

Now it's time to prepare a meal. Everything is cooked on an open fire. But wood is needed for the fire. Who better to get the firewood than the teenage girls and women!

Each of these baskets of firewood weighed from 120 to 150 pounds! Incredible!

BEREAN MISSION, INC.	<u>A F R I C A</u>	B.A.M.S. — Katanti
3536 Russell Blvd.		Shabunda par Kindu
St. Louis, Missouri	The Dark Continent!	Congo Belge, Afrique

Prayer Letter   * * * * *   August 1955

Dear Faithful Friends:

As I write to you the voices of Africa are sounding in my ears — the occasional chatter of monkeys in the jungle, a million voices of a myriad of insects, the raucous cries of the big birds, and the gentle songs of the tiny birds. We can also hear the voices of the natives as they walk through the jungle to their gardens. Often these voices are raised in songs of glory to a Risen Savior, songs which rise from hearts overflowing with joy because once they sat in darkness but now the light of the glorious Christ shines in their hearts.

Yes, we rejoice to hear the songs of the Savior's love rising above the other forest sounds. But sometimes the songs we hear in the jungle are not songs of gladness, but the songs of heathen darkness sung in minor chords — the chants of the young boys as they go deep into the forest for the Satanic rites of circumcision — weird, haunting melodies. Then our hearts are burdened. The work is far from finished. So very many souls are still bound by the chains of darkness, blinded by Satan. Oh God, help us to be faithful in proclaiming the gospel of Thy saving grace. Enable these stammering tongues by the power of Thy Holy Spirit to bring many, many dear ones to Thee through faith in our Lord and Savior Jesus Christ.

Off in the distance I can hear the ominous rumblings of thunder. Not a breath of air is stirring. Sure signs that a storm is brewing. Hope all our houses stand. We need housing here on Katanti desperately: houses for missionaries, school buildings for our Africans, a new school building for our missionary children. Every time a storm blows up, Mrs. Ernest Green hurriedly shepherds the children out of the school house. Why? Because we are afraid the school house will fall in on our children.

One of our missionaries received a gift from home. Undoubtedly a dozen different ways to use the money flashed before her eyes. Perhaps she needed the money to buy vitamins. Maybe she needed shoes, or maybe she just wanted to spend it on something pretty that all young women love. Yes, even missionaries love pretty things! But do you know what she did with it? She has asked to place the money on a school building for the Africans. Will you join those of us who are on the field in praying and giving, if the Lord lays it on your heart, for buildings on all four of our stations. We Spainhowers are praising the Lord daily that almost enough money has been given in order that we can build our house at the new Uku Station. We want to thank each one of you for praying and giving toward this need.

While we are waiting to start building at Uku, we are not idle. We have many duties here on Katanti for there is always far more work than there are missionaries to do it. We spend many hours endeavoring to prepare simple messages in Kilega. It is a slow, difficult, oft times discouraging process. We are hearing and speaking more Kilega, but please don't think because we have been here a year that we know Kilega well. Pray that the Lord will continue to give us an ever increasing grasp of this language. We earnestly desire to speak Kilega fluently, and not just to get by. The better Kilega we speak, the better we can tell these Balega people of the unsearchable riches of God and win precious souls to our Lord Jesus Christ.

I am now the oft-times harassed mother of 21 African daughters. The Girls Work of Katanti Station has been assigned to me. My 21 "daughters" are lively, lovable, and mischievous. Never a dull

moment! I really have my hands full when all 21 come to prayer meeting in a slightly naughty mood. We clothe them, feed them, house them, educate them, and most important of all, lead them to the feet of our blessed Lord. Their "mother" will be their school teacher when the semester begins in September. Jeanette and Marian are real helpers with the girls. The African girls adore their white sisters and fight for the privilege of carrying Jeanette's accordion home from services and of sitting next to Marian.

Beginning in September, Les will be gone a good part of the time as the evangelist for Katanti Station. He and SaJacque, our African evangelist, will stay in the villages preaching, teaching, examining our out-schools, and many other tasks that go along with village work. His Kilega will probably increase by leaps and bounds as he lives among the people — sitting where they sit and bearing their burdens with them.

Pray for us both as we take up our work for Christ in a more definite way. Pray that souls will be saved. That is our reason for being out here. You pray for us and we'll pray for you, and God will accomplish great things both here and there.

                Yours in making Him known,

                Les, Gertrude, Jeanette, and Marian

Jeanette's Comment: The Fence Girls

The official term for what Mom was overseeing was "The Girls Work." Unofficially, these school girls were called "The Fence Girls." They were usually ten to fourteen years old—right at marriageable age. It took a lot of faith for the Africans to send their girls to Katanti Station to go to school. The Africans kept a careful eye on their daughters—a virgin girl would bring a much better bride price when she was sold into marriage. So we had to do everything possible to keep the girls safe and sound—and still give them a chance for a bit of an education.

After consulting with the elders and others for the best way to handle this situation, a special compound, near to the church and schools, was built. It was surrounded by an eight- to 10- foot pointed bamboo fence. There was only one opening into this compound—through the main room of SaBuseni and NyaBuseni's house. Even their older sons were sent to stay with others in the main village. Smaller houses for the girls jutted off the main house, and there was plenty of room for cooking fires and other activities. The girls were always chaperoned—and they were taught separately from the boys. The African women taught them what they needed to know to become good wives and mothers; our mother taught them how to read, write, and do simple math, as well as the Bible.

Mom's taking charge of the Girls Work meant that Marian and I pitched in, too. From helping to hand out clothing and blankets each fall when the girls came to school to listening to them read, we were expected to help as much as we could. Often, there would be several girls who would come up to our house on the edge of the forest and stand to call, "Jeanetta! Jeanetta!" until I would come out and visit with them. But for all of that, I never did learn to speak the language well. I could understand a lot of it, but I never was comfortable speaking it.

But I knew enough to understand when they'd say, "But Louisa always did such-and-such with us." They were talking about Louise Vander Ploeg, whose mother had been in charge of the Fence Girls before we came. The Vander Ploeg family was home on furlough and didn't return until after we had returned to the States because of Mom's health. I really disliked Louise—the Fence Girls thought she was so perfect! Two years later when I ended up in the dorm, Louise and I had a good laugh because, after she returned to the field, all she heard was "Well, when Jeanetta was here, we always did such-and-such."

On most Wednesday evenings, I went with Mom to the Fence Girls compound for prayer meeting. I carried a big flashlight so we could see as we headed down the main road, then turned off on a little path to the compound. One evening as we were coming home, I didn't have that flashlight focused on the path. Instead, I was waving it around seeing how far the beam would go before it was lost in the star-studded sky.

And then, I stepped on something. I guess it was the Lord that told me to keep my foot firmly in place. As I pointed the big flashlight to the path, I discovered I was standing on the head of a black mamba, one of the most poisonous of all local snakes. It was young—probably only three or four feet long instead of the ten to twelve feet of an adult snake. I was glad I had sturdy shoes on.

Imagine my horror, then, when Mom told me to give her the flashlight, and she would hurry up the road to get Dad! The moon was shining brightly, but she needed the flashlight to safely reach the missionary compound and bring Dad back. I had to stand there in the relative darkness with that snake twisting around my leg, making sure I never let up the pressure on its head.

It wasn't long before people were thronging around me—Africans and missionaries alike. *Bupangas* (machetes) were flashing in the moonlight. One of the Africans pointed out that they would have to cut right next to my foot to make sure the snake was dead. If the head was cut off too far down the body, it wouldn't kill the snake. I declared that no one but my father was going to do any chopping around my foot!

Now, that obviously put a lot of pressure on my father! I never stopped to think that the Africans were probably much more proficient with a *bupanga*—all I knew was that nobody was going to swing a *bupanga* at my foot except for my father. I'd heard about too many people brought into the dispensary with terrible wounds from a careless swing. One of the Africans pulled the snake out to its full length. I know Dad and Mom must have been praying mightily—and Dad swung that *bupaga* with all his might. It sliced neatly through that black mamba, right next to my foot. The snake stopped wiggling, but Dad wasn't taking any chances. He lifted me straight up and swung me to the side away from the snake. Needless to say, from that point on, the flashlight was always pointed at the path!

But that incident actually served a very good purpose. The very next Sunday, the African elder preached from Psalm 119:105, "Thy word is a lamp unto my feet, and a light unto my path." Just as I needed the light from the flashlight to see the path, despite a bright moon, it is only by hearing the preaching of God's Word—and daily reading of the Bible—that we can hope to overcome the temptations that face us each day. God's word is our guide and our comfort.

And that little story has been told over and over across the country as Mom and Dad were on deputation work and, finally, as I worked with children all over the country when Larry and I were traveling in evangelistic work. Whoever would have thought that such a frightening incident could be used to help bring men, women, boys, and girls into a deeper relationship with Jesus!

Jeanette's Comment: Schooling in Congo

After having had little to no formal schooling during our time in France, Marian and I weren't sure we were really ready to start school again in the Fall of 1954! But then, missionary kids from other Berean Mission stations—and other missions—began coming in to stay at the dorm. That made life look a whole lot more interesting!

Our first school year, I was in 7th grade and Marian was in 3rd grade. Every morning we trudged from our house down to the rickety mud schoolhouse with a leaky leaf roof. That was about one-half block from the first large house we lived in, about a block from the little house on the edge of the jungle. We could go home at recess and at lunch.

We started about 7:30 a.m. because everything was cooler then. We had a break mid-morning and an hour and a half at lunch—and everything on the mission station shut down at that time. That was the hottest part of the day, and everyone—African and missionary alike—was to rest and be quiet. Since our mission station was located two degrees south of the equator, the heat could easily reach 120 degrees in the shade. A "siesta" was a necessity to maintain good health. Life—and school—buzzed back into action about 1:30.

Aunt Hallie Green was our teacher. Before going to nursing school, she had taught in a small one-room school in Nebraska years earlier and, thus, was the most qualified person to do it—until the Hendry family would arrive in October 1955. Mom generally taught our Bible classes and subbed when Aunt Hallie was called out for a medical emergency—she was the station nurse as well. Mom also taught any children below third grade who lived on Katanti Station.

Because of never really knowing who would be teaching the missionary children school up to this point, all of the curricula were ordered from Calvert School—the only "home" schooling available in the 1950s. Missionary mothers on stations other than Katanti had to teach their own children from kindergarten through second grade. By third grade, they could be sent to the school on Katanti and live in the dorm. That was awfully hard for such young children! With Calvert schooling, the kids worked through textbooks/workbooks, and the teacher was there to answer questions. This setup actually worked out quite effectively because Eldon Green and I were the oldest students—and we were in 7th grade that first year, 8th grade the next year. All the other students were in elementary school.

The one thing that I noticed during these two years is that it became increasingly difficult for me to see the blackboard, and I had to squint to read. For someone who constantly had her nose in a book—or looking at music—that was a real hardship. After returning to the United States in the Spring of 1956, I finally got glasses and that took care of the problem.

Jeanette's Comment: Why I'm a Writer, Not a Nurse

The missionary nurses were our heroes. The Africans would bring in their dying families or friends and expect our nurses to do the work that even most doctors could not do. With God's help, the nurses were often able to do wonderful things. So we older girls, especially, all wanted to be nurses.

One day the African dispensary helper came running up the path to the mud schoolhouse, knocked on the door, and without waiting for an answer, ran in to speak urgently to Aunt Hallie, the nurse on Katanti. Since it was almost the end of the school day, she dismissed classes. And five of us older girls followed her down the path to the dispensary.

The dispensary was surrounded on all sides by small hills where the Africans would normally sit in the morning while awaiting treatment. One of the African elders would come and lead in a brief devotional, then Aunt Hallie and the dispensary helper would see patients. Except for emergencies, the dispensary usually had patients only in the morning. Since it was mid-afternoon when this emergency arose, the hillsides were empty.

The building was located at the bottom of these hills with a wide veranda on all sides. Aunt Hallie would establish herself on one side and see the patients in order. There was a small examining room when privacy was needed. As we got to the dispensary, Aunt Hallie indicated that we five girls were not to come any closer than on one hillside.

Turns out, a man had gotten one foot entangled in the spokes of a bicycle wheel and nearly cut off his big toe. The dispensary helper had put the man's foot to soak in permanganate water while he ran for Aunt Hallie. So Aunt Hallie lifted the man's foot out of the pan to get a closer look at it—and the toe fell backwards, held on only by a tiny strip of skin.

Immediately, three of the missionary girls fainted completely; two of them drew closer to watch Aunt Hallie sew the man's toe back on. The dispensary helper was almost frantic. What should he do about the three girls lying on the hillside? Aunt Hallie calmly told him that when the three came to, he was to send them home.

I was one of those girls. Oh, no! Not one of the two who got closer to see what Aunt Hallie did to help the man. Both of them actually did become nurses.

Nope, I was one of the three who fainted. It was at that point that I realized I would never have the stomach for nursing and had better rethink my career plans!

Katanti
August 24, 1955

Dear Mr. and Mrs. Wright:

Just read a letter from Mrs. Amie in which she said that God gave you a blessed time at the Conference. Praise the Lord! We were all praying for you. Received your lovely card containing the two pair of hose. Thank you so very much. You are always so thoughtful.

I had quite an experience last night. About ten o'clock I heard someone calling me outside our bedroom window. It was Hallie Green. They had an emergency at the dispensary and would I please come down and help. I crawled out of bed, threw on my robe and rushed to the dispensary. There I found Hallie working feverishly over a young girl. This girl, she was hardly more than a child, had gone to the forest the morning before to have her first baby. The baby was delivered, but no one cut the cord and the afterbirth remained in the womb. She lay in the forest all that day, and all the next day. They finally brought her to us last night. The baby was still attached to the cord. Hallie said she had never seen a human being as filthy as this poor young woman was. She and the baby were quickly bathed, and Hallie called me to administer ether while she tried to remove the after birth. She worked a long, long time on the girl but was unsuccessful. We committed the young woman to the Lord and came home. This morning the baby died and the mother is running a high fever and is in much pain. Death lingers close to these people.

Nya Aziza, helped mom in the women's work

I asked Hallie why the village women wouldn't come to our dispensaries, why they still went into the forest. She said that it is a shame to have a baby. That's why they sneak off into the forest like animals. Besides that, the witchdoctors tell them that we eat the babies or we take their spirits from them, so they are afraid to come. They wait until it is hopelessly too late, then they come dragging into the dispensary and often they die. The witchdoctor can say, "I told you so."

I'll probably be helping Hallie quite frequently as Hazel Leigh is unable to do any work at all. I suppose you've heard that she is pregnant. She has been so sick and weak that Hallie has again taken complete charge of the dispensary. Hallie has a tremendous amount of work to do; teaching, caring for the dorm children, so I am taking over all her Women's Work. Pray for me that our Lord will give strength and wisdom. I'll be teaching all morning in the missionary school; teaching one hour in the afternoon in the African School; caring for my 24 daughters, managing the women's work, which includes a message in Kilega each week plus all the extra curricular, Sunday School for missionary children, also a choir for them, plus the duties as housewife. I get a bit staggered when I think of them all. I feel so woefully inadequate in the Kilega but God said, "My grace is sufficient," and it is.

Pray much for Les' ministry in the villages. Pray for many souls to be saved through his ministry. Pray that his Kilega will increase by leaps and bounds. Of course, you know that we have asked to remain in Balega territory because of our difficulty with the language. Pray for this matter, too. We felt so definitely that this was God's will for us even though our hearts felt the challenge of Uku.

It was also a hard decision to make because pride entered in. We really hated to admit that the language was just about to get us down, and we didn't feel capable of learning another. Since making the decision, and telling the others, we have had such peace in our hearts, and strangely enough, God seems to be increasing our Kilega. So we are resting in Him, and trusting our fellow workers and the Home Board to understand. It is good to leave all things in His hands.

I believe I'm beginning to be a "meat" Christian instead of a "milk" one—but I do suffer growing pains at times.

Must close and get ready for prayer meeting. Even Ernie Green has a hard time understanding at prayer meeting because the people "mutter" their Kilega, but they derive comfort in our being there.

Much, much love,

Gertie

Katanti
September 28, 1955

Dearly Beloved of the Lord Jesus,

Have just finished typing Gertie's fine prayer letter so will try to write a few personal lines to send along with it. All here are well, praise the Lord. Gertie and George Pearson and I made a trip recently to Ikozi to have Dorothy fix our poor, decaying teeth. How wonderful it is to have our own mission dentist! It was only a round trip of 154 miles to Ikozi and back to have our teeth worked on, whereas it would have been a round trip of 450 miles if it had been necessary for us to go to Bukavu for the work. And won't it be wonderful when we have our own mission doctor! We are all certainly looking forward to the arrival of Dr. Zemmer and his family.

While at Ikozi, we saw the Crumleys again and welcomed them to Africa. They are comfortably settled in the large mud house in which the Lisles lived. After Mrs. Amie and Amanda left on furlough, the Lisles moved into the large stone house of Mrs. Amie. They are nearly finished with another large mud house for the Dr. Zemmer family and are putting up an office building with four offices in it for the single girls. The Lisles are preparing to build the first concrete block house on Ikozi, but there is such a scarcity of good sand and gravel, and the cost of cement is so high that it is really posing quite a problem.

We still do not know where we are to be placed since our request not to be sent to Uku. The executive committee met last month but decided to postpone any decision until the regularly scheduled executive committee meeting in December. So we don't know. Gertie and I have offered our services as dormitory "father and mother" of the missionary children, which we could handle along with other station duties, when the Greens go home on furlough. However, the Greens feel that perhaps the Hendrys will want that job along with the school teaching. So we will have to wait until the Hendrys arrive to find out their mind in the matter.

As Gertie mentioned in her prayer letter, we are beginning to enter into the work somewhat, even though our Kilega is woefully lacking. She is teaching the youngest missionary children, has classes in the African school, the African girls' work, and the women's work. I am the evangelist for Katanti territory and spend most of my time out in the villages. I'm not much of an evangelist when I can't speak the language, but it is coming a little at a time. Of course, I take our African evangelist with me, and he does the real preaching.

Love to all,

Les

BEREAN MISSION, INC. 3536 Russell Blvd. St. Louis, Missouri	A F R I C A _____ The Dark Continent!	B.A.M.S. — Katanti Shabunda par Kindu Congo Belge, Afrique

Prayer Letter　　　　　　　　　　＊ ＊ ＊ ＊ ＊　　　　　　　　　　November 1955

Dear Ones in Christ Jesus:

Come and go to prayer meeting with me tonight. We won't go to the church where the adults have prayer meeting because I have 28 African daughters waiting for me in their little village. At 7:30 P.M. I light the small kerosene lantern and start towards the girls' homes. On the way I stop for Maxine Gordon, and we continue on together. The path is narrow and we must walk single file. As we near the "Lupango," which is the name for the girls' village, we hear youthful voices singing an African hymn. What lovely, natural harmony the African has! Maxine and I stop and listen for a moment. Our hearts are gladdened with the music of praise to our God.

Then the girls see our light. "Bavua! Bavua!" they cry. "They come! They come!" Little stools are quickly brought for us to sit on, and all gather around. Above our heads, the bright stars of God's heaven; on every side, the mysterious shadows of the forest; the soft glow of the campfire reflects on young faces; the presence of God is near. We lift our voices in glad songs of praise. Five of these dear girls have just become new creatures in Christ Jesus through the ministry of Miss Gordon. After several songs, Maxine reads to us from God's Word. I'm sorry you don't understand what she's reading, but the girls do for it's God's Word in their language, Kilega, and it speaks to their hearts.

Now it is prayer time. Do the girls have prayer requests? A quiet voice speaks, "My father does not know Christ. Pray for him." "My relative is sick. Pray for her." "Pray for Utamusonga (that's me!) that she might hear and speak Kilega." And so the requests are made known to all. We bow our heads to pray. All is quiet except the crackle of the fire, the buzz of insects. Then, in a shy voice, one begins to pray, then another, and another. Simple prayers are theirs, but prayers of faith. We sing another hymn and prayer meeting is over. Rather reluctantly Maxine and I leave the girls. "Muende busoga," the girls call. "Go well." "Musigale busoga," we respond. "Stay well." Once again, Maxine and I walk the narrow little path to our homes. We are tired. We have both had a busy day. But aren't you glad you came to prayer meeting? We are.

Maybe now you would like to go to one of our out-villages with Les, Sa Jacque, the African evangelist, and Katindi, our cook, who always travels with Les. The car is loaded. How much equipment he has to take! Food for a week, camp cot, air mattress, mosquito net, bedding, cooking utensils, trumpet, brief case, and a gun. Les kisses Jeanette, Marian, and I on the cheek (it's very uncouth to kiss on the lips here in Congo) and we wave goodbye. In our hearts we are praying, "Go with God."

They arrive in the village of Naganzi, and a house is made ready for them. The extensive cleaning consists of sweeping the dirt floor and chasing the chickens out of the house. There is a combination living room and dining room, a room for Les, and a small room for Katindi. To the rear of the house is a small shed-like kitchen with a clay fireplace where Katindi will do the cooking for Les. Sa Jacque will sleep in another home. Shouts of excitement ring through the village as the car turns in "main street," a cleared space between two rows of mud houses. The people swarm around to shake Les' hand, "Samba, Tata, Samba," they say. "Greetings, my father, greetings." Little black, naked children duck in and out of the crowd, worming and squirming their way as close to Les as possible. The people are happy. A missionary has come to sit in their village.

Soon the drums beat out the call to worship. Some bring their small stools, and some sit on the ground. They gather in a cleared space in the center of the village and sing hymns. Les greets them

and brings a short message in Kilega. Some of them are amazed to hear the white man speak their language, and all of them are amused at his peculiar inflection. Their language is a tonal language, and the missionary can only approximate these tones. Then, Sa Jacque, the African evangelist, teaches them from the Word of God in a way that the missionary will never be able to do. God speaks to many precious hearts in these village meetings.

Les returns to the mud hut to eat the dinner Katindi has prepared for him. There is no privacy. The place is swarming with curious people who want to watch the missionary eat. Gently Les tries to get them to leave the house so he can wash and eat. Not so gently, Sa Jacque shoos them away. Feeling akin to a monkey in the zoo, Les washes and eats. Most of the people are out of the house, but they are peeking in the doors and windows, and walking through at will.

After dinner, by lamplight, Les is reading his Bible when he hears a commotion in the dining room. A tense voice calls out, "Vua na bupanga." "Come with a big knife." Les quickly steps into the other room in time to see some villagers kill a snake in the house. A little girl about eight years old, the daughter of the owner of the house, had stepped on the snake as she walked through the dark house, and it had bit her on the ankle. Hurriedly Les gets a razor blade, and they cut the child's ankle around the marks of the snake bite. Then they rub and rub down the child's leg and rub native medicine into the wound. The native medicine is an extremely fine gray powder, much like Fullers Earth, but very effective in drawing out or neutralizing the poisonous venom. The next day the girl is limping and the swelling reaches the calf of her leg, but it goes no higher, and in the following days it gradually recedes.

The next morning at six o'clock another service is held. Later in the morning, while all of the people are working in their gardens, Les, Sa Jacque and Katindi go hunting. They tramp through the humid, dark forest looking for monkeys. The Lord enables, and they provide the villagers with meat. In fact they eat so much that Katindi goes to bed early that night complaining of a stomach ache. A Mulega (a person of this tribe) just can't stop eating as long as there is a morsel of food left in the pot. The afternoon is spent sitting in the huts visiting with the people. In the evening, another service.

The time has come to return home. Katindi packs all the equipment and loads it in the car. The villagers press around to tell Wemaninua (Les) "Muende Busoga" - "Go well." Are they glad he came? Three people give him chickens as a love gift. Others give eggs. Out of their poverty, they give in love. Les is happy. He is going home, but he has left a bit of his heart in the villages where he "sat where they sat, and bore their burdens" with them.

For six days Les lived in the African environment — never a word of English — never a white face. On this trip, thirteen services were held. Unbelievers were urged to come to Christ. Christians were encouraged. They came with their problems and were helped from the Word of God.

Yours in His glad service,

Les, Gertie, Jeanette, and Marian

Marian's Comment: Serving the Lord in the Congo

During our first term in the Congo, a lot of Dad and Mom's time was spent just learning the Kilega language and the culture. A new missionary doesn't show up on the mission field fully prepared to jump right into the work. A huge obstacle to doing so is not knowing the language of the people. Other hindrances are learning and understanding a vastly different culture; living in mud houses with leaf roofs along with all the critters that come with them; preparing and eating foods they never thought was possible—such as monkey meat.

The other missionaries helped Dad and Mom, as much as they could, to get settled and acclimated to their new way of life. Uncle Ernie tutored them in the Kilega language. But after living in France for a year, they knew the best way to learn a foreign language is to walk among the people themselves. So they would frequently walk to the Katanti village, mingling with the Africans. The Africans loved that because it showed that Dad and Mom cared about them, and it also gave them the opportunity to help them learn not only the language but a lot of their customs as well.

Dad's Ministries

Once they were able to say more than just "Samba" (hello), Dad started going to distant villages with African elders to hold meetings. Some villages could be reached by car but others were deep in the jungle so they had to walk. Thankfully, Dad was always sure footed and had no trouble keeping up with the Africans who accompanied him. Naturally, he wasn't able to preach, but he could sure play his trumpet, and then do a lot of impromptu sign language to communicate. If another missionary went along, Dad could give his testimony through an

interpreter until he was more fluent in Kilega and could handle it himself. During both our first and second terms on the mission field, Dad became the missionary evangelist for Katanti or Kamulila station. He had a burning desire to reach Africans in distant villages for the Lord.

Dad was also in charge of the workmen on Kamulila Station during our second term on the mission field. The workmen did all types of jobs around the station, including building school buildings for the Africans, repairing buildings or replacing the leaf roofs, making

desks, and many other jobs that came their way. Dad paid the workmen every Friday. They may not always have shown up on time for work, but they all were there promptly on pay day! Dad really enjoyed working with these men, and they told others that Tata Wemaninua was fair and treated them well.

This is Dad and one of his workmen securing the poles for the school building roof together with bamboo strips, wrapped around and around the poles.

All these poles had to be cut by machete. No chain saws!

One of Dad's best workmen was named Luimbo. Dad took this picture just as Luimbo had finished cutting down a large tree. How would you like to cut down a tree using nothing more than this rustic "axe?" All in a day's work for Luimbo!

On our second term when we were living on Kamulila, Dad worked closely with the church elders. These men truly loved the Lord, and it was the desire of their hearts to see many of their Balega people come to know the Lord as Savior. (By the way, that's Dad's plaid, flannel shirt on the elder to the right of the picture. He didn't have a good shirt to wear to church, so Dad gave him one of his.)

Mom's Ministries

While on Katanti during our first term and Kamulila on our second term, Mom was put in charge of the young African girls who were brought to the mission station to go to school. Several of our supporting churches made dresses of different sizes for the girls and sent them to us along with blankets so we could give each girl a new dress and a blanket when she arrived. The girls stayed in chaperoned huts not far from the school. These girls would soon be sold into marriage, if their fathers were not believers. Women and girls were considered no better than animals—to be bought and sold.

Mom had a great love and burden for the salvation of African children. It didn't matter how dirty they were, Mom loved each and every one and tried to show them her warmth and love whenever she could. This little one wasn't too sure about standing with this missionary lady, but the child's mother was thrilled to have Mom's attention directed towards her child and kept yelling at her to stand still. Mom was telling Dad to take the picture quickly or else she would sure get away from her grip.

Mom also loved her work with the African ladies. She had Bible studies with them to tell them the Good News of Jesus Christ and to strengthen their knowledge of Him. She tried to teach some how to sew simple seams by hand. The funny thing is that they would hold a piece of cloth between their toes, and sew away from them. Somehow they managed to get the job done. She also taught them to read, write, and do simple math.

So many of the women loved Mom with her gentle, kind, and patient spirit. Mom worked long hours with the women teaching them to read and how to care for the children. She was their counselor and friend.

One interesting sidelight: Katanti was on one of the main roads crossing the jungle, and the Africans in that area were a little better educated and understood "modern" life a bit more than those on Kamulila. Because of the long-standing schools on Katanti and Ikozi, it was accepted that the girls and women would learn how to read and write.

However, that wasn't the case on Kamulila. When Dad's workmen realized their wives had earned Kilega church songbooks because they could now read, write, and do simple math and they couldn't, they told Dad to make Mom stop teaching their women because the women would think they were superior to the men. Dad told them that, instead, they should learn to read, write, and do simple math, too. If their wives could do it, why couldn't they? One of the African schoolteachers was asked to have special classes with the workmen—and it wasn't long before they earned their Kilega songbooks, just like their wives had done. Marital peace was restored.

The preceding pages tell about the main roles Dad and Mom had as missionaries. However, it would be impossible to mention everything they did. Most days they were up early and to bed late. There were many times when they had to stop everything they were doing to help a missionary nurse in the dispensary, or drive a seriously injured or ill patient to the hospital in Shabunda. Every day was a new day with new challenges and adventures. There was nothing boring about missionary life.

Shabunda
Wednesday, December 21, 1955

Dear Loved Ones,

"God is our refuge and strength; a very present help in trouble." How we praise Him for grace and strength sufficient for each task and for each day.

I'm writing you from Shabunda where we have brought Gertrude to the doctor. About three weeks ago she became sick with a bad cold. She was in bed for a few days and then started back into the work again. After a few days of activity she was back in bed sick again. She gained some strength and then tried to work again, but had an attack of some sort on Wednesday, the 14th, in the morning.

I had gone to a distant part of our territory that day, along with most of the men missionaries, to look over a proposed new mission site and didn't return until after 6 o'clock that evening. We found Gertie very ill, but in the hands of our two nurses, Mrs. Parcel and Mrs. Green. This past week has brought further spells of suffocation, and in one final effort we have brought her into Shabunda in order that the doctors (two of them here) may be able to take x-rays and other laboratory tests. She seemed to stand the 50-mile trip over twisting mountain roads fairly well. We bedded her down in the rear of our Suburban, and she didn't have too much difficulty breathing. In her last attack before coming in to Shabunda she almost entered upon her journey "Home," but as she expressed it later, "The Lord turned me around at the valley of the shadow and sent me back. He has more work for me to do."

This morning they x-rayed her chest and the doctor said it was not too bad—she does have pneumonia—but the x-ray did not disclose the amount of congestion that would cause such acute shortage of breath. They have also taken blood tests and are coming back today to establish a further course of treatment other than the penicillin and streptomycin which she is now getting. We are trusting in the Lord, who is ever faithful. We feel confident, as Gertrude does, that the Lord has turned her around and sent her back to finish the work He has given her to do in this life.

I will hold this letter for a few days, adding to it from time to time, so that you may have the full story when it reaches you. Because of the stress that Mother Wilson is undergoing at the present moment we have not let her know that anything is amiss. We are trusting that there will be a definite improvement by the time I mail this letter, and then, Brother Wright, perhaps you could let Mrs. Wilson know that the crisis is past.

In the meantime, let me acknowledge your letters of October 20 and November 28, which I simply haven't been able to answer as yet. I want to thank you, too, for the lovely birthday greetings enclosing the S-T-R-E-T-C-H socks. It was so good to hear all the news: of your Missions Conference, who the speakers were, and how the Lord blessed hearts, of the many young people who went forward to re-affirm their decision to serve Christ. So good to know how the Sunday School is growing, and we praise the Lord for the way He is leading His people to provide for the new Sunday School and church building. My! We won't know Edgemont when we return in 1958. Praise God for His goodness. *"O give thanks unto the Lord for He is good."* Oh yes, we want to thank you for subscribing to the *Moody Monthly* for us for Christmas. It was so kind of you.

Thursday, December 22, 1955

Let us bless the Lord again. *"Bless the Lord, O my soul, and all that is within me bless His Holy Name."*

The doctor came to see Gertrude again last night and said that after further study of the chest x-ray, blood specimens, etc. that she does *not* have pneumonia. The blood tests were all good except for one which indicates "sediment" (or something like that); the heart is strong. Still the difficulty seems to be with her breathing. She has been doing very well since last Tuesday's attack, except for being so weak.

Tomorrow (Friday) they are going to examine the digestive tract through a fluoroscope. As yet the doctor says he cannot explain the severe attacks which she has had. But we are praising the Lord for strengthening her. Her breathing is considerably better at the moment. I feel that she is past the crisis, barring another attack, and we are trusting the Lord to keep her in the hollow of His hand. He is able!

Tonight begins our African Christmas Conference at Katanti—and on the other stations, too. Satan has certainly been fighting the conferences this year. Last Saturday night or early Sunday morning the 2-year-old son of one of the Uku Station elders died as they were rushing him to Katanti for medical help. It seemed to be pneumonia. Then Gertrude's critical condition with all the anxiety and long, difficult trips various ones have had to make in connection with it has been tiring on all. The Parcels are finding it necessary to take a vacation at this time for Hazel Leigh's sake, and Ernie Green is about worn out with a deep bronchial cold. With so much to combat, we feel that the Lord is preparing the way for the most blessed conference yet—for His strength is made perfect in weakness.

Friday, December 23, 1955

Must finish this letter hastily and get it in the mail today. We had Gertie to the hospital again this morning to take some more x-rays, but they indicated nothing. I believe the Lord has been clearing up the congestion in the lungs so fast that the doctors can't catch up in their diagnosis. We certainly praise the Lord for her wonderful improvement. She still isn't able to sit up and is very weak, but the crisis seems to be past. Praise God!

Give the news gently to Mrs. Wilson, and tell her I'll write her direct next week—and perhaps Gertie may be able to write a line or two. Please continue to pray for her.

Much love to you both in Christ,

Les

Marian's Comment: Mom's Illness

As I prepared to write some of my thoughts pertaining to the illness of my mother, I started by reading all the letters written by Mom and Dad that are included in this book. As I read their different accounts of her illness and then typed out a "timeline" for that period, I began feeling emotions that I had not felt for many, many years. I was drawn back to that time when I was just a few months from turning 11 years of age.

Dad was the evangelist for the Katanti Station, so he and our African evangelist were gone a lot visiting African villages deep in the jungle to bring them the Gospel. The day Mom became critical, Dad was on an evangelistic trip out in the jungle.

I was walking slowly on the dirt road that led back to our two small houses at the edge of Katanti and the jungle which surrounded the station. As I looked up toward the house, I saw Aunt Hallie Green, a nurse, running from our house towards me. I asked her what was wrong, and as she ran right past me, her reply was, "Don't go home!"

I remember becoming immediately afraid and did exactly what she told me not to do—I ran home to Mom. When I entered her bedroom, she was just lying there, barely breathing, saying nothing, not moving. Jeanette was there and stopped me from rushing up to the bed to ask Mom what was wrong. She told me to be quiet and wait for Aunt Hallie. I must have realized the gravity of the situation because I just quietly stood there, with Jeanette's arm around my shoulders. I don't recall if we were crying or not. We might have been too frightened.

When Aunt Hallie returned, she brought Aunt Hazel Leigh Parcel, another nurse, back with her. They told us to go outside so they could take care of Mom. We obeyed, reluctantly. We didn't realize that they were thrown into action trying to save our Mother's life. Mom's breathing was extremely shallow and difficult. They had to give her shots to stimulate the heart and her breathing and to relax her body. I started giving Jeanette grief about why we couldn't be with Mom; why we had to wait; where was Dad; etc. Jeanette comforted me as best she could while she tried to reassure herself. I knew if Dad would just come home, everything would be all right. He would fix it!

Word was sent to our Africans asking them to quickly send a message by drums from village to village in the jungle until Dad and the evangelist were found. The native language, Kilega, is very tonal so villages would often send messages back and forth to each other by beating on large drums. I don't know how long it took or how many villages had to respond, but they eventually found where Dad was and gave him the message to come home quickly. Jeanette and I watched the road at the entrance of Katanti for a long time, anxiously awaiting his arrival. By the time Dad arrived at 6:00 p.m., a truck was blocking the road down by our African village. Dad parked the car behind the truck and ran up the hill as we ran down to him. We cried with joy at seeing him, and I knew Mom would be all right now. Dad was home!

But Mom wasn't all right. Her condition worsened, and our nurses ministered to her day and night. Dad would allow us to quietly come in to see her any time we wanted to. We would stand beside her bed, but most of the time our beautiful Mother didn't move, didn't open her eyes, and didn't know we were there.

Dad finally told Jeanette and I that he needed to talk with us. I'll never forget him slowly and carefully telling us that he was going to have to take Mom away to the State Hospital in Shabunda where there was a Belgian doctor, but we wouldn't be able to go with them. Then he said the words I will never forget, "Your Momma is very sick, and she may not make it to Shabunda. The Lord might take her Home." After that, I hardly even heard him say that Aunt Maxine Gordon, a single missionary lady, whom we loved dearly, would be taking care of us.

The next morning, Dad made a bed in the back of our Plymouth Suburban and with the help of other missionaries, gently placed Mom on the bed for the trip. Uncle George Kennedy drove his truck in front of Dad to make sure there were no obstacles blocking the road along the way. Aunt Hallie rode with Dad, prepared to give Mom injections should she have another serious attack. Aunt Lydia Frank, another nurse who had come from Ikozi, drove behind them so Mom would have two nurses caring for her at the State Hospital in Shabunda. Mom was conscious as they were leaving and tried to smile as we kissed her goodbye—perhaps for the last time. Jeanette and I choked back our tears because we didn't want Mom to feel sad. As the caravan made its way down the hill, Mom weakly smiled and slowly raised her arm to wave goodbye to Jeanette and me. I will remember that forever! That very well could have been the last time we would have seen our dear Mother on this earth. Jeanette and I clung to each other and cried with broken hearts until Aunt Maxine, through her own tears, lovingly and gently took us home.

The accounts of Mom's struggles are in the letters so I won't go into any more detail about that. But I know for a fact that we love and worship a truly awesome God. Our God had His hands on Mom through her entire ordeal, which lasted several months, and in His infinite wisdom and grace, God did not take our Mother home to be with Him. For that I am truly thankful!

However, in the midst of everything Mom was going through, she received a letter from her sister towards the end of January letting her know that their step-father had passed away into the presence of our Lord on January 9, 1956. Since we had no telephones, the only way we could be told was to wait for my aunt's letter to arrive which took anywhere from two to three weeks. When Mom and Dad returned to Katanti from the Methodist Mission in Minga, they gave Jeanette and me the news. I knew my beloved Grandpa had been ill but with all we had gone through with Mom, it never occurred to me that he would die. I cried as if my heart would surely break. Mom and Dad assured me he was no longer suffering, and we would all see him again one day in Glory. But at that moment, it didn't help this little girl in the jungles of Africa, who suddenly felt very homesick for the family she missed so much in America.

Jeanette's Comment: Seasons of Difficulty

Christmas has always been a special time for me. Mom and Dad always emphasized two things— that it was the time to celebrate Christ's birth and that it was family time. It didn't matter where we were, how many gifts we had, or how bright the Christmas tree glowed. The true meaning of Christmas and being with family took first place.

In our little two-room garage house when we were very young, Dad and Mom cleared off the top of a small cabinet behind Dad's desk—and there they set a tiny tree. But Santa Claus never had a part of our thinking. Oh, we knew the stories about Santa Claus, but to Marian and me, they were always just stories—no different than *The Poky Little Puppy* or *The Three Little Kittens Who Lost Their Mittens*. The Christmas pageant at Edgemont Bible Church, the choir cantata, and then spending Christmas Day at Grandma and Grandpa Wilson's house—this is what was important.

While our Christmas in France brings back very happy memories for me, our two Christmases in Congo in 1954 and 1955 have only sad memories. In 1954, none of our crates and other equipment, including Christmas decorations, had yet arrived on Katanti Station. And right before Christmas is when we had to move to that little two-room guest house on the edge of the jungle, with all four of us squeezed into one small bedroom.

Grandma Wilson and Aunt Frances (Mom's sister) had mailed out packages months earlier for Christmas, so there were a few presents. But Mom and Dad hadn't been into Bukavu or anywhere they could have gotten gifts. Mom's sewing machine had not yet arrived, so she couldn't even make new dresses for us. We had no Christmas decorations—and no way to make any. Finally, one of the other missionaries lent us a string of Christmas lights, and we draped them across the doorway leading from the one bedroom into the bathroom, and for the two or three hours each night when the station generator might run, we'd turn off the lights in the bedroom and talk by the light of those dim Christmas bulbs. Christmas just didn't seem like Christmas.

Christmas in 1955 held out greater promise for us. Boxes had already arrived from Grandma Wilson and Aunt Frances—even Dad smiled secretly at a couple of boxes from Montgomery Ward, whose catalog Marian and I had carefully pored over a few months earlier. The second two-room building had been built, so we had room for a tree. Our equipment crates had arrived from the United States, so we had decorations—if we could figure out what to use for a tree. There were no conifers at all in the Congo—and palm tree branches didn't have the right holiday feel. Uncle Carl Blackburn, who lived on Ikozi Station, came by one afternoon and brought a bunch of tall ferns. When tied together, they looked a lot like a Christmas tree.

Before Dad had left for his evangelistic trip, he got the tree set up in the living room area of the new two-room building and told Marian and me we could decorate it—but not to worry Mom with it because she still wasn't feeling very well. Aunt Maxine Gordon would check in and make sure everything was going okay.

Marian's comment about Mom's illness says everything about how we girls felt and what happened to us while Mom and Dad were in Shabunda seeing the Belgian doctor. At night, I'd sit on the sofa in our new living room, lit only by the Christmas lights on our tied-together tree, and cry until Aunt Maxine would send me to bed.

As a young, selfish teen, I not only cried for my mother—but for another ruined Christmas. It wasn't fair! Two miserable Christmases in a row!

But things went from bad to worse. We received word that Grandpa Wilson was desperately ill in the veteran's hospital. To top that off, Great-Aunt Minnie, who was living with Grandma and Grandpa by that time, was driving home from visiting Grandpa one evening when she was in a terrible car accident on the icy roads. She was not expected to live—and Grandma was traveling back and forth between two hospitals to spend time with both her husband and her sister. And we weren't there to help! These were dark days indeed.

Grandpa Wilson

Grandpa never recovered and died in January after spending four months in the hospital. But Great-Aunt Minnie lived—however, the doctor said that she'd probably never walk again. He didn't know Great-Aunt Minnie! Three months later, she was walking just fine, thank you—and she efficiently ran Grandma's house until the Lord called her home more than twelve years later at age 90.

Great-Aunt Minnie (Grandma's sister)

Shabunda
December 28, 1955

Dearest Mother and All:

Honest, this is my very own handwriting so you can stop worrying now. We wrote to Mr. Wright first because I just couldn't bear the thought of you coming home from the hospital, sitting all by yourself and reading a letter saying I had pneumonia. I much preferred the thought of Mr. and Mrs. Wright being with you when you heard.

"The Lord has done great things for us; whereof we are glad." Just a week ago yesterday at about this very time I was struggling to breathe. I was dying, and I knew it. So did the others. They had done all they could. I knew the exact moment the Lord laid His hand upon me and gently turned me from entering the valley of shadows and gave me life. Praise His name. I remember wanting so very much to tell Les that God had given me back to him, but I couldn't speak. Breathing was too difficult. I lay for an hour, maybe two, so exhausted from the crisis that I couldn't move a muscle or even lift my eyelids but I *knew* I was going to be all right. God had given me life, new life, when mine was gone.

I've always wondered if a child of God would have any fear at death but I can truthfully say "There is no fear." I had a feeling of regret at leaving those I love so much but peace in my heart that I would see my Savior face to face.

It was decided to attempt the hazardous trip to Shabunda and the doctor. When I could speak I told Les to have no fear. I could stand the trip. God had given me life. Hallie was about exhausted. The physical and mental strain of caring for me through these attacks was really showing on her. Under God's guidance I give her credit for saving my life three times. Les fixed the back of the car as a bed. They put me in and away we went. George Kennedy and Ernest Green went first in George's truck to clear the road. Hallie rode with Les in our car.

On the way we met Lydia Frank who came to lift the burden of nursing off Hallie until she could get some rest. We made the trip to Shabunda without incident. I just felt stronger all the time. After the doctor saw me, he told Lydia Frank that my lungs were much worse and he didn't know if I would live. I have gained strength so fast that he says, "C'est bizarre" — "It's unusual, peculiar." Just between you and me, it's miraculous. One week from the day I was dying, I took my first steps around the room supported by Les. Today, I am able to stand alone. Tomorrow I'll be walking alone. Praise the Lord. He is the Great Physician.

I'm turning into a pin cushion. Have had between 50 and 60 shots in two weeks. Hallie says there isn't much space left to shoot. Lydia has returned to Ikozi but Hallie has stayed on here. Since I have improved so much, she is getting a much needed rest. Maxine Gordon is caring for the girls.

Ernie Green brought his four children and our two girls here on Monday, and we opened our presents and had Christmas.

Please don't worry, Mother. Our Lord doesn't do things by half measures. He has returned me to life. He will return me to full strength. I won't be able, for some time, to again shoulder all the responsibilities that I had. I promise not to abuse the strength the Lord has given me. All the missionaries have been wonderful. Hallie, Lydia and Hazel Leigh, especially, because the work fell on their shoulders. Les, of course, continues to be the dearest husband in all the world. In some ways this has been harder on him than me, but God was and is his strength.

Love,
Gertie

Another letter was received, written on January 3, 1956, saying that they had made the return trip home. Gertrude is slowing regaining her strength. She says: "We've had a regular stream of people coming to see me. They all prayed so much for me, so they came to see the answer to their prayers. Bless their hearts. It did our hearts good to see each one of them."

Katanti
January 14, 1956

Dear Brother and Sister Wright:

*"My voice shalt thou hear in the morning, O Lord; in the morning will I direct my prayer unto thee, **and will look up**.*" And will keep on looking up! K. L. U. finds Scriptural authority in Psalm 5:3.

We have received your two newsy letters of December 27 and 31, and certainly thank you for your faithfulness in writing to us. We have not been so faithful in writing and acknowledging gifts of late because of Gertrude's serious illness and all that it involves, but I'm sure the folk will understand as the news makes its way around.

Gertrude is still not making any progress, although I don't think at the moment she is slipping back any, except still losing a little weight. She is a complete invalid; even the least exertion exhausts her. We are just trusting the Lord for her. He has brought her thus far and we know He will see her through. Ebenezer!

As you will note from the enclosed prayer letter, we will be taking her to Dr. Hughlett of the Methodist Mission at Tunda. The Lord willing, we trust to leave Katanti on Tuesday, January 24, and arrive at Tunda the evening of the 25th. It will be two long, hard days of driving, but we will fix Gertie a bed in the back of the car by folding down the rear seat and making a bed on an air mattress for her. It just seems such a long wait from now until the 26th when Dr. Hughlett will be there to see her. But the Lord is the strength of her life. Of course, by the time this letter reaches you we will have already seen the doctor, but I'm sure Gertrude will still need your prayers very much. It looks as though it will take a long, long time for her to gain back her strength. God is able! Pray for her.

You inquired as to whether or not any of the dresses for the African girls, which were sewed by the ladies of the Guild, had arrived as yet. No, but there are three packages for us at Shabunda now, and one of them may well be those dresses. Bob Hendry and Glenn Crumley will be going on Monday to get them. The dresses cannot come too soon because Gertie has given out to the girls all the dresses she had on hand already. Of course, Gertie is unable to do anything at the present, and so Maxine Gordon has taken over the girls work from her, as well as Gertie's two classes in the African school; Hazel Leigh Parcel has taken over the teaching of the first-grade missionary kids from Gertie; Mrs. Green will take back the women's work from her; Helen Hendry will take the missionary children's Sunday School from her.

You also inquired about the African Conference at Christmas, but we were in Shabunda with Gertie at the time and missed the entire conference. Ernie Green said there were well over 1,000 Africans in the church on Saturday night and again on Sunday morning at the close of the conference. I was scheduled to speak at the Saturday night meeting and conduct the communion service on Sunday morning, but Brother Leonard Parcel stepped into my place due to the emergency. Of course, Ernie Green really had the great load of the preaching and organization on his capable shoulders.

The Greens will be flying from Bukavu on May 25 to be in Leopoldville the 26th, and in New York the evening of the 27th. Their fares amount to approximately $675 per adult, which is very little more than going by boat, and probably no more by the time you consider all the extra expenses of the boat trip.

Word has reached us that the Vander Ploegs sailed from America on January 11, and that their four oldest children will fly from Belgium, arriving in Bukavu on January 25. That will be the same day we are scheduled to arrive at Tunda with Gertie. Just think, the Greens will fly from Bukavu to

New York in the same time it will take me to drive Gertie to Tunda, which is only about 500 miles from here!

We have been remembering the Darrel Handel meetings in prayer, trusting the Lord for some real decisions for Christ. How well we remember the blessings received from the "Christ For You" meetings about three and one-half years ago. Today you are drawing near the close of another series of meetings, and we know the Lord has been very precious.

Must close now. Enclosed is our prayer letter. The Lord bless you both, and all the dear ones at Edgemont. We remember you daily at our devotions.

Pray on.

Les

BEREAN MISSION, INC.	AFRICA	B.A.M.S. — Katanti
3536 Russell Blvd.		Shabunda par Kindu
St. Louis, Missouri	The Dark Continent!	Congo Belge, Afrique

Prayer Letter   * * * * *   February 1956

Dear Faithful Ones in the Homeland:

Many were the lovely Christmas Cards, letters and gifts that you sent to us in Congoland, gentle reminders of your love and faithfulness to your missionaries who are so far away. We have been unable to acknowledge most of them because of the serious illness of Gertie. May we use the medium of this prayer letter to thank you one and all in our Savior's dear name.

We have been in Congo for only one and one-half years, but it seems that Gertie was endeavoring to carry too heavy a load of work with the result that her strength was undermined and she became quite "run-down." She caught a cold which worsened until she finally had to go to bed for three days. Then she tried to work again for a few days, but had to return to bed again. This went on for two or three weeks, trying to work but having to give up and go to bed each time.

Finally, on Wednesday morning, December 14, following a siege of coughing, her breathing suddenly became extremely shallow and difficult. She could feel herself "blacking out" and her arms and legs becoming numb. Gertie was alone in the house, and it was only the grace of God that brought our nurse, Mrs. Green, to the house at that particular moment to see how she was feeling that day. Mrs. Green quickly called for Mrs. Parcel, another nurse, and they gave Gertrude shots to stimulate the heart and the breathing and to relax her body. I returned home from a trip to distant villages about 6 o'clock that evening to find her extremely weak and breathing very shallow. The nurses had placed her under an improvised vapor tent to aid her breathing. Other of our missionaries had driven to the State Hospital at Shabunda, some 50 miles away, to bring the doctor, but he was unable to come.

Gertrude's condition remained about the same from Wednesday until Friday, when she again had a crisis and almost slipped away. Once again the various injections seemed to give just enough stimulant to keep her breathing. Then on Sunday, she had her third crisis. While we were working with her to keep her breathing Rev. George Kennedy again drove into Shabunda, and this time the doctor returned with him. Mr. Kennedy drove so fast over these hazardous roads that he blew a tire. The doctor examined Gertie the best he was able with the limited equipment available and said that he felt reasonably certain it was pneumonia. He told us that as yet there were no facilities at the State Hospital in Shabunda to accommodate white patients, but that he needed Gertie there for further tests and x-rays. We told the doctor that we could stay at the Mission which is situated at Shabunda, but he felt the risk was too great to move her there. The doctor left medicines with Mrs. Green and asked to be kept advised as to Gertie's progress.

Two days later she again suffered a crisis, more severe than before. The medicines seemed ineffective. How helpless we all felt as we watched her desperate struggle for breath. I silently bowed my will to my Lord, leaving all things in the hands of Him who is able. He gave me grace to say, "Thy will be done." The hardest job was to tell Jeanette and Marian that their mother might not live, that perhaps the Lord might take her home. They took it like good soldiers of Jesus Christ. Everyone was praying, missionaries and Africans together. Gertrude told me later that she knew she was dying. But just as all sensibility was fading away and she was entering the "valley of the shadow of death," she had the realization that the Lord was turning her around and sending her back to those of us who love her so much. She ceased to labor for breath, and instead, her breathing became almost imperceptible. She lay that way for several hours, unable to talk and at first even unable to lift her eyelids, yet fully conscious.

After much prayer we felt God would have us attempt the trip to Shabunda in an effort to obtain further medical attention. Oh, dear Lord, hasten the day when our own mission doctor, Dr. Harry Zemmer, will arrive on the field, and supply him with the equipment he needs! We fixed a comfortable bed in the rear of our Plymouth Suburban, and Gertie made the hazardous trip with no ill effects. Praise God! As we were leaving, the road through our mission compound was lined on either side with our faithful Africans, many of them with tears streaming unashamedly down their black faces. All of them with a prayer in their hearts for "Mama."

You should have seen the procession to Shabunda. George Kennedy went ahead in his truck to clear the way. Our roads are really just one car wide and we didn't want any sudden stops. Our Suburban was second in the procession. Mrs. Green rode with me to keep an eagle eye on Gertie. She had her hypodermic needles sterilized and ready for any stimulants that might be needed. In the car behind us was Miss Lydia Frank, our nurse from Ikozi Station, who was coming to share the nursing responsibilities with Mrs. Green. Three cars in a row is really a traffic jam in the Congo.

When the doctor re-examined Gertrude in Shabunda, he shook his head. He gave us very little hope. Gertie just laughed when I told her. "Because," she said, "God has returned me to you. I'll be all right." The doctor took x-rays the next day. He said her lungs were not too bad. He could not tell us what had caused the four severe crises which, if God had not intervened, would have claimed her life. We still do not know. The State doctor dismissed the case and sent us back to Katanti, December 31. He gave us no further advice or medicine. Gertie is not progressing at all. She has very little strength. The least exertion, and she is exhausted. Our splendid nurses who have cared for Gertie so lovingly feel that she must have further attention. By radio, Mr. Green contacted the Methodist Mission some 500 miles southwest of us. They have a very fine American doctor, who has kindly consented to give Gertie a thorough physical. On January 23 we will begin the long and difficult journey to the doctor. We will again convert our Plymouth into a bed on wheels, and Gertie will be able to rest as we travel.

Our Lord has been so precious to us during these weeks of distress and pain. Our times are in His hands for whatever the future may hold. "Our future is as bright as the promises of God." Let us join hands in prayer before the Throne of Grace.

Yours in His Never-failing Grace,

Les, Gertie, Jeanette, and Marian

February 11, 1956

Dearest Family:

We're still at Minga and so homesick for Jeanette and Marian. Don't know yet when we'll be able to go home, but we're going to ask the doctor this evening so I won't seal the letter until after we talk with him. Just think, it's been three weeks since we left Katanti. I'm beginning to really gain in strength, although I'm afraid I overtaxed myself today, and now I'm quite weary. But a good rest will fix me up. I surely do get bored having to rest all of the time. Soon I'll be as yellow as can be, for I am taking an Atabrine cure now for malaria.

This is the second cure. The first was with a drug called Aralen. Then I took Quinine, now Atabrine. All that ought to do something, shouldn't it?

The after effects of the operation have been quite painful. The cyst was quite large, the size of a marble so it has left a large cavity. The doctor is afraid that as the cavity heals it will have a tendency to close the channel. So every other day I have to take a treatment to keep it open. We can't go home until the wound has healed.

We wonder now if I'll really be able to stave off further attacks of malaria. It is a treacherous enemy. Les feels very strongly that if I don't strengthen completely, or if I have more attacks, he will ask that we be recalled home. An ailing missionary is of no use to the Lord and actually a hindrance to the work. When we first arrived, the doctor asked if it would be possible to return to the States. Les said only if urgently recommended by him as the only course to follow. The nurse here told us that if we were missionaries under their board, we would immediately be sent home as soon as I had the strength to travel.

One of the missionary families has a little boy who suffers repeated attacks of malaria, not just ordinary ones but with convulsions. If the boy doesn't pull out of it, they will be permanently sent home. So we can't help but wonder what the Lord has in store for us. I tremble now when I realize what a risk we took with Marian when she was so sick. The Lord was so good to raise her up.

That all sounds kind of gloomy but actually we don't feel gloomy about it. We are in the Lord's hands and know that anything He brings to pass will be right and good. Isn't it wonderful to trust Him!

Les and I are so hungry for news. The last letter we received was the one from Frances telling of Dad's death (January 9, 1956). It seems years since we have heard from you. I think I'll stop now and rest a bit. Will write more after we've talked to the doctor.

Sunday we asked the doctor about going home but he wasn't the least bit encouraging. He says that he isn't completely satisfied with the way it had been healing. Don't know exactly what he means by that.

I'm feeling a bit perkier than I did yesterday. Not quite so down in the dumps. Don't fret over my health and the remote possibility that I might not strengthen. Les and I both have felt the assuring presence of the Lord all through this trying time. All I want to do right now is get back to Jeanette and Marian as soon as possible. The Lord can arrange the future. We leave it entirely up to Him.

The people here continue to be gracious, especially two nearing 60-year-old spinsters who have really brightened our otherwise dreary days. They even feed us Cokes. Think of that! We seemed to immediately be friends at first meeting.

Lots of love to you all,
Gertie

BEREAN MISSION, INC.	AFRICA	B.A.M.S. — Katanti
3536 Russell Blvd.		Shabunda par Kindu
St. Louis, Missouri	The Dark Continent!	Congo Belge, Afrique

Prayer Letter * * * * * March 1956

"And it shall come to pass, that before they call, I will answer; and while they are yet speaking, I will hear" (Isaiah 65:24).

Dear Loved Ones:

How often this precious verse from God's Word has been literally fulfilled in our lives during this trying time of illness. Our Lord has surely gone before us, straightening the crooked places and making the rough places smooth. We left Katanti on Tuesday, January 24, headed for the Methodist Mission Station at Minga, some 500 miles distance, where I could be examined by an American doctor. Les had arranged a full-length bed for me in our Plymouth Suburban where I could lay in comfort during the long trip because I was too weak and sick to possibly make the journey sitting up. It really wrenched our hearts to kiss Jeanette and Marian goodbye, to see the tears well up in their eyes though they were striving gallantly to smile.

Les was supplied with a hypodermic needle and two medicines which had proved effective in enabling me to keep on breathing when these attacks would occur. Our nurse had given him minute instructions on how to use them, but he eyed them with much apprehension. I teased him saying that I simply refused to have an attack on the way because I did not want an amateur to "stick" me. The Lord heard us while we were yet speaking, and I suffered no further attack until we had reached the first Methodist station at Tunda. Here Dr. Hughlett met us in order that he might make a preliminary examination a day sooner than waiting until we arrived at Minga.

After examining me, Dr. Hughlett felt it advisable to have a consultation with another of their mission doctors at their Wembo Nyama station. Dr. Sopy gave me an exhaustive examination of heart, respiratory system, and every kind of blood test. His diagnosis was "chronic malaria," which had attacked the respiratory system, together with heart fatigue and anemia. Dr. Sopy told us that during his years of experience in the Congo, he had seen only four cases of this type of malaria: mine, his own, and two others, and all were very critical. He felt that a stiff malarial cure and a protracted rest would arrest the malaria but that I would have to be extremely cautious to prevent a recurrence.

We then went to Minga where Dr. Hughlett resumed the case. These people are all Southerners, and they received us with gracious Southern hospitality, which made us feel immediately welcome and among friends. Dr. Hughlett began the malarial cure, and I began to improve and gain some strength. After reviewing my past medical history, the doctor felt that a complete physical would be advisable as I had not been examined since leaving the United States. Upon completion of the physical he informed Les and me that an operation should be performed at once. Delay could precipitate a serious, even dangerous condition. We were dumbfounded. There had been no indication that anything was wrong. We praised God for leading us in this way. Two or three more months and the condition probably would have become critical. *"Before they call, I will answer."*

It has been three weeks since the operation. Strength has returned so discouragingly slow. The malaria still plagues me. Besides that, I'm so homesick for Jeanette and Marian, and when we ask the doctor about going home, his reply is, "Still too early to tell." The missionaries here are doing their best to help us pass the time. The nurse, Miss O'Toole, comes by for Les and me to take us to the leper colony. She has complete charge of all the work there. It was the first leper colony founded in this part of the Congo and is the second largest in the whole Congo with almost 300 patients. The people are so pathetic in their painful deformities. Their love and devotion to Miss O'Toole, who has spent 26 years in their midst, is really an inspiration. It is truly the love of Christ being shown forth to these needy people through the tender compassion of this servant of God.

As strength allows, we want to visit the school and also the Girls' Home in which I'm vitally interested. I think I'm busy with my 30 girls, but they have more than 100 girls here, so we have much to look forward to. It has really been a rewarding experience to see this work of God which was founded about fifty years ago. They have beautiful brick buildings and so much wonderful equipment that we so lack on our stations, but Berean Mission is a young mission. God is blessing. He will expand and supply His work in His own time. We must be faithful to labor and pray for the advancement of the Gospel in our area of Congo.

Dear friends, it has been good to have this chat with you. Les and I know you will be praying for us, even as we remember you in our prayers. It has been three months since I became ill, and we do not know how long it will take for me to recover my strength and be able to work again for my Lord. Isn't it wonderful just to leave it all in His loving hands? *Thou wilt keep him in perfect peace, whose mind is stayed on Thee, because he trusteth in Thee*" (Isaiah 26:3-4).

In His strength and love,

Gertrude and Les Spainhower

March 6, 1956

Dear Praying Friends:

We wish to take this opportunity to thank you for your prayer ministry and gifts to our dear missionaries, and especially in behalf of Mrs. Spainhower. Word has reached her loved ones here in East St. Louis that they have arrived back at their mission station in Katanti safely. We do thank the Lord for that and covet your continued prayers for Mrs. Spainhower, and the family, and for each dear missionary at this time. *"Call upon Me in the day of trouble, I will answer thee, and thou shalt glorify Me."*

Sincerely in Christ,

Rev. G. Joseph Wright
Pastor, Edgemont Bible Church

EDGEMONT BIBLE CHURCH
WORLD-WIDE MISSIONS COUNCIL
Box 806, Edgemont Station, East St. Louis, Illinois

"Call unto Me, and I will answer thee, and show thee great and mighty things, which thou knowest not" (Jeremiah 33:3).

March 16, 1956

Dear Christian Friends:

We have just received the following cablegram relative to our dear missionary family, the Rev. and Mrs. Les Spainhower and girls of Belgian Congo, Africa.

"IMPERATIVE GERTRUDE RETURN AMERICA IMMEDIATELY - MEDICAL AND EXECUTIVE COMMITTEE URGE EMERGENCY FURLOUGH - AIRMAIL THREE THOUSAND DOLLARS - SPAINHOWER - KATANTI - Signed - Carl Blackburn, Chairman of Field Council."

Your interest in the movements of the Spainhower family throughout their missionary experiences has been a source of great encouragement to them and to us. We thought that you would want to know the latest happenings so that you could pray with us for their safety, as they come by plane from the Congo to St. Louis, within the next few days. The three thousand dollars has been cabled to them from their accounts, by the Berean Mission Office in St. Louis, Missouri.

Mrs. Spainhower, evidently, is not recovering sufficiently from the recent bout with malaria and then the surgery which she had to experience. The Field Council of the Mission has been close to the situation and after much prayer has no doubt decided that it would be best for Gertrude to be taken back to America for treatment and rest. As "good soldiers of Jesus Christ," the dear Spainhowers are accepting this emergency as a part of their missionary experience, and believe that Romans 8:28 is God's word for them at this time. We as their supporters and prayer helpers are called upon at this time to stand by in faithfulness to these dear servants of the Lord Jesus Christ. We need to keep up their monthly support as well as designate any special gifts to meet this emergency.

The Christian and Christian missions are subject to the exigencies of this world. But our God doeth all things well and we are confident that Satan will not gain the victory in these circumstances of life. I urge you to bear these dear servants of Christ to the Lord in prayer continually. We will keep you informed of further developments.

Sincerely in Christ,

Rev. G. Joseph Wright
Pastor, Edgemont Bible Church

Katanti
March 25, 1956

Dear Brother and Sister Wright and all,

"My soul, wait thou only upon God; for my expectation is from Him. He only is my Rock and my Salvation: He is my Defense; I shall not be moved."

While resting from labors this Lord's Day will endeavor to write you a much belated letter. Because of the length of time it takes to get mail through, we are receiving letters from various ones expressing their thankfulness to know that we are back at Katanti and that Gertrude is better. Actually Gertrude is at Ikozi where Miss Lydia Frank can give her the many injections she must have, and where she is closer to the mine doctor—some 40 miles from there. The children and I are at Katanti unpacking cases, which have never been opened because we had no place to put anything, sorting, and repackaging some things to ship home. Other things will be sold or given to the missionaries here. It is difficult to see the hand of the Lord in all of this, but *"we know that all things work together for good to them that love God, to them who are the called according to His purpose."* Whatever His purpose it will be for our good, and to the glory of His blessed name!

Gertrude wrote Mother Wilson last week, and I added a hasty postscript while in Bukavu when making arrangements to come home as quickly as possible. You undoubtedly know of my cabled request for three thousand dollars to bring us home. Needless to say, we do not have this amount to our credit at the mission, but if we may include our housing fund as return passage, then we would have nearly enough to meet this amount.

We have *tentative* reservations by plane leaving Bukavu Saturday, April 14 at 7:00 A.M. and arriving Leopoldville at 5:15 P.M. same day. Leaving Leopoldville at 12:00 noon Sunday the 15th, and arriving New York City 8:55 P.M. Monday the 16th. Leave New York City at 1:30 P.M. Tuesday the 17th, and arrive Lambert Field, St. Louis at 4:35 P.M. same day via TWA. We are waiting now for confirmation of these reservations and word from the bank in Bukavu that the money was received by cable. Of course, by radio and cable the word passes more quickly between Bukavu and St. Louis (some 10,000 miles) than it does from Bukavu to Katanti (225 miles). We receive word once a week via dilapidated truck (barring any breakdowns or accidents or landslides, etc.) So, we are still waiting to hear.

Wednesday, March 18—The courier truck passed by today and brought word from the Bank in Bukavu that the emergency funds have arrived and have been credited to my account. But there was no word from the plane reservations, so I still won't be able to confirm the dates until next week when the courier will come again - maybe! If we don't hear then, we'll get home before the letter. Word from Ikozi is that Gertie is just holding her own—not much sign of improvement. Pray much for her. This has been a long struggle.

Love in Christ,

Les

Jeanette's Comment: Getting Ready to Leave

While Mom was being tended over at Ikozi, Dad was left with deciding what to do with everything we had shipped to Africa—but hadn't really used yet. As he noted in the March 1956 letter to Pastor and Mrs. Wright, he did ship some things home—but foodstuffs and many other things he wanted to disperse among the missionaries.

Even Marian and I had choices to make. I was 14—and too old for any of the toys I had, including my beautiful Ruthie doll. One of the other missionary girls was delighted to get her. But my books! Grandma Wilson had kept me well supplied—and it was quite traumatic to have to leave them behind. We donated them, of course, to the missionary children's school—and they became the basis of good lending library. My only consolation was that my accordion and music would go home with me.

Marian had the hardest time because she had to leave all of her toys, too, but she was still young enough to want to play. One of the missionary girls got her Eileen doll and all its clothes. But she finally donated her Susie doll to the fence girls. Now, Susie was a rubber "Betsy-Wetsy" doll—you gave her water in a little bottle, and let's say politely, it came out the opposite end, just like a real baby. Even Susie had a big box of clothes that Grandma Wilson had made for her. Well, Susie survived for another year, well loved by the younger fence girls. They were all entranced by the "wetsy" apparatus, but they lovingly took care of her, bathing her often—until all the paint was scrubbed off her features and, finally, the rubber disintegrated in the hot tropical air.

One day, Dad decided to hold an "Open House" for the missionaries on Katanti Station to come and choose what they wanted from our household goods. One of the newer missionaries, Barbara Pearson, arrived with a big, black baby buggy that she, somehow, managed to get into our living room where everything was set up. She said it reminded her of shopping at the supermarkets back in the States—a phenomenon that we had not yet experienced.

In some respects, it was probably a good idea that Mom wasn't there to watch our home denuded. She was slowly gaining a little strength on Ikozi with Aunt Lydia Frank, a nurse, watching over her. But our family was being torn up by the roots—and we didn't know what would happen next.

Jeanette's Comment: Homeward Bound

All arrangements were finally made—the couple of crates going back to the States were shipped, airline tickets purchased, even the Green Hornet sold. Uncle Carl Blackburn would drive us into Bukavu and bring the car back. Dad generously paid the houseboys for the final time, plus giving each of them a shirt and a tie. The missionaries, the African elders, and our houseboys gathered in the circle to bid us farewell and to pray for our safety.

And then as we drove down the long Katanti hill, the Africans lined the road, tears streaming down their faces. Even though I was really looking forward to going home, it was a very emotional moment. All along the road to Ikozi, the Africans ran to the road to wave to us. The drums had told our story: Tata Wemaninua and his family were going back to America because Mane Utamusonga was too ill to stay in Africa.

But Mom was waiting for us at Ikozi. She still had to spend a lot of time resting in bed, but she looked wonderful to us. Unfortunately, that night both Marian and I came down with malaria, only adding to Aunt Lydia Frank's patient list—and Dad's anxiety about getting us all out of Africa and back to the States.

But we made it! On Saturday, April 14, Uncle Carl Blackburn dropped us off at the tiny airport in Bukavu. Marian and I were both weak and wobbly from the malaria, and Dad had to carry Mom up the steps of the little gully hopper we were going to take out of Bukavu to Usumbura. It was a short flight, and then we waited in the airport for a couple of hours before boarding a larger plane that would take us to Brussels, Belgium.

We did not keep any kind of record of our homeward flight—all of us were too exhausted and weak to care. I know we flew from Usumbura to Athens, Greece, arriving in the middle of the night. Usually, everyone would have to disembark while a plane was being serviced and fueled, but because of Mom's condition, they let our family stay on board.

From Athens, we flew non-stop to Brussels. I remember looking out the window to see the Alps below us. Otherwise, I don't remember much of the trip. I think we slept a lot.

We had a number of hours to wait in Brussels before boarding the plane to take us to New York. Sabena surprised us at the airport and said they were putting us up in a hotel in Brussels so that Mom would be more comfortable. It was a ritzy place—lots of gold and chandeliers in the lobby. I remember the huge, fluffy bathrobes that all of us wrapped up in after good, hot baths. Then we slept like babies for several hours.

From Brussels, we flew to England, where we landed in the middle of the night—and again our family was allowed to stay on board during refueling. The crews on our Sabena flights were very helpful and made all of as comfortable as possible. That makes me wonder how awful we must have looked—Mom so weak Dad had to carry her, Marian and I with yellowed skin from our last Atabrine treatment for malaria, and Dad, I'm sure, must have looked totally exhausted.

Finally, we landed in New York City—America, at last! And Marian will tell you what happened in New York.

Marian's Comment

"We're going home!" I can honestly say when Dad told Jeanette and me that we needed to take Mom back to the United States so she could be treated by the doctors there, I wasn't filled with conflicting emotions at all. In my heart, I was so excited because I knew we would soon be with Grandma and the rest of our family, and we would be with people we loved at Edgemont Bible Church. In my young mind, I had no way of understanding what it must have meant to Dad and Mom to leave Africa and the work they had struggled for so long to become a part of. Their love for the Africans of our Balega tribe was deep within their hearts, and they wept as we left. Myself? I couldn't wait to get to Grandma Wilson's house again. I knew Grandpa would no longer be there but that wasn't uppermost in my mind. I just wanted to go home!

We were all worried about Mom and how she would be able to make the trip back to the States. She was terribly weak and Dad even had to carry her up the steps to board the plane at first. But I can remember how completely excited I was about going home again. I don't remember much about the trip back home except that we flew Sabena World Airlines (no longer in existence), and they were wonderful. They made Mom as comfortable as possible. They also gave me a special kid's lunch box which had all kinds of specially wrapped foods and a box with compartments that I'm sure was designed to help keep a child entertained for a while and encourage the child to eat. However, I thought the box was so very special that I didn't want to open everything. I wanted to save it and show Grandma.

However, when we arrived in New York City and had to go through customs, things became very tense. Here we were, four poor missionaries straight from the jungles of Africa needing to come home because Mom was not well. But the customs officials had a "tip" that diamond smugglers were coming from Africa, and they were ready to catch them. Unbeknownst to us, they had already caught one smuggler and had him sitting on a bench close to customs as "bait" for the other smugglers. Naturally, that was the very bench my Dad carefully had Mom and Jeanette and me sit down on to wait while he tried to go through all the paperwork with the custom officials.

The man on the bench was grumbling and talking under his breath. Mom thought he had a problem and asked if she could help him. Well, police and custom officials pounced on us, sure that we were his accomplices! — one thin man, one sick woman, a young teenage girl, and a ten-year old girl — yeah, right!!!! I was holding my treasured Sabena lunch box, and it was immediately taken from me, over my protests, to be searched. Our suitcases were opened, and Dad was questioned and questioned again. Finally, when they realized we were probably who we said we were, they returned my Sabena lunch box to me — and I burst into tears. They had torn open every single thing and demolished what was inside looking for diamonds! My sandwich was torn apart and squashed. The cookies were broken up into many crumbly pieces. Dad, Mom, and Jeanette knew the gravity of the situation, so they were very relieved that it was all over, and we could pass through customs. However, I was heartbroken that my cherished lunch box was in ruins. I wept as I threw it into the trash can with some of the custom officials looking a little guilty — at least I hoped so!!

Getting off the plane in St. Louis, Missouri into the loving arms of Grandma and the rest of our family was emotional and sweet. It had been three years since we had said goodbye to our family, and the reunion was wonderful. Grandma must have been so relieved to finally see Mom after fearing she would not live to return home again.

We lived in Grandma's basement for a while. Mom received medical attention at Barnes Hospital. Eventually, Dad resigned from Berean Mission, feeling certain that our missionary days were over, due to Mom's declining health. He contacted his former employer and was able to return to work for them again after all these years.

God's hands were always on us — in California, France, and Africa. It was God's will for Dad and Mom to be missionaries, but the Lord had His reasons for bringing us back home again sooner than expected. They were in God's hands, and their faith was strong enough to not question God but to follow his leading.

Jeanette's Comment Continued

I'm not sure what airline we took from New York to St. Louis. It didn't matter — every minute in the air brought us closer to home. On Tuesday, April 17, the plane touched down at the St. Louis airport. Aunt Minnie, Grandma Wilson, and Aunt Frances, as well as Pastor and Mrs. Wright, were waiting to welcome us home. But Grandpa Wilson wasn't there. That made our homecoming bittersweet.

A lot had changed since we had left East St. Louis nearly three years earlier, including the advent of supermarkets! We could see the many changes as Grandma drove us down State Street to her house on 86th Street.

A lovely spring awaited us — but we four missionaries from the tropics nearly froze while everyone in the St. Louis area was enjoying the "warm" 60-degree weather.

When we started opening suitcases at Grandma Wilson's house, everyone started coughing. All the dampness, humidity, mold — whatever made the "tropical" smell — pervaded her house. All of our clothes were immediately tossed into the washing machine. Our suitcases, the accordion case —

and the accordion, bellows extended—were set out in the sun for several days. We finally had to replace our shoes and our Bibles because, even though they went outside into the sun, too, we just couldn't get that smell out of them. Leather did not fare well in the tropics—but we never noticed the smell out there.

Mom was thoroughly checked out at Barnes Hospital where it was confirmed that she'd had respiratory malaria—and there was no way she could have recovered from that while remaining in the tropics.

Marian and I didn't go back to school until the fall. There were only a few weeks left, and it just wasn't worth our entering school and facing new curricula for only four or five weeks. And we needed to regain strength as well.

And so we settled down to start a new life in the United States.

BEREAN MISSION, INC.	A F R I C A	563 North 86th Street
3536 Russell Blvd.		East St. Louis
St. Louis, Missouri	The Dark Continent!	Illinois

Prayer Letter	* * * * *	April 1956

"The Lord shall preserve thy going out and thy coming in from this time forth, and even for evermore" (Psalm 121:8).

Dear Prayer Partners:

This time we send our love and greetings to you from East St. Louis, Illinois, U.S.A. We are far from Katanti Station, Belgian Congo, where we have labored in His service for these past many months. Marvelous has been the loving watchcare of our blessed Lord during the long journey home. He went before making the rough places smooth.

Gertrude was so weak that we wondered how she would ever make the trip, but moment by moment God sustained her and gave her strength. When we started our journey, I had to carry Gertrude up the steps into the plane, much to her embarrassment. But God continued to strengthen her until she was able to slowly make it up the steps at other stops along the way, with just a little "pushing and shoving" on my part.

We thank you for your prayers, dear ones, for we know that we came home on wings of prayer just as surely as we were borne upon the wings of the airplane. We were fully conscious all the way that "underneath were the everlasting arms." We left Bukavu, in the heart of Africa, Saturday morning, April 14, and landed in St. Louis, Missouri, Tuesday afternoon, April 17. In just four days we had crossed three continents, a sea, and an ocean.

Our hearts were filled with conflicting emotions as we left Congo. There was deep sorrow as we left our work and loved ones both among the missionaries and our dear Balega people; joy and anticipation as we winged our way homeward; and, finally, peace in our hearts that this was God's will for us. We are not asking "why," because it is not our part to question the wisdom of God, our Heavenly Father. We do not know what the Lord has in store for us in the future, but we do know that He doeth all things well. Whatever His purpose in all of this we are sure that it will bring glory to His Name, and will be for our good.

At the present writing, Gertrude is spending her time in bed. Since arriving in a different climate she has contracted a severe cold which has again weakened her somewhat. The Lord willing, she will enter Barnes Hospital Clinic, St. Louis, Missouri, on Monday, April 23 for a complete checkup. We covet your prayers in her behalf that soon she might be returned to health and strength again.

Naturally, this is a period of great adjustment for us all, but *"The Name of the Lord is a strong tower: the righteous runneth into it, and is safe"* (Proverbs 18:10). Words fail us as we seek to express our heartfelt appreciation to you dear friends who have travailed in prayer for us; who have so unselfishly given of your means for our needs. Only eternity will reveal the depths of your faithfulness.

                        Sincerely in Christ,

                        Les, Gertie, Jeanette, and Marian
                        The Spainhowers

Part Six

Starting Again
1956-1958

"Casting all your care upon him; for he careth for you."
1 Peter 5:7

When Jeanette and I decided to compile these letters from our missionary days into a book, we asked Dad to write a brief account of what happened once we came back to the States and how we became missionaries again. The following is what he had to say on the subject.

BETWEEN TERMS

July 16, 2010

Today, at age 93, I again take pen in hand (actually it's a Dell computer) and will endeavor to search back through the foggy recesses of my imperfect memory in an effort to recall the events in our family's lives between our first term in the Congo and the second term, and to explain why we felt led to return to Congo.

We arrived home from Congo on April 17, 1956, and took up residence with Gertrude's mother in East St. Louis, Illinois. Gertrude spent a great deal of her time in bed-rest to gain back a little strength. Then, six days later, on April 23, 1956, she reported to Barnes Hospital Clinic, St. Louis, MO, for a complete physical checkup. This was followed by several months of rest and recuperation. During that time, I followed the admonition of the Scriptures and returned to my former livelihood as a design draftsman/engineer because 2 Thess. 3:10 tells us that *"if any will not work, neither shall he eat,"* — and I had a family of four to feed.

Gertrude and I felt that we would no longer be able to return to tropical Congo, and so we resigned from Berean Mission, notified all of our supporters that we would no longer be receiving their contributions and encouraged them to continue to support missions as God led them. We mortgaged my income for the rest of our lives and purchased a home in East St. Louis, Illinois, in Loisel Village. We moved in, settled down, and began serving the Lord in Edgemont Bible Church, our home church.

When we arrived home from Congo, Jeanette was 15, and Marian was 11 years old. That fall, we enrolled Jeanette in the ninth grade at Clark Junior High School in East St. Louis, and Marian in the fifth grade at Edgemont Grade School without any difficulty. Their transcripts from the mission school in Africa were accepted.

As time passed by, we settled down comfortably in our new home—a home with smooth plastered walls and ceilings instead of mud walls with spiders running all over them and leaky leaf roofs, a home with windows you could open and close instead of just framed openings in the walls with screens over them. We were so comfortable that I felt ashamed about living in such luxury while our Balega people were living in mud houses.

Also, we received a few letters from time to time from some of our dear Africans asking when we were coming back—they missed us! They also mentioned that they needed clothing, food, etc. One of our houseboys wrote saying how badly he needed "bisalapata" (shoes)! All of this was very hard to take. Gertrude and I felt that the Lord was sort of nudging us to return to Congo. By this time Gertrude's health and strength was much improved, and it became more and more difficult to resist this appealing prospect.

After much prayer, we decided to seek the counsel of our pastor, Rev. G. Joseph Wright of the Edgemont Bible Church, who was also a member of the Home Board of Berean Mission, Inc.

He had concerns about Gertrude's health, in the light of past experience, and thought it wise to take this matter to the Home Board of the Mission for further consideration. After much discussion, the Mission Board decided that Gertrude should have another thorough physical checkup and bring the doctor's report to the Board for a final decision. The doctor's report was affirmative, the Mission again accepted us as candidates for a second term, and our missionary life was resumed!

The Lord enabled us to sell our home with only a small financial loss, but we again faced the tremendous task of raising support, money for equipment, transportation, etc. And so the following chapters will take you on the long trail back to the Belgian Congo, Africa, which began September 14, 1957, as we headed for California on deputation—one year and five months after returning home because of Gertrude's illness.

Marian's Comment: Regular People

It wasn't difficult at all for me to feel perfectly comfortable back in the United States again. After being gone for three years, it was absolutely wonderful to be with Grandma Wilson again as well as the rest of our family. We were almost treated like "celebrities" at Edgemont Bible Church with people hugging us and asking us all kinds of questions about living in Africa. That was okay, but all I really wanted to do was to blend in with everyone and just be a part of them, as if we had never been gone. I can remember telling Mom that I wanted to be a "regular" person.

While we lived with Grandma Wilson in her basement, I was delighted to be able to play again with my "buddies." Bobby and Tommy Kohnen lived two houses down; Bonnie Touchett lived one block away; and Chuck Hill lived a couple of blocks from Grandma's. We had all been friends together since we were little. We spent many an hour riding our bikes around the neighborhood or walking to the corner market to buy candy or ice cream if we could talk our folks out of a few cents. There were no stores in the jungles of Africa so this was a real treat for me. The joys of being home again!

Mom and Grandma Wilson, 563 N. 86th St., East St. Louis, Il

We were quite happy when we moved into our own home on Bougainville Drive in Loisel Village in East St. Louis. It was a brand new home and seemed like a dream come true. It was a lovely red brick home with real shingles on the roof, instead of a mud house with a leaf roof. Jeanette and I shared a spacious room so the extra room could be a study for Dad and Mom. Dad had returned to his former job, Jeanette and I attended school, and as Mom's strength returned, she was again a busy wife and mother. We were "regular" people now.

What I didn't know was that the hearts of Dad and Mom were still in the Congo with the Balega people. So after a year had passed, they felt God was calling them to return to Africa. How did I feel? Well, at 12 years of age I understood what that would mean. Once again we would be leaving our family and friends. There was no question in my mind that I wanted to be wherever my parents and sister were because we were a close family. But I have to admit that I was very sad the day a "For Sale" sign was put in our front yard. I knew we were headed for another separation from loved ones but also for new "unknown" adventures. Again, we would no longer be "regular" people.

Jeanette's Comment: Ninth Grade in East St. Louis, Illinois

When we returned home, it seemed as if I were immediately caught up in a whirl of activity. It was the end of the school year, so there were all kinds of parties and church activities. Toward the end of May, one very pretty high school senior asked my parents if they would allow me to go with her and her boyfriend on a double date to the Youth for Christ banquet. They would provide the date—a boy that I'd known for a long time from Sunday School.

Now, Mom and Dad were kind of reluctant. Here I was fresh from the boonies—and just entering ninth grade in the fall. I wouldn't be sixteen until November, and they didn't want me dating until then.

But Carolyn persisted—it wouldn't be a real date, we wouldn't be alone at any time, we were going to a church/youth function, etc. So I ended up with a new lavender dress (an early birthday present from Grandma Wilson)—and had a wonderful time on my first [non]date.

Notice in the photo that I'm wearing glasses. One of the first things Grandma did when we came home was to take me to the eye doctor who said I was very near-sighted. I really only needed glasses when reading or for classwork, but it was such a relief to see well that, at first, I wore them all the time.

I became actively involved in the youth and music work at Edgemont Bible Church. I played the piano for services on occasion but also went to the St. Clair Detention Center and played for the song service there just before Sunday School. I sang in the choir and learned to sing alto. The church gave me a full-sized accordion shortly after we returned, and my smaller accordion went to Marian.

But the greatest excitement was when Dad returned to full-time employment—and bought a nice, brick house in Loisel Village! Marian and I still shared a room, but we actually had twin beds this time. But that simple house also became the scene of fun parties with the youth group—Halloween, Christmas, singspirations after church. Mom loved hosting our small teen group.

But as returned missionaries and Dad just starting his job, there really wasn't much money. Our house was furnished sparsely, but Marian and I dressed nicely, thanks to Grandma Wilson's talented fingers and sewing machine!

I started in ninth grade at Clark Junior High School in East St. Louis in the fall of 1956. It was kind of a frightening experience for me. I had to "travel" between classes—and I had my first real experience with the fact that anything mechanical hates me. I finally just carried all my books with me for the day because I never could get the combination lock on my locker to work! NEVER! I always had to ask for help. I had no trouble with book learning, however, and ended up inducted into the National Honor Society at graduation.

With everything going so well, I could easily have gotten swell-headed, but God had a very effective way of bringing me to my senses. That first winter was coming—but Dad and Mom couldn't afford a winter coat for me. Someone gave them one for me to wear. I still shudder when I think of that awful thing! It was kind of a rust-colored knit with a huge, gray, fluffy fur collar—a monstrosity!! I was humbled very quickly, believe me! I had no choice but to wear it for a couple of months because there was nothing else. Finally, my Grandma Spainhower got a new coat and gave her old one to me—it was just a plain dark forest green, but it seemed wonderful in comparison to the other one.

All the other ninth-grade girls wore nylons to school, but that, too, wasn't in the budget. I had nylons to wear to church and youth events, but not as an everyday part of my apparel. I lived a mile from the busline—and I walked to catch a bus every day that winter with bare legs because I refused to wear slacks under my clothes. That really wasn't cool! I was sure I would have been laughed out of school!

We had a pleasant Christmas that year. Dad had always thought that buying a Christmas tree every year was a waste of money, so he bought an artificial tree. Marian and I spent hours that December making ornaments out of Styrofoam balls covered in sequins and beads and other things. We really had a great time working together to decorate that tree.

By spring, that dreadful coat and the lack of nylons were forgotten with the news that we would be returning to the Congo—after spending another year in California on deputation work. It hurt to see the house and all the furniture sold, but there was an underlying current of excitement to see what would happen next.

The first thing that happened was the purchase of a bright red Chevy carryall that Dad named "Kasoga." That's the Kilega word for *good*. The Africans used a version of the French word *camion* for a truck, and they called a really good truck *kamio kasoga*. That's why Dad chose that name. In addition, he requested the carryall be the brightest red *(kisimana)* available because the Balega dearly loved anything red. The Africans would cheer whenever they saw that red carryall coming round the bend: "Kamio kasoga—kisimana-kisi-kisi-kisi!" They emphasized how good and how red it was.

After the house was sold, we moved into Grandma Wilson's basement again until we left for California.

3427 North Vineland
Baldwin Park, California
September 27, 1957

Dear Ones in Christ,

Greetings in the Saviour's Name from smoggy California. It is nice and sunny, too, but the sun must penetrate through a dense smog, particularly in the morning hours. We arrived here a week ago today (Friday) after a very nice trip. We took it slow and varied the speed between 30 and 50 mph until we arrived at Tucumcari, New Mexico, which is about 950 miles from East St. Louis. There we had the "break-in" oil drained and fresh oil put in. After that we were able to hold a more constant speed for the rest of the journey. We had absolutely no trouble with the Carryall. It brought us right along on the trip—pulling the trailer, too.

After due reflection upon the matter, we have decided to name our new Carryall "Kasoga." In Kilega, the language of our people, this means, "a good one," and truly it has proven to be a good one. We bought such a bright red truck because our Africans are so fond of bright red, and we feel sure they will agree with us that it is "Kasoga" ("a good one").

When we arrived in Baldwin Park last Friday afternoon, we found that Mr. and Mrs. Kellogg had their little garage-house all ready for us. They had just newly painted the interior and put up nice fresh, clean curtains. They are lovely Christian people and have made this little garage-house available for our use while we are here in California.

Kasoga in front of Kellogg's garage-house – our California home

We are so thankful for their kindness and just praise the Lord for so working in their hearts. So we are all settled comfortably and about our Father's business. And, of course, the work He has set immediately before us is that of deputation work, endeavoring as He leads, to raise the units of support needed to send us back to the Congo, as well as the necessary funds for passage and equipment.

Last Sunday, morning and evening, we attended the Calvary Baptist Church in Monrovia, and received a very warm welcome from these dear ones. They had about $40 a month of our support last term, and their interest is very keen. They all told us how very much they enjoyed our prayer letters, and how they looked forward to receiving the next one. Needless to say, this has all been very heartening and encouraging as we continue in our efforts to start all over again.

Calvary Baptist has a new Pastor, Dr. Wesley H. Goshorn. I understand he has just been with them for about three weeks. We attended a Men's Fellowship supper on Monday night, which occasion happened to be family night, so we had opportunity to renew many old acquaintances. Tuesday, we called on Rev. and Mrs. Claude Parkhill of the Pico Union Church, whom we also knew quite well. Brother Parkhill has given us the Sunday School General Assembly, as well as both the morning and evening services for Sunday, October 27, which is their Missionary Sunday. This will give us a wonderful opportunity of presenting our work to this congregation, and we thank the Lord for it. These people do not know us yet, as we have never before been in the Pico Church. We knew the Parkhills when they had the church in Puente. So this is really a new door which the Lord has opened wide before us.

Wednesday night we attended prayer meeting at the Cogswell Road Community Church and made the acquaintance of the Pastor and people there. Their Pastor and his wife were missionaries to Venezuela, South America, but had to return because both of them suffered broken health. He still does not look like he is in very good health. As I looked at him, I found encouragement in the fact that we were not the first nor the only missionaries who have had to return from the field because God permitted their bodies to be touched. How we praise the Lord that He has graciously restored Gertrude and that He is making ready to send us back to the Congo and to the people we have learned to love so much.

This afternoon we are going to La Puente to meet the new pastor there. We have been in that church before when Brother Parkhill was Pastor, so no doubt many will remember us. Also, the Myra Lou Missionary Circle of that church has already taken two of our units in response to our first prayer letter. There are many others yet to be contacted, but we will get around to them one at a time. And then, of course, we must constantly move around among the different ones if we are to know them and if they are to know us. Our experience has been that people support a missionary whom they know personally.

Have you heard anything more concerning Dr. Zemmer since the word of his serious illness and that he was in the hospital at Bukavu? We are praying for him and anxious to hear of his condition.

Give all at Edgemont our love. We are thinking of you and praying for you.

With Christian love,

Les and Gertie

P.S. Both Jeanette and Marian are enrolled in school and well into their classes at this writing. They were a week late in entering due to the delay in waiting for "Kasoga" to be delivered, but have caught up in this first week of school.

Jeanette's Comment: Tenth Grade in California

We made arrangements to go to the Kellogg's missionary house on our return to California. It was only slightly larger than the two-car garage-house we'd lived in before going to Africa the first time—but since it was rent-free, that helped with expenses while we were raising support and transportation costs for our return to the Congo. That missionary house was in almost constant use. I'm sure the Lord richly blessed the Kellogg family for their generosity to missionaries who needed a place to live while preparing to go to the field.

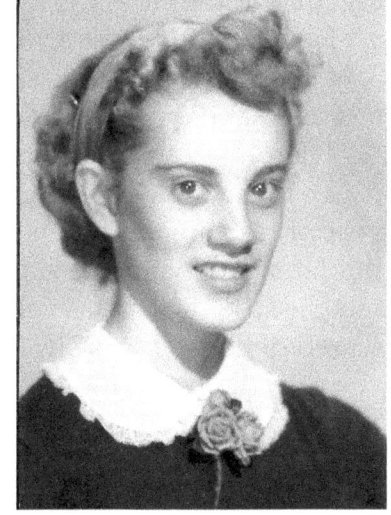

If I'd thought that Clark Junior High School was big, Baldwin Park High School was even larger! It was also wide open. The classrooms were enclosed, but the lockers and hallways were only roofed over. If we had wind and rain, we just got wet going between classes! Fortunately, that didn't happen too often in Southern California!

One of the classes I really enjoyed was French class. A distinguished-looking older Frenchman taught the class, and I was the only one who really paid attention. I knew we were heading back to the Congo, and I figured I'd better get to the place where I could understand some of what was being said. The teacher said I had a very good accent—although he couldn't figure out why since what little French I knew I had picked up in Marseille, of all places! But that one year of French really came in handy!

Dad had to pull all of his mathematics training from the deep recesses of his brain to help me through geometry. I'd had no problem in ninth grade getting through algebra, but the theorems and axioms and visualizing cubes were absolutely beyond me! It was the last math class I took until I had to take psychology statistics 25 years later when I finally got to college! I knew what my gifts were even back in 10th grade—and I knew quite firmly that math wasn't one of them!!

Gym was also very important in California—to everyone but me, of course! I hadn't had to go to gym class in East St. Louis because I ended up with severe eczema that infected and couldn't take the mandatory showers, etc., so they excused me and gave me an extra study period. The first semester at Baldwin Park High School, I had a calisthenics class. That's where I learned I had shortened tendons in the back of my legs—just like Dad's—and a lot of those exercises were almost impossible for me. The second semester was supposed to be volleyball. But by the time I had sprained my wrist a couple of times and hurt my fingers, my Dad got me out of volleyball. As he pointed out to the principal, playing the piano and accordion was much more important for me than playing volleyball. It could very well end up my life's vocation. Surprisingly, they listened to him. So back to the calisthenics.

Even though we lived in Baldwin Park, we attended Calvary Baptist Church in Monrovia again. I became quite involved again with the music program and in the youth group. Remember way back in the first section of this book that I spoke about a nice boy who had come to my aid when a mean boy had dumped a bunch of heavy books on my head on our first trip to California—and I then I had outspelled him in a spelling bee? Well, that nice boy grew up into a very nice teenager. On our first Sunday visit to Calvary Baptist Church, he came up to me with a big smile and asked, "Can you still spell *mosquito?*" We both laughed and immediately started talking. He definitely made my life very interesting for that year we were in California. It turns out that he also grew up with a magnificent baritone voice. I often played the piano for him when he sang, and he took me back and forth between Baldwin Park and Monrovia in an old 1948 Hudson for youth events. So it was with considerable regret that I left California after finishing tenth grade!

Marian's Comment: Vineland Elementary School

It didn't take us long at all to get settled in the Kellogg's garage house because it was small, and we didn't have very many things with us anyway! It reminded us a lot of living in our little garage house in East St. Louis before we went to Africa the first time. We basically had a small kitchen, bathroom, and an "L" shaped room with a table for eating, Mom and Dad's bed, and a bed for Jeanette and me with curtain separating our bed from theirs. Good thing we had a great family life together or the closeness would have done us in for sure!

Jeanette and I were a week late entering school. I was very blessed to have Vineland Elementary School right down the street from our home, so I could walk to and from school every day. I was in 6th Grade and quite fearful that absolutely no one would want to be my friend.

There were three classes of 6th graders, and I was put into Miss Nichols classroom.

To my eyes, Miss Nichols was ancient! As I discovered later in the school year, that was her last year of teaching and then she retired. She was a short, gray haired woman with a lot of wrinkles. But let me tell you, she was one tough lady. Even with three 6th grades, we had a lot of students in our classroom. She was very strict and didn't put up with any nonsense at all. I have to admit I was scared of her so I was always on my best behavior.

I did make friends that year with several girls in particular and a few of the boys. In fact, two of the boys, who were best friends, were named Johnny and Lonny. Johnny was short and Lonny was tall. They decided they liked me, so instead of fighting over me, they both decided to be my boyfriends at the same time! I'll never forget one day when they both showed up at our home to give me a box of peanut brittle—together. I think Mom, Dad and Jeanette were just about to crack up with laughter! When we left California, Johnny and Lonny vowed to wait for me until we returned from Africa. Needless to say, I never heard from them again. Sigh!!

Vineland had a "fair" in the spring. I was permitted to go to the fair with my friends, and we had a marvelous time playing the various games that had been set up. One of fun things I did was to toss a ping-pong ball to try to get it into a small jar that had a goldfish in it. I won! They put it in a plastic bag with water for me, and I happily started walking home. But I stopped quickly and began to worry that Dad and Mom wouldn't let me keep it. So I returned to the school to think about this. Then I finally realized I was just going to have to take it home and hope they didn't flush it down the toilet! To my surprise and relief, they were delighted we had a new "pet." We bought a small fish bowl, and every day you could see Dad leaning over the fish bowl talking to it! I think the fish actually became Dad's pet! We named it but I can't remember the name. It finally went to fish "heaven" before we left California, but we enjoyed it for a while.

BEREAN MISSION, INC.	A F R I C A	Deputation Address:
3536 Russell Blvd.		3427 North Vineland
St. Louis, Missouri	The Dark Continent!	Baldwin Park, California

Prayer Letter	October 1957	No. 3

"And when He putteth forth His own sheep, He goeth before them, and the sheep follow Him: for they know His voice" (John 10:4).

Dear Christian Prayer Helpers:

Thank you for remembering us in prayer as we have once again left family and friends behind and have stepped out in faith following Him whose voice we know. Once again we have heard our Lord Jesus Christ say, "Go ye." He has overcome our frailties and fears and bids us but to follow Him as He goes on before leading us one step at a time. How good it is simply to trust in Him.

In our last prayer letter we told you of the purchase of a new Chevrolet Suburban Carryall to be used in deputation work and to take with us to the Congo field. We received delivery of the Carryall on Friday, September 13, at about 5:30 P.M. On the way home with it, I picked up a rental trailer. By 10:00 o'clock that night we had the Carryall and the trailer loaded and ready to go. At 5:45 A.M. the next morning we eased out of Mother Wilson's driveway and started our trip to the Southern California area.

How we praise the Lord for our new, bright red, Carryall! We purposely specified the most brilliant red available, because our Africans are fascinated by "kisimana" (red). If something is a brilliant red, they call it, "kisimana kisi-kisi-kisi." We pondered just what name to give our new Carryall. At first we thought of calling it "Saul," because it stands head and shoulders above all the other cars (it's really a truck). But we finally decided to name it "Kasoga." Our Balega people call a truck a "kamio," which is an adaptation of the French "camion." And, they would speak of a good truck as a "kamio Kasoga." By contraction then, they would speak of a good one (meaning a good truck) as "Kasoga." We are sure that when they see our bright red Carryall, they will agree with us that it is truly "Kasoga" (a good one).

A dear Christian family in Baldwin Park, California, has written to us offering to put their little 3-room rental at our disposal, free of charge, while on deputation work in Southern California. How we praise the Lord for so leading these dear ones to meet our need. When we arrived at 3427 North Vineland, Baldwin Park, California, we found that Mr. and Mrs. Kellogg had newly painted the interior of the little house, had put up fresh, new curtains, and in every way had prepared a lovely place for us. We are grateful to them for their kindness to us. This is another evidence of the Lord's leading. *"And when He putteth forth His own sheep, He goeth before them."*

We have been given a very warm Christian welcome in several churches in this area where we are known. God has been graciously undertaking for us and many doors of opportunities for the glory of our Lord Jesus Christ, whose we are, and whom we serve. The Lord bless you all richly.

Yours in His Missionary Service,

Les, Gertie, Jeanette, and Marian
"The Spainhowers"

Marian's Comment: Deputation Meetings

It was necessary for us to go on deputation meetings to various churches as representatives of Berean Mission in St. Louis and to raise support for our time on the field. At those meetings our parents presented the work they did as missionaries during our first term and the work they would be doing upon our return. As people would hear the message, some would respond to the Holy Spirit's direction to help us with financial support. Sometimes the church as a whole would agree to give us a particular amount of money each month. But many times it was individuals who felt the burden to reach lost souls in Africa. We thank the Lord for each and every one who gave financially but also for those who prayed for us each step of the way.

People seemed to really enjoy our ministry to them because Dad and Mom put a lot of thought and planning into it. First, the Chevy Carryall had to be loaded with what we would need for our presentation. The following picture shows Dad holding the screen for showing slides.

On the tailgate of the Carryall is the projector for the slides, Dad's trumpet case, and a box or two full of African items to put on display as well as prayer cards to be handed out. The two cases waiting to be loaded into the truck were Jeanette and my accordions. One of our music stands is on top.

We would always arrive at the designated church early so we would have plenty of time to get everything set up. Dad and Mom would also meet with the Pastor prior to the service to verify how much of a program the pastor wanted. Our full program included several musical numbers, the slide presentation, and a brief message from Dad.

God had given Mom a beautiful soprano voice so she frequently sang "Down From His Glory" with Jeanette accompanying her on the piano. The chorus of the song began with a high note as she sang, "Oh, how I love Him, how I adore Him…." When she would get close to the chorus, I would always close my eyes and ask God to help her voice hit that note strong! Mom said she used to look at me for courage, knowing I was praying.

Dad played a melodious, sweet trumpet. He had a beautiful arrangement of "Overshadowed" while Jeanette did a fabulous job accompanying him on the piano. One line of the song says, "I'm overshadowed by His mighty love..." and that was how Dad felt in his great love for our Lord and Savior. It radiated from his playing to those listening. I never grew tired of hearing it.

Then Jeanette and I would play our accordions together. Sometimes we played "My Anchor Holds," and at other times we played "Stand Up For Jesus." I mostly played the songs as they were written but Jeanette had the ability to fill in and add special touches that made us quite a hit with those listening. (By the way, Edgemont Bible Church first gave Jeanette the accordion I am holding for our first term. Then they gave her the full-sized accordion when we started out on deputation meetings for the second term. But before we left for Congo, they gave me one just like Jeanette's. It sort of overpowered me for several years until I grew more!)

Jeanette would run the slide projector while Dad or Mom made comments about each one. The slides were such a wonderful tool for people to be able to visualize the jungle, see the work that the missionaries were doing, and to understand the need to reach the Balega people with the gospel.

Sometimes the pastor wanted Dad to tie everything together in a brief message. Dad never considered himself a pulpit-pounding preacher but he did such a good job of quietly giving God's message of *"Go ye into all the world and preach the gospel...."*

We also had jobs to do once the meetings were finished. While Dad and Mom greeted people and answered their questions, Jeanette would pack up the projector and slides and fold up the screen. I would put each of our instruments and music in their cases. With Jeanette being older, people liked talking with her, too. Frankly, I was terribly shy and really appreciated putting away our music and instruments and leaving the talking to others.

Quite frequently, we had a table set up with our African display. A lot of people would come by to ask questions or look through the items we had brought. The closed book in the front of the table was an African hymn book (words only) written in Kilega, the language of our Balega people. The opened book is the Kilega New Testament.

Dad had a great map of the world and had colored the Congo in red so it would stand out. Frequently, people wanted to know exactly where we would be in the Congo, so we could show them.

The most difficult time for me during these meetings was if we were at the church on a Sunday morning and had to attend Sunday School. Jeanette and I were always in different Sunday School groups, which meant I had to go alone.

Jeanette was always my security. I dreaded what I knew was coming. In general assembly, before they went to their individual classes, I was brought up front while the kids would stare at me. The leader would say, "We have a *real* missionary with us today! Tell us something about Africa!" I wanted to crawl in a hole as frequently I would hear kids snickering. One time I saw some of the kids making fun of me by calling me a "Jungle bunny"! Before I crawled in a hole, though, I would have gladly slugged them! I would usually mutter something about living in a mud house and a leaf roof and eating monkey meat. That usually provided a shock factor that shut them all up temporarily!

December 12, 1957

Dear Brother and Sister Wright,

Gertrude wrote to you at length earlier this week, so I will just write a short letter at this time transmitting our prayer letter for December, together with some more names for our mailing list. How we do thank the Lord for the interest evidenced in our prayer letter by so many. We trust that the Lord will use this as a means of keeping us in the thoughts and prayers of many.

We have sort of poured out our hearts in this latest prayer letter, but we have felt led of the Lord to do so. We trust that He will make it a blessing to many and that He may be pleased to use it as a means of challenging many to more determined prayer—perhaps to have a definite part in our support.

Several have sent us programs of Edgemont's 8th Annual World-wide Missions Conference, and it all looks so interesting. We were praying for you all and wishing that we could have been with you at that time. As mentioned in our prayer letter, we have had the privilege of participating in some missionary conferences, and what a blessing we have received from them. We have another conference scheduled for January.

We wish you both a blessed Christmas holiday. We will be thinking of you and praying for you. Pastor and Mrs. Goshorn of the Calvary Baptist Church in Monrovia have invited us to their home for Christmas Day.

                                        Lovingly in Christ,

                                        Les and Gertrude

Excerpt from a December 19, 1957 letter to Pastor Wright:

Have had only three meetings so far this month, but have certainly been caught up in a whirl of pre-holiday activities in the various churches. Just now people are thinking of Christmas and loved ones at home—not missions and needy ones on distant shores.

                                        All our love in Christ,

                                        Les and Gertrude

Jeanette's Comment: Wishing You a Merry Christmas!

When it came time for Christmas, we looked at that little garage-house and just shook our heads. There really was no room anywhere for a Christmas tree—and that was just one expense we could do without. Besides, when it was nearly eighty degrees outside, it didn't feel much like Christmas.

But the Kellogg's son (in his early 20s) was absolutely horrified that Marian and I wouldn't have a tree. So one evening, a few nights before Christmas, he knocked on the door. There he stood with the scraggliest little Charlie Brown Christmas tree I'd ever seen. He'd found an extra tree stand in his basement and an extra string of lights and brought the little tree to us. Well, Mom moved a few things around and found a space to put that little Christmas tree. But what to put on it? We didn't want to spend the money buying ornaments for such a tiny tree!

Marian and I remembered how much fun we'd had making ornaments for the last year's tree, so we got busy again. We had plenty of pine cones from our trips up into the mountains, so we bought a small bottle of gold paint and some glitter and made more ornaments. Mom found a few other things that would work, including making small chains out of aluminum foil. Pretty soon the tiny, ugly tree with its one strand of lights blossomed into a shining work of love.

Love is the most important ingredient for any situation. In this case, we were remembering God's only Son who was born in circumstances far less fortunate than ours! We also thanked the Lord for a gentle young man who had been concerned that two missionary kids didn't have a Christmas tree.

3427 North Vineland
Baldwin Park, California
January 10, 1958

Dear Mr. and Mrs. Wright:

Your long, newsy letter was received just at Christmas time and was a blessing to our hearts. It is always so good to hear from home. We enjoyed the tape of the Edgemont Choir singing the Christmas Cantata, too. And our hearts were encouraged by the personal word from so many as recorded on the tape that evening at the Martins.

This afternoon we finished making a tape for the folks at Edgemont and trust to have it in the mail tomorrow morning, so you should have it by Wednesday, the 15th. We are mailing it to you, Brother Wright, to be used in any way the Lord may lead. It is recorded at 3 ¾ speed and will play for 20 minutes. We enjoyed making it and trust the Lord will make it a blessing to you all. We felt as though we were right there in the church speaking to you.

You made mention in your letter of folding and stapling our future prayer letters in order to mail them more economically as bulk mail. By all means do so. I will keep this in mind in typing them up and try to send in the master copy spaced out so as to utilize an 8 ½ x 14 sheet with one flap for addresses, permit number, etc. I can see where it will cut the cost to less than ¼ of the cost of mailing in envelopes at 3 cents per letter, plus cost of envelopes. We think Adele did a superb job on our last letter, both in neatness and in time. She must have worked night and day to get it in the mail so quickly. She definitely deserves a great big "THANK YOU in Jesus' Name."

Yes, response to the appeal for our support and incidental expenses is very slow. But we are reminded that God is never late, never early, but always right on time! We realize, too, that the position we are in with respect to our missionary status is of our own making. Perhaps God is giving us time to learn our lesson well. Nevertheless, we are asking of Him the impossible because I firmly believe that delights His heart. We are asking the Lord to perform a miracle in supplying our need in order that we might begin our journey back to the Congo by July of this year. In the face of all that must be supplied and must be done, such a goal is an impossibility, humanly speaking. But with God, nothing shall be impossible. Gertrude and I were becoming rather discouraged with the lack of response, but lately it seems that God has been encouraging our hearts with the definite conviction that He is just about to do something great, and we are prayerfully waiting for it to happen. He will bring it to pass.

Our latest statement from Berean Mission showed a gift of $30 for our passage and equipment from Edgemont Bible Church, but did not indicate from whom. We want to thank the individual or group for this generous offering. Little by little the "thermometer" is slowly making its way up once again. We also received a generous offering toward our passage and equipment from the little church in Moselle, Missouri, which is pastored by Don Schroder.

God graciously supplied an item recently that will be of great use in the Congo. A young couple here in California felt led of the Lord to purchase a small, lightweight, transistor-powered public address system for us. It operates on 8 ordinary flashlight batteries for approximately 100 hours. Then, just change batteries. It weighs about 15 pounds complete with microphone, speaker, amplifier, and phonograph turntable. It will be the perfect thing for use in village evangelism. They said it would be about three weeks before they can make delivery of it. How we praise the Lord for His unique and useful instrument to be used in getting out the gospel in the villages.

Trust the tape recording will arrive in good time and prove to be a blessing to all. The Lord bless you both, and all at Edgemont.

Love in Christ,
Les and Gertrude

3427 North Vineland
Baldwin Park, California
February 28, 1958

Dear Mr. and Mrs. Wright,

Greetings in the Saviour's dear Name! We received your postal card some time ago and then your letter day before yesterday. We were so sorry to hear that you have been sick, Mrs. Wright. That flu bug simply is no respecter of persons, is it? What a great sorrow it must have been there in the Congo where the pagans would believe that it was an evil spirit instead of a flu bug. They are so terribly superstitious. And then the news that has been reaching us of the home-going of dear ones: Mr. Breeding, Mr. Lyons and Mrs. Arney, Sr. I could sense the great weight of it all upon you, Brother Wright, as I read your letter. Yes, it is in the time of need that our Lord increases our strength. *"He giveth power to the faint; and to them that have no might, He increaseth strength."*

You mentioned that John Sanford would be coming out this way for deputation work. We received a letter from him last week saying he would be coming, perhaps sometime in March. It will be good to see him again. He said he had a 1958 Chevrolet Carryall, just like our '57 except twin headlights, and his is Teal Blue. The truck that Carl Blackburn mentioned in his prayer letter is a much heavier truck than our Carryall. It is a 2 ½ ton Ford truck, given to him by their church in Akron. According to word from them both, John Sanford is expecting to sail in July of this year and the Blackburns in August or September.

When we mentioned coming home in April or May, it was only a prayer request and the desire of our heart that we might have our needs met by then so we could come home and pack to sail by July. But that does not seem to be the Lord's will in the matter. Out of twenty-four letters I recently sent out to Pastors in independent churches, a little more distant from Baldwin Park, only two had the common courtesy to even reply: one in the negative, and one in the affirmative. I can readily understand why they do not want us in their churches, but I cannot understand the cold indifference and lack of Christian courtesy. So many of the pastors on whom we have called simply tell us that they are unable to fully take care of their own missionaries, so why would they open their doors to us. Others say their missionary budget is full, so why waste our time in presenting our work to their people. These same pastors preach a Christ with wide open arms pleading, *"Come unto Me all ye that labor and are heavy laden, and I will give you rest,"* but they tell us to go away because they have a sufficient missionary burden with their own. They stand in the pulpit and preach a Christ who said, *"Whosoever will may come"* — but they tell us to go away, their missionary budget is already full. They preach a Christ who said, *"Come. And let him that is athirst come. And whosoever will, let him take the water of life freely,"* but they tell us to go away because there is not enough for them and for us too. If these were modernist churches it would be different. But they are churches where the gospel is preached to "overstuffed" congregations, who are not willing to share a dry crumb with the multitudes in the regions beyond their own comfortable pews.

Carl Blackburn has been corresponding with us about the possibility of our returning together in August or September. He wanted to know definitely before March 5, when he starts out on a month of meetings, so he could make their own reservations in advance. I told him that at the present rate of interest in our behalf it would by 1960 before we would be ready and for him to go ahead and make his reservations. John Sanford, of course, is going in July so he can get the children in school in Congo in September.

We have a Missionary Conference coming up March 16 to 23, inclusive, at the San Gabriel Union

Church near here. They could not give us a speaking place but will permit us to set up a booth in the Lower Auditorium to present the work of Berean Mission. I have prepared a large wall map of the world showing our various fields of missionary activity. We have our little smattering of curios, and all of the various tracts, Missiongrams, and other literature to display. I printed a sign reading, "THE SEWING NOOK—Missionary Projects", and beneath it we will display some African Fence Girl dresses, aprons for the houseboys, rolled bandages, etc. I wish we had more to display, such as large pictures of Africa and of the natives, more curios, etc., but it is too late to get anything here from the Mission. Besides, that would cost money, which we don't have. The San Gabriel Union Church is quite a large, independent work, with a missionary budget of $53,000 last year. But it is more or less the same story. They have so many of their own missionaries coming in for the conference that they were not able to give us a place to speak. They are even flying one of their missionaries home from South America to speak at the Conference.

We did have a blessed time at a tiny little church in McArthur, California, where Gaylen Dedmon, formerly of the Navajo Field, is now pastoring. It is way up in Northern California in a beautiful valley high in the mountains. I believe the valley is over 3,000 feet elevation. The ranchers were so very kind and interested in what we had to say. Here in the Los Angeles area they have so many missionaries the folk dread to see another one coming. But the folk up there don't see missionaries very often. There couldn't have been more than 100 people present in the little church the Sunday we were there, although it was filled to overflowing with seats set up in the nursery to accommodate the crowd. They gave us the largest single offering we have ever received anywhere of $107.05. We did not send it in through the Mission as we needed it to defray expenses of the 1300-mile round trip and to hold us over until our Mission check arrives. One of the ranchers took 2 units of our support, and Brother and Sister Dedmon took 4 units personally. Gaylen seemed to think there might be another couple of units develop. The rancher and his wife who took the two units of support were also interested in the monkey hunting for food. He had given his wife a Marlin 30-30 caliber Carbine for a wedding present about seven years ago, which has had only 7 shells fired in it, and so they gave me the gun to take back to Congo to shoot monkeys. We had a wonderful time with them up there in the mountains. It was a real spiritual oasis in a dry desert of deputation work.

I guess that is about all for this time. As I re-read the letter it sounds a little discouraging, but then we are discouraged at the present time. We are quite weary of simply not being wanted. *"But they that wait upon the Lord shall renew their strength; they shall mount up with wings as eagles: they shall run, and not be weary; and they shall walk, and not faint."* We are weary—but we are waiting upon the Lord.

                        Yours in His Never-failing Grace,

                        Les and Gertrude

3427 North Vineland
Baldwin Park, California
March 6, 1958

Dear Pastor and Mrs. Wright,

Just a short letter this time to transmit our March prayer letter.

 You will be pleased to know that the Pico Union Church in Pico, California, has taken ten units of our support, with possibly another unit coming from a Sunday School Class. This, together with the units from McArthur, California and other recent additions, will make a total of nearly 100 units toward the required 170. Perhaps the Lord intends to move that mountain yet! Keep praying—the light is breaking through!

 The dear ladies at Pico Union Church have really been sewing for us, too—that is, for our Africans. They have made 96 dresses for our African girls; 54 aprons for houseboys; 24 small boys shorts; and given us many worthwhile items of used clothing for the Africans. Also, four lovely quilts for our own use in Congo. They have certainly been lovely to us and so interested in our Africans. We just praise the Lord for them. No matter how bitter the discouragements, the Lord always sweetens the way with dear folk like these.

 Have a note from Mrs. Amie today. She has airmailed a copy of the Kilega New Testament to me in care of the Mission Office for forwarding. I asked them in Congo to mail one just as soon as it arrived. I'm so anxious to get my eyes on one. She says Irving is losing weight, not eating, and not sleeping. He certainly needs our prayers.

            In Christian love,

            Les and Gertrude

BEREAN MISSION, INC.	AFRICA	Deputation Address:
3536 Russell Blvd.		3427 North Vineland
St. Louis, Missouri	The Dark Continent!	Baldwin Park, California

Prayer Letter	March 1958	No.5

Dear Christian Friends:

> *"Casting all your care upon Him; for He careth for you"* (I Peter 5:7).
> *"Cast not away, therefore, your confidence, which hath great recompense of reward"* (Hebrews 10:35).

This reminds me of an incident which took place in a lonely part of one of Congo's motor roads. An African chauffeur, who was a Christian, was driving his truck from one large town to another. In a lonely part of the road, many miles from any native village, he overtook an elderly woman with an extremely heavy load on her head.

He stopped the truck, and she hurried off terrified to try and hide in the forest. "Come on, mother," he called, "Don't be afraid. I only want to help you. I'll take you along in my truck. I'm going right past your village." The old African woman was still dubious, but finally allowed the driver to lift her into the truck. The truck started off, but the first thing the woman did was to pick up her load again. She wasn't going to risk leaving that.

There she sat in the back of the truck with her load on her head. She was unaccustomed to the movement of the truck, and she found it difficult both to keep her balance and to hold on to her precious load at the same time. The load jogged up and down, bumping her head and pressing her neck right down on her shoulders. She perspired freely and was almost exhausted at the end of her journey.

When they reached her village, the driver stopped the truck and went behind to help the old lady down. Imagine his surprise to find her sitting there, panting for breath, but still hanging on to her load. "Why mother, you haven't been carrying that all the way, have you?" he exclaimed. "Yes," she said, "you see, I did not want to lose it!"

We smile at the incident, but how like so many Christians. How often we bring our burdens to the Lord, and even though trusting in Him ourselves, we still pick up the burden and go on carrying it along the way, when we might rest the whole weight of it upon Him. *"Cast thy burden upon the Lord, and He shall sustain thee."* We trust the Lord concerning our eternal interests, but how often we are afraid to trust Him completely to care for our temporal needs. We fail to realize that the very breath we draw is His gracious provision. We need to learn again and again that the Lord cares and keeps; He guides and guards His own; and He will meet us in every circumstance and situation.

Sometimes we allow ourselves to get *under* the circumstances, whereas God would have us to always be *above* them. Such was the case with us recently. Gertrude and I were fretting about how and when we would ever get back to the Congo. It seemed so impossible, and it seemed that no one really cared. So few churches would open their doors to us and give us the opportunity to present our work. And it seemed that when we did speak, the people were not challenged. We were under the circumstances of fruitless deputation meetings. You see, we were looking in the wrong direction. Disappointment had caused us to be downcast, and so we failed for the moment to look up to the One who cares—our Lord Jesus Christ.

And then God sent along a letter that caused us to rejoice once again and to praise Him who cares for us. No, it was not a letter of encouragement from one of our many friends and prayer helpers. Nor was it a letter from some faithful steward of God, enclosing five thousand dollars for our passage and equipment to send us back to the Congo. No, there wasn't a cent in this letter. It was a letter from the Belgian Congo, written in Kilega, which is the language of the Balega tribe. It was from Katindi, our cook. I would like to share a portion of his letter with you, dear friends. Permit me to give you a very literal translation into English, in order that you might sense the feeling of his African heart:

> A letter to my father 'The Called One' (that is the meaning of my Kilega name). I greet you again in the name of our Lord Jesus Christ. Truly many days I have not sent you a letter. Truly I am here in the strength of God. But I am with sorrow because my little baby has died. And because of this, I am with much sorrow, my father. But I am with hope because some day I will see him in the arms of God. For this reason I am again with happiness; some day I will see him there in heaven.

Precious faith of an African Christian! The simple trust of a child of God. Katindi, believing and trusting that he will one day behold his dear little departed baby in the arms of God — that he will see him there in heaven. Katindi, who but a few years ago was a pagan lad living in the dense forest, now knows the One who cares, and is trusting in Him. Oh, how his letter rejoiced my heart. And it made me ashamed of myself, too. Why, if Katindi can trust God to hold his little baby safe and secure in His Almighty Arms until eternity dawns, surely we can trust Him to supply our material needs now and send us back to the Belgian Congo — back to Katindi — back to thousands of other Balega like him, who are precious in the sight of the Lord.

And now I would like to share one more short portion of Katindi's letter with you. He wrote:

> Now I want to know what day you will arrive here. Truly when you arrive here, I want to become your cook again because I am with happiness to do your work.

When I replied to Katindi's letter, I told him that only God in heaven knows what day we will arrive there at Katanti, our former Mission Station. But that He who now holds Katindi's little baby in His Almighty Arms is also able to send us back to him soon.

Pray for us, won't you, dear friends, that God will burden His people somewhere, somehow, to send us back to our beloved Balega Tribe. Yes, our needs are great — but the need of those poor, lost souls over there in the forests of the Belgian Congo are greater. And our God is greater than all, and HE IS ABLE!

Jesus said, *"Ask, and ye shall receive, that your joy may be full"*. Will you join with us in asking God in Jesus name to send us back to the Congo this summer, if it be His blessed will?

Your African missionaries,

Les, Gertrude, Jeanette, and Marian
"The Spainhowers"

3427 North Vineland
Baldwin Park, California
April 22, 1958

Dear Mr. and Mrs. Wright:

Have been working over a new list of names to be added to our mailing list as a result of our most recent meetings, so I thought I would write a line or two and forward this latest list to you.

We have just concluded another week of Missionary Conference, this time at the Bethany Baptist Church of West Covina, California, a Conservative Baptist work. We have several very good friends in this church, and so they were able to hurdle the denominational barriers for us. The Lord led and blessed, and we were graciously received.

Our blessed Lord continues to open doors for us, and we are speaking two, three, or four times almost every week. We are usually in one church Sunday morning and in another that evening. Just as we begin to feel that we have "run our course," the phone rings or a letter arrives, and we have more meetings and more opportunities. Surely, out of all the multitudes we have spoken to God will burden some hearts to send us forth once again! We are waiting upon Him and trusting in Him.

The girls have only nine more weeks of school, and then they will be through for another year. We are still asking God that we can start them in our mission school in Africa next Fall. If we can see the Lord's leading us out this summer, we are thinking of flying the girls on ahead of us by plane, while we take a slow freighter with our equipment around South Africa and up the East Coast to Dar Es Salaam, Tanganyika, and drive in from there. That is more or less the route taken by Lydia Frank and Iola Baker.

Jeanette would be with us for two and one-half more years in Congo to finish high school, and then we would send her home with another missionary family returning on furlough in order that she could begin her training. She still feels the Lord would have her to train as a missionary teacher, and Marian feels certain the Lord wants her to be a missionary nurse. And we are anxious to get back to the field as just plain missionaries, making known the Lord Jesus Christ as Saviour to those who know Him not.

We will be sending along another prayer letter in a couple more weeks. Until then,

Much love in Christ,

Les and Gertie

BEREAN MISSION, INC.	A F R I C A	Deputation Address:
3536 Russell Blvd.		3427 North Vineland
St. Louis, Missouri	The Dark Continent!	Baldwin Park, California

Prayer Letter   May 1958   No. 6

To Our Many Friends and Loved Ones:

"Behold, now is the accepted time; behold, now is the day of salvation" (II Corinthians 6:2).

One of our African Christian elders was asked if he would like to attend Bible School in order to better prepare himself to lead his people in the ways of the Lord. He reflected for a long moment and then, in true African custom, gave his reply in the form of a long tale.

He said that all of the animals were gathered together in the forest one day when suddenly into their midst ran a tiny squirrel, chattering with excitement and scampering to and fro. The animals immediately noticed something different about their little friend. As he scurried about there was a big, bushy "something" trailing behind him. When the squirrel finally quieted down enough that they could talk to him, the animals asked what that "something" was behind him. The squirrel replied that it was a "tail." He said that way deep in the forest there was a person giving them away for free and urged all the other animals to go and get themselves a pretty tail like his.

The animals talked excitedly between themselves as they watched the squirrel scamper about with his big, bushy tail flipping this way and that. For, you see, up until this time none of the animals had tails. Finally, the lion stepped forward and with a loud roar said that since he was the king of beasts, he would go and investigate this matter. The rest of the animals waited impatiently for the lion to return to see if he, too, would have a tail. At last they heard a happy roar and into their midst bounded the king of beasts — and there, trailing behind him was a big, long, beautiful "something." Yes, the lion had a tail also! And what a tail it was! He could swish it back and forth, and there at the very end was a beautiful tassel. The animals couldn't contain their excitement and they all wanted to be the next one to go and get a tail — that is, all except the chimpanzee. He just sat on the limb of a tree, eating bananas, and wondering what all the fuss was about.

Next, the elephant decided he would go and get himself a tail. He reasoned that since he was the largest of all the animals he would probably get a tremendous tail in keeping with his size. The rest of the animals heard the elephant trumpeting for joy as he made his way back through the forest. They all looked expectantly as he came thundering into their midst, but they had to look a second time before they could find his tail because it was so small. The elephant hastened to explain that since he had such a long trunk hanging from his nose at the front of him, he only needed a short tail behind him.

Now, who would be next? All of the animals were eager to go. All, that is, except one, the chimpanzee! He couldn't see what all the fuss was about. "There's plenty of time," he said. "I'll go when all the rush is over." So the monkey decided to go and get his tail. And what a useful tail his turned out to be! It was long and strong, and he could hang by it from the trees, and use it in so many ways. The rabbit came hopping back with his new tail — a beautiful powder puff sort of a thing. And so the animals went one by one to get their tails.

Finally, after all the other animals had their tails, the old chimpanzee stirred himself, and stretched. "Well," he yawned, "now that the rush is over, I guess I'll go and get my tail." He wandered sleepily off into the forest while the rest of the animals waited to see what sort of tail the chimpanzee would get. They waited, and waited, and waited. After a very long time they heard him coming through the forest. But it was a sad, dejected chimpanzee who returned sheepishly into their midst. They all looked at him with anticipation, but when he turned around, there was nothing there. He had no tail! "I was too late," he said remorsefully. "By the time I got there, all the tails were gone."

The African Christian elder had finished his story, and he just sat there silent. He had not said "yes" he would like to go to Bible School or "no" he did not want to or "maybe" he would go later. However, after reflecting a moment upon his story, his answer was quite evident. What he was really telling us in an African's round about way was that he thought it would be well for him to attend Bible School while he had the opportunity. If he delayed, the opportunity might pass, and he would find himself without this valuable training in the Word of God. He did not want to be too late! He did not want to get there after the opportunity was already gone. He did not want to be like the chimpanzee!

How like the chimpanzee are so many people here in America! The Word of God tells us in II Corinthians 6:2, *"Behold, now is the accepted time; behold, now is the day of salvation."* But so many people simply put off being saved. They say, "There's plenty of time. I want to do this or that first, and then I'll turn to the Lord." They know full well that they are sinners in the eyes of a Holy God, and they know that *"the wages of sin is death,"* and they know that *"Christ died for our sins according to the Scriptures, and that He was buried, and that He rose again the third day, according to the Scriptures,"* and they know that *"as many as receive Him, to them gave He power to become the sons of God, even to them that believe on His name."* And still they procrastinate! They put off receiving the Lord Jesus Christ as their Saviour. They defer to believe on His name. And worst of all, many of them wait too long! They wait until the opportunity has passed, until their soul is required of them, and then they go out into a lost eternity, without Christ, without God, and without hope.

But how about those poor heathen out there in the forests of the Belgian Congo who do not know these things, who have never heard the gospel message? Yes, they too are sinners in the eyes of God! For in His Word we read that *"all have sinned, and come short of the glory of God"* (Romans 3:23). They are under the condemnation of sin and must pay the penalty—DEATH! How can they be saved from this awful penalty? By trusting in the Lord Jesus Christ as their Saviour—*"For whosoever shall call upon the name of the Lord shall be saved"* (Romans 10:13). But the question is raised, *"How then shall they call on Him in whom they have not believed? And how shall they believe in Him of whom they have not heard? And how shall they hear without a preacher?"* (Romans 10:14). The answer is obvious. Let someone go and preach Christ to them! Let someone take the gospel message to them! But the final question is asked in verse 15: *"And how shall they preach, except they be sent?"*

Yes, *"now is the accepted time – now is the day of salvation!"* But while Christians procrastinate, untold millions are perishing—UNTOLD! While God's people put off praying, and defer in their giving, and simply wait for someone else to shoulder the burden, countless multitudes of the heathen are slipping away into outer darkness without Christ and without hope, because they have never been told that there is a Saviour.

"Pray ye therefore the Lord of the harvest, that He will send forth labourers into His harvest." While we wait to be sent, there is a great harvest of souls "rotting" in the field

                        Yours in Christ (because someone told us about the Saviour),

                        Les, Gertrude, Jeanette, and Marian
                        "The Spainhowers"

3427 North Vineland
Baldwin Park, California
May 17, 1958

Dear Ones in Christ,

    It was just two weeks ago that we mailed our last prayer letter to Adelle, and here we are already with another one! It seems that the Lord has just literally driven us to make this appeal while there is still enough time for us to sail this year. We feel so definitely that God wants us back there this year. Surely He will burden hearts.

    We do praise the Lord for leading in another way, too. We believe He has led us to someone who will be willing to secure all of our clothing, linens, and many household sundries at wholesale prices. This will represent a great saving in equipment costs if this party is willing. We will know in a few more days. Then, if Brother Chester Arney will be willing again to order certain hardware items for us wholesale, it will represent a great saving of the Lord's money.

    How is the new Sunday School building progressing? Trust you are able to be in it by this time. We have rejoiced to see how abundant have been the Joash offerings each month.

    The Lord continues to open many doors before us. We have a Missionary Conference the 21st – 25th of this month, as well as many meetings already scheduled for June and July. We pray the Lord will bring about a response to the enclosed letter, that will enable us to return home to pack even sooner than we could ask or think. Am also enclosing a very short mailing list for Adelle.

    Give our love to all at Edgemont, and we will be seeing you in the Lord's own time.

                                    Much love in Christ,

                                    Les and Gertie

May 18, 1958

Dear Brother and Sister Wright,

Am writing you hurriedly in an attempt to catch up with the prayer letter which we airmailed to you just this morning (Sunday morning). We found out this evening immediately before the service at San Gabriel Union Church that they have undertaken $100 per month of our support (40 units). Praise the Lord!

In the prayer letter mailed to you this morning, we mention the need of *60 more units* — there is now a need for only *20 more units* of support. I believe it would be a better testimony of God's grace and goodness in providing for us, to leave the text of the letter as is, but to add a "P.S." saying that "since receiving this prayer letter from the Spainhowers, word has come that a church in San Gabriel, California has taken $100 per month of their support (40 units), and that leaves a need for only 20 more units."

I believe this evidence of God's readiness to move us out to the field will be an encouragement to many to send in their gift toward our passage, don't you?

We are so thrilled and happy and praising the Lord that we cannot get to sleep tonight (this is Sunday after service). I'm going to send this letter off airmail early tomorrow, and hope that it arrives before Adelle cuts the stencil on the prayer letter. With the addition of the "P.S." it will probably be necessary to print the prayer letter on 8 ½ x14 instead of 8 ½ x 11. No wonder I had a feeling of "urgency" as I prepared that letter. God is moving us out to the field again — and He is moving fast!! Praise His name!

In haste,

Les

KELLY TRAVEL AGENCY
76 Clinton Street
Brooklyn 1, New York

May 28, 1958

Rev. Leslie J. Spainhower
563 North 86th Street
East St. Louis, Illinois

Dear Brother Spainhower:

We are able to give you a tentative date for departure to Dar Es Salaam. We can accommodate you on a Robin Line ship scheduled to leave New York around October 5. The rate would be $650, subject to 15% discount.

I am enclosing a folder describing this service, and if it is acceptable will you please send me a deposit of $200 before June 5.

We shall appreciate your reply, and if you have any questions, please contact me.

Yours in Him,

B. W. Kelly

3427 North Vineland
Baldwin Park, California
June 3, 1958

Mr. B. Wm. Kelly
Kelly Travel Agency
76 Clinton Street
Brooklyn 1, New York

Dear Brother Kelly:

Your letter, dated May 28, advising of possible accommodations to Dar Es Salaam via the Robin Line, scheduled to leave New York about October 5, is acknowledged.

Inasmuch as the sailing plans of individual missionaries of Berean Mission are subject to the approval of the Home Board, we have referred your proposal to them for action. Should this proposal be acceptable to them, it is obvious that the deposit could not possibly be made by June 5, as suggested in your letter.

Nevertheless, the matter is under consideration, and you will hear from the Home Office of our Mission in the due course of time.

In the meantime, I would like to have the following additional information from you. If we do not employ a freight forwarder, then to whom do we consign our cases of equipment for loading as excess baggage? How about items coming from Servel, Inc., Montgomery Ward, etc. for consolidation with our equipment? Will the Robin Line receive such shipments in advance? We would not want to wait until the last minute to have our freight shipped to New York for fear of missing the boat. Perhaps you can advise me a bit more in detail as to what is involved in this respect.

Sincerely yours in Christ our Savior,

Leslie J. Spainhower

bcc:Rev. G. Reuben Lindquist
Berean Mission, Inc.

bcc:Rev. G. Joseph Wright, Pastor
Edgemont Bible church

For your information and guidance.

3427 North Vineland
Baldwin Park, California
June 3, 1958

Dear Reuben,

Today's mail brought a reply from the Kelly Travel Agency to an inquiry I recently made regarding accommodations from New York to Dar Es Salaam via South Africa. You will find a copy of his letter enclosed, together with a copy of my reply. This leaves the matter hanging in the air until a decision is reached. He requested the deposit by June 5, so this particular booking may or may not be available even if you should decide to take it.

We are certainly faced with a dilemma, and only the Lord knows the right answer. We must prayerfully seek His leading in the matter. Our problem is this: If we do not accept this sailing, or one no later than November, then we are caught by the cold weather and will not be able to sail until the next year (about May). Other major problems would be involved in that event regarding Jeanette's age, etc., but we won't go into that at this time. On the other hand, if we are to sail in October or November, we must quickly raise about $5,000 in order to do so. In my June prayer letter, I set the figure at $3,500, so as not to shock our readers' sensibilities. However, the cold, hard facts and figures substantiate the larger sum. I am setting out my estimates below for your perusal:

$1500 - Actual cost of flying Jeanette and Marian from St. Louis to Bukavu
       (including $90 expense money for trip).
 1105 - Actual cost of passage for Gertrude and Les by Robin Line
  300 - Estimated cost of excess baggage (includes all equipment)
  200 - Estimated cost of shipping equipment to New York pier
  650 - Approximate cost of shipping Carryall on freighter with us
  400 - Estimated cost of shipping equipment inland in Africa
  200 - Estimated customs duty (???)
  700 - Estimated need for initial supplies, food, and equipment to be purchased in
       Congo upon arrival.
$5055 - Minimum Total Need

The above estimates and figures do not include any of the following: Travel expenses for Gertrude and Les from St. Louis to New York; expenses for several days in New York awaiting sailing (you know these freighters); travel expenses for Gertie and Les 1500 miles inland in Africa; payment in advance for Jeanette and Marian's tuition in Mission School; payment in advance for a couple of months in the dormitory; cost of passports, visas, etc.; various port charges; and all the miscellaneous and unforeseen expenses.

Another very important factor to consider is the support which has already been pledged. Praise God, I believe it is all in now except for about five units! However, as mentioned in a previous letter, I am afraid we might lose some of this support if our departure is delayed beyond this year. Rev. Hemphill of San Gabriel Union Church was particularly interested in knowing when we would be returning to the Field in connection with their $100 per month.

So — what to do? We are continuing with our plans to leave here June 24 for home, inoculations, dental work, packing etc. in an effort to sail this year. If our needs are not met, then we will have to seek the Lord's will further. The matter of accepting or rejecting Mr. Kelly's accommodations for

October 5, per enclosed copy of letter, is referred to you for decision and reply. You are more familiar than I am with what is involved in paying a deposit. If we found later that we did not have funds to go ahead, could the reservations be canceled without losing the deposit? At any rate, as you pointed out in your letter to me of May 23, sailing plans must be approved by the Home Office, and therefore I am referring Mr. Kelly's letter to you for reply. We would appreciate knowing what action is taken, as well as your views and advice in our particular circumstances. I am sending a copy of this letter to Mr. Wright, as our pastor, in order that he may also be fully apprised of the situation.

Sincerely in Christ,

Leslie J. Spainhower

P.S. Funds currently in our Reserve Account will probably all be needed for the purchase of equipment, clothing, refrigerator, range, beds, mattresses, etc., inasmuch as we are starting with nothing again.

Cc: Rev. G. Joseph Wright, Pastor
    Edgemont Bible Church

I am taking this means of spreading out the matter before you, too, Brother Wright. We feel very definitely that the Lord wants us back in Congo this year, and that He is "shoving" us out. Therefore, we are proceeding as though every need had been met, and we are trusting Him to supply. As stated, we are coming home to pack and make ready to sail. We will be leaving here June 24 and trust to be home by Saturday, June 28, or Sunday the 29th. Pray with us that God will work it all out according to His own will and purpose. We can only follow His leading and trust in Him. All I can see is a huge mountain ($5,000 still needed), and no way to get over it or around it. But my Lord not only knows the way, He is the Way. I'll trust in Him!

With Christian Love,

Les

BEREAN MISSION, INC.	AFRICA	Deputation Address:
3536 Russell Blvd.		3427 North Vineland
St. Louis, Missouri	The Dark Continent!	Baldwin Park, California

Prayer Letter	June 1958	No. 7

Dear Co-laborers:

Only a short time has passed since we last visited with you in your homes by means of our prayer letter. Ordinarily we would not be "dropping in" to your mail box for another visit so soon. However, the time has come when some important decisions must be made, and these decisions depend upon you, as together we seek God's will and guidance.

First of all, we want to tell you how grateful we are to you, our co-laborers and prayer partners, for the interest you have taken in our ministry. Your faithfulness in praying for us is evidenced by your consistent giving that our needs might be met. God is answering your prayers, and ours, and so we want to take this opportunity of giving you an up-to-the-minute report, indicating the Lord's blessing and provision as He is leading us out once again to our beloved Balega tribe there in the heart of Africa.

You will rejoice with us to know that God's people have already pledged 110 units of our monthly support. A total of 170 units of support are required for our family of four. That leaves only <u>60 more units</u> to be pledged before we can return to the field. The fact that new units of support have been coming in slowly but steadily is certainly an indication of the Lord's blessing and guidance, and is proof that there is no recession with God. His program goes right on! We know that He has His stewards who will be willing to pledge these remaining 60 units of our support as He leads them and lays the burden of our pagan tribe upon their hearts.

For the benefit of some of our readers who may not be familiar with Berean Mission's plan of support, may we say that a "unit" of support is $2.50 per month, pledged for a period of five years (one term), and may be remitted monthly, quarterly, semiannually, or yearly. Individuals, as well as Bible classes, Sunday School classes and departments, missionary societies, or other groups may take as many units as they desire. Under this plan, the individual Christian, as well as organizations, is given an opportunity to have a direct part in the support of a missionary family of their own choice. This brings about a personal acquaintanceship and relationship between the missionary and his supporters, as well as a prayer fellowship that is pleasing unto the Lord. In this manner we truly become "laborers together with God" in His great missionary program.

This brings us to the purpose of sending you this message at this time. We feel that God wants us back in Congo this year! And He is moving in that direction. Word has come from the field that we are desperately needed. But there are many time-consuming matters that face us before we can return to the Congo. Passports and visas must be secured; equipment must be purchased and packed; shipping and passage must be arranged, etc. However, before we can enter into these final arrangements, our financial needs must be supplied.

Beloved, we firmly believe that God's program, carried on in God's way, will have God's provision in God's time. And, we believe that God's time has come for us to return to the Congo! As you pray for us, will you also ask God what He would have *you* to do about the remaining 60 units of our support still needed? If you honestly and earnestly would like to see us back in Africa doing the work God called us to do, then please don't wait for someone else to shoulder the burden God wants *you* to bear.

We are so happy to be able to report to you that we now have sufficient funds in hand to purchase all of our equipment for Africa. Truly, *"The Lord hath done great things for us; whereof we are glad"* (Psalm 126:3). But there is still another great need which must be supplied in order that we may return to the Congo. We still need approximately $3,500 for our passage and for freight on our equipment. This would, indeed, be a staggering sum for any single donor!!! But, this is something in which we each may have a small part, thus supplying the total need without placing an undue burden upon any.

Our prayer letter goes into nearly 450 homes across America, absolutely free of any charge, and most of you have been receiving it for a number of years. If *each family* who receives this prayer letter would send in to Berean Mission a gift of ten dollars, designated "for Spainhowers' passage," the total amount would be met, with enough left over to cover all incidental expenses in getting us back to the Congo.

We do not like to use this prayer letter as a means of making a plea for funds, but dear friends, if you desire to have part in returning us to God's great harvest field there in Africa, *now is the time*!!! If each of our readers (as a family) will respond to this letter, *this month*, we will be ready to sail for Africa by September of this year. May God grant it! If you will mail your gift, designated "for Spainhowers' passage," to Berean Mission, Inc., 3536 Russell Blvd., St. Louis 4, Missouri, we will be notified by the Mission of *all* gifts in order that we may *personally* acknowledge them.

We have but one request to ask of you, dear ones, concerning all of this—PRAY! And when you pray, ask God what *He* would have you to do, and then do it as unto Him!

                              Your Missionaries to the Congolese,

                              Les, Gertrude, Jeanette, and Marian
                              "The Spainhowers"

P.S. Since receiving this prayer letter from the Spainhowers, word has come that a church in San Gabriel, California, has undertaken $100 per month of their support (40 units) and that leaves *a need for only 20 more units*. Praise the Lord!

                              Rev. G. Joseph Wright
                              Pastor, Edgemont Bible Church

Jeanette's Comment: My God Shall Supply All Your Need

A sense of urgency began filling our hearts after months of discouragement. We were actually going back to the Congo in 1958! And the scariest—and most exciting—part is that Marian and I were actually going to fly out by ourselves, months ahead of Dad and Mom, so we would be entering school on time. We would be living in the dormitory on Katanti and attending the missionary children's school.

My French teacher was probably as excited as our family to think that what he had been teaching me for a year would actually be put to use. He gave me a list of phrases that might be helpful while we were traveling.

The summer was filled with the usual pre-departure activities: getting vaccinations, applying for passports and visas, making reservations for Marian and my flight and for Dad and Mom's freighter, crating the equipment to be shipped to the Congo on the same ship as Dad and Mom were sailing.

The money kept pouring in, the needed units supplied, and most of the passage and equipment funds were paid for before Dad and Mom left. Everyone receiving our prayer letters, but especially the dear people at Edgemont Bible Church, were just as excited as we were to see how God was answering prayer.

Yes, we were definitely being "shoved" back out to Africa so quickly that it almost made our heads spin. The need was so great—and a great God was answering prayer!

Part Seven

Africa — Second Term
1958-1960

"The eternal God is thy refuge, and underneath are the everlasting arms."
Deuteronomy 33:27a

Marian's Comment: Saying Goodbye Again

Our return trip to the Congo was far different from our first journey. Instead of traveling as a family, this time Jeanette and I would fly to Africa by ourselves so we could start school on time. Dad and Mom, along with our truck and belongings, would come later by ship, traveling with another missionary family, Carl and Barbara Blackburn and their children.

August 28, 1958, came faster than we wanted it to. It's one thing to say goodbye to our extended family and friends, but it's another thing entirely to have to say goodbye to Dad and Mom. Even though we knew we would see them again in a few months, it was almost unbearable. We had never been separated from them for any length of time before. Dad and Mom, Grandma Wilson, Pastor and Mrs. Wright, and Mr. and Mrs. Leo Williams, friends from Edgemont, came to the airport to bid us farewell. You can tell by the lack of smiles on our faces that we were already feeling the sadness of separation as we prepared to walk into the Lambert Airport Terminal.

Now let me tell you a little about Lambert Airport. The terminal was built in 1956, the year we came home from Africa the first time. The original terminal had an uncovered ramp, or walkway, jutting out from the middle of the terminal. This is where our family and friends went outside to watch our plane lift off the runway at 8:15 A.M. With all the jets taking off and landing at Lambert these days, can you imagine standing outside like that?

We had all stood in a circle holding hands while our dear Pastor Wright prayed for our safety before we walked out of the terminal. Hugs and kisses were done quickly, and then we walked out the door towards our TWA 4-propeller plane. No boarding ramps to protect us from the weather back then! It was a cloudy, windy morning as we boarded with tears streaming down our faces. The stewardesses seemed to understand and as cheerfully as possible helped us get settled into our seats. As the plane glided down the runway and lifted up towards the sky, we could briefly see our loved ones waving to us on the ramp. More tears flowed—ours and those waving to us!

We flew into Laguardia Airport in New York. From there we were taken by an airport limousine to Idlewild International Airport which, since 1963, has been called the John F. Kennedy International Airport. We then made our connection with Sabena Belgium World Airlines for our flight overseas. Dad did a terrific job of booking our flights and planning our itinerary, but Jeanette did a marvelous job of taking the lead and making sure we were where we were supposed to be at all times. I just followed along, not really aware of the responsibility she must have been feeling.

Sabena Airlines was absolutely the best airline we had ever been on. They took very special care of us and would frequently come to our seats to ask if we anything or just to talk to us. Even the navigator, who didn't speak English, came by. We tried to talk together using simple English and

Jeanette's one year of French with a lot of sign language. We laughed a lot with him.

We flew from New York to Gander, Newfoundland. From there to Shannon, Ireland, to Manchester, England, and on to Brussels, Belgium. Well traveled girls, right? Well…..all we saw were airports! No time for sightseeing. When we left Brussels, we flew across the Mediterranean Sea. It is hard to imagine, but while we slept through the night we flew high over Europe and above the Sahara Desert, arriving at Kano, Nigeria, early in the morning. Our next stop was Leopoldville, the capital of the Belgian Congo, where we stayed the rest of that day and overnight. Our final destination was Bukavu where we were met by Uncle Bob Hendry, the missionary who taught our mission school.

It took a lot of faith for Dad and Mom to put their only daughters on a plane and send them halfway around the world by themselves. But they knew we weren't really alone. Our heavenly Father was watching over us each step of the way.

Note: I know Dad's letter said that we stayed for a full day and overnight—but that wasn't accurate. We arrived in the afternoon in Leopoldville, went through Customs and entered officially into the Congo, ate supper with a very nice man who was staying at our hotel, and then headed for the airport at 6:00 a.m. the next day.

Jeanette's Comment: Off we go!

It was really hard to see as Marian and I walked across the tarmac at the St. Louis Airport and climbed the boarding ramp onto that TWA plane. The tears were flowing freely—and my heart was absolutely pounding. I was responsible for getting my younger sister and myself safely to Katanti Station in the Belgian Congo almost 10,000 miles away from everyone we knew and loved! I would have given anything to turn around and run back down the ramp and climb into Kasoga once more!

As the stewardesses met us at the door of the plane, they were kind of taken aback by the tears. They probably thought we'd just left one divorced parent and were heading off to spend the next six months with the other one. They'd seen it before—poor kids. But they took us to our seats—several rows apart! We weren't even going to sit together but with strangers!!

I tried to mop up my face so as not to alarm the businessman sitting next to me, fastened my seatbelt and took the gum the stewardess offered. While the motors revved, I even managed to watch the demonstration of what to do if we had a problem in the air—happy thought! But then, I remembered the verse Marian and I had chosen for our trip—Deuteronomy 33:27. *"The eternal God is thy refuge, and underneath are the everlasting arms."* As we headed down the runway, I began to pray.

Once we were in the air and could remove our seatbelts, I was preparing to find Marian and see how she was doing. But a man came and knelt beside my seat. "Are you traveling with another little girl?" he asked, kindly. "She's been crying ever since we boarded, and I don't know how to get her to stop." I told him Marian was my sister—and that we had just left our parents on our way to the Belgian Congo. He looked totally stunned. Then he motioned for the stewardess. "I'm exchanging places with this passenger." When the stewardess began to protest, he told her, "You can change the boarding manifest. She needs to be with her little sister!" He helped me move my things back to where he had been sitting, then moved up to my former seat.

Marian and I shared a fresh burst of tears, but then it was over. We were together, and that's all that mattered. Two young girls flying halfway around the world alone—no, that wasn't right! We were backed up by the shield of faith and *"underneath [were] the everlasting arms."*

One thing I noted was that our stewardesses seemed to spend a lot of time giggling up front with the pilot and other officers—or with the first-class passengers—and not paying much attention to the rest of the peons on the plane.

The flight was quiet—none of those possible emergencies the stewardess had talked about—and we landed safely at LaGuardia Airport in New York. I checked with information and found the correct bus to board that would take us to Idlewild for our international flight. The bus driver was brusque and seemed annoyed to have two teens to bother with. I told him we were going to the Sabena World Airlines terminal, and he nodded. So off we drove, watching out the windows and wondering why anyone would ever want to live in a busy, noisy, crowded place like New York! To make it worse, it had started to rain, covering everything with a dismal, gray mist.

As we approached the various airline terminals at the airport, passengers would pull the cord to let the bus driver know to stop in front of a particular terminal. Marian and I were both watching, but we almost missed the Sabena terminal. The bus came to a screeching halt when I pulled the cord, and the driver started cussing at us. "Whyn't you give a guy some warning?" he fussed. I was a little impertinent and shot back, "Because I've never been here before and didn't know where the terminal was!"

The driver didn't park under the sheltered area. Oh, no! He parked out in the open where Marian and I got completely soaked as he off-loaded our two big suitcases and two accordion cases. If it were any consolation, he got soaked as well, which made him cuss even more! We were both shocked—in East St. Louis in 1958, men just didn't curse around women.

A porter hurried over and helped us in the door of the small Sabena terminal. The lady looked at our tickets and passports and loaded our luggage onto the conveyer belt. "My goodness! You're all wet!" she exclaimed. She told us to come around the counter and follow her. She took us back into the area where the airline personnel stayed, had us go into the restroom and take off our wet clothes, which she put into a dryer back in the personnel area. So dry and only slightly disheveled, we waited back with the airline personnel until we were personally escorted to our plane and turned over to the care of the overseas crew.

As Marian mentioned, they really took good care of us. The food was delicious—even in Economy Class—everyone quite attentive. I think they probably all got a good laugh later when Marian and I pulled out the curlers and rolled up our hair just before the lights were turned out. No way were we going to arrive in Brussels, Belgium, looking like a couple of bedraggled orphans!

The airport in Brussels was far larger than in St. Louis. We had several hours to wait before our flight for the Congo. I found the area where we would be boarding the plane bound for the Congo, and we settled in.

Of course, the first thing we needed to do was use the restroom. We gathered up our purses, books, and little bags and headed for the restroom. It was nice and clean and a smiling woman handed us towels to dry our hands on. No paper towels here! But then came the shock—she wouldn't let us out of the restroom. She kept jabbering at us and pointing to a little saucer with coins in it. She wanted a tip for handing us clean towels!

I tried in my hesitant French to explain that I had no Belgian francs and that my American coins couldn't be changed. (Later, I found out that in an international airport, all currency could be changed.) I even offered to leave Marian and our things there in the restroom while I went to the exchange counter to get a few Belgian francs. No deal! She blocked the door. Now, of course, she wouldn't have dared such an action if any other passengers had been in there. She just knew she could bamboozle an inexperienced teenager. Finally, I handed her a dime, and she released us. I told Marian that if we used the restroom again—and that woman was still in there—we'd just wipe our hands on our skirts in front of her! Fortunately, that wasn't necessary—but I knew to give the next woman a dime!

We had been seated for just a little while when a number of young airmen came in through one of the gates. "They're Americans!" Marian said as they passed by. "Let's go say 'hi'!" It was with great effort I restrained her. Although it was wonderful to hear good ole American English being spoken, Mom and Dad had warned me about getting friendly with men on this trip. So we sighed as they walked on down the concourse.

We were really tired by the time I heard our flight announced—in both French and English—and we headed for the proper gate. I asked if this were the correct gate, and the lady at the counter smiled. "Oh, yes! I've been watching you, and I was just getting ready to come and get you." So it had been noted that two young American girls were traveling alone and needed special care.

After a delicious supper, the lights were turned low so people could rest on our long overnight flight to Leopoldville, the capital of Congo. No curlers tonight. Marian and I just slept peacefully. We didn't even know when the plane refueled. They just let us sleep.

It was mid-afternoon when we arrived in Leopoldville. There were several things that I had to do: get through customs, be properly registered into the Belgian Congo, and change the rest of my travel money into Congo francs. There would be no more use for American dollars. Getting through customs was no problem—that's where all passengers were taken. Since we were carrying no contraband, it was a breeze. The customs officials pointed us to the area where we would register. Someone who spoke English took care of us—and we were soon authorized to be in the Belgian Congo.

Then, we stood in the middle of the airport, people swirling around us, as I searched for the counter where I could exchange my money. None of the Africans spoke a word of English, and fewer of the Belgians seemed to speak it. A tall, older man finally stopped and asked what we needed. I started to tell him in French, but then he spoke English to us. What a relief!

After helping us exchange our money, the man asked where we were headed. I told him that we had reservations at a particular hotel. He said he was going there, too. He helped us onto the shuttle bus, ordered people around at the hotel, made arrangements for a wake-up call, and then asked if we would join him for dinner. That's when I hesitated. He smiled and took out his billfold. He showed us photos of his wife, his children, and all his grandchildren. "You don't have to be afraid," he said. He pointed to a dining room. "We will meet there in the doorway at 7:00 p.m."

I was still a bit reluctant, but I figured I was going to have trouble getting us any food otherwise, so I agreed. We followed the porter with our luggage. This wasn't like an American hotel with several stories in it. It was almost a maze of open hallways, surrounded by palm trees and lush tropical flowers—reminded me a lot of the high school in Baldwin Park, California!

Safe in our room, Marian and I bathed, took a nap, then put on nice clothes to meet our guardian angel—that's how I had finally designated the grandfatherly Belgian. We met him promptly at

7:00, he ordered our meals for us (but we paid for our own, to his amusement), and we had a really good time talking about our families. Afterwards, he called one of the porters and told him to escort us to our rooms. We thanked him profusely, and he waved us off. That was the last we saw of him.

I had awakened before our wakeup call and was already dressed before I got Marian up. She was ready in no time, and everything was ready when the porter knocked at our door to pick up our luggage. We waited with the luggage in the dark in front of the hotel until a small shuttle bus arrived to take us to the airport. I stood by the bus and made sure the luggage was loaded before we got on.

We checked in at a gate at one end of the airport. Just a few other people were around—and when we saw our plane, we understood why. It was basically a gully-hopper and held no more than 20 people. Many of them were Africans. We flew much lower and could really enjoy watching the scenery—the lush green canopy of the jungle, brown rivers meandering through the jungle, small villages where the children would run out to wave at the plane.

We were offered a continental breakfast and, later, a sack lunch. Surprisingly, both were very good!

Mid-afternoon, we landed at the Bukavu airport, where our family had left a little more than two years earlier. We went into the tiny terminal—but no one was there to meet us. Not one familiar face! The porter brought in our luggage, and we sat on benches to one side to wait and see who was going to come. Uncle Bob Hendry, our teacher at the mission school was supposed to pick us up—but he was nowhere in sight. I got a little worried because the airport was quite some distance from town, and I didn't know how we would get into town if no one came for us. The last taxi had already huffed out of sight.

The African at the terminal desk kept looking over at me—and Marian whispered, "What are we going to do?" I just shook my head, trying to think.

Suddenly, the terminal door burst open—and a man ran in, looking quite distressed. He didn't see us at first, sitting over on the side, and ran to the African at the counter who just calmly pointed over to us. By that time, Marian and I were halfway across the floor. It was Uncle Bob! Even though we had only been on the field together for a few months before we Spainhowers had to leave because of Mom's illness, we hugged him like a long lost uncle!

All was well. The burden rolled off my shoulders and onto Uncle Bob's broad ones. But we had one more adventure to undergo before we reached Katanti. You can turn to the October 1958 prayer letter where Mom and Dad included my letter about the trip from Bukavu to Katanti to see what happened on this part of the trip.

BEREAN MISSION, INC.	AFRICA	B.A.M.S. - Kamulila
3536 Russell Blvd.		Bukavu, D. S.
St. Louis, Missouri	The Dark Continent!	Congo Belge, Africa

| Prayer Letter | September 1958 | No. 9 |

Dear Prayer Partners:

"The eternal God is thy refuge, and underneath are the everlasting arms" (Deuteronomy 33:27).

How precious this verse became as our daughters, Jeanette and Marian, began their flight back to the heart of Africa, where they will attend school with the other missionary children. As they winged their way across the heavens, we realized that they were now entirely beyond the reach of Mom and Dad's care and protection. They were like little birds leaving the safety of the nest for the first time. How good it is to know that God is their refuge, their hiding place, safe and secure, and that underneath the wings of their airplane are the everlasting arms of the Almighty bearing them up safely on their long journey back to the Congo.

It was 8:15 A.M., Wednesday, August 28, that a TWA Constellation roared down the runway at Lambert Airport, St. Louis, rose into the air, made a long, sweeping curve across the heavens, and in but a few moments became a tiny speck disappearing into the rising sun. Aboard that airliner, Jeanette and Marian no doubt waved a last "good by" through the window as they rushed past the air terminal, then were whisked all too quickly into the vacant blue sky. Their journey of nearly 10,000 miles back to the Belgian Congo had begun! As we turned our faces homeward, our hearts were heavy because of the parting, and yet we had perfect peace as to the girls' safety, for did we not have God's promise? *"The Lord is thy Keeper... The Lord shall preserve* (keep, guard) *thy going out and thy coming in"* (Psalm 121:5, 8).

Jeanette and Marian's first stop was Laguardia Airport in New York, from where they made their way to Idlewild International Airport and boarded a Sabena transoceanic airliner. From New York they flew via Gander, Newfoundland across the broad expanse of the North Atlantic to Shannon, Ireland, to Manchester, England, and on to Brussels, Belgium. From Brussels they flew across the Mediterranean Sea, and while they slept in the night they were carried high above the Sahara Desert, arriving at Kano, Nigeria as the dawn of an African day crept across the sky. Then, after the plane was refueled, they made their way on to Leopoldville, capital city of the Belgian Congo, where they had a full day and night of rest from their long journey. They left Leopoldville very early Sunday morning, August 31, flying over a vast area of dense, virgin, tropical forest, arriving at the small but somewhat modern frontier town of Bukavu late in the afternoon of that same day.

Although we have not received word from them at this writing, Jeanette and Marian were to be met in Bukavu by their schoolmaster, Rev. Robert Hendry, who will conduct them on the two-day journey back into the mountain vastness of the forest, to Berean Mission's Katanti Station. At Katanti, the girls will attend the Berean Christian Academy together with the children of our fellow Berean missionaries, as well as children from four other missionary societies. How we do praise God for calling Bob and Helen Hendry to this essential service of educating the missionaries' children right on the mission field. Should the Lord tarry in His coming, I'm certain that the efforts of this dedicated couple will pay great dividends in the lives of precious, second-generation missionaries returning to the African tribe of their childhood to labor among them for Christ.

Perhaps some of you are wondering, "What about Mom and Dad? When are they going to be reunited with the girls in the Congo?" We are so happy to be able to tell you that we are now in a position to proceed with arrangements to sail from New York on October 7th aboard a freighter, as originally planned. The Lord willing, this sailing should enable us to reach our Berean Mission stations there in the Congo in time to be with Jeanette and Marian for Christmas. What a joyous Christmas that will be. Not only to be reunited with our girls, but once more to be in the midst of our beloved Balega Tribe, the people we have learned to love so much in the Lord. Praise His name!

We are also rejoicing in the fact that we have been able to secure passage together with our very dear friends and fellow missionaries of Berean Mission, Rev. and Mrs. Carl Blackburn and their four little girls. Brother Blackburn's home church in Akron, Ohio has given him a new 2 ½ ton Ford truck to take back to the Congo. We will be able to haul the combined load of our equipment in his truck, while his family rides with us in our Carryall. This will effect a large saving in shipping costs as well as afford us many hundreds of miles of wonderful Christian fellowship as we travel. Truly, *"all things work together for good to them that love God, to them who are the called according to His purpose."*

Now, may we lay a prayer burden upon your hearts? On the basis of the number of gifts being received for our passage and the general interest indicated in our outgoing to the Congo, the Mission has felt led of the Lord to authorize us to proceed with arrangements to sail. However, all of the necessary funds are not yet in hand. There is still a minimum need of $900 to cover our outgoing expenses.

Berean Mission has been willing to advance that amount to our credit in order that we may go ahead and return to the Congo together with the Blackburn Family to relieve the pressure in the Field at the present time due to a shortage of missionaries to carry on the work. This amount must be repaid. As your missionaries, we are asking you to pray that this $900 might be supplied even before we sail on October 7 and that it will not be necessary to put our account in debt. I do not believe that financial indebtedness in the Lord's work is Christ-honoring. Pray, will you?

Well, dear ones, you have stood by us so faithfully down through these past years of missionary activity, and we just thank the Lord for each one of you. Now that He is thrusting us forth once again into His harvest field there in the Belgian Congo we covet your continued, faithful prayers in our behalf. Only eternity will reveal how much the harvest and how great the reward. Pray on, beloved, and never cease.

Your missionaries to the Congo,

Les, Gertrude, Jeanette, and Marian
The Spainhowers

Marian's Comment: Arrival at the Dorm

During our first term in the Congo, our family was stationed at Katanti where the missionary kids went to school. From third grade up, if their parents were on other mission stations, the kids had to live at the dormitory on Katanti run by Uncle Ernie and Aunt Hallie Green. Fortunately, on our first term we didn't have to live at the dorm.

However, on our second term in the Congo, our parents were to be stationed on Kamulila. So for the first time, Jeanette and I had to live in the dorm so we could attend school. We knew we would be away from our parents for four months, then home for Christmas vacation one month, back to the dorm for four more months, and home for three months during the summer. This is not always an easy transition for missionaries and their kids. Unfortunately, back then we didn't have home school materials available to us like they have today. So we had no choice.

We arrived around midnight at the dorm, which was named Jansen Hall after one of our pioneer missionaries Albert Jansen. We were exhausted and taken to the girls' dorm room right away. The three windows over the porch was where we stayed with several other girls. None of the girls awakened to greet us so we quietly slipped into our night clothes and literally fell into bed.

The next morning, the dorm girls woke up and never made a sound as they dressed and prepared for breakfast. Jeanette and I never heard a thing. A little later we heard laughter below us and realized everyone was up and having breakfast in the dining room. We quickly got up, dressed, and headed downstairs. There wasn't much of a welcome by anyone sitting at the two long tables, but we were told where to sit and, as inconspicuously as we could, ate our breakfast. Our journey was over, and we were now back at Katanti but under totally different circumstances than our first term. At that moment, I would have gladly walked all the way to Bukavu to get back on our plane again and go home!

When we were just about finished with our breakfast, the dorm's African cook came into the dining room and quietly said something to Aunt Hallie. She turned to Jeanette and me and said someone was waiting out front to see us. We couldn't imagine who that would be. We quickly left the table and headed to the front door. We almost cried for joy because standing there was Katindi,

the African man who had been our cook during our first term. He was so overjoyed at seeing us again and wanted to know when Dad and Mom would arrive because he was waiting to assume the position of cook again for our family. That was such a sweet reunion because we thought a lot of Katindi. We assured him Dad and Mom were coming in a few months and would want to see him. Of course, all of this was said through someone interpreting for us since we didn't know the Kilega language.

Since Uncle Bob Hendry was the school teacher, and he had been through the ordeal of bringing us to Katanti, our first day there was the first day of school for that year. We had a very nice new concrete block school building with a tin roof. Our school building and the dorm were the only buildings on Katanti that weren't made of mud with leaf roofs. The dorm was built with bricks made from mud.

The younger children from grades 1-6 were in one room with Aunt Helen Hendry as their teacher. All the other grades were in one large room with Uncle Bob teaching everyone else. Jeanette was starting her junior year of high school, and I was starting 7th grade. Eldon Green was in Jeanette's grade but I was the only kid in my class for that year. So we attended a "country school" but it was actually deep in the jungles of a completely different country!

So that's how our first day back in the Congo began. Jeanette was always gracious and had a good way of adapting to anything that came her way. Unfortunately, I struggled more with changes because I resisted them—especially if I didn't want to do it in the first place. In another "comment" I will share some of my struggles, anger, and loneliness during that first year and how years later God opened my eyes which allowed me to forgive and finally find peace.

Marian's Comment: Berean Christian Academy

Welcome to Berean Christian Academy on Katanti Station in the Belgian Congo, Africa!

We missionary children were very blessed to have a new concrete block school building with a tin roof, which was built just a year or so before Jeanette and I arrived. There were two entrance doors in the front. The door on the left opened into Aunt Helen Hendry's classroom for Grades 3—6. On the right was Uncle Bob Hendry's classroom for Grades 7—12. The small room to the back side of the porch was our bathroom.

The camera did not capture Jeanette and me, along with a few others, in these pictures.

Berean Christian Academy was a lot like going to school on "Little House On the Prairie" — only in the jungle. Each classroom had the teacher's desk at the front of the room with all individual student desks facing the front, from lowest grade back to the highest. There were wicker chairs to the side of Uncle Bob's desk. Those were our "recitation" chairs. Uncle Bob would call a particular grade (which could be one student or perhaps several), to come forward for recitation on a particular subject. All the other students in different grades were supposed to just continue on with their own studying. Quite often, though, we would all just listen — especially to the higher grades. They would frequently get into lively discussions that were very interesting and often humorous.

The back wall of our classroom was nothing but shelves full of books and National Geographics. Some teachers in the United States had shipped them out to our school. We had encyclopedias, reference books, and quite a few novels — both fiction and non-fiction. Jeanette was fascinated and thrilled with a large number of Grace Livingston Hill books. To this day, Jeanette has purchased hardcover copies of every one of her books and continues to read them over and over again. I spent many an hour browsing through the National Geographics. I was fascinated by the many colorful photos and interesting stories. Also, that's when I started developing a love of reading novels. No, I didn't particularly like Jeanette's Grace Livingston Hill books, but we had other Christian novels that I began to enjoy.

Occasionally, we would have excitement in the classroom, thanks to living in Africa. One time I was sitting at my desk when suddenly I heard a "plop" on my paper. When I looked down, there was a huge, black tarantula looking rather stunned. Needless to say I screamed and got out of my desk faster than humanly possible! Our brave boys argued briefly over whether to kill it or capture it. Thankfully, the decision was made to help the tarantula into its eternal resting place!

Another time, Jeanette and Eldon went to the recitation chairs for their discussion time with Uncle Bob. Eldon sat down first, but when Jeanette started to sit down, he quickly gave her a hard shove, making her fall forward onto Uncle Bob's desk, scattering papers. The reason? There was a large cobra in her chair, ready to strike had she sat down! Praise God for Eldon's quick reaction. Uncle Bob and one of the boys grabbed a bupanga (machete) and killed the snake before it could do any damage.

The door of our classroom was always open to help keep the room as cool as possible. One day, as we were all studying, a snake quickly slithered through the classroom, whipping over some of our feet. It all happened so fast, we hardly had time to react. It ended up quickly slithering back out the way it came in! Guess the poor snake figured there was way too much commotion inside with us girls screeching and jumping on our desks! It wasn't long after that before a screen door was made and installed.

School commenced at 8:00. Our morning studies took place until noon, with one break mid-morning. At noon those of us who lived in the dorm would rush back for lunch. The others would go to their homes. We were usually starving, to say the least. After lunch, we were required to go to our dorm rooms for one hour of rest. The hottest part of the day was between 1:00-2:00. Everyone, missionary and African, was quiet for at least that one hour. We could take a nap, read, or write letters but not talk to each other. Then at 2:00, we returned to school. We were dismissed in the afternoon by Uncle Bob after our studies were completed. Unless we were studying for exams, we usually did not have homework in the evening.

The following is a picture of those who attended Berean Christian Academy for the 1958-1959 school year, our first year back in the Congo. It was taken towards the end of that year.

*Jeanette is the third person standing from the right. This was her junior year of high school.
Marian is sitting in the second row, first person from the right, her 7th grade year.
The picture was taken on the front steps of the dorm.*

Our Berean Christian Academy "orchestra." Five played accordions and four trumpets. We played every Sunday for the congregational singing at the African church.

Jeanette and Marian are standing in the front row with the accordions Edgemont Bible Church had provided for us.

Marian's Comment: BCA Sports

A year before Jeanette and I arrived for school on Katanti, the Green's sons, a couple other missionary boys who lived on Katanti, along with some helpful African friends, dug out a tennis court behind the school. That meant they had to use machetes to cut down vines, bushes, small trees, and whatever else was there, to clear the land. Since this was the side of a hill, they had to use shovels to dig down to make the ground flat. I can only imagine how much work this must have been for them in the tropical heat of summer! But look at the end result!

Yes, it was a mud tennis court so, of course, when it rained, we couldn't play for a while. But it was wonderful. Look at the beautiful background, too! Linda Hendry (shown here) was the best tennis player of all of us. She could serve that ball with force right across the net, and it was almost impossible to return. That's Eldon Green sitting up high as the official referee.

Some friends of the Hendrys had sent out a lot of sports equipment to the school for tennis, badminton, volleyball, and softball. We actually were well equipped for these sports.

Uncle Bob was not only our school teacher, but he was also the coach/referee of our softball and hockey games. Every Friday after school, all the missionary teenagers with Uncle Bob, would gather at the field by the African church for a game of softball. That was the only time on the mission field that we girls were allowed to wear jeans. Trust me....that was the ONLY thing about playing softball that I enjoyed, too!

Jeanette and I, along with a couple other girls, just were not athletically inclined. Unfortunately, the boys really liked to win. The boys were divided into two teams, and then the captains of those teams would choose between the girls. Poor Jeanette always felt like she was the last one to be chosen each week, but had a good attitude about it anyway. I would have definitely been the last one chosen, too, except one of the boys was my "boyfriend," and he was kind enough to put me on his team.

Jeanette surprised everyone at the last game we played for our final school year there. Our parents had come for graduation and to take us back home with them. So they were there watching our last softball game. Lo and behold! Jeanette connected with the ball and everyone started cheering for her!

Eldon was standing on the sidelines telling her to RUN! She did, and ended up with a grand slam homerun! What a fabulous ending to her softball days.

You can tell by the huge grin on her face below that she was feeling good!

Whoo hoo!!!

Another sport the boys enjoyed was field hockey. It was played on the same field as our softball games. They didn't have helmets, knee pads, or equipment of any kind! They even had to carve their own hockey sticks out of a certain kind of tree growing in the forest. But they enjoyed playing hockey, and the Africans really enjoyed watching them.

The picture below shows the boys having a water break. I included the picture to show the field, along with the African church at Katanti in the background. That's where we went to church every Sunday with the Africans from our village.

Marian's Comment: BCA Dating

Having teenagers on Katanti attending Berean Christian Academy, meant that there would be the inevitable boy/girl attraction. Aunt Hallie and Uncle Ernie really tried to discourage "romance," but that never worked.

But one thing is for sure about living in the jungles of Africa on a mission station the size of two city blocks—there was no place for dating. We had no stores to go shopping in, no movie theaters, no fast food restaurants for junk food, no bowling alleys, and I could name more but the idea is evident. So what did we do?

Well, at the dorm every Friday evening after dinner, the "couples" could sit on a couch (we had several), with a throw pillow between them, and play board games. There could be absolutely NO physical contact of any kind—including holding hands. My boyfriend, Tim, lived in another house with his family, but he was allowed to come to the dorm on Friday evenings so we could play games. Trust me when I say Uncle Ernie and Aunt Hallie kept a close watch to make sure we didn't try to hold hands under the pillow. Little did they know!! Where there's a will, there's a way!

The times we looked forward to the most were when there was a full moon. Uncle Ernie would go outside on the porch, and if he thought the moon cast enough light, he would allow "dating couples" to stay outside and ride bikes. The boys would peddle the bikes, and the girls would sit on the handlebars. We could ride from the dorm, down to the front of the African church, and back again. Uncle Ernie would monitor the activities carefully to make sure no couple got off their bikes or stayed out of sight at the church area for any length of time.

Well, riding our bikes slowly down to the church and back gave us the opportunity to have our hands "touching" on the handle bars—once we were out of Uncle Ernie's sight, of course—and to grab a quick kiss at the bottom of hill. It had to be quick, because couples were coming and going all the time. Naturally, some of the younger boys, who didn't have girlfriends, would sometimes ride their bikes down to the church and try to spy on everyone else. They knew better than to tell Uncle Ernie what they might have seen because revenge would have been swift!!! They didn't dare!

So that was the extent of our dating in the Congo. Doesn't sound like much, does it? But I can attest that we all greatly anticipated our Friday evenings and the full moon "dates."

Now, I realize our dating experiences may sound ridiculous and juvenile to young people today, but this was all we knew. In reality, there was nothing else we could have done, so we just made the best of it. I am thankful Uncle Ernie and Aunt Hallie allowed us this enjoyment, no matter how insignificant it might seem to others. It definitely gave us something to look forward to.

Jeanette's Comment: Confessions of a Non-Dater

It's always hard to start attending a new school. It's doubly hard to suddenly find yourself living in a dormitory situation in one room with six or seven other girls—and your parents are totally out of reach.

Along with new school materials and a new teacher, you have to learn new societal rules. You have to cope with acute homesickness. You have to try and fit in somewhere.

But sometimes, you can't fit in. Sometimes, you're shocked to discover that you are purposely being snubbed, that you are considered an outsider, someone who doesn't belong. It was that kind of closed society that Marian and I entered on our return to Katanti Station.

We quickly discovered that unless you were part of the "in" clique, you had no say about anything, and your life was circumscribed by their rules of behavior. For instance, if a classmate was part of a "couple," then you were not supposed to speak to the person of the opposite gender of that couple. That big no-no would bring frowns and muttered recriminations. Dorm couples were allowed to "date," as Marian described, by sitting in the dorm living room and playing board games or talking. On rare occasions, they were permitted to ride together on bicycles.

If you weren't part of a couple, then you were expected to stay in your dorm room on Friday nights and not disturb the couples. Not only did you avoid the living room, but you also were not supposed to ride your bicycle if the couples were riding theirs.

Couples ruled dormitory society and spilled over to other school activities. Anything anyone did had to be approved by the older of the couples. In other words, a person wasn't supposed to run for an office in Katanti Scouts, the all-school club, unless approved. One couldn't work on the school newspaper—unless approved. Every area of life had to be approved.

Marian and I were shocked by the rigidity of the school society—and lonesome to boot. It wasn't too long, however, before Marian became part of a couple—but the young man wasn't in the dorm. His family lived in another house on Katanti. This proved to be an advantage because she occasionally was allowed to visit and eat supper with that family.

But there were others that were left out on Friday nights, too. And I'm telling you, it was b-o-r-i-n-g sitting in that dormitory room every Friday night! Sometimes, a couple of us older girls got together at another house. But we were careful not to interfere with the "couples."

Well, I tried to be a good girl—and I managed to survive that first year. But I determined over that first summer at Kamulila that the whole "couples" system was rotten, and I was not going play that game another year. Fortunately, some of the leaders had to go back to the USA with their parents for furlough that summer, something that really decimated the whole system.

The new school year started, and the very first Friday night, I called together all the non-daters and proposed a game night—in the dining room, right off the living room where the few remaining daters were making googley eyes at one another. We began holding game board tournaments on Friday nights. It was a blast! In fact, we had so much fun that the remaining "couples" could hardly resist joining us. Oh, they grumbled at first, to be sure. But the rest of us just ignored them and had a great time!

And thus, I confess. I was a hide-bound non-dater—a rebel at heart—and our second school year progressed with a great deal more light-hearted fun that included everyone. No one had to sit in a dormitory bedroom on Friday night again!

Marian's Comment: From Deep in My Heart

All kids go through difficult stages in their lives as they are growing up. Some can be devastating, and the effects can go with them into their adult lives. What seems totally demoralizing to one may not seem like much to someone else, but that doesn't take away the pain for the one going through it. My first few months at the dorm was such a time for me.

I was 13 years old. My parents were on a completely different continent. We had no telephones in the jungle so I couldn't even call them. Letters could take up to 2 to 3 weeks to arrive. I felt totally disconnected. Thank God, Jeanette was with me or I never would have made it through that difficult time.

It's well known that kids can be cruel to other kids. It's sad to say but the same cruelty goes for some preacher kids or missionary kids, too. As soon as we took up residence at the dorm, the three girls who were around my age decided to follow the lead of one of them and completely shunned me. They wouldn't talk to me unless it was necessary, they wouldn't include me in any of their activities, and they would look at me while whispering together and snickering. They made sure I knew that they had formed a "private" club—and I was not invited to join.

On top of that, from the beginning I felt that my dorm mother, Aunt Hallie, didn't like me. Numerous times in my loneliness I tried to talk to her, but each time she would either say she didn't have time or she was too busy or I should just go on and find something to do. I realized I couldn't confide in her or share my loneliness with her, so I backed off and tried to avoid her as much as possible.

I'm not going to go into all the details of the many ways we didn't get along. It wouldn't be good reading, nor would it benefit anyone. But I will just say that my relationship with our dorm parents never seemed to be very good. There were moments when it was tolerable, but even as the Lord allowed my relationships to improve where the other girls were concerned, those first few months in the dorm were ones I pretty much wanted to forget. The second half of our school year and the next year were better as far as friendships were concerned, so I was thankful for that.

Then in 2011, God opened my eyes to something else. When I was re-typing all Dad and Mom's prayer letters into my computer in preparation for this book, I spent many hours reading and sorting the letters. But as I was reading the letters and typing, the Lord unfolded a truth to me that I had not known in my immature, self-centered, young mind.

I knew that Aunt Hallie was our dorm mother with all the planning of meals, mending of clothes, overseeing the houseboys who did the cooking, laundry, and cleaning, plus she was the nurse for our mission station and worked every day in the dispensary. But what I didn't know was that on top of that she was in charge of the African women's work, she taught in the African school and sometimes in the missionary kids' school in the lower grades. She also prepared Bible lessons. I had no idea that there were many times in the middle of the night, while we were all sleeping peacefully in our beds, she would be called for medical emergencies. She was not only the nurse but she had to stand in as a doctor as well since she was the only medical person for miles around. She had very little rest in the midst of so many demanding responsibilities. It took its toll on her physically, and she had several breakdowns while on the field. I didn't know this.

The Lord impressed upon me as I was working on this book that, in spite of the fact that Aunt Hallie and I weren't close, Aunt Hallie was His willing servant in the jungles of Africa for years and years as she struggled to cope with the everyday situations that would occur. Both Aunt Hallie and Uncle Ernie were faithful to God's calling and won many of the Balega people to the Lord. In God's kingdom, that's what counts

Marian's Comment: Dad and Mom's Congo Return

At the time Dad and Mom were hoping to return to the Congo, there was a shortage of missionaries on the field. The missionaries who were there were struggling to keep up with the work. So the Board of Berean Mission gave Dad and Mom a credit of $900 that was still needed to cover the cost of their journey and told them to go ahead and return to the Congo so they could help relieve the pressure. However, these funds would have to be repaid to the Mission as our supporters gave for that purpose.

The Lord's timing is perfect. At the same time Dad and Mom were preparing to leave, so were their fellow missionaries and friends, Rev. Carl and Barbara Blackburn and their four little daughters. God went before them and made it possible for all of them to secure passage on the freighter Robin Kirk together.

The Blackburns' home church in Akron, Ohio gave them a 2½-ton Ford truck to take back to the Congo with them. That enabled the two families to haul all their equipment, crates, and barrels to New York City in Uncle Carl's truck, while Aunt Barbara and the children rode with Dad and Mom in our Carryall. This saved both families the huge expense of shipping everything to New York. To God be the glory!

Dad and Mom received a letter from the Kelley Travel Agency letting them know that their sailing date on the Robin Kirk had been set for October 3, 1958. So on September 25, they said their goodbyes to our family and friends in Illinois and drove to Akron, Ohio, to join up with the Blackburns. They loaded both vehicles and had a great time traveling together to New York City.

While in New York City, on October 2, they received word from Kelley Travel Agency that they would not be sailing on October 3 as planned due to a workman strike on the docks. A tentative departure date of October 6 was given to them, but they were told that was not for certain. They all immediately started praying for God's intervention. Praise the Lord, God did enable them to sail on October 6, 1958.

Since the ship was a freighter, they had many layovers at South African ports. It would take them six weeks to finally arrive at Mombasa, Kenya, on the east coast of Africa on November 19, 1958.

The following letters are the only ones we had available to us to include in this book. Dad didn't write a Travelog on this trip.

Thursday, October 2, 1958

Dear Mr. and Mrs. Wright,

When we returned from a sightseeing trip around New York City with the Blackburns, your good letter was waiting for us. Also waiting for us was a message from the Kelley Travel Agency informing us that due to the strike our boat would not be sailing October 3. A tentative date of October 6, Monday, was set but that *nothing* was certain. We believe God can break the strike deadlock and are praying to that end.

We have enjoyed good traveling with the Blackburns. The home in which we stayed in Lancaster, Pennsylvania, was not the same one in which you stayed. The elderly couple with whom we stayed were named Cooper. They had a lovely old home. We enjoyed a real time of fellowship with them. We attended the Calvary Church in Lancaster and heard Dr. Torrey preach. In the evening, Carl preached in a small independent church.

Tuesday, Carl and Les delivered the two trucks and equipment to the docks. They ran into some difficulty with the longshoremen and had to unload the truck themselves.

Wednesday, they went to the British Consulate and obtained our East Africa visas. All the business is taken care of now. We are just waiting and praying for the departure time.

We miss you all back home but have an urgency to press forward for Christ. The Lord bless you richly.

Rejoicing in Christ,

Les and Gertie

POSTCARD TO PASTOR AND MRS. WRIGHT....

October 3, 1958

Dear Ones,

We are on top of the Empire State Building just now awaiting nightfall so we can view the lights of New York. Your package arrived today. We were supposed to sail today, but are caught in this shipping strike. It may be days or weeks before we sail.

Love,

Les and Gertie

BEREAN MISSION, INC. 3536 Russell Blvd. St. Louis, Missouri	<u>A F R I C A</u> The Dark Continent!	B.A.M.S. - Kamulila Bukavu, D. S. Congo Belge, Africa

Prayer Letter	October 1958	No. 10

Dear Prayer Partners:

    Rejoice with us. Jeanette and Marian arrived safely in Bukavu, Sunday afternoon, August 31. They were met at the airport by Rev. Robert Hendry, headmaster of Berean Christian Academy, and his two children, Linda and David. Jeanette, I'm sure, breathed a quick prayer of thanksgiving when she saw "Uncle Bob," for now she could place in his capable hands the many responsibilities which had rested so heavily upon her slender shoulders as they traveled. Permit me to quote a portion of her letter which describes so graphically their trip into the forest-covered mountains to Berean Mission's Katanti Station.

    We've had quite an initiation to Congo! Three guesses what happened. We were stuck behind four trucks on the Bukavu road. Guess I'd better start right at the first to tell my tale. We finished shopping in Bukavu and left at 12:00 noon, Monday. Uncle Bob had something to deliver to the missionaries at Mushweshwe (Conservative Baptist Mission Station), so we started on our way. Of course, we got on the wrong road! We wandered over it for about an hour until Uncle Bob finally realized what was wrong. When we finally arrived at Mushweshwe, we met the Vans again (Rev. Neil Vander Ploeg of Berean Mission, and four of his children). We both got ready to leave in about half an hour, but we didn't make it. Something was wrong with the gasoline line or something. We finally left Mushweshwe at 3:00 P.M.

    We stopped for an hour by the side of the road for supper and then drove on. We hoped to make Ikozi (Berean Mission Station) by 1:00 A.M. The roads were quite muddy and slippery. At 8:00 P.M. we had a flat tire. It took us half an hour before we left again. At 9:00 P.M. we turned a bend in the road, and there were four trucks, two of them stuck in the mud side by side! Uncle Bob just sighed and turned off the motor.

    At 9:30, the Vans and us had 'lights out.' That was some night, believe me! I was squished between Marian and Uncle Bob. At one time both Marian and Uncle Bob used my shoulders as pillows. Talk about being squished!! We got up at 3:00 A.M., but it was 3:00 P.M. that afternoon before the four trucks were finally out of our way so we could proceed to Ikozi. We arrived there by 6:00 P.M., ate a hurried supper, and left by 7:00 P.M. I slept a good part of the way to Katanti. We arrived at Katanti at 11:00 P.M.. We 'honked' all the way up the hill to the Dormitory. We got to bed at twelve midnight. Boy, did it feel good!

    That was quite an introduction to Congo for Jeanette and Marian. So typical, too. Thank you for praying the girls right to their destination. God answered your prayers. But please don't stop praying for Jeanette and Marian just because they have arrived at Katanti. Surround them in prayer that God will protect them from malaria fever, as well as from the many things, creeping and otherwise, that could hurt them, and for the many adjustments they must make. Should you desire to write to them, their address during the school term is:

Mlles. Jeanette and Marian Spainhower
B.A.M.S. - Katanti
Shabunda, par Kindu
Congo Belge, Africa

Now for a word about Mother and Dad. We received a letter from the Travel Agency advising us that our sailing date has been advanced to October 3. Could we be ready? I'll say we can be ready! Lord willing, we will leave the St. Louis area Thursday, September 25, for Akron, Ohio, where we will join the Carl Blackburn family, who will drive with us to New York. If all proceeds according to schedule, the "ROBIN KIRK" will hoist anchor and set sail for South Africa on October 3. Praise the Lord!

Photo of the Robin Kirk taken by Dad in the New York harbor

At this writing we still lack about $600 of our passage. Will you join us in laying the burden before the Throne of Grace? We thank God for each one of you who have had a definite part in our outgoing, both in praying and giving. The Lord bless you, and may your gifts to us bring forth fruit that may abound to your account.

It would be so nice to have a letter from *you* waiting for us when we arrive at our mission station around the first of December. We will be so hungry for news from home. As a sort of gentle hint, our address will be:

Rev. and Mrs. Leslie J. Spainhower
B.A.M.S. - Kamulila
Bukavu, D. S.
Congo Belge, Africa

It is best to write airmail, as it takes about three months for regular mail to reach us.

This will be our last prayer letter written from the United States for several years, but we will endeavor to keep them coming to you from the Congo. The lines of communication will be long, and sometimes uncertain. But the faith line, through prayer, is short, sure, and never-failing. We welcome with open hearts your letters. We covet your faithfulness in prayer. Once again we are launching out, depending upon <u>YOU</u> to hold the other end of the prayer rope.

In His Keeping,

Leslie and Gertrude Spainhower

Dad took this picture of the Statue of Liberty while touring New York City with the Blackburns before sailing for Africa. You don't know how much seeing this statue means until you leave your country, knowing you won't be returning again for a long time.

November 1, 1958
Aboard Ship

Dear Ones:

How we have enjoyed the daily calendar which you fixed for us. We think of you each new day as we read our thought for the day.

We were supposed to dock at Capetown this evening, but terrific head-winds have slowed us up. It will be tomorrow before we actually set foot on land. I'll be so glad to have something solid under foot. I cut Les' hair this morning, and that is quite a feat with the boat rocking and rolling. I was afraid he might wind up with an unintentional crew cut or minus an ear. So far, no casualties.

I've been the only one bothered with seasickness and, praise the Lord, it hasn't been too bad. The little Blackburn girls are good sailors. They have completely captivated everyone. Some crew member is always giving them a handful of candy bars, some soda, or something. They are precious children and have really been a blessing.

We had services last Sunday afternoon. Not many crew members came, only six. But the Lord doesn't need a crowd to be "in the midst." Our hearts were especially blessed because four of the six were Negroes. Little Africa! Carl brought a fine message. The three older girls sang "Jesus Loves Me" so sweetly, in Kilega as well as English.

We are so longing to see Jeanette and Marian. Seems like years since we waved goodbye to them at Lambert Field. Les mentioned something about our daughters to one of the stewards. He said, "Daughters! We thought you were newlyweds!" That was a nice compliment but we would much rather be a family. We have the girls' pictures on our dresser to keep us company.

Someplace en route to Kamulila we will celebrate our twenty-first wedding anniversary, Jeanette's seventeenth birthday, and Thanksgiving.

Give the dear ones at Edgemont our loving greetings. Thank them for praying so faithfully. We are counting on them. May the Lord richly bless you in your corner of His great vineyard.

In Christian love,

Les and Gertrude

November 14, 1958
Off the East Coast of Africa

Dear Pastor and Mrs. Wright,

Greetings to you and to all at Edgemont in the name of our Lord Jesus Christ. We received your good letter of October 20 at Capetown passing along all of the news. We have laid over in so many South African ports that it is getting to be difficult to keep track of them or to keep track of the passing days. We have now been at sea for five weeks and have one more week to go. We are scheduled to land at Mombasa on the 19th, but one never knows until one gets there.

While we were in Durban, we were met at the ship by a Dr. and Mrs. Bennet from Carl Blackburn's home church in Akron, Ohio. They are out under TEAM and were in Durban for three months of intensive language study (Zulu) before going in to their mission station up country. The Blackburns didn't even know they were in Durban, but someone from their home church had written Dr. Bennet telling him that Carl and family were coming. They took us all to a large home for transient missionaries where they were staying while studying the Zulu language, and we had supper with them there. During the evening, Rev. and Mrs. Genheimer arrived, having word from you that we would be in Durban, and so we all spent the evening together.

Durban, South Africa

The next morning the Genheimers met us at the ship and took us for a drive around Durban, ending up at their lovely home for tea, and then back to the ship. Sunday was such a threatening day that we were afraid to attempt the long walk from the ship in to the Baptist Church in Durban with the four Blackburn girls. Carl had a raincoat, though, so he went in alone, and who should he

meet in church but Rev. Marvin Olson, brother to Ivan Olson. They had just moved from Johannesburg to Durban about three months ago.

We are enclosing our December prayer letter and will prepare another some time after we are finally home at Kamulila. We should arrive in time for the big African Christmas Conference, followed by a conference of all the out-teachers. So we are going in with our sleeves rolled up and ready for work. Pray for us as we trek inland because this is the rainy season and the going may be difficult. Give our love to all at Edgemont.

Love in Christ,

Les and Gertrude

Jeanette's Comment: A Joyous Celebration

November 29, 1958, was a banner day for Marian and me: Mom and Dad finally arrived on Katanti Station! Our long wait was over! We could hold them, hug them—and cry over them.

They were billeted to stay at the Hendrys' home. The Hendrys graciously invited Marian and me to share supper with them. We just couldn't bear to be separated from our parents that first evening!

After supper, we all sat on the bed in Mom and Dad's room—underneath the mosquito net—and talked until late. I'm afraid we totally disregarded any of the dorm rules and regulations—with our parents' permission! Finally, Dad walked us back to the dorm, and we quietly got ready for bed.

We only had a couple more days with Mom and Dad—and a lot of that time they spent visiting with the other missionaries and with the Africans, who were delighted to see them. It was during this time that Dad made arrangements with Katindi and Ngabo, both houseboys from our first term, to come and work for us on Kamulila. The family was taking shape once more!

But no tears were shed when Mom and Dad left on December 2. Only two more weeks, and they'd be back to pick us up for a whole month for Christmas vacation!! Even though we practiced hard for the school Christmas program, we would have been glad to skip the whole thing and just go home with Mom and Dad. Fortunately, cooler heads prevailed (Mom and Dad's, of course), and we did all the things we were supposed to do. But we were packed and ready to go long before we needed to be!

Our family was also going to increase on our trip home. During the first term, we had not had a cat because I was allergic to them. Instead, we had large rats that ran across the straw mat ceiling, especially at mealtimes, and all the straw would come sifting down. Dad determined that we would have a cat this term. The Hendrys' cat had a litter of kittens that were weaned and ready to place in new homes. Dad let us choose which one we wanted—and we chose the runt of the litter, a tiny, coal black kitten. She didn't have a spot of white on her anywhere!

I really don't know how we got her back to Kamulila without her running off in fright every time we stopped, but we did arrive at our first home on Kamulila with Midnight Cuddles Spainhower safe and sound. She rapidly adjusted to life in the Spainhower household and was dearly loved by all four of us.

It was nearing dark when we arrived on Kamulila. The trip on the ferry across the Ulindi River is really exciting at night! Fortunately, it was a clear evening, not rainy at all. As Dad drove up the hill to the station—honking all the way—both the missionaries and Africans came running up to our house.

Helen Gow, Evelyn Nickerson, and Iola Baker greeted us with great delight. The other missionary family, the Fernando Fasts, were at the state hospital in Shabunda where their baby would be born. I don't ever remember meeting them because I think they returned to Kamulila after we went back to school and then went back to the States on furlough before we came home for summer vacation.

We really liked Kamulila Station. There were three missionary houses—the usual mud houses with wide verandas and leaf roofs. The three single missionary women lived in one house, the Fernando Fasts in one closer to the village, and the Ivan Peterson family would be returning to the "house on the hill" where we were staying when they came back from furlough. We moved into the Fasts' house once they left for furlough. Dad liked it better because it was closer to the workshop where he supervised the African workmen. For Marian and me, it didn't matter where we lived as long as Mom and Dad—and Katindi and Ngabo—were there. Oh, yes! Not to forget Middy, the newest member of the family!

We immediately plunged into working with the missionaries and African leaders for the Christmas conference where Christians from all over the area came together to worship the Lord. Dad had all kinds of work to do—including hunting for monkeys and birds for the Africans to use for food during the conference. Mom was busy with the "fence girls" and the women's class she regularly taught. Marian worked with Aunt Evelyn at the dispensary for a while but also helped with the children's meetings during the conference. I helped Aunt Helen with the African school Christmas programs and also played my accordion for all the meetings.

Another thing I really enjoyed was being able to play Aunt Helen's piano whenever I wanted. At the dormitory, piano time had to be regulated so that everyone taking lessons had a chance to practice—and we didn't drive Aunt Hallie Green, the dorm mother, to absolute distraction. But I thoroughly enjoyed playing the piano during the day while the lady missionaries were busy working with the Africans.

Despite all the things Marian and I were doing to help with the mission work, we had plenty of time at home, too. Since the Blackburns had brought all of our equipment across to the Congo with theirs, we now had the box with our artificial tree and all of its decorations. Dad even rigged up a battery, so we could use the lights for just a few minutes each evening. Marian and I made extra ornaments and gave them to Katindi and Ngabo, who were delighted if a little unsure what to do with them.

New Year's Eve brought a special treat for everyone—although the Africans weren't quite sure what to make of it at first. In the heavy-duty ammunition cases Dad had brought with stuff for his guns, he had also packed a lot of fireworks. Dad loved fireworks as much as any kid. So from our hilltop, he shot rockets and whirligigs into the air. Boom! Bang! Lights in the sky! The Africans wondered what was going on. They hurried up to the house to ooh! and aah! just like the missionaries. We had quite a fireworks show!

Marian and I enjoyed an extra week of Christmas vacation because of huge landslides that blocked the road from Kamulila to the crossroads with the main road. Landslides in rainy weather weren't unusual but these were very large and had us totally blocked in. So we had many reasons to celebrate that first Christmas on Kamulila.

It was difficult to go back to school once more, but every Saturday morning, we could talk briefly on the ham radio with Mom and Dad. By this time, each of the mission stations had ham radios to keep in contact with each other—and to know what was going on in the world. The time would come when those radios would save the lives of the Berean missionaries. But in 1959, we just knew that we could reach Mom and Dad if we really needed to.

BEREAN MISSION, INC. AFRICA B.A.M.S. - Kamulila
3536 Russell Blvd. Bukavu, D. S.
St. Louis, Missouri The Dark Continent! Congo Belge, Africa

Prayer Letter February 1959 No. 11

Dear Prayer Partners:

Greetings in our Saviour's dear name from Berean Mission's Kamulila Station in the Belgian Congo, Africa. How good it is to be sitting in our mud house, in the light of our own pressure lantern, writing a prayer letter. Traveling days are over — but that is an ambiguous statement because one travels constantly in Africa, and that is a different story for another time.

When we last wrote to you we were still aboard ship, waiting to dock at Mombasa, Kenya. On November 18, 1958, the Spainhowers and the Blackburns left the good ship "ROBIN KIRK" with nary a backward glance — so happy were we to put our feet on *terra firma* once more. All our belongings were unloaded and went through British customs without incident due to the considerate help of Rev. Lyons, a veteran missionary stationed in Mombasa. Rev. Lyons kindly offers his help to bewildered missionaries debarking in Mombasa as an extra service to the Lord. Truly, this is a service above and beyond the call of duty.

We will spare you the details of our long, arduous trip inland except to say that the loving watchcare of our gracious Lord was evident with every revolution of the wheel. We traveled nearly 1,500 miles in two trucks without a single flat tire or motor failure of any kind. Praise the Lord! We traveled with the Blackburn's four small children, constantly changing water and eating strange foods, and yet not one of them became ill. *"When He putteth forth His own sheep, He goeth before them"* (John 10:4). You were praying, dear friends, and your prayers were answered.

November 29, we came "honking" up the hill to Berean Mission's Katanti Station, where our two daughters are attending the Berean Christian Academy. As we drove up in front of Jansen Hall, the dormitory for the missionary children, there were Jeanette and Marian alternately laughing, crying, and hugging each other until we could hug them. Why do women cry when they are happy? That is a riddle no one has solved. They just do. The four of us talked, talked, talked. When night came we all crawled under one mosquito net and talked some more. Both girls were healthy, happy, and working mighty hard in school. We left Katanti and our girls on December 2 for Kamulila, which was to be our new home. It wasn't so hard to say "goodbye" to Jeanette and Marian this time, because in just two weeks their Christmas vacation from school would begin and then we would have them at home with us for one whole month.

At about 4:00 P.M., as we crossed the Ulindi River on a ferry boat of native dugout canoes, we heard the furious beating of drums. We didn't know it then, but the drums were saying, "They are coming! They are coming!" The message was being relayed to Kamulila just one and half kilometers away.

The road was lined with Africans shouting, "Samba, Tata! Samba, Mane!," which is to say, "Greetings, Father! Greetings, Mother!" We could hardly make our way to the top of the hill to the mission station. Standing on the porch of the mud house which was to be our new home were our good friends Helen Gow, Evelyn Nickerson and Iola Baker, our co-workers on Kamulila Station. The Fernando Fast family, also of Kamulila, were in the government hospital at Shabunda awaiting the arrival of their fourth child.

As we greeted our friends, we heard singing in the distance. The Africans were coming, rejoicing that their missionaries had returned to them. Nearly 200 school boys, in orderly ranks of four, came marching up the road beneath the Belgian flag and the flag of the Belgian Congo. Also coming were the afternoon rains, but that did not daunt the Africans. Dripping wet they came to us, singing their marching song at the top of their lungs. Along came the villagers, shouting greetings. Many clasped our hands in both of theirs and said, "We prayed for you many days, and now God has sent you back to us. Ganuna Kalaga Yehowa!" Praise God! Our hearts were touched by their sincerity and their love. How glad we were to be back with them again. Our hearts were saying with their hearts, "Ganuna Kalaga Yehowa!" Praise God! From St. Louis, Missouri to Kamulila Station was 12,500 miles. We were home.

December 19 we brought Jeanette and Marian home. They created quite a sensation because they were almost as big as mother. The Africans took the girls to their hearts just as they had received us. The girls like it here on Kamulila. Marian spends quite a bit of time at the dispensary with Evelyn Nickerson, our nurse. Jeanette helped Helen Gow with the presentation of the Christmas program by the African school. Marian helped in the children's meetings during the Christmas conference. Jeanette played her accordion at the services. The Africans say that we are not two missionaries with two children, but that we are four missionaries.

As soon as we arrived at Kamulila, Les was plunged into the planning of the Christmas Conference with our African elders and Christian workers. The conference began on Christmas night with the Christmas program. Friday and Saturday there were five meetings each day. Sunday morning at 9:00 o'clock was the Communion Service, and at 10:30 the regular morning worship service, and in the afternoon a baptismal service. Africans walk for miles to come to these conferences. Some walked for four days. From the out-villages came 853 people. These people must be fed and housed. For two days Les and the African elders went out in our truck to gather food for the conference. One day they went hunting, and Les brought back some monkeys and birds for them to eat.

The Lord blessed in a marvelous way in the conference. Sixteen precious souls accepted Christ as Saviour. Sixteen precious souls delivered from the darkness of sin and Satan into the glorious light of Christ, the Son of God! Fifty-six Christians yielded to the convicting power of the Holy Spirit, confessed sin in their lives, and rededicated themselves to live for Christ daily. Great victories were won in some of their lives. Sunday afternoon, Les and two of our Christian elders, Lutete and Kiamunene, baptized fifty-nine Christians. To qualify for baptism an African must be a Christian for at least one year, *and* their lives give evidence that they are "new creatures in Christ Jesus." *"Wherefore by their fruits ye shall know them"* (Matthew 7:20). We missionaries do not judge the candidates

for baptism. The African Christian elders do, and their standards are high. I must confess that I had a few uneasy moments when Les entered the Ulindi River, since crocodiles have an abode there. We hoped that the noise of the large crowd would keep the crocodiles away, and apparently it did because we did not miss anybody! Seriously though, our hearts were blessed as we saw these black jewels enter the waters of baptism, following the example of their Lord and Saviour Jesus Christ.

Friday night of our conference, Les and I, together with our nurse, Evelyn Nickerson, made an emergency trip to the mine doctor at Kigulube, some thirty miles away. An African woman was in critical condition in childbirth. It was raining, and the road was a quagmire. It took us two and one half hours to go thirty miles. The poor woman was in agony with every bump of the road. To our sorrow she died just a couple of hours after arriving at the hospital. She was a Christian and is now in the presence of her Lord, but she left five little children and a heathen husband who blames us for her death. Les has made three emergency trips in our truck in the few weeks we have been here. Life and death are close companions here in the depths of the tropical rain forests. How good it is to know that we have a loving Shepherd ever watching over us.

It is difficult to stop writing. There is so much to tell you. But some of our experiences will just have to wait for another day and another letter. Thank you, dear friends, for your prayers, gifts, letters and lovely Christmas cards. We appreciate them so much. Continue to bear us to the Throne of Grace in prayer, even as we remember you.

Your missionaries in Africa,

Les, Gertrude, Jeanette, and Marian
The Spainhowers

African church on Kamulila

Dad's workshop (our red truck in the background

Two-room African school building

Marian's Comment: So You Want To Be a Nurse

Ever since I was a young child, I had dreamed of one day becoming a nurse. My Grandpa Wilson had made me a wonderful large, wooden box with a hinged lid that had different sized compartments in it. I had my medical instruments from store-bought nursing kits in that box along with medicine bottles of different sizes and shapes (filled with candy pills), cotton balls, bandages -- you name it, I had it. I doctored and healed more dolls and friends than anyone could imagine. So I knew as I was growing up that I was definitely going to be a nurse.

When Aunt Evelyn Nickerson, the missionary nurse on Kamulila Station, asked me to go to the African dispensary with her, I thought that was the best thing ever. I was almost 14 years old and already I was going to start fulfilling my dream. I spent quite a few days with Aunt Evelyn as she helped pregnant mothers and hurt or sick Africans.

One day a man came with his foot wrapped in a filthy cloth. Aunt Evelyn turned to me and asked if I would remove the cloth from the man's foot so she could examine it. I carefully began to unwrap his foot, making sure I wasn't hurting him in any way. The cloth was wrapped around his foot many times. When I finally pulled the last piece of cloth from off his foot, I froze in shock and the entire contents of my stomach wanted to make a quick exit. The poor man's toes were almost completely gone and the bloody, puss-filled stubs were crammed with white, squirmy maggots! My nursing career abruptly ended right then and there.

I went home and told Mom and Dad that I no longer felt God wanted me to become a nurse. And I was true to my word!

March 7, 1959

Dear Brother and Sister Wright:

Greetings from Africa on a cool, rainy day. The rain is so welcome. Besides being our major source of water supply, rain serves to cool down the heat waves. Didn't rain for two days and I found the heat oppressive. Les said with vigor, "Isn't this wonderful weather?" I replied rather limply, "Yes, dear."

Helen, Evelyn and Iola returned from Shabunda last night. They brought the encouraging news that Cay Vander Ploeg's eye infection isn't as bad as they thought. She has three boils on the *eyeball*. The doctor told Cay that this condition would clear up in a few months, and her eyesight would not be impaired. Praise the Lord. Iola is not in good health. The doctor found that she has rheumatism of the spinal column. Between the disks of the vertebrae are swollen places. It's quite painful. Do remember her in prayer.

Last week when we took the little Blackburn girls back home to view with wonder that precious baby brother, we went on over to Katshungu to spend a couple of days with the Lisles. Everett is doing a magnificent job on the hospital. Everett and Les went over to Katanti and brought our four precious daughters back to Katshungu. We had a lovely weekend together. I began to regain some of my strength which I had lost during a bout with the flu and the constant care of the three little girls.

Les and I took all four girls back to Katanti Sunday afternoon. We ate supper at the dorm, then headed back to Katshungu. About half way there, we developed car trouble and had to sleep in the car all night. These African nights get pretty cold, too. The next day, Les fixed the car and away we went. He is getting to be a first-rate mechanic, of necessity, of course.

We received word over the radio this morning that Ernie Green had received word of the arrival of the money from our reserve account. Praise the Lord. It will take a couple of weeks to transfer it to our account, then we'll be able to "bail" out our much-needed equipment. Do send our thanks to those in the office for so promptly taking care of this. We appreciate it so much.

The Lord bless thee and keep thee. We are praying for you.

In our Savior's love,

Les and Gertrude

Marian's Comment: Furry Family Additions

Jeanette mentioned in her comment about Midnight Cuddles Spainhower, our newly adopted black kitten. We were delighted to welcome Middy, as we nicknamed her, into our home. She was playful, loving, and did a wonderful job taking care of our mice and rat population.

One evening after Jeanette and I had returned back to school on Katanti following that first wonderful Christmas vacation, Middy fell into a bucket of kerosene Dad had sitting around his workshop. Mom quickly went over to Aunt Evelyn Nickerson's house (our station nurse) to ask her what she should do for poor Middy. Aunt Evelyn suggested keeping her warm and seeing what would happen in the morning. So Mom wrapped Middy in an old towel and took her to bed with her. She told us later that Middy kept burping kerosene in her face all night long! But by morning, Middy crawled out of the towel, staggered over to her food bowl, and ate heartily. All was well. The funny thing is that she never had parasites like other cats—and she had the thickest, silky black fur we had ever seen. Even though she wasn't a long-haired cat, you couldn't part her fur to see her skin; her fur was simply too thick—all thanks to a good dunking in kerosene early in her life!

Now, as Middy matured, she became very fond of our Dad. She loved all of us—or at least endured us—but she would allow Dad to pick her up and lay her on her back in his arms while stroking her head. She was quiet and reserved, and definitely a part of our family.

In due time, Middy gave birth to her first litter of kittens—two fluffy, striped little kittens who didn't look a thing like their sleek, black mother! Middy didn't fuss when Dad picked up these two little bundles of fur for the picture. They were named them Smudgy and Nudgy, which sounded a lot like names Dad would pick out. Jeanette and I could hardly wait to see them when we came home the next time.

The kittens looked identical but they were quite different. Nudgy was very affectionate and loved to be held or sit on our laps. As time passed, we all realized that Smudgy was downright retarded! She meowed a lot and instead of walking in a straight line, she would stagger like she was drunk or would walk around in circles. When she would catch a prey, instead of killing it, she would bring it—alive—to the front door and whine for us to come see what she caught. She always wanted to bring her catch into the house and play with it. When we killed it, she would stagger away! Smudgy just disappeared one day and never returned.

Middy had one more litter while we were still on the field. She gave birth to three kittens—two black and white ones and one pure black like her mother. They were named Eeney, (no Meeney) Miney

and Moe. Moe was the all black kitten. They were adorable!

Jeanette and I didn't have the opportunity to watch them mature since we returned to the States not long after this picture was taken. But we certainly had a lot of fun with them while we were there.

We always looked forward to returning to Kamulila from school so we could see our pets. We enjoyed Middy and her kittens a lot. We spoiled them, and they gave us love and affection in return.

Jeanette's Additional Comment:

One day while Marian and I were going through these Prayer Letters, we realized that we didn't know what had happened to the cats when Mom and Dad had to evacuate from Kamulila in July 1960. Dad was living with Marian at the time, so we could ask him.

Dad said that shortly after Marian and I left the Congo, Middy seemed to go wild and simply disappeared. She always had the freedom to leave the house whenever she wished, but she started spending more and more time outside. About four weeks before the evacuation, Middy simply disappeared and didn't come back to the house again.

Dad couldn't remember what had happened to Eeney, Miney, and Moe, but we found a letter he wrote to Uncle Ernie Green (see September 24, 1960) specifying what to do with all of our belongings that had to be left in the Congo. In that letter, he "willed" the three cats to the mission.

BEREAN MISSION, INC. 3536 Russell Blvd. St. Louis, Missouri	**AFRICA** The Dark Continent!	B.A.M.S. - Kamulila Bukavu, D. S. Congo Belge, Africa

Prayer Letter	April 1959	No. 13

Dear Friends in the Homeland:

"O give thanks unto the Lord; call upon His name: make known His deeds among the people" (Psalm 105:1).

    Early one morning word was received that the chief of the entire district had been poisoned by his political foes and was in a desperate condition. Chief Mubaki sent word to the Mission asking us to come and get him because his relatives refused to carry him in on kipoi. They are very antagonistic to the Gospel, but the chief realized that the white missionary could override the objections of his family and bring him to the Mission for medical aid. Chief Mubaki is not a Christian but has always been kindly disposed to the Mission. So we felt constrained of the Lord to aid him all we could.

    I summoned Lutete, our head elder, and together with one of our African male nurses we drove to Mubaki's village and entered into his house. There we found a very sick man and a house full of belligerent relatives. The chief was in bed, running a high fever, and his knees and ankles were dreadfully swollen as a result of the native poison. His relatives argued that this was the poison of the Balega and only the medicine of the Balega could help. What could the white man know of the black man's medicine? I listened to their arguments for a while in an effort to gain time in order to decide what course of action would be best. Finally, I turned to Chief Mubaki and asked, "Do you want to go to the Mission?" He raised his eyebrows in true native assent and said an emphatic, "Yes." Turning to his relatives, I said, "It is his life, not yours. Let us go. Put him in our car." With much noise and many protests they carried their chief to the car, and we drove back to the Mission, where he was put into the competent care of our registered nurse, Miss Evelyn Nickerson.

    Miss Nickerson does not know the antidotes for the various native poisons, but we have a great God—a God of infinite wisdom and tender compassion. He gave Miss Nickerson wisdom in her choice of medicines, and He gave strength to the chief. We all prayed that Chief Mubaki would find Christ as His Savior, as well as healing for his body while on our Mission Station. Every effort was put forth both by the missionaries and the African Christians to witness to the chief of his need of Jesus Christ. In about three weeks, Chief Mubaki was able to return to his village healed in body—but not in his soul. He has resisted the Gospel message. Pray for Chief Mubaki that his heart will be opened to the love of God, which is in Christ Jesus our Lord, and that he will trust Him as Savior. As a result of this experience, our daughters, Jeanette and Marian, have a new name for their Dad. They now call me the "chief snatcher."

    While on this same trip to "snatch" the chief from his relatives, Lutete asked if I would take along a young couple who had just been married the day before at the morning worship service. The bride's father was a hard, pagan man and had opposed the marriage because the husband, one of our Bible School graduates, was going out as a village preacher. The father hated the very name of Christ, and so he refused to come and see his daughter married in the church, even though he was willing to sell her into the marriage in order to obtain more riches. Nevertheless, the bride wanted to see her father once again before she left with her husband to go to a distant village.

    The trip began in happiness, but ended in great sorrow for the bride. Upon arriving at her village, she heard this sad news. The day before, at the very time she was being united in Christian marriage in our church at Kamulila, her pagan father had been bitten by a snake out in the forest and died almost instantly. Lutete seized the opportunity to point out to the villagers that if this man had come to the church to see his daughter married, he would still have his life, and perhaps would have eternal life besides for he would have heard the Gospel and had an opportunity to accept Jesus Christ as his Savior. Now it was forever too late!

On January 23, we returned Jeanette and Marian to Katanti Station for school after a wonderful Christmas vacation with us at Kamulila. They enjoyed an extra week of vacation because we were sealed off from the world by tremendous landslides which covered our single, winding road for a distance of about two or three miles. It took an extra road gang of some 200 Africans more than two weeks to shovel off the thick "oozy" clay and clear the narrow road once again for traffic. "Traffic" consists of one or two trucks per week in addition to the occasional passage of one of our missionaries. Gertrude and I find it very difficult being separated from our daughters, but we can testify that *"His grace is sufficient"* in all circumstances.

Muddy landslide. White man in center was the Belgian foreman of the road gang.

On our way back to Kamulila after returning Jeanette and Marian to school, we stopped at Ikozi Station and picked up three little girls, Ruth, Mary and Martha Blackburn. They visited with us for five weeks while their daddy and mother, Rev. and Mrs. Carl Blackburn, went to the nearest State Hospital to await the arrival of a little one. We had a real good time in spite of finding a vicious "spitting" cobra under Martha's bed, our kitty falling into a bucket of kerosene (she is minus one of her proverbial nine lives), and all of us except Martha having a bout with the flu. We praise God for His loving watchcare over the Blackburn children while they were in our care. Ruth, Mary and Martha's joy was full to running over when at long last they held in their little arms a wonderful new baby brother.

You dear ones at home probably know more about the uprisings in the Congo than we do, since we have no radio, and newspapers do not exist back here in the bush. These are turbulent times for the Congo and for all Africa. There is much fear among our Christian leaders as they contemplate the possibility that their missionaries may be forced to leave the country. "If you have to go," they tell us, "we black people will return to the darkness we knew long ago. The old hatred between tribes is not gone. They have been held in subjection by the white man. If you leave, tribal wars will resume. We Christians will have to run into the forest and hide. We will be as sheep to the slaughter." Such is the fear of our African Christians.

There is a growing resentment on the part of the pagan villagers up and down the road against the white man, including the missionaries. The spirit of rebellion has reached back into the forest-covered mountains where our Balega tribe dwells, as word of the uprisings has trickled into the area by word of mouth. The word we hear is "Muzungu, kuenda kumputu!" — "White man, go home!" But their attitude in no way lessens their need of the Lord Jesus Christ.

Beloved, pray much for this country, its people, its missionaries. Let us join hands around the Throne of Grace and put forth every effort to reach these dear ones with the Gospel of the grace of God, so long as He leaves us an open door.

In His Keeping,

Les, Gertrude, Jeanette, and Marian
The Spainhowers

BEREAN MISSION, INC. 3536 Russell Blvd. St. Louis, Missouri	**A F R I C A** The Dark Continent!	Kamulila B.A.M.S. - Kamulila Bukavu, D. S. Congo Belge, Africa

Prayer Letter   June 1959   No. 14

Dear Friends in the Homeland:

The past two months have been a time of testing and of blessing; of sadness and of joy. Though circumstances vary, yet the Lord is invariable. *"Faithful is He that calleth you."*

I was sick for nearly six weeks with a combination of Asiatic flu, malaria and anemia. Strength has been so slow in returning, but I have been standing on His promise, *"As thy days so shall thy strength be."*

Les has been busy as the proverbial beaver in keeping the industrial work humming and organizing his duties as chairman of Kamulila Station. Three weeks ago, he made a week-end trek back into the forest to visit some remote villages. It had been almost a year since a missionary had been in there. Les walked for many hours over narrow forest trails. We are situated in a mountainous terrain. It's really rugged hiking. Up on one side of a mountain, plunging down the other side, repeating the process again and again. After about five and one half hours, Les' legs refused to climb another hill. His Gospel Team, consisting of nine of our mission workmen and SaAziza, the evangelist, promptly made a *kipoi* to carry him to the farthest village.

Les claims it is quite an experience being carried on *kipoi*. As they descended, he had the sensation of toppling out on his face; as they ascended a hill, of doing a backward somersault. The carriers never slackened their pace. They would come pell-mell down a mountain, dash over a roaring mountain stream on two slippery logs and right up the side of the next mountain. Talk about thrills!!! Coney Island has nothing on the Congo.

That evening, the men built a fire in front of the house where they all slept. Around the fire, they held their first service. Les was proud of his men. Most were illiterate workmen, but they loved the Lord and gave a good testimony. After the service, they ate a good meal of rice with palm oil and hot pepper gravy and then went to bed. Les slept fully clothed with three other men in a tiny, windowless room of a mud hut. Services were held at daybreak—then they traveled to the next village, hunting monkeys along the way. No decisions were made, but we know that God's Word will not return to Him void. Pray for the seed that was sown in this remote area of our Lord's vineyard.

When our bright red Chevy pulled up in front of our house, I was not at all sure that I wanted to accept the mud-spattered, rain-soaked, unshaven, limping man as my beloved husband. In the eyes of the Gospel Team, the trip was a huge success. The Word of God was faithfully preached to hungry hearts, and Les killed forty-three big red monkeys to fill hungry stomachs. The whole village of Kamulila feasted like kings—African kings, that is.

May 7 we went to Katanti Station for the graduation exercises of the Berean Christian Academy. Five young people were graduating from the eighth grade and two young women, Louise Vander Ploeg of our mission, and Nancy Brooks of E.S.A.M. graduated from the High School. It was a lovely service. The school was decorated in palm fronds and beautiful flowers. Mr. Sam Vinton of another mission brought a challenging message to our young people. About fifty missionaries attended the graduation exercises. Two other missions send their children to our school.

Immediately following the graduation exercises, we gathered up Jeanette and Marian and all of their belongings (how can two girls in the heart of Africa accumulate so much stuff??) and headed for Kamulila. The girls will be home for four wonderful months. As usual in Congo, we were delayed for over an hour because of a bridge that "died," as our Africans say. After much work on the part of Rev. Roger Reed, one of our missionaries, Les, and some Africans, the bridge was finally safe enough to cross (since "underneath were the everlasting arms"), and we were once again on our way home.

We had been home just a week when Les became quite ill with a high fever. Naturally, our first thought was "malaria," but a cure-dosage of an anti-malarial didn't faze the high temperature. On the fifth day of his sickness, our nurse, Miss Evelyn Nickerson, advised that we must seek a doctor. This poses quite a problem as our own mission doctor is in America on furlough. We must, therefore, make the 150 mile trip to the State Hospital at Shabunda. A mattress was placed in the back of Miss Iola Baker's Chevy station wagon. At 10:00 A.M. we left Kamulila; and at 9:00 P.M. we pulled up in front of the doctor's home. Arrangements were made for us to sleep at the hospital. In the morning a series of tests were made and a thorough examination given. Dr. Pieter's diagnosis was Rickettsial Fever, brought on by a tick bite.

It was thought best, in view of the possibility of further complications, for us to remain at our Katshungu Station which is only fifty miles from the Shabunda Hospital. Rev. Roger Reed drove back to Kamulila with Miss Baker and Miss Gow to bring Jeanette and Marian, and our car to Katshungu. We praise the Lord that, at this writing, the fever seems to be broken. Les is pathetically weak. The doctor advises *at least* a month's convalescence here at Katshungu, then a very gradual re-entering into the work.

We do not understand why these things come into our lives. There is so much to be done and seemingly such a short time left to us here in Congo. We are not to question, only to trust our gracious Lord. Romans 8:28 is still one of the precious promises of God. *"And we know that all things work together for good to them that love God, to them who are the called according to His purpose."* Even Rickettsial Fever is one of the "all things." Won't you pray just a little more for your missionaries, the Spainhowers? Pray, too, for the African Christians. There are trying times ahead for them.

Trusting in Him,

Les, Gertrude, Jeanette, and Marian

June 14, 1959

Dear Loved Ones,

So glad to be able to report that Les is so much better. We are once again back at good old Kamulila. Be it ever such a humble mud house, there's no place like home. Les still feels quite tired all the time. Continue to pray for him. We praise the Lord for raising him up so quickly.

The work is heavy, pressing in upon him. Saturday morning he had to make an emergency trip with a sick one—a drain on his strength over these rough roads.

Today has been such a nice day. This morning at the worship hour was the Graduation Exercises for the Fifth Grade. Our head elder, Lutete, brought an inspiring message on II Timothy 4:2, I Timothy 6:13-14, and I Timothy 6:20. All but one of the young people in the graduating class have accepted the Lord as their Saviour, several within the last few months. They all looked so nice, just shining, as they sang "Onward Christian Soldiers," then came forward one by one to receive their certificates.

This afternoon, we missionaries were invited to a feast in the village. We enjoyed a precious time of fellowship with the Africans as we feasted on a dish pan full of rice for just we missionaries, and a luscious chicken cooked in palm oil and native peppers. As we parted company, we all sang "Take The Name of Jesus With You," a favorite song of the Balega. We Spainhowers went to Helen and Iola's house to drink a coke and help Iola eat her birthday cake. Then the six of us gathered around the piano to have a Singspiration. A good day of fellowship with the Lord in our midst.

The Conference begins next week at Ikozi. Some of the missionaries we haven't seen for some months. Conference is always like a big family reunion.

We are praying for you and our beloved church.

Rejoicingly yours,

Les, Gertrude, Jeanette, and Marian

Marian's Comment: Chee Chee

One day when Dad was out in the forest hunting monkeys to give to the Africans for food, he made his shot and the monkey immediately fell out of the tree to the ground. When Dad and his African helper reached it, a baby monkey was sitting next to its dead mother. Dad felt badly for the little thing and had the African catch it. They wrapped it in an old towel Dad had with him and brought it home to Kamulila.

As soon as he arrived with the monkey, Helen Gow, one of our very sweet single missionary ladies, took it in her arms, and Dad knew right then and there the monkey had a new home. Aunt Helen named her Chee Chee. She had her houseboys build a large, wire cage around a small tree in her yard for Chee Chee with wire across the top, too, so she couldn't escape.

The next time Jeanette and I came home on vacation from the dorm, Aunt Helen took me to meet Chee Chee. It was love at first sight! She smelled bad, was a messy eater, and had a bad temper, but I didn't care. Chee Chee took to me right away. Anytime I would come to the cage and open it, all I had to do was hold out my arm, and she would jump on it and hang on. When Aunt Helen saw how we bonded together, she said I could consider Chee Chee my own pet monkey anytime I was at home on Kamulila. I didn't even have to ask to take her out of the cage.

Chee Chee loved bananas, but she was a little stinker when it came to eating them. I found out that she would chew a few bites and hold them on either side of her cheeks. Then when she felt like it, she'd spit them at me or anyone else who was around at the time. So when I fed her bananas, I started massaging her cheeks and neck so she had to swallow!

Mom stressed one very important rule, though. I was never to bring Chee Chee into our house. However, one afternoon as I was playing with Chee Chee, I wanted something from the house. I don't even remember what it was. I knew Mom and Dad weren't home, but Jeanette was. I didn't want to take the time to put Chee Chee back into her cage just so I could go into the house for a minute to get what I wanted. So when I entered the house with Chee Chee, Jeanette did what all older sisters are supposed to do and warned me that Mom said Chee Chee was not to be in the house. I'm sure I probably gave her one of those impatient, younger sister looks and said I would only be a minute. Mom would never know.

Unfortunately, Chee Chee must have suddenly felt exhilarated by being in new surroundings. She immediately jumped from my arm and started climbing

across all the living room furniture, tables, and anything in her path. Then she grabbed onto the curtains at the window and started swinging from one to another! Jeanette and I desperately tried to catch her but to no avail. It was almost as if she was laughing at us!

Finally, I remembered that Chee Chee was afraid of the Africans. So I quickly called Katindi and Ngabo and asked them to stand in the two doorways and make a noise to frighten her. Chee Chee screeched and quickly jumped onto my arm, holding on for dear life. Needless to say, I ran out of the house as fast as I could and put Chee Chee back into her cage.

I thought I was in the clear until Mom and Dad returned. As soon as they walked into the living room, Mom stopped and called to me. She asked if I had brought Chee Chee into the house! I forlornly admitted I had. But before Mom could scold me, Jeanette assumed the role of my protector and tried to explain that I was just there a minute but Chee Chee accidentally got loose. By the time she finished telling the story—and it was humorous—even Mom and Dad couldn't be angry with me any longer.

I've never known how Mom knew Chee Chee had been there. Perhaps it was Chee Chee's lingering smell. Perhaps it was the guilt written all over my face. But you can bet that I never brought her into the house again!!

Where did Chee Chee end up? Well, Aunt Helen finally had to let Chee Chee go free after Jeanette and I came back to the States. She started getting mean, and Aunt Helen couldn't handle her any more.

July 24, 1959

Dear Mr. and Mrs. Wright,

Thank you very much for your letter and prayers. Please thank the people at church, too. I sure needed their prayers and yours.

We have been in the big city of Bukavu. It was the first time in almost a year that Jeanette and I have been in civilization. It felt good. Now that we are in the bush, we miss the good old paved roads.

I don't believe I ever told you that I finished painting the pictures you sent me. Well, I did. One of them is hanging in our room and every time I look at it I remember you. I sure do miss your wonderful messages, Mr. Wright. Out here they're all in Kilega, and I can't understand them.

Aunt Minnie sent me some pictures to paint, too. I'm on the third one of them. Two of them are of Jesus, and two are of horses.

Night before last one of our little third grade boys in Kamulila village died. He was a Christian and so are his parents. The father adored the boy and was just numb. Poor guy! Just when they put the boy in the grave the father said, "He was like a cut goat." (Referring to the boy.) It meant that his son had died quickly with no sickness. It was really sad, but we can praise the Lord that he and his parents are Christians.

Thank you again for your prayers.

Love always in Christ,

Marian (14 years old)

July 26, 1959

Dear Brother and Sister Wright:

I'm way behind in answering letters, almost six weeks actually. I didn't have our address file with me at Katshungu, and it seems as though we've been at Katshungu more than home on Kamulila. At this writing, all the Spainhowers are once again home and in good health.

I'll back up a few weeks and tell you about the Annual Field Conference at Ikozi. We all had a wonderful time. Les and I were bedded down at Blackburn's house. Jeanette and Marian were at Adeline Fast's home with all the single girls. Quite appropriate. All of us really enjoyed being together, catching up on all the news from all the stations. Getting acquainted with the Ed Moyers and Fern Sanford. Lovely people. The business part of the conference just went like greased lightening. We sure were a bunch of agreeable people.

All joking aside, the Lord led the conference in a precious way. There was wonderful cooperation and harmony. As we were discussing whom to ask to be our guest speaker at conference next year, it was hoped we would have two - a Rev. G. J. Wright from a place called Edgemont, and a Rev. C. R. Lindquist from St. Louis—a "suburb" of Edgemont! Jeanette and Marian just said that they objected. If you were out here at conference, you wouldn't be home when they got home! Yes, they are both going home next year. We've prayed much about it and feel the Lord definitely leading in this direction. Marian is unhappy at the thought of being out here without Jeanette. Also, the main reason is the precarious political situation in this area.

Jeanette will have to work for a while after returning home. She is an excellent typist right now. This year Helen Hendry is going to teach Jeanette and Eldon shorthand. Eldon also is a good typist. We're thankful for this training. The youngsters at the Academy are really going to miss Eldon and Jeanette. There go their piano teachers.

Had a precious service this morning. Kikumunene, our Kamulila evangelist, had a precious service this morning, preaching on Proverbs 18:10. At the close of the service, a sweet young mother came forward to accept Christ as her Saviour. I stayed beside her as Kikumunene dealt with her. It was really precious to see an African tenderly leading a lost sheep into the fold. After we had all prayed I asked her, "Is the Saviour in your heart?" She looked at me and said with a radiant smile, "Yes, because I accepted Him." Simple faith as a little child.

Our old elder, Miseka, is quite ill. He is such a sweet old man. When the Lord calls him to glory, a big gap will be felt in our work here on the Station, and in our hearts. Every morning he comes to the door and says, "Ndi muayuka busoga?" "Did you get up well?" Which is their way of asking if you have had a good night's rest. When Les is gone, Miseka comes at least twice a day to see if the wife of Wemaninua is all right. We really love that old man.

Evelyn has gone to north Congo to a Dr. Becker of the Africa Inland Mission. She isn't a bit well. Has a temperature every day. Do pray much for her. Helen is much better now. She has a difficult year ahead of her teaching sixth grade for the whole mission. (We had two sixth grades before.) She is also head of the first five grades, too. Iola is going to help her but it is still a lot of responsibility on Helen, and she is getting tired. Pray much for her, and for Iola as she takes on this new work of the school.

Les has a hard trip to make in our big, old, mission truck. He is working on the truck now to get it in shape. He is going to put our Bible School Graduates (Kamulila had twelve) into their villages. I always am uneasy when he goes out in the big truck. Our roads are so dangerous, and the truck isn't exactly reliable. About the time you receive this letter, he'll be making the trip. Pray for him and all our missionaries as they make trip after trip on these hazardous roads.

I won't be able to afford postage if I don't stop writing. The Lord bless you, and we're praying for you.

Love in Christ,

Les, Gertrude and Girls

Elder Miseka with his young family. Miseka helped to start the work on the Kamulila Station.

BEREAN MISSION, INC.	AFRICA	B.A.M.S. - Kamulila
3536 Russell Blvd.		Bukavu, D. S.
St. Louis, Missouri	The Dark Continent!	Congo Belge, Africa

Prayer Letter	August 1959	No. 15

Dear Praying Friends,

"God is our refuge and strength, a very present help in trouble" (Psalm 46:1).

So much has happened since our last prayer letter that it is difficult to know just where to begin. Many of you have written, assuring us of your prayers for Les' complete recovery from his illness. Your prayers have been answered. He is back at work again, although a few pounds lighter.

On June 15, all Berean Missionaries gathered at Ikozi Station for the Annual Field Conference. We did enjoy a blessed time of fellowship, as well as a fruitful time of business. Rev. and Mrs. Raymond Florence, missionaries under Child Evangelism International, were our guest speakers. While we had our business session in the morning, Mrs. Florence had Daily Vacation Bible School for the pre-teen children. Our Jeanette assisted her by playing her accordion during the singing. Jeanette was also one of the conference pianists. In the afternoon, Mrs. Florence had a class for our teenagers. For handwork, she taught them to decorate cakes. Marian was an excellent rose-maker. Jeanette figured she will stick to her piano. One evening the teenagers decorated four beautiful cakes and served them to the conference. Marian made all the roses.

Every morning Rev. Florence brought us meditations from the Epistle to the Galatians. In the evenings, we enjoyed a singspiration, special music furnished by the various missionaries and their children, Gospel films, and a message from the Word. Our souls were refreshed. As for the business side, I've never attended a conference more obviously led by the Holy Spirit as evidenced by complete unity and harmony.

The last few days of the conference, Marian complained of pains in her abdomen. The last day of conference, the pains were so severe that we made an emergency trip to the doctor at the State Post of Shabunda, the same doctor who treated Les. Miss Lydia Frank, one of our nurses went with us. I suppose you can guess what it was—Hepatitis. She was a very sick girl. The doctor would have preferred for us to remain at Shabunda, but there are no facilities at the hospital for the care of white patients. Dr. Pieters has the utmost confidence in Miss Frank. He detailed his instructions to her, gave her medicine for Marian, and sent us back to Katshungu. We sent in runners every few days, keeping the doctor informed as to Marian's progress.

Marian was so sick. Food was repulsive to her. All she could think about were apples. She longed for apples as a man in the desert longs for water. "No apples are grown in Congo," I kept telling her. She would look so pitiful. We had no fruit at all. A Belgian stopped by Katshungu. In the course of the conversation, Rev. Roger Reed mentioned how sick Marian was. The man went on his way. The next day, an African came driving up in a big truck. "The Monsieur has sent a gift to the sick girl." When Roger opened the box, he shouted with glee and came dashing over to Miss Frank's where we were staying. The "gift" was four pounds of luscious A - P - P - L - E - S and one dozen naval oranges flown from South Africa for the Belgian's own luxury. He had shared them with our sick girl. We were instantly reminded of how God sent the ravens to feel Elijah. That was no greater miracle than apples back in the Kivu forests of the Belgian Congo. Isn't God good to us?

Marian is as perky and bouncy as ever now…well, almost, that is. She can participate in no sports for a year because of damage to her liver. We are so thankful to our Lord for His loving watchcare over us all.

After Marian had regained most of her strength, we drove in to Bukavu, our closest city, about 250 miles away. We did enjoy being in a city again. The first time the girls and I had been back into civilization since we entered the forest nearly a year ago. We had a good time looking at all the pretty things in the shops; enjoying such things as electric light, hot and cold running water right out of a faucet instead of running in on the shoulders of a black boy and dumped into the tub. My, it was nice, but we're *so* glad to be back in our dilapidated mud house again. After all, it's home.

The girls have just one more month of vacation. Why do vacations have to fly by on jet-propelled wings? Les and I are thankful we are so busy, otherwise we would be unbearably lonesome with our daughters away.

Dear friends, thank you for praying, for giving, for writing. I'm sure no other missionaries have more faithful prayer warriors behind them than we Spainhowers do. The Lord bless you each one.

Standing on His promises,

Les, Gertrude, Jeanette, and Marian

Marian's Comment: Hepatitis and God's Miracle

Every year around June, the missionaries and their kids looked forward to the Annual Field Conference. That's when all the missionaries would meet for a week on one of our stations to go over mission business matters. It was also a good time of fellowship together, and a time to refresh our souls by having a guest speaker.

For the conference of June 1959, we all met at Ikozi Station. The missionaries who lived on Ikozi, opened their homes to the rest of us for lodging and meals. Meals were always a lot of fun because we rotated among the various homes for our meals. That way we were able to enjoy fellowship with different missionaries at each meal.

At this conference, our guests were Rev. and Mrs. Raymond Florence, missionaries under Child Evangelism International. While the missionaries were at their morning business meetings, Mrs. Florence held Vacation Bible School for all of the younger kids. We teenagers were there to help her. Mrs. Florence gave some of the teens the opportunity to tell a Bible story to the younger kids each day, using flannelgraph figures to illustrate the lesson. I was assigned a story and given the figures I was to use so I could practice. But getting up in front of others petrified me, and I really didn't want to do this at all. My turn was supposed to be the last day of the conference. This was a completely new experience for me, so I was quite nervous and scared. I was afraid I would do a bad job of it, and the kids would laugh at me.

As the week went by, I started getting a pain in my right side. To be perfectly honest, I thought it was because I was so nervous about telling the Bible story. When I finally complained about the pain to my parents, I wonder if at first they possibly thought the same thing. But the pain persisted and increased in intensity. I really started feeling quite ill. I heard Mom and Dad talking to Aunt Lydia Frank, the missionary nurse on Katshungu. Then, my fear wasn't so much of telling the Bible story, but instead, I was very afraid of being taken to the African hospital at Shabunda to the Belgian doctor there.

But that is exactly what happened. The good thing is that Aunt Lydia went with us. The doctor examined me and said I was very ill with Hepatitis. I had to spend the night in the hospital. I begged Mom not to leave me. Of course, she never wanted to leave me, but it was more important for Aunt Lydia to stay with me instead of Mom, since Aunt Lydia would be needed to take care of me that night. It turned out to be a very wise thing because I got quite sick during that night. She was very kind and gentle with me. She comforted me with her words and never left my side all night.

The next day, the doctor gave Aunt Lydia everything that was needed for my recovery, and we made the trip to Katshungu Station, where Aunt Lydia would take care of me. Mom, Jeanette, and I stayed in a small guest house situated behind Aunt Lydia's house. Dad had to return home to Kamulila since he'd already been gone so long with rickettsial fever.

My memory is vague about those first few days, as I was terribly sick. I couldn't force myself to eat anything, but I finally started asking Mom for apples. She kept reminding me that apples aren't grown in the Congo. But I kept asking.

As Dad mentioned in his prayer letter, a Belgian man stopped by Katshungu on his way to some other place, and one of our missionaries, Rev. Roger Reed, happened to tell him about a missionary girl who was very sick, and how I kept asking for apples. Then the man left.

The next day, an African driving a big truck, came to Katshungu. When Uncle Roger went to meet the driver, the African told him that his boss (the Belgian man) had sent a gift for the sick missionary girl. He then took some crates of APPLES and ORANGES out of the back of the truck. The fruit had been flown to the Belgian man from South Africa for his personal use, and he wanted me to have them so I would get well. Coincidence? Not with our God!

If you don't remember anything else from this story, I want you to remember the awesomeness of our God. Who would have ever thought a very sick missionary girl, deep in the jungles of the Belgian Congo, Africa, would actually get apples and oranges practically delivered to her door by a perfect stranger. This was nothing short of a direct miracle from God. Yes, I started eating apples and oranges, and it wasn't long before I began gaining strength again. Praise God from Whom ALL blessings flow—yes, even apples!!

This is a picture of Aunt Lydia Frank, a single, missionary nurse, who spent many years serving the Lord in the Congo. The African next to her is one of her helpers in the African clinic.

Jeanette's Comment: Vacation in Bukavu

It had been nearly a year since Marian and I arrived in the Congo with Mom and Dad to follow. We'd already been through some rough times—being separated from Dad and Mom at the mission school, Dad's bout with rickettsial fever in May 1959, and Marian's battle with severe hepatitis in June. It was time for a vacation!

Missionaries were supposed to take a vacation every year, primarily to get out of the jungle into a different climate. Many of them would spend a couple of weeks at a conference grounds called Kumbiya in Ruanda-Urundi on the shores of Lake Tanganyika. But that meant living in grass huts—a big step down from our mud houses!—eating in a dining hall, and using communal bathhouses. If you recall Dad's reaction to communal living in Oklahoma in 1952, that was definitely not the kind of vacation that would rest and relax him!

We preferred to spend only one week on vacation—in Bukavu, the largest city near us, about 250 miles away. We wanted soft beds in a hotel, hot and cold running water, steak and French fries—a wonderful taste of city life, so different from life in the jungle!

So Dad made reservations for a week at a nice hotel in Bukavu near the end of July. That gave Marian time to regain most of her strength from her bout with hepatitis. Dad asked Ngabo to go with us, too, so we'd have an African with us for the trip. He'd very faithfully stayed with us at Katshungu to help during both Dad's and Marian's illnesses, and Dad wanted to express his thanks. Ngabo had never been to Bukavu—he was both excited and a little scared. He would stay in the African village on the outskirts of town. Dad would pay for his lodging and meals.

Mom, Marian, and I packed very carefully. We could wear our best dresses, nylon stockings, heels, jewelry—things we didn't often get to wear in the jungle. I was delighted that I could wear makeup. I had felt so grown up back in America because I was allowed to start wearing makeup when I was 16. But I couldn't wear it back in the jungle. The only women who wore "makeup" (made from berries) were prostitutes, so the mission wisely banned the use of makeup on the mission station. But since the Balega rarely traveled to Bukavu, we could feel free to wear it there.

The big day arrived—we put our suitcases in Kasoga, including Ngabo's little metal bag, and off we drove into the cool of the early morning. It was a long trip, and we arrived mid-afternoon. We dropped Ngabo off in the village, and Dad gave him money for the first night. Just to keep tabs on him, Dad arranged to meet with Ngabo every day to give him money for the next day's lodging and food, plus a little extra to spend as he wished.

We pulled up to the hotel—a three-story stucco building—and a bellboy came out to gather our luggage. As soon as we got up to our room on the third story, Marian and I hurried out onto the balcony that overlooked the lake and the rest of Bukavu. This was a beautiful little city—the pastel stucco houses surrounded by palm trees reminded us a lot of Southern California. There were shops and electricity and....

Suddenly, Mom uttered a cry of despair. Where was her suitcase? Dad had just come into the room from parking the car, but he turned around and hurried back out to check again. No suitcase! In fact, he didn't even remember packing it into the car. (And when we got back to the Kamulila, we found it sitting off to the side of the living room door!) So that meant we had some shopping to do right away!

Mom's new blue dress! Mom made all her own clothes so having a new store-bought dress was a special treat for her.

We left the nice big room with two beds in it, the gleaming white bathroom—with hot and cold running water—and took the elevator down to the main floor. Dad asked the desk clerk where we could buy women's clothes, and we headed off on a spree to get Mom properly attired. She purchased one new dress, a change of underclothing, and a nightgown. She alternated clothing every day between what she had traveled in and the new clothes. Every evening she washed out what she had worn that day and hung the clothes in the bathroom to dry.

We decided to have supper right at the hotel that evening since we were all tired from the trip and the added shopping. It was a lovely dining room—and we were very brave: we ordered a salad to go with our steaks and French fries! We were taking our chances because sometimes tropical bacteria wouldn't be totally destroyed from the fresh vegetables or lettuce and could cause gastrointestinal problems. But we yearned for a salad! We couldn't get the fresh vegetables for salads back in the bush. Fortunately, we had no problems.

After our late dinner, we took turns taking a soaking hot bath, then climbing into our nice, soft beds, expecting a good night's rest. But we must have been near an elevator shaft or something because all of a sudden we heard the strains of "Volare" by singer-songwriter Domenico Modugno. For hours we heard "Volare, oh, oh! Volare, oh, oh, oh, oh!" We slept in late the next morning.

The next few days were spent walking and walking and walking, as was always customary for the Spainhower family. We usually ate lunch at Le Gourmet—it would probably be designated as a delicatessen today. They had wonderful breads, plus a great selection of meats and cheeses for making sandwiches. We could get potato chips and ice cream sodas! In the afternoon, we'd generally stop at one of the sidewalk cafés and get a Coke. We'd have dinner in one of the small cafés—then back to the hotel to listen to "Volare" for hours! (I checked online, and it was an award-winning Eurovision song, even translated into English and other languages, and many famous artists worldwide sang it over the next few years.)

Along with ordering supplies for the mission, foodstuffs to be shipped to Kamulila, and other necessities, Dad bought one other item that brought us much joy during our last year in the Congo: a battery short-wave radio with a phono-pickup. We could receive programs from all over the world—and we could play records, too. We really enjoyed the music on BBC from South Africa.

Here's a short aside. We had two records of church music by the famous country singer Tennessee Ernie Ford. The Africans loved to listen to him. They called him "the man with the big voice." On a whim, Mom wrote to Mr. Ford to tell him how much we enjoyed his music out in the middle of the jungle and that the Africans really liked it, too. He sent her two more records.

But our vacation had one other interesting misadventure the evening before we returned to Kamulila. Here is how Mom described it to her sister:

> We went to a nice little restaurant for steak, salad, and French fries before we went back into the bush. We enjoyed a luscious dinner. The waiter brought the tab and retired to a discreet distance. Les reached back for his wallet; his face fell a foot. No wallet! He had left it at the hotel. Now how do you explain *that* in halting French?
>
> Les quietly got up from his chair, and with his "most reverend" dignity headed for the door. His wife and two daughters kept on eating *very* slowly and trying to control our slightly hysterical laughter. I've never felt so hilarious in all my life. Les made the trip to the hotel and back in nothing flat. He entered the restaurant, again with utmost dignity, walked to our table where Jeanette, Marian, and I were still eating French fries. Calmly he helped us on with our wraps, paid the check, and escorted us to the car where we promptly collapsed in laughter. A fitting ending for our series of misadventures!

Ngabo was waiting for us at the specified spot the next morning. He thanked Dad for bringing him to Bukavu but emphasized that he preferred living in the jungle! The lovely vacation was over—and in less than a month, we would be heading back to school again.

Jeanette's Comment: Pardon, Madame

Sometimes, the simplest and most natural human functions can cause unbelievable complications when dealing with another culture in a foreign country. It seemed to be Mom's lot to be on the receiving end of many of these complications.

Before they started working for us, our houseboys had been trained to let Mom know when they needed to take a short break. Most Africans knew nothing about bathrooms; they just went a little way into the forest to take care of such needs. So they'd explicitly tell Mom what they needed to do out in the forest—and probably wondered why she always blushed.

Mukenge seemed to have somewhat finer sensibilities. He would speak to Mom in French and say, "J'ai un petit besoin," which meant, "I have a little need." She'd just nod. Mukenge seemed to understand that too much explanation wasn't needed, so he trained the houseboys to simply say, "I need to go to the forest." They thought that was kind of strange, but it kept Mom from blushing so much.

The first incident Mom endured happened while we were living in the two-room, plus bathroom-in-the-middle, house. The houseboys were in the "kitchen" room, and Mom was in the bathroom that separated the general room from the bedroom. One of the houseboys knocked on the door of the bathroom, which had no lock, and called for her.

Now, in the Kilega language, many words sound similar, and poor Mom experienced that now. She called out "lingila," which means "wait." Unfortunately, the houseboy thought she said "ngila," which means "enter." So while Mom was enthroned (and completely covered), he entered the bathroom. She just asked him what he wanted, answered his questions—and he went back into the kitchen area and closed the door. He may not even have known the difference—but Mom was completely mortified. Dad installed a lock on that door in less than an hour!

A couple of times a year, especially in the second term, our family would go into the city of Bukavu just to enjoy civilization and its benefits for awhile. But this was still a different culture, a European culture. On one of our little vacations, while we were eating at Le Gourmet, one of our favorite restaurants, Mom excused herself to go to the restroom. None of us realized it was a unisex bathroom with no doors on the stalls.

As she was once again "enthroned," a distinguished Belgian gentleman walked in. As he passed the stall where Mom was sitting, he stopped in front of her, bowed, and cheerfully said, "Bonsoir, Madame"—"Good evening, Ma'am." Then he went into another stall. When Mom came out of the restroom, her face was as red as a beet, while Dad, Marian, and I were sitting there in shock. From then on, whenever we ate at that restaurant, we three females always went to the restroom together, so two of us could shield the open stall by holding our skirts out to the side—and Dad stood outside to forestall any gentlemen from joining us.

Not having a lock on bathroom doors seemed commonplace in European buildings. When we were at the boarding house in Bukavu before Marian and I flew home for the last time, Mom got into trouble again. She was once again enthroned in an unlocked toilet closet (that's all that was in there—she had to go to another bathroom to wash her hands). Even though she had her hand on the doorknob, the door was suddenly wrenched from her hand and flung open.

Mom said that the most handsome Belgian man she'd ever seen was standing in the doorway. He actually clicked his heels together, bowed from the waist, and crisply said, "Pardon, Madame," and smartly closed the door. She managed a civilized nod to him as she quickly departed. And once again, Dad was called into door duty every time one of us females had to use the bathroom.

August 28, 1959

Dear Mr. and Mrs. Wright:

Here I sit at Katshungu once more. Don't worry. None of us are sick, praise the Lord! Les and Roger Reed are off on a trip to Kindu to buy some lumber. We took Jeanette and Marian to school. The Greens have fixed up the dorm just lovely. They worked so hard this summer plastering, painting and arranging. The children will have charming surroundings for their home away from home.

You would never guess what met our eyes when we arrived on Katanti. It was quite a sight, believe me. The old mud house in which the Hendrys were living just collapsed. Saturday at noon, Helen was fixing dinner in the kitchen when a huge chunk of the wall crashed down, just missing her. She heard a grinding, crunching sound. The Lord literally held that house up until they could get moved out. They are down in the old Parcel house now. The whole wall of David's room fell down flat. What if the boy would have been in it? The Africans looked at the house, and watched while the missionaries moved everything out. They would say, "Don't go in there. Don't you know death when you see it?" Truly we can thank the Lord for His watchcare.

The need for housing, *good* housing, is acute. Katanti is in a deplorable state. Ikozi is a lovely station. Kamulila has just mud houses but they are in reasonably good condition. We had hoped to start Kamulila's first permanent house but since that boulder decommissioned our truck, we are forced to start another mud house or we will find ourselves in the same condition Katanti is in. I don't mind living in a mud house, as long as it isn't going to fall in around my head. They are nice and cool when this Congo sun gets to beating down. With the political situation what it is, you just wonder if we should put the money into permanent buildings. We surely need the mind of the Lord.

The drive to Katanti was one of the most hazardous we've ever made. It rained for nearly 24 hours. The roads were almost impassable. The Lord enabled us to pull Lydia Frank out of the ditch and also a Belgian. We surely feel His protecting hand upon us.

All our love,

Les and Gertrude

BEREAN MISSION, INC.	AFRICA	B.A.M.S. - Kamulila
3536 Russell Blvd.		Bukavu, D. S.
St. Louis, Missouri	The Dark Continent!	Congo Belge, Africa

Prayer Letter — September 1959 — No. 16

"The Lord shall preserve thy going out and thy coming in from this time forth, and even for evermore" (Psalm 121:8).

This letter brings our greetings to you in the Savior's dear name. Gertrude has been writing to many of you from time to time, but this time I would like to share with you some of our recent experiences and blessings as we have been *"holding forth the Word of Life"* here in the heart of Africa.

How happy and thrilled we were to know that all twelve of the young men sent to our Berean Mission Bible School from Kamulila Station passed the course, three of them graduating with the highest grades in the entire class. These new preachers are sorely needed in the many African villages scattered throughout this area. Twelve new lights to shine for the Lord Jesus Christ in the heathen darkness of these dense forests! What a joy and privilege to place them in their respective villages where they will conduct services every morning at 6:00 A.M., and each evening at about 5:00 P.M., when the people return to their villages from hunting and gardening in the forests. They will also gather together the children of their village and of nearby villages to teach them in the first and second grades of school, as well as to teach them the things of the Lord. These out-village preachers, together with our mission elders, are the spiritual backbone of the African church among our tribe.

Mom with Bible School graduate Sa Mongosa and his family

But we were confronted with the problem of how to get these new preachers to their far-flung villages, together with their wives and children and all of their household effects. Our mission truck, a 1952 Chevrolet, 2 ½ ton Van, had died of overwork long months before. Three of the big tires were flat and there was no useable spare tire; the brakes were no good; and one of the rear springs had four broken leaves, including the main leaf. I placed two of the new preachers in their villages with my ½ ton Chevrolet Carryall, but the cost of making a special trip with each preacher and his family would be prohibitive inasmuch as some of their villages were sixty and seventy miles from the mission. The only solution was to repair the big mission truck and make one trip with all of their household goods. To this plan the remaining ten teachers readily agreed, as they were anxious to get out to their villages and begin to preach the Word. Together with their families they "put their feet in the path" and walked many, many miles to their villages carrying the barest necessities of cooking utensils, clothing, etc. on their back and heads.

I worked for a week on the old truck, wrestling 20-inch tires off the rims, repairing some tubes and replacing others. I purchased a new rear spring for $42 and installed it. The brakes were beyond my mechanical ability due to the condition they were in, so we just had to trust the Lord for the stops and starts. After changing the oil and greasing the chassis we were finally ready for the trip.

I parked the truck in our mission village in front of the native evangelist's mud house for loading with the household goods of our new preachers. There were many willing hands to help, for the people love and respect their preachers. Into the truck went crude wooden bed frames, cloth mattresses stuffed with dried grass, heavy wooden mortars and pestles for pounding rice, large woven baskets bulging with native pots, pans and metal dishes, bundles of rather dingy-looking blankets and clothing. In America, we would have driven it all to the nearest rubbish heap and burned it, but among these people it represented every single earthly possession of ten families.

There were no TV sets; no, not even a single radio; only one cheap little phonograph which was furnished by the missionaries to a teacher in a particularly large village in order that he might play Gospel Recordings records for the villagers. There were no soft, easy-chairs, nor overstuffed furniture; only a variety of crude, wooden benches and native stools. Naturally, there were no electrical appliances of any kind, nor anything to make life more pleasant or comfortable—this was remote, interior Africa, where living is primitive and life is hard! But out there in ten distant villages were ten families anxiously awaiting the coming of the mission truck bearing their precious belongings.

The first day of our trip was rather uneventful. We dropped off belongings to a number of the new preachers as we traveled along the winding, rugged, mountain road. They greeted our arrival with the greatest of enthusiasm and fairly hugged to themselves their meager but precious belongings. The first night we spent at the little African village of Isezia, in the home of a friendly African Christian named Amuli. He had a nice-sized rabbit in a box on his porch. I noticed him take the rabbit from the box and go with it to the rear of his house. Then we heard a couple of high-pitched squeals, and Sa Musene (our African evangelist) turned to me and said, "Amuli has killed his rabbit for your supper tonight." This was real Christian hospitality because that rabbit was worth the equivalent of $2 among these people, which would be more than a week's salary. How many of us in America would put out a week's salary to entertain a stranger in our midst? How many of us go out of our way so much as to shake hands with the stranger that comes into our church? But this African, though poor in this world's goods, was rich in the grace of our Lord Jesus Christ. And, the Lord soon opened a way of returning Amuli's kindness.

While the rabbit was being cooked, a young man came in from the forest path with word that he had seen a couple of large black monkeys nearby. I grabbed my 30-30 carbine from the truck, and we followed the young fellow along the path to where he had seen the monkeys. Our efforts were rewarded, and soon we returned to the village with a forty-pound monkey which we gave to Amuli. Needless to say, we all feasted sumptuously that night on rabbit and monkey meat cooked in palm oil and hot peppers, and palm oil gravy poured over steaming hot rice. Ummmm! That evening we held a service for the people of the village and then gathered around a campfire in front of Amuli's house and talked of the things of the Lord until bedtime. How hungry these Christians are to learn more and more of what God has to tell them in His Book.

The next morning we had more rabbit and palm oil and rice for breakfast (Ugh!), and were on our way to deliver the rest of our goods and to return to the mission that night. By about noon we had reached the farthest village along a branch mine road and had delivered the last of our load. We ate lunch and started back along this treacherous mountain road. We were driving along, tired but happy that our mission was accomplished, when suddenly there was a sharp jolt and a ripping of metal, and then a split second later there was a rending crash. I felt the truck literally dragged to one side of the road. I could not imagine what we could have hit for I had seen nothing in the road.

Sa Musene and I leaped out of the truck expecting to find the whole front end of the truck smashed in, but it wasn't even scratched. A second glance caused us to freeze in our tracks. There on the top of the truck, one end resting on a rocky ledge, and the other end smashed part way into the van of the truck, was a tremendous boulder weighing perhaps three or four tons!

Apparently the top corner of the truck van had struck the overhanging boulder, and it had ripped into the truck body. The impact dislodged the boulder from its ledge, and the tremendous weight of it came crashing into the truck body, pinning us to the spot. The boulder came to rest about two and one-half feet from our heads. It was so heavy that it sheared off 9 leaves in the right front spring as if they were popsicle sticks and broke several leaves in the left front spring. The body damage was quite extensive, and in general, the whole truck is now a wreck. We praise the Lord, however, that Sa Musene and I escaped without a single scratch. We just felt sort of "shook up," especially after seeing the size of that boulder.

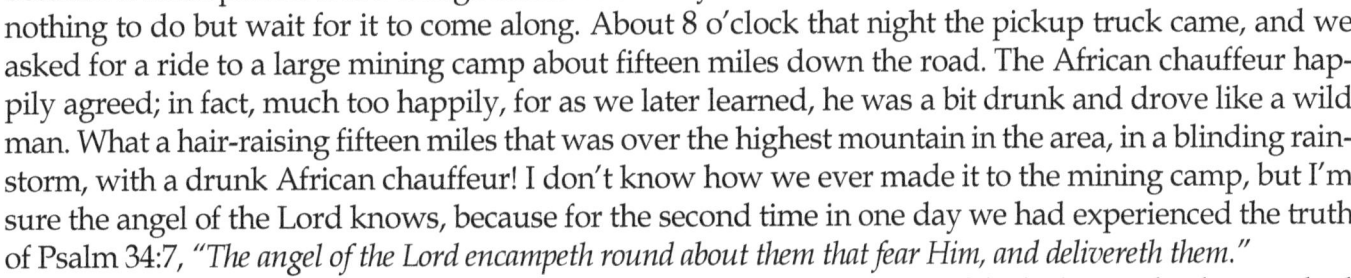

We walked back about a mile or so to the nearest village, where I ate a sandwich and some cookies which Gertrude had put in a lunch for me. After eating, we held a service in the village, and the Lord blessed the preaching of His Word in the salvation of a small lad about twelve or thirteen years old, who trusted the Lord Jesus Christ as his personal Savior. That one precious soul was worth infinitely more than the truck which was smashed.

We knew that there was one other truck on the road that night because we had passed it at a village earlier in the day. So there was nothing to do but wait for it to come along. About 8 o'clock that night the pickup truck came, and we asked for a ride to a large mining camp about fifteen miles down the road. The African chauffeur happily agreed; in fact, much too happily, for as we later learned, he was a bit drunk and drove like a wild man. What a hair-raising fifteen miles that was over the highest mountain in the area, in a blinding rainstorm, with a drunk African chauffeur! I don't know how we ever made it to the mining camp, but I'm sure the angel of the Lord knows, because for the second time in one day we had experienced the truth of Psalm 34:7, *"The angel of the Lord encampeth round about them that fear Him, and delivereth them."*

The African Christians at the camp received us gladly, and at ten o'clock that night they cooked some rice for us, and one of them even persuaded the African storekeeper to open up so that he could buy a can of herring in tomato sauce with hot peppers for me to eat with the rice. That one can of food cost him one-half of his day's pay, but he knew that a white man could not eat the other food they had prepared for my evangelist. Surely the Lord has enlarged the heart of His people, even out here in the African bush.

The next morning I called at the mine workshop and told the Belgian in charge of the camp of our predicament. He gave me two of his African mechanics and some equipment and sent us back in a pickup truck to the scene of the accident. The mechanics, with the help of the African Christians from a nearby village, fastened a steel cable around the boulder and ran the other end of the cable to the trunk of a large tree higher up the slope of the mountain. Then, with the aid of a heavy chain hoist, they were able to draw the steel cable taut. When they were reasonably sure that the cable would support the weight of the boulder, they used a large steel chisel and sledge hammer to split off chunks of the boulder where it was imbedded in the body of the truck.

Finally, when we felt that most of the weight of the boulder was being supported by the steel cable, I climbed into the driver's seat and started the motor. I must confess that I did not feel too secure with that three or four-ton rock hanging over my head. I put the truck in reverse gear and let in and out on the clutch in an attempt to tear the truck loose from the rock. At last, with a rending of steel, the truck lurched backwards leaving the huge boulder swaying on its rocky ledge, supported by the steel cable. I turned the truck as far to the left as the narrow road would allow and went around the dangling boulder. After everyone had moved to a safe distance, the mechanics loosened the cable by use of the chain hoist, and the boulder came crashing down onto the road, only this time it was *behind* the truck instead of on top of it. They will have to heat the rock with fire and then throw water on it to break it in pieces in order to get it off the road.

We loaded in the mechanics and their equipment and started back to the mine camp. As we were going over the big mountain on a very narrow road, we groaned as we caught sight of another car approaching us. That meant real trouble to find a spot where we could get around one another, and it meant that one of us would have to back up on that mountain slope. Our dismay was soon turned to joy, however, when we discovered that the oncoming car was that of Miss Helen Gow, one of our own missionaries, and in the car with her was Gertrude, Jeanette and Marian, out looking for their overdue husband and daddy.

We limped back to our mission station, riding with the front end down on the axle. The brakes wouldn't work without pumping them, and the brake pedal would stick down each time it was depressed, greatly complicating matters. The gas pedal would stick, too, and would have to be released by lifting it with my toe. But, once again, God proved His faithfulness and watchcare by bringing us safely back to the station that night, even though we had to finish the trip in another torrential rainstorm. Truly, *"the Lord shall preserve thy going out and thy coming in from this time forth, and even for evermore."*

We are so thankful for the Lord's preservation on this trip, but how we do regret the loss of our much-needed truck. We were contemplating the construction of the first permanent-type missionary dwelling on our Kamulila Station. At present we are all living in mud and stick houses with leaf roofs. But without a large truck to haul heavy loads, it would be impossible to undertake such a construction job. There would be no way of hauling the necessary loads of sand and gravel, of cement, lumber, and steel roofing. Yes, dear friends, out here in the African bush living is primitive and life is hard—but He who said, *"My grace is sufficient for thee,"* has also promised, *"as thy days, so shall thy strength be."* How very thankful we are for a delivering, preserving God and Savior.

We are thankful, too, for such faithful prayer warriors and stewards of God as you dear ones. How many of our battles against Satan and his darkness have been won on *your* knees while we have been doing the fighting; how many of our deliverance's have been wrought on *your* knees while we were experiencing the danger; how much of our need has been supplied *"according to His riches in glory by Christ Jesus"* as He has burdened *you*, His faithful stewards, to meet that need for His glory. Only eternity will reveal your labor of love, and the reward that shall be yours, and ours, at His coming.

Thank you for your faithfulness in keeping us before the Throne of Grace. Please pray for us as we take Jeanette and Marian back to Katanti for their final year of schooling in the Congo.

We are a close family, and it is only by the grace of God that we can endure the separation. Pray, too, that the necessary funds for the girls' return to America will be forthcoming during this school year. Pray without ceasing!

Yours in His never-failing grace,

Les, Gertrude, Jeanette, and Marian

BEREAN MISSION, INC.	AFRICA	B.A.M.S. - Kamulila
3536 Russell Blvd.		Bukavu, D. S.
St. Louis, Missouri	The Dark Continent!	Congo Belge, Africa

Prayer Letter	December 1959	No. 17

Dear Friends:

"Knowing therefore the terror of the Lord, we persuade men" (II Corinthians 5:11).

This verse became the text of our African Evangelist, SaAziza, as he began a four-week evangelistic trip. At the beginning of each day, he would read this verse and the Holy Spirit gave him new zeal to "persuade men" to come to the Savior.

When he returned from his journey, we stood amazed as he unfolded to us the marvelous way God had worked in the hearts of the people through his ministry of the Word. We could not help but compare him to the Apostle Paul - *"In journeyings often, in perils by the heathen — in perils in the wilderness — in weariness — and beside these things that are without, that which cometh upon me daily, **the care of all the churches**"* (II Corinthians 11:26-28).

First, he traveled on the mission bicycle to the village of Bulumbu. There he conducted a three-day Bible Conference.

The Lord poured out His blessing. Christians were built up in the faith. Nine precious souls received the Lord Jesus Christ as their Savior. Fourteen backslidden Christians repented of their wanderings and returned to the Lord. What a glorious beginning to an evangelistic trip!

SaAziza bicycled more than 100 miles along the mine road, preaching the gospel in village after village; encouraging our village preachers in the remote areas; strengthening the church; "persuading men"; and the Lord blessed mightily. He left the mission bicycle at the house of Bikamba, one of our out-village preachers, and accompanied by a young Bible school graduate and three older school boys, entered into a narrow forest path to take the precious gospel message to remote villages hidden deep in the vast forests. They trekked nearly 200 miles over forest-covered mountains, in places where no white man has ever been, an African missionary to his own people. They trekked through gorilla-infested forests, and, in one instance came upon a gorilla in the path. They quickly hid themselves in the underbrush and waited, praying, hardly daring to breathe. The gorilla crashed off in another direction, and SaAziza and his companions were able to continue their journey.

All in all, SaAziza traveled more than 200 miles by bicycle, and nearly 200 miles on foot. Eighty-eight Africans accepted Christ as their Savior. Forty-six Christians repented of their backsliding and returned to fellowship with their Lord. The church, the body of Christ, was strengthened. SaAziza summed it up in this simple way: "Lugendo luane luabezaga muezi umozi. Kalaga anlagile nunse busoga." ("My trip was one month. God watched over me very good.") The quiet statement of a humble servant of God.

While we are on the subject of what the Africans are doing, here is some news about a school. It is not a schoolroom full of squirming children, but a room where about eight earnest men, all of them fathers, are struggling with reading, writing and arithmetic. They are some of our mission workmen who work all day at manual labor, in oppressive heat, and after work go to school for an hour to learn to read and write. They are mature men who were illiterate until about two years ago when this school was started for them. Their objective? To be able to read the Word of God! This is certainly cause for some honest heart-searching. How many of us, who read so easily and rapidly, spend much time reading and studying the precious Word of God? And these dear ones are struggling mightily just to be able to read their Kilega Bibles.

Mom with some of the ladies she is teaching to read Kilega.

We also have a school for women. They, too, meet for an hour each day after hard labor in their gardens and in their homes. Sometimes they are so tired that they fall asleep during class. Always they are caring for their children as they struggle with trying to learn. The men know they can learn, but the women aren't so sure. They have been taught for centuries that they are only animals and not capable of learning. As one young woman said to Gertrude after a particularly trying session with reading, "Mama, I am a fool. I cannot learn." Then Gertrude stopped teaching reading and taught that women are *not* fools. They *can* learn. And for proof, she called their attention to the young African woman who helps Gertrude teach the women's school. Then the lesson was continued with renewed zeal and encouraged hearts.

Now just a word about we Spainhowers. We are getting ready to make a trip to Katanti to see Jeanette and Marian (end of October). It will be the first time we have seen them since school started August 28. Such a long time! Then we will not see them again until Christmas, when they will have one wonderful month at home. That, dear friends, will be our last visit with our girls for a long, long time. When school is out in May, they will be winging their way to the United States. Jeanette will have graduated from high school, and Marian has expressed her desire to return to the States with her. Because of the turbulent political situation here in the Congo, we are agreed that she would be safer in the homeland.

Their airplane fare will be approximately $1,500, which should be in hand by April 1960. If you feel led of the Lord to help return Jeanette and Marian to the United States, you may send your gift to Berean Mission, Inc., 3536 Russell Blvd., St. Louis, 4, Missouri. Be sure and designate your gift "Spainhower Girls' Passage Fund". You may be assured that all gifts you send to Berean Mission are handled *exactly* as you designate them.

These are perilous times in the Belgian Congo and in all of Africa. We missionaries feel that the Congolese are plunging headlong into a nightmare. We do not know how much longer we will be permitted to stay at our posts, but we rest in the knowledge that we cannot be forced out unless our Heavenly Father permits it, or wills it.

Occupying until He comes,

Les, Gertrude, Jeanette, and Marian
The Spainhowers

Jeanette's Comment: Katanti Scouts

The mission school grew very quickly once the Hendrys took charge of it—and the Berean Mission children got older. Not only had the Hendrys brought out a lot of sports equipment and a good library for the school, but they really worked on keeping all of us occupied. To have so many young people basically confined to a relatively small space on the compound with little activity would have been a disaster.

The Hendrys suggested that the students form a club to come up with ideas for entertainment, for helping others, and the like. Katanti Scouts was formed during the time we were in the United States. All of the meetings were run by the students. Uncle Bob was the faculty advisor.

By the time Marian and I returned to the field, Katanti Scouts not only planned entertainment events for the school but often for all of the station missionaries. Softball and hockey teams were chosen during Katanti Scouts meetings, as were the editors/reporters for the *Katanti Kourier*, a small newspaper mimeographed once a month, and the editor/staff for the *Safari*, the yearbook.

During the first school year, neither Marian nor I were ever chosen for anything—except as one of the last ones chosen for softball teams. A small group of students were in charge of everything. By the second year, however, the situation eased considerably, and we could become more actively involved. I became one of the reporters for the *Kourier* and, in my last semester, the editor of the *Safari*.

The annual Katanti Scout Fair took place in October. Basically, it was a good excuse for having all the parents of the students come to Katanti for a couple of days to visit with their kids. From the beginning of the school year, there had been all kinds of tournaments—chess, checkers, as well as badminton, tennis, hockey, and softball. Those so inclined also created craft projects, from slingshots to embroidery.

In 1958, Mom and Dad were on the high seas returning to the Congo, so Marian and I felt lonely and left out of all the fun. But in 1959, Mom and Dad arrived from Kamulila on Thursday. The first thing Mom did was give me a permanent. Grandma Wilson would send permanents out to Congo three or four times a year for me. Dad, Mom, and Marian all had naturally curly hair. I was the only one who had to have some help.

Most of the parents were going to arrive on Friday afternoon, so all of us students had to finish our week's assignments in school. I'm afraid our concentration wasn't very good.

But in the afternoon, Marian and I spent the time with Mom measuring and sewing hems on new dresses she had made for us. We planned to wear them on Sunday. At least, Mom didn't have to worry about our out-growing our clothes this term because we were both fully grown.

In the evening, all of the girls went down to the softball/hockey field to practice their cheers for the hockey game on Saturday morning. Dad and Mom went with us and carried pressure lanterns—so we could see well and avoid any snakes or other critters that preferred the night hours. Of course, the noise and the lights also attracted the attention of half of Katanti village who came rushing to the field to watch the crazy missionary girls yelling on the field.

Saturday was the big day! It started out at nine o'clock with a hockey game—complete with cheerleaders. In the next picture, I am behind the letter "B" and Marian is to the left side of me. I'm sure we must have looked a sight trying to do our cheers but we had fun anyway! Then came badminton and tennis tournaments. After lunch the judges were busy judging the various craft entries. Marian won first prize in the embroidery category. Grandma Wilson had mailed her a red checkered tablecloth to embroider with black thread. She really enjoyed embroidery work like Grandma did.

The big-ticket item was the softball game in the afternoon. All of the missionaries brought lawn chairs or blankets to sit on. The Africans ringed the field.

Mom is sitting in the center of this picture with her sunglasses on. Marian is standing behind her. I am sitting to her right behind Aunt Ferne Sanford.

First, we raised the American flag on the pole by the backstop. Since we were living in a Belgian colony, usually the Belgian and the Congo flags were flying. But there it was—the American flag—waving proudly against that blue tropical sky.

I strapped on my accordion, and Eldon led all of the missionaries in singing "The Star-Spangled Banner." The Africans couldn't figure out why so many of the missionaries were wiping tears from their faces. I think that sometimes we just take the benefits of the United States for granted. But as we discovered, when you're in a foreign country and suddenly the red, white, and blue reminder of America flies in front of you, tears are a natural result.

Most of the visiting parents stayed over Sunday, attending the Katanti church in the morning. Then, we had a singspiration on Sunday evening. I was asked to play the piano for it. It was great for all of us to sing the choruses and hymns—in English!

Mom and Dad headed for Kamulila on Monday morning. There were only five-and-a-half weeks until Christmas vacation—and we could hardly wait!

Jeanette's Comment: Kamulila Christmas 1959

Throughout this book, I've written about nearly every Christmas over those years. Some were joyful; some brought us sorrow. But it was a precious time when we were together as a family, wherever we happened to be.

During our last term in the Congo, our family was separated most of the year because Marian and I were living in the dormitory on Katanti while attending school. So the two Christmases on Kamulila meant a lot to us.

Jim and Tom Lindquist came back to Kamulila with us for Christmas 1959. Their parents and little sister were on their way back to the field after their furlough but had sent the boys ahead so that they wouldn't lose any schooling. Uncle Irving and Aunt Betty Lindquist had founded Kamulila in 1952, so the Africans there considered Jim and Tom to be "their" boys. Such rejoicing as they saw how big the boys had become—Jim was in 10th grade and Tom in 6th grade.

Kamulila was all a-buzz in preparation for the African Christmas conference when we arrived home. Mom wrote in a letter to Grandma that some Africans walked almost a hundred miles—for over a week—to come to the conference. Dad and Uncle Pete Peterson hauled in food by the truckload from nearby villages. They even hunted monkeys way back in the forest. Dad shot 31 and Uncle Pete 5. The Africans ate well!

Mom and I decorated the tree the day after we got home, so thankful for the artificial tree that we'd brought back to the Congo with us. Marian had a light case of malaria and didn't feel like helping. We even opened our presents on the 21st because we knew that, once the conference started, there wouldn't be time for our family celebration.

On Christmas Eve, the Africans presented their Christmas program. Mom wrote to Grandma, "It was so good. Everyone knew their parts and really shouted them out. A young married couple were Mary and Joseph. NyaMandelena is a beautiful girl, and she looked like a bronze Madonna. Very sweet. The crowd was terrific."

The Africans loved to sing Christmas carols that had been translated into Kilega—and they loved to go caroling on Christmas Eve. Large groups of them sang from house to house in Kamulila village—and on the missionary compound. Mom said the first group came by at 10:30 p.m.; the last group arrived at 3:15 a.m. "They sing until you get up to wish them a Merry Christmas," Mom wrote. Our house is so close to the village that they kept us awake most of the night. But how could we complain? They were rejoicing over the birth of Jesus Christ. They understood what the Bible means when it says that Jesus came to save people from their sins.

The conference officially began on Friday, Christmas Day, and would end after the last service on Sunday. There were four meetings each day with *two* preachers at each meeting. Dad preached at one of the afternoon services for the three days. Mom held a huge women's meeting on Saturday morning. Uncle Pete preached at several of the services, too. Otherwise, African pastors and elders conducted the services. A baptismal service took place on Sunday afternoon. (See " A Baptismal Service—Balega Style")

The missionaries all took turns attending various services. Marian and I attended only a few of them. Since we didn't speak Kilega very well, four services a day with two preachers in each service was more than we could handle.

After the conference, all of us could begin to relax for a little while. Aunt Helen Gow, especially, wanted to make sure that we four kids had a good time together. She had badminton and croquet—and we played the games almost every day.

One afternoon, Dad decided Jim, Tom, Marian, and I should do some target practicing. In a large field, away from people, he set up a target. He stayed with us, of course, as we took turns using his 22 rifle. Here's what I wrote in my diary about this experience: "At first, Tom and I couldn't even sight in the target, but Jim and "Annie Oakley" [Marian] shot away. Finally, I managed to sight in but couldn't hold the gun, so Jim found a pole for me to rest the gun on. Then I did pretty well. Once, I hit the bullseye!"

We had a few parties, too. Aunt Helen Gow had one party at the single women's home, and then, we had a "backwards" party at our house for all the missionaries on the station. Everyone arrived at our back door, and we told them goodbye. As they left, we greeted them enthusiastically and welcomed them. We all wore our clothing backwards. It was a hilarious evening.

But on Saturday, January 16, we bid farewell to Mom and Dad. Since Dad had not been well, Uncle Pete drove Jim, Tom, Marian, and me to Ikozi in his truck. We spent the night there and continued on to Katanti on Sunday.

Even though our lovely Christmas holiday was over, I was kind of excited. Just sixteen more weeks — and I would graduate from high school! To top it off, Marian and I would then return to the United States. We could handle just about anything for sixteen weeks!

Jeanette's Comment: A Baptismal Service — Balega style

Here in America, most of us are used to nice, sterile conditions for a baptismal service — a tile-lined baptistery, maybe even a mural on the wall, spotlights focused on the baptistery, with microphones to catch every word.

The pastor wears protective rubber gear over his suit, under a white robe. Those being baptized often wear white robes as well.

Before being baptized, these people may meet once with the pastor or, according to the denomination, take a pre-baptismal class so that everyone is sure the person is saved.

But it was different in the Congo back in 1959. After a person professed Christ as Savior, he or she had to wait for a year, be faithful in church attendance, and live a righteous life before baptism — and this ruling was set forth by the Balega elders, not the missionaries. The elders knew, as did we missionaries, that people might profess conversion just to please the white missionaries or in hopes of gaining some benefit. This year-long waiting period was long enough for the elders to see a changed life.

So on this Sunday afternoon in the summer of 1959, a large group of Balega believers — both from Kamulila station and some from nearby villages — were literally going to "gather by the river" for a baptismal service. The Ulindi River was just a short distance from Kamulila Station. Christians and heathen alike gathered on the banks of that river, deep in the heart of the Congo, to watch a baptism. This service presented a wonderful opportunity to give the gospel because the unsaved Balega were very interested in why these Christians were going to be baptized.

But there was a big problem — there were lots of crocodiles in that river. Just a few days earlier, one had grabbed a woman doing her laundry at the river's edge and had dragged her off. They never did find her body.

As the time approached, we missionaries walked down to the river, and the elders pointed to a safe place for us to stand. The Africans lined the banks, sat up in the trees — and shouted at the children to stay back from the river's edge. The elders worked hard to keep order.

When all was finally ready, Balega voices rang out that old hymn, "Shall We Gather at the River." Then, one of the elders faced the crowd and gave a wonderful evangelistic message that clearly indicated why these people were being baptized — they had committed their lives to the Lord Jesus Christ and wanted their friends and loved ones to witness their testimony. The elder had to shout for everyone to hear. Fortunately, since we were at a bend of the river, the sound carried well.

Finally, two or three of the elders waded into the water and beckoned for the first of the 20-25 Balega Christians to come to them. The baptismal area had been cordoned off

Elder Lutete baptizing

by a half-ring of canoes topped with boards. Standing on those boards were four sharp-eyed African hunters—and Tata Wemaninua (Dad) with his rifle. No crocodiles were going to carry anyone off from this baptismal service!

A hush fell over the crowd as the first men waded out to meet the elders. Each of them clearly gave their testimony. Although it wasn't as mortally dangerous for a person to become a Christian among the Balega as it would be today in a Muslim country, these African men and women knew that they would be facing trials and troubles because they were cutting customs and traditions. For example, it might mean that young men would have trouble getting a wife—they had to buy them—and their relatives wouldn't help raise the bride price. Sometimes, the family of the proposed bride refused to allow a woman to marry a Christian man.

The women were shyer and quieter, quite unused to speaking at all in public, especially around men. Generally, they just nodded as the elders would ask them pointed questions about their faith. A married woman, especially, faced a different set of problems if her husband weren't a Christian. At the least, he could beat her—at worst, kill her with no repercussions.

So baptism meant far more to those Balega than a simple service does here in America. It was consecrating themselves to the Christ they professed—and they knew there would be a price to pay.

Kamulila, December 28, 1959

Dear Pastor and Mrs. Wright,

Thank you ever so much for the tablecloth to embroider. It is so beautiful. (I'm not just trying to be polite for it really is!)

Starting with Christmas Day, we have had a four-day conference for the Africans here on Kamulila. Thursday evening was the Christmas program put on by the school boys and girls. It went off perfectly. "Mary" and "Joseph" were so sweet and are a fine Christian couple. Friday and Saturday there were five meetings a day. I would have enjoyed them so much more if I could have understood more of the language.

Today was our big day. Before the communion service, Dad ordained Lutete Daniel as one our first Balega pastors. On each of our other stations, one or two pastors were ordained. Lutete then served the communion himself for the first time without a missionary officiating. It is a great step forward when the Africans can have one of their own instead of a missionary to be their "pastor." Of course Dad will still oversee and advise, if necessary, but Lutete will begin to serve the African Church and all its affairs himself. He is a wonderful man. This afternoon 45 were baptized, so Lutete had Dad and Sa Aziza help him. Pray that these Africans will really be good testimonies for Him. This was the last service of the conference.

Thanks again for the tablecloth.

Love in Christ,

Jeanette

Lutete with an old Christian man at Kamulila. Dad loved and respected Lutete a great deal — and the feeling was mutual.

Marian's Comment: Crime Doesn't Pay

During our last year at the dorm, we all experienced a shocking event that we will never forget.

It was Sunday morning. We all got dressed for church and ate the breakfast that the dorm's faithful cook, Kibekiangabo, had prepared for us. After breakfast, those of us who played musical instruments for the African service grabbed them and headed out the door for the walk down the hill to the mud church building. It was a typical Sunday morning, nothing out of the ordinary.

Songs were sung, a message from God's Word was given in Kilega by one of our African elders, and soon we were chatting and laughing as we walked back up the hill to the dorm.

But when we girls entered our upstairs bedroom, we gasped in horror. Clothes were strewn all over the beds and floor. All the drawers of the chests and dressers were opened with everything scattered all over the room. Our underwear drawers had been ransacked with many items gone and others thrown over the room. Jewelry, notebooks, pens, everything was either scattered around the room, or completely missing. I don't think anything was left untouched. Poor Jeanette was distressed because she had been saving money for college from giving piano lessons to other missionary kids, and that was missing.

We called for Uncle Ernie and Aunt Hallie. Naturally, the boys came, too. After showing them that we were robbed, the boys ran outside and tried to find a trail. They were successful, too. They found stolen items at the back of the dorm and out into the forest that had been dropped in the robbers' haste to get away from the dorm with their loot.

A runner was sent to get the elders of the village to let them know what happened. We had no police to whom we could report the crime. But the missionaries knew that the Africans themselves might be able to find out who did it. But frankly, we figured that was probably the end of it, and we would never find whatever they got away with.

How did we feel? To be honest, we girls not only felt angry, but we felt personally violated. Just knowing that the thieves had handled our personal belongings was unnerving, to say the least—especially not knowing what diseases they might have left on our clothes and other things.

Several days later as we were all in school studying, we heard a commotion from the Katanti village. Voices were raised and kept getting louder. We realized a group of people were coming up the hill, past the church and our school, towards the dorm. We were all straining to see out of the school windows. We immediately realized that the African chief of the Balega tribe was being carried on a kipoi with great pomp and ceremony. This was a big deal! The Africans coming with them were talking excitedly.

As they passed our school, we saw people walking behind the chief's kipoi with a teenage boy, whose hands were tied together with bamboo ropes. That got our complete attention, and some of us begged Uncle Bob (our school teacher) to let us go outside and follow them up to the dorm. We wanted to see what was going on. Obviously, in Uncle Bob's wisdom, his answer was an emphatic "no"!

The school wasn't far from the dorm so we could still hear the commotion. Uncle Ernie and another missionary man met the chief on the porch of the dorm. We couldn't hear what they were saying, but one thing a missionary knew: they had to be very careful where an African chief was concerned. He had jurisdiction over the Balega tribe, and the missionaries really had to be careful to respect his position.

As we were sitting at school, straining to listen—and trying our best to catch a glimpse of what was happening—we suddenly heard the most terrifying screams of pain. It didn't last long, but it sent a chill down our spines. We found out later that the teenage boy had been caught by other Africans with some of our stolen items. The chief was summoned, and he was bringing the boy to our dorm to get a confession out of him. The chief knew he had not acted alone, and he also wanted the names of the others involved. So before Uncle Ernie knew what was going to happen, the chief's men put chains around the wrists of the boy and quickly started twisting them. The pain was instant and horrible. Needless to say, he fell screaming to his knees and immediately confessed, giving the names of the other boys. They were all caught, and we heard they were sent to an African prison.

Some of our possessions were recovered as they were caught—including Jeanette's piano money! From then on Uncle Ernie had us keep any money we might have (which wasn't much) in a locked cabinet in his office.

One of the disturbing things about this story is the teenage boy. His name was Buseni, and he was the only son of one of our Katanti elders, Sa Buseni, who really loved the Lord. Let me tell you how I knew Buseni.

On our first term in Africa, I was riding my bicycle when Buseni, who was a little older than I was, approached me, wanting to ride my bike. I had seen him around frequently, and I didn't like him. So I shook my head no. He had a stick in his hand, and promptly proceeded to hit me once on the head with it. Then he ran. I hurried home to tell Dad and Mom what happened.

There were some other African boys who saw what Buseni did. They ran to the village to tell his father, Sa Buseni, what he had done. Sa Buseni was horrified and embarrassed. He caught Buseni and brought him to Dad. He asked Dad to bring me outside so I could watch Buseni get a thorough whipping by my Dad! Dad quickly explained to his beloved elder that discipline is to be done in the privacy of his own home and by him, not by Dad. Well, Sa Buseni grabbed a stick and began beating Buseni in our front yard. When he was finished, Buseni ran into the forest. I almost felt sorry for him.

However, on our second term in Africa, there was a lot of political unrest as the Africans wanted their independence from the Belgian government. Most Africans in the jungles really didn't understand what independence actually meant. Some thought they could get their independence given to them in a bag. Others thought that what was ours would now be theirs. By this time Buseni and I were both teenagers. I happened to come face to face with him one time, and he mumbled that when independence came, I would be his woman! I think that was one of the deciding factors that led Dad and Mom to send me home with Jeanette when she graduated from high school before their independence occurred.

The last time I saw Buseni was the day the chief brought him to the dorm and put chains around his wrists. It was Buseni who screamed in pain. It was Buseni who ended up in prison for theft at the dorm. I have always wondered if he just became hardened as he got older, or if he ever accepted the Lord as His Savior.

Jeanette's Comment: Dramatic Changes

The adults knew, long before we missionary kids, what was happening in the Congo—the unease, even the change in behavior of the village Balega as we drove along the roads. Independence fever had hit the Congo! Dad wrote this in the April 1959 prayer letter:

> These are turbulent times for the Congo, and for all Africa….There is a growing resentment on the part of the pagan villagers up and down the road against the white man, including the missionaries. The spirit of rebellion has reached back into the forest-covered mountains where our Balega tribe dwells, as word of the uprisings has trickled into the area by word of mouth. The word we hear is "Muzungu, kuenda kumputu!" —"White man, go home!" But their attitude in no way lessens their need of the Lord Jesus Christ.

Mom wrote to Grandma on Christmas Day 1959: "Congo is simmering. Fire is going to break out one of these days. Not here in the bush but in the cities."

Eldon Green was quietly listening to BBC (British Broadcasting Company) on the radio in the dorm one evening in January 1960, when he suddenly started shouting for everyone to come into the living room. There it was—Belgium was granting independence to the Congo on June 30, 1960. But I glibly wrote to relatives at home early in February, "We don't expect any trouble, of course, seeing that they're getting what they want, but the Balega have no conception of what independence is. They think that it simply means that they will now boss the whites, and they can come up to us and to our homes and take anything of ours that they want."

Now, the Balega did actually think that the new, Africa government would hand out independence to each person—in a bag. "Uhuru!" they shouted at us now. "Freedom!" Instead of friendly greetings as we drove past villages, they shook their spears and shouted obscenities. The houseboys who always rode with us were horrified at the things the villagers shouted at us. Fortunately, Marian and I didn't know enough Kilega to understand what was being said—we just knew that life as we had known it had dramatically changed!

But I was only beginning to understand what all of this meant. Patrice Lumumba, one of the candidates for president of the liberated Congo, promised a white woman for every African man—and the death of every white man.

On February 2, 1960—while Dad and Mom were staying at the dorm—the grade school missionary girls were playing with their dolls under some trees on the back path (behind the missionary houses) when a group of Balega schoolboys began groping them. Dad heard the houseboys yelling and ran out. As the schoolboys ran away, they laughed and shouted, "Uhuru!"

Life changed immediately for all of us kids. No more trips to the African store at Bomboli unless an adult drove us there. All of the girls were restricted to the area of the missionary homes—but only on the main road at the front of the houses. That meant we could walk from the Hendrys' concrete block house (located where our two little houses had been during the first term) to the school building—an area of about two blocks. We couldn't even go to the ballfield, located just past the last house, unless adults were present. The boys didn't have quite as many restrictions, but they had to report where they were going and with whom if they left that area.

I noted in my diary during our final semester that Belgian state officials came several times to Katanti. The adult missionaries held station meetings almost every week, and the Executive Council (made up of representatives from each station) met at least once a month at Katshungu. There was talk that the President of Berean Mission might come out in June to be with the missionaries when independence came. (He was firmly told to stay home—the missionaries and African Christians didn't need to be worried about his safety, too!)

I finally understood what all of this meant—and I was really scared! To be so far away from Dad and Mom, with all of this ugliness swirling around us, was almost more than I could handle. But I was the oldest girl, and I had to calm the fears of the others. I often couldn't sleep at night, but to keep from disturbing the other girls, I would creep as silently as possible out to the hallway with a flashlight. I shed a lot of tears.

One night, Aunt Hallie Green must have heard me because she came out of her bedroom and asked what I was doing. When I told her that I was frightened and couldn't sleep, she just patted me on the shoulder and told me that it would do me more good to read my Bible than to cry. From that point on, I always brought my Bible—and that's where I found all those wonderful, comforting passages where God told us not to be afraid, that He would always be with us—even in the "valley of the shadow of death." My favorite verse during this time was Psalm 4:8—*"I will both lay me down in peace, and sleep: for thou, Lord, only makest me dwell in safety."*

Could I sleep at night? Yes, once I decided to turn everything over to the Lord. Was I still afraid? From time to time. Did I still get up at night? Yes—but less often. I learned more and more to trust in the Lord, and I matured both as a Christian and as a young person because of this situation.

Marian's Comment

At the end of my comment "Crime Doesn't Pay," I told about one incident I had with a teenage boy named Buseni. That's when the realization truly hit me that our lives were changing, and I became afraid of what was going to happen. From then on I was fearful when we would travel because, instead of the Africans cheerfully waving and calling out "Samba" (hello) to us, their faces were unsmiling and cold. One time we had to stop at one of the villages to give something to the African pastor there. I had my arm resting on the open window. Suddenly, I felt someone's hand rub up and down my arm. I looked into the mocking eyes of a young African male. His eyes and mannerism frightened me. As I quickly shut my window, he laughed and yelled something to his friends that I didn't understand. From then on, Dad always made sure all of our windows were closed if we ever had to stop.

I didn't awaken and get up in the night like Jeanette did. Instead, I started having a recurring nightmare. I dreamed that our family was still living in the two houses by the jungle at the end of Katanti Station like we did on our first term in Africa. The dream was always the same. I could hear the screams of terror of our missionaries all being slaughtered by the African rebels. They would go from the Sanford's house, to the dorm, to Parcel's house, and then to the Vander Ploeg's. Our houseboys would be trying to help us run into the jungle to escape a brutal death. I would always awaken just before the rebels reached us, but I would be shaking and didn't want to go back to sleep again for fear the dream would return. When I finally told Jeanette about them, she told me to try to recite Scripture verses or sing hymns in my mind to take away the horror of the dream. I had that recurring dream many times until Jeanette and I returned to the States. Then it stopped and never returned.

I have to admit that I relied on Jeanette's outward calmness and strength during this time. Jeanette has always been my rock and protector when our parents weren't around. She was learning to trust in the Lord, and I was trusting in my sister. Oh how we missed Dad and Mom being with us!

BEREAN MISSION, INC.	A F R I C A	B.A.M.S. - Kamulila
3536 Russell Blvd.		Bukavu, D. S.
St. Louis, Missouri	The Dark Continent!	Congo Belge, Africa

| Prayer Letter | March 1960 | No. 18 |

Dear Friends in the Homeland:

"As cold waters to a thirsty soul, so is good news from a far country" (Proverbs 25:25).

Thank you, dear friends, for the many lovely cards, newsy and encouraging letters, gifts, and packages which gladdened our hearts at Christmas. Few of you will ever know how much a letter from home means to those of us who are in a far country. It refreshes our hearts *"as cold waters to a thirsty soul."*

About a week before we were to go to Katanti Station to bring Jeanette and Marian home for Christmas, our nurse, Miss Evelyn Nickerson, came to us with an urgent request. NyaAziza, wife of our African Evangelist, SaAziza, about whom we wrote in our last prayer letters, was critically ill and needed to be taken to the State Hospital at Shabunda, 141 miles away. There was one main obstacle, however. We had not been able to leave the station for over a week because the river was too high for the native ferryboat to carry us across. Miss Nickerson came with the news of this emergency at about 7:00 o'clock in the morning. In faith we made preparations to leave. By 11:00 o'clock we received word that we could cross the river. God had answered prayer.

When we asked SaAziza who was going along to care for his wife at the hospital, he answered, "I am." If you were familiar with the customs of these people, you would realize how unusual this was. The women *always* go to care for their sick husbands, but rarely does a man accompany his wife to care for her. That is women's work! Not only did SaAziza care for his wife, but he also took along their small granddaughter and an orphan boy who lives with them.

NyaAziza was in agony all the long journey. Every bump was torture, and the road is nothing but bumps. Often she would moan, "Mama, help me. I die of pain!" But there was nothing we could do for her except pray. About six o'clock in the evening we arrived at our Katshungu Station. We fully expected to drive on to Shabunda that night, but when Miss Lydia Frank, our Katshungu nurse, examined NyaAziza she advised us to remain at Katshungu for the night. NyaAziza was too spent to continue the hard journey. Miss Frank made her as comfortable as possible for the night and early the next morning we left for Shabunda.

Because it was Sunday, we had a difficult time getting NyaAziza admitted to the hospital. There is only the one Belgian doctor for hundreds of patients, and he is off duty on Sundays, except for emergencies. We finally located the African in charge and arranged for NyaAziza to be admitted. Out of curiosity, many Africans gathered to watch us. As Gertrude helped NyaAziza from the car, we heard one of them say, "Look! The white woman helps the black one from the car. Tuangama! We are amazed!" Then Les placed his arm around SaAziza and we gathered in a small circle to pray. "Listen," the Africans whispered, "the white man prays in our language." As we started to leave, NyaAziza caught Gertrude's hand, "Mama, you're not leaving me!" "Hush," said her husband gently, "God is with us."

And God was truly with them. NyaAziza had a very serious operation in a very weakened condition, but God raised her up again. SaAziza was a faithful witness for Christ during their stay at the hospital and was able by God's grace to lead two precious souls to the Lord and to bring comfort and consolation to many others as he prayed with them and talked to them. God always uses SaAziza for His glory wherever he goes.

December 19 we returned to Kamulila with Jeanette and Marian. How happy we were to be united as a family again. The girls trimmed our Christmas tree (an artificial one we brought from America), decorated the whole house, much to the astonishment of our Africans, and made plastic ornaments to give to the two young men who help us around the house. They played their accordions in church, and in many ways once again endeared themselves to the Africans on Kamulila Station, who call them "Bakinga beitu" (our girls).

We enjoyed a wonderful month with them. Then, January 16, they returned to school for four more months. May 6, Jeanette will graduate from High School and Marian from the eighth grade. We will enjoy one month with our daughters and then on June 4 they will fly home to America. We dread the time of parting but know it is God's will. Many of you have assured us of your prayers for this trying time. We do appreciate it.

You will be glad to know that $50 was received in December for the girls' passage home. We praise the Lord for this. A total of $1500 is needed to bring the girls home. Please pray that all will be supplied by the time it is needed.

Yours in His service,

Les, Gertrude, Jeanette, and Marian
The Spainhowers

BEREAN MISSION, INC.	AFRICA	B.A.M.S. - Kamulila
3536 Russell Blvd.		Bukavu, D. S.
St. Louis, Missouri	The Dark Continent!	Congo Belge, Africa

Prayer Letter	May 1960	No. 19

Dear Praying Friends,

"For the eyes of the Lord are over the righteous, and His ears are open unto their prayers" (I Peter 3:12).

Many and varied have been the activities of the past few months. Due to the illness of Mrs. Hallie Green, dormitory mother of our Berean Christian Academy at Katanti, Les and I were asked to be the substitute dorm "dad and mom" while the Greens sought medical help. Our own medical doctor had not as yet returned to the field from his furlough in America. We stayed at the dormitory three weeks, and a busy three weeks they were.

There is quite a difference between planning three meals a day for Les and me, as compared with planning three meals a day, plus two snacks, for seventeen healthy, always hungry young people ranging in age from eight to eighteen. Fortunately, Mrs. Green has a well-trained cook who has been with her since the dormitory was first begun. I planned the menus, but Kibekiangabo (whose name means "a piece of a shield") knew the proper amounts to cook for such a large group.

Gallons of drinking water had to be boiled, filtered and cooled each day. After a "hot" baseball game, it was nothing for the kids to troupe in and quaff two gallons of water before you could blink an eye. Les took over that tremendous job completely. I think he deserves a medal because we never once ran out of cool water.

As Les had no particular duties on Katanti for these three weeks outside of the dormitory, he had some time to devote to the older boys. They love to go hunting. Nearly every morning, just at sun-up, some of the older boys would go into the forest with their African friends to hunt squirrels. Their weapons were slingshots which they themselves had made. They came home with game, too. They would carefully skin the squirrels and tan the hides. They cleaned the meat and put it in the freezing compartment of the refrigerator. When they had enough squirrels they would build a fire out back and have a feast. The hides were mounted on the wall in their room.

That sport seemed kind of tame after "Uncle Les" came with his gun. On Saturdays he took them on hunts way back in the forest. They had a wonderful time spotting the monkeys for Les to shoot. Les received a new name while we were at Katanti. Because he killed 87 monkeys for the villagers to eat, they gratefully bestowed on him the name, "SaNsisa," which means, "father of red monkeys." Can't say that name exactly appeals to *me*, but he was proud of it. Les preached on Sunday, and it seemed like old times. We were stationed on Katanti all last term, so the Africans there are old friends. We really enjoyed sweet fellowship with them.

But what a difference we notice in the villages up and down the road. There is such a change in the attitude of the villagers. No longer are we greeted with a friendly "samba" (hello). Now they insolently yell, "Uhuru" (independence). They shout obscenities; shake their fists and spears at us. Independence Day in Congo is scheduled for June 30. Many expect demonstrations and uprisings at that time. Pray much for the safety of missionaries all over Congo. Pray constantly for the African Christians, that they will be able to stand for Christ in the midst of turmoil and confusion.

Each of our five stations has a short-wave radio (of a sort). Our scheduled time to talk together is 6:30 A.M. Imagine our surprise on the morning of April 5 to hear the news from Katanti that Jeanette had been rushed to our hospital station at Katshungu the night before with acute appendicitis.

How we thank the Lord that our mission doctor, Dr. Harry Zemmer, had returned from furlough just three weeks before. Jeanette arrived at Katshungu about 8:30 P.M. By 9:30, Dr. Zemmer was giving her a spinal anesthetic. By 11:30 she was tucked in bed, one exhausted young woman minus an appendix.

The excitement was all over by the time Les and I arrived at midnight of April 5. That was more than 24 hours after the operation. Jeanette was very calm, cool and collected during the ordeal. In fact, Dr. Zemmer said she was about the calmest surgery patient he ever had. Poor Marian, though, was nearly beside herself with worry. Her beloved sister going off for an operation and she couldn't go with her. Jeanette didn't have time to feel sorry for herself; she was too busy comforting her little sister. That "little" sister, incidentally, is bigger than the "big" sister. On April 13 we took Jeanette back to Katanti and school.

We returned to Kamulila in time for Easter Sunday. Such a tumultuous welcome! There were hundreds of Christians gathered on Kamulila for our Easter Conference. The shouting was deafening as we drove up the driveway. I'm sure Les and I shook hands with at least a hundred people in less than five minutes. Our hearts were warmed by their loving greetings. Quite a contrast to the insolent "Uhuru" and hatred of the unsaved. It made us realize all the more what a change the Lord Jesus Christ makes in the heart and life of the believer.

We are now in our routine once more. Yesterday Les drove out to pick up our mail and supplies. It is a 60-mile round trip and takes about six hours because the road is so bad. On the way back he picked up a sick old man who was trying to walk the thirty miles to the mission for help. The old man was very primitive, dressed in just a dirty loin cloth and his dignity. He had obviously never been in a car before and he was terrified. As soon as the car started moving, he covered his head with a filthy old blanket he was carrying. It was a scorching hot day and he nearly roasted under that blanket. To top it all off, he became violently car sick. Do you think he would come out from under that blanket? No sir! He took the can reserved for that purpose, put it under the blanket, and proceeded to "up-chuck" in it for the next 20 miles. When Les finally arrived at the mission it took a lot of persuasion to get that poor befuddled old man out from under that blanket. I really think he wished he had stayed in his village and died peaceably beside his fire.

May 6 is graduation for our girls. In our next prayer letter, we will tell you all about it. We'll tell you, too, about their take-off from Bukavu on June 4. Many of you have sent gifts of passage money for Jeanette and Marian's trip home. We thank you in our Saviour's Name. About $800 is still needed. Will you continue to pray that all will be supplied?

Rejoicing in the Saviour,

Les, Gertrude, Jeanette, and Marian
The Spainhowers

Marian's Comment: A Little Bit of Heaven

In February of 1960, Aunt Hallie became very ill. I think a lot of it was complete fatigue from the responsibilities of the dorm, her medical work as Katanti's nurse, women's work, and the list goes on and on.

Uncle Ernie decided to take her to Shabunda to the Belgian doctor there. Our own mission doctor, Dr. Zemmer, was usually stationed on Katshungu, but he had not yet returned from his furlough to the States. After being told by the Belgian doctor that Aunt Hallie probably had bleeding ulcers, the Greens decided to go to the Methodist mission station, Wembonyama, a couple of hundred miles away to see Dr. White.

Uncle Ernie contacted Dad by short wave radio and asked if Dad and Mom would come to the dorm to oversee the care of the missionary kids until they could return. I was sorry Aunt Hallie was so ill, but my heart was doing flip flops at the thought of Dad and Mom being with us at the dorm for a while. This was truly a dream come true.

Now mind you, Dad and Mom were both strict disciplinarians. They didn't put up with foolishness. But they were loving, fair, and kind. It doesn't get any better than that.

One of the first things Mom did when she took over the kitchen in the dorm was to throw out the white flour. You may wonder why she would do such an extravagant thing since we didn't have stores there to replace it. The supplies for the dorm were brought to Katanti on the back of an old truck, which bounced and tossed for miles on our poor, mud roads. On one particular trip, by the time the dorm received the supplies, kerosene that was being hauled in the truck had leaked onto the flour sacks. It permeated the flour, making it smell and taste like kerosene. Unfortunately, Aunt Hallie couldn't just run to a store to replace it, so she had to use it anyway until the next truck could get there.

Every Saturday we always looked forward to delicious, marvelous pancakes. What a treat from having rice meal or corn meal for breakfast! The first time pancakes were prepared with the kerosene flour, however, we took our usual big bites and nearly threw up right then and there. Instead of the taste of Hungry Jack pancakes, we had kerosene pancakes!! UGH! They tasted horrible. We burped nasty kerosene all through the day. Of course, the kerosene flour was also used in the homemade bread and pie dough!

Well, Mom brought her flour along with her after remembering the letter I had written to her about our gross kerosene pancakes. Were we ever delighted when we bounded into the dining room that first Saturday and had tasty pancakes with no trace of kerosene! Mom immediately won over all the kids—including the Green boys!

Dad won over all the boys by taking them hunting with him, as mentioned in the prayer letter of May 1960.

Dad and Mom brought one other treat with them: the makings for Cokes—Coke syrup and seltzer water. Both Sunday afternoons, they fixed a Coke for everyone in the dorm. Special treats like that never happened at the dorm before, and the kids were delighted.

At the end of the school year, someone asked some of the kids what was the best thing that happened that year. Several kids, including one of the Green boys, quickly replied, "When Uncle Les and Aunt Gertrude came to the dorm." The kids saw in those few weeks what Jeanette and I knew all along—that God had truly blessed us with remarkable parents!

All in all, those three weeks were terrific. Jeanette and I felt like we were enjoying a little bit of heaven just by having our parents with us for that time.

Jeanette's Comment "Ouch! I felt that!"

The first week in April was test week. Every quarter Uncle Bob Hendry tested us over everything we had learned during that time. So the weekend had been relatively quiet with everyone poring over their books in preparation for their tests.

On Monday morning, I felt a slight pain in my right side but didn't pay any attention to it. By noon, it was much worse, but I was determined to finish the school day before I mentioned it to Aunt Hallie Green, the station nurse. By 4:00, I had severe pain in my shoulder and all up my right side. Aunt Hallie notified Aunt Maxine Gordon that I might need to go over to the hospital station on Katshungu to see Dr. Zemmer if the pain didn't ease up. She said she was so thankful that the mission doctor and his family had returned to the Congo just three weeks earlier after a year's furlough at home.

By 6:00 p.m., Aunt Hallie decided that I'd better go to Katshungu. But there was no way to notify Dad and Mom about the medical trip or get their permission for treatment. They only talked on the short-wave radio once a day at 6:30 a.m. Out in the jungle there was no such thing as getting parental consent to start treatment.

Marian wanted desperately to go, too, but since it was test week, the powers-that-be decided that wasn't a good idea. They decided that she should just stay put and take her tests. Marian put up quite a fuss and pleaded with Aunt Hallie to let her go with me, but to no avail. I'm not sure, however, that Marian really was able to concentrate that well anyway.

As I climbed into Aunt Maxine's car, the kids all lined up on either side of the road to wave me off. Marian was almost beside herself as we drove down the long Katanti hill headed for Kamulila.

It was a dreadful trip! As was customary when a missionary traveled, Aunt Maxine had one of her houseboys along. As was also customary, she stopped in nearly every village along the way to deliver a message or give something to someone. She finally picked up another sick person—and a family member--to take to the hospital at Katshungu, too.

It started to rain and, before long, the roads were a muddy mess. Of course, the car slid and got stuck in the mud. Despite my pain, I had to get out to help push it free.

We finally arrived at Katshungu, and I was placed in the "sick room" at Aunt Lydia Frank's house. As the station nurse, all missionary patients were cared for at her house. That's why missionaries would bring along a houseboy—and usually, some food—to help during a medical stay.

Dr. Zemmer came in with a large safety pin in his hand. First, he pressed around on my abdomen for a while. Then, he opened that safety pin and started "marching" it across my abdomen from left to right. There was only a slight pricking feel on the left side. But as that pin came across to the right side, my abdomen heaved up and down. He pronounced that I had acute appendicitis, and he would have to operate immediately.

Aunt Maxine nearly fainted. She hadn't thought I had anything very serious—and she was frightened that she had taken so long to get to Katshungu from Katanti. I asked Dr. Zemmer why my shoulder hurt so much if it were appendicitis. He told me that the appendicitis had probably inflamed the diaphragm, which radiated the pain up my right side and into my shoulder. And that's precisely what he discovered when he operated.

Aunt Lydia wrapped a clean sheet around my waist, and we all drove over to the mission hospital. Now, the operating room was spotless, but I imagine most American physicians would have considered it very primitive. I lay down on the table while Aunt Lydia and Dr. Zemmer bustled around getting things ready. Uncle Ed Moyer arrived to keep a check on my blood pressure. Even Aunt Maxine stayed to help in any way she could. Shots and instruments were laid out. Finally, all four adults got into sterile gowns, caps, and masks.

First, Aunt Lydia gave me a shot—a painkiller that would relax me and make me doze off. They had me sit up and bend over, putting my head on Aunt Maxine's shoulder while Dr. Zemmer gave me a spinal anesthetic. They couldn't use ether or anything like that out in the jungle because there was no oxygen available to help the patient. Only spinals were available.

It took effect almost immediately. My legs became a dead weight, and they had to help me lie down. Then, they covered me with white sterile sheets, leaving open only the small area where Dr. Zemmer would operate. They concocted some sort of shield, so I couldn't see what was happening. Dr. Zemmer had asked if I wanted to watch, but I had told him that I would only throw up and would, therefore, forego the pleasure.

Uncle Ed Moyer strapped me to the operating table—as if I could have gone anywhere with totally numb legs! I waited and waited for them to start, just chattering away. I wasn't about to go to sleep! Finally, I asked what was holding up the process and was informed that the operation was already well underway.

About that time, Uncle Ed started messing with the blood pressure apparatus and pinched my arm. "Ouch! I felt that!" I said. Dr. Zemmer nearly fainted until I assured him I felt nothing from the operation, only from the blood pressure stuff. That brought about a lot of joking—but I also ended up with a bruise on my arm for proof that the apparatus had pinched me!

Until just a few moments before the end of the operation, I was wide awake. Dr. Zemmer told me later he'd never had so much fun operating on someone because we'd told jokes and stories all the way through. I think Uncle Ed just egged me on—he had quite a sense of humor—and they were all amazed that I seemed to be having such a good time during an operation!

Of course, by the time, I was settled in the "sick room" at Aunt Lydia's, the painkiller had worn off—and I was wide awake the rest of the night.

As soon as Mom and Dad received the short-wave radio message about my appendectomy, they arranged things about their work on Kamulila, packed up, brought along Ngabo, and arrived on Katshungu a little after midnight that next night.

That weekend, Aunt Maxine brought Marian over to Katshungu, so she could see that I had survived and was doing okay—studying hard for the tests Marian was bringing to me.

By April 13, I was back at the dorm again. Although I healed, I didn't fully recover from having an operation out in the middle of the jungle until I returned to the United States that summer. How thankful I am that our good American doctor had been there to take care of me! A burst appendix meant certain death in the jungle—and they might not have been able to get me into Bukavu to a good doctor in time. But God was merciful and spared my life.

Jeanette's Comment: Food, Fun, and Festivities

Graduation! Eldon Green and I were graduating from high school and Marian and Skip Sanford from eighth grade. It seemed as if the missionaries on Katanti Station were determined that all of us missionary kids would have wonderful memories to take with us of the end of this 1960 school year. Looking back, I think many of them suspected that it might not only be the end of the current school year, but it might also be the end of the school, depending on what happened on June 30, 1960, Independence Day for the Congo. So they went all out to make sure we had a memorable time.

Shortly after I returned from Katshungu after my appendectomy, two swimming parties took place. There was a swimming pool at the Belgian club in Shabunda for the state officials and their families, who graciously allowed people from our mission to enjoy a safe, sanitary swim (no amoebic dysentery as was found in the rivers and creeks back in the jungle). So on one Saturday, all of the boys went to Shabunda to enjoy a day at the club. The next Saturday, all the girls went — except for me. It was too soon after my appendectomy, and Dr. Zemmer had strongly advised that I not go.

But that was just the start of the festivities! The excitement kept building over the next couple of weeks. Since our grades were so high, neither Eldon nor I had to take final exams. We had to finish all scheduled assignments and exercises, but we didn't have to worry about finals.

Friday, April 29

Senior Sneak Day! The two graduates in 1959 had sneaked off early one Saturday morning to go to Shabunda for the day, so naturally, Eldon and I decided to do the same thing. We invited Barbara Vander Ploeg, the only junior, to join us. Barb spent Thursday night at the dorm. Since she often did that, no one seemed to suspect a thing. The two of us were up at 5:00. As we quietly dressed, Charlene Kennedy stirred a little bit—but didn't awaken. By 5:30, we had picked up the breakfast and lunch that Aunt Hallie Green had put in the refrigerator after everyone else had gone to bed and hurried over to wait at the Parcels' car. Uncle Leonard Parcel would drive us to Shabunda and chaperone our activities.

The night before, Eldon had been sure that he and Uncle Leonard would have to wait for Barb and me—taking too much time to primp, he said. Ha! Barb and I were at the car first, and by the time Eldon arrived, Uncle Leonard had already joined us. We were waiting for Eldon! We teased him all day about it.

We left Katanti about 5:35 and arrived in Shabunda about 8:30. We went directly to the native stores, which were quite a bit larger than the one at Bomboli, and we did some shopping there. But by 9:00, we were in the pool at the club — freezing! Yep, even in the tropics, the water got cold overnight. We lasted all of 45 minutes.

After changing back into our other clothes, we went miniature golfing at the club. By 11:30, we headed back to the pool — and now, the water was nice and warm. We ate our lunch by the pool — but Uncle Leonard bought ice-cold Cokes for all of us. What a treat!

We had another couple of hours at the pool, then headed back to Katanti. By that time, my side was really aching from all the activity and the rough roads — it still probably was too soon after surgery to have been doing all of that.

The rest of the kids all swore that they hadn't heard a thing until we were driving down the Katanti hill. I wonder, sometimes. The whole idea behind a "sneak" day is that if someone catches the seniors before they sneak away, they get to go on the trip, too. I have a feeling that all the rest of the kids were given explicit instructions not to catch us! And, poor things, they had to go to school all day while Eldon, Barb, and I were playing at the club!!

But that wasn't the end of the festivities for that day. The Parcel family had invited all of the missionary kids from the school to their house for games and good food — and they provided plenty of both. I was really tired and weak — and quite sunburned — but I smiled all through the party. I noted in my diary that it was worth it all! What a great day!

Saturday, April 30

This was a special day for we four graduates—the banquet. Uncle Bob and Aunt Helen Hendry, our teachers, always prepared a special banquet for the graduates. Marian and I got dressed in our new banquet dresses—thanks to Grandma's expert sewing! We felt so elegant, especially as Skip and Eldon escorted us down to the Hendrys' house. (The Hendrys' own two kids had to go to the Vander Ploegs for supper!)

We had ham, fried potatoes, cranberries, canned corn, salad, and lemon chiffon pie. The canned ham, cranberries, and corn came from South Africa—they simply weren't available in the Congo—and had been ordered months earlier. The potatoes and salad stuff had come by truck from Bukavu earlier in the week. Salads were very rare out in the jungle because of the possibility of dysentery or other exotic germs on raw food. Especially the lettuce was thoroughly soaked and cleaned in permanganate to make sure it was free of dysentery. The lemons grew on a tree behind the Hendrys' house.

We had a marvelous time with games afterwards. All in all, it was a most satisfying experience in every way.

Wednesday, May 4

I had officially finished with my studies on Tuesday, so I was free to do what I wanted on this day. For me, that meant playing the piano and reading—and taking a long nap at rest hour.

Class Night was after supper. Uncle Bob and some of the boys built a big bonfire on the tennis court down below the schoolhouse. And was it ever hot!! We four graduates were tied together at the neck and "dragged" down to the bonfire. There were predictions for our futures, admonishments for our behavior, and jokes galore. It was a good time, topped off with roasting marshmallows. Admittedly, they were a little stale since they'd been shipped out from the States, but hey! What's a bonfire without marshmallows!

Thursday, May 5

All of us dorm girls were up bright and early! We dragged out our suitcases and started packing. Our room was a total mess! Our parents were all coming to attend the concert that night and the graduation on Friday—and we were all determined to be ready to go as soon as possible on Saturday. Time with our parents was precious!

All of us students who were involved in music in any way had been practicing for several months to present a concert. Uncle Ernie Green had carefully coached all of us—and we knew we were ready to do our best. Our orchestra was five accordions, plus several trumpets. We played together during group hymn singing. Eldon and I alternated accompanying various soloists and groups. Everyone who took piano lessons was to play a recital piece.

Mom and Dad arrived just a little before lunch. I had seen them only a few weeks before when I had my appendectomy—but we were definitely overjoyed to be together again! In the afternoon, I decorated the high school room, now bereft of the desks we'd worked so hard at all year long. They were stacked in the much smaller grade school room. The boys set up chairs, and we made sure everything looked really nice.

After supper, we all put on our concert clothes. Since Charlene Kennedy, Marian, and I were singing a couple of trio numbers, Grandma had made matching dresses—in different colors—for all three of us. Mom had sent our sizes to Grandma who made the lovely dotted-swiss dresses, each with a matching velvet ribbon sash, plus a corsage of artificial flowers. Mom had hemmed the dresses during the time she and Dad were staying at the dorm. We really felt grand in those dresses!

All of our hard work paid off. The concert went off beautifully. Parents were proud—and kids were glad it was over with! One step nearer home!

Friday, May 6

The big day finally arrived—graduation! I guess it's always kind of bittersweet. We were so anxious to go home—and on to the States—and yet, we knew we'd probably never see these people again.

Marian and I had special store-bought dresses. Grandma had asked us to pick out what we wanted from a *Seventeen* magazine. She purchased the dresses at Famous Barr in St. Louis, along with new high heels, nylons, and other pretties. We felt absolutely elegant—and so much prettier than girls in America who had to wear graduation gowns!!

The service was really nice—but unlike the two girls who had graduated in 1959, I didn't find anything to cry about. But it was very special. I won the scholarship award for a 93.7 grade average for the year, beating out Eldon by one-tenth of a point.

There we were, surrounded by friends in a small concrete block schoolhouse out in the middle of the jungle. A most unusual setting! After lots of photos of the affair, all of the students went to the Hendrys' house for cake and candy bars.

Such simple pleasures—but they meant so much to all of us!

Some of the folks who were not from Berean Mission headed home right after graduation. But those from Berean stayed until Saturday morning. All of the Berean missionaries were going to meet on Saturday afternoon at Katshungu. What we kids didn't realize was that there was a very serious purpose for this meeting—planning the activities of the mission and missionaries around what might happen on June 30, Congo's independence from Belgium.

But Marian and I were just so happy to be going home with Mom and Dad to Kamulila that we didn't even fuss about the extra time that had to be taken for the meeting. And we had 25 days before we left for Bukavu—and America!

Part Eight

The Final Chapter
1960

"God is our refuge and strength, a very present help in trouble."
Psalm 46:1

Jeanette's Comment: The Further Travel Adventures of Jeanette and Marian

The title almost sounds like a travel book for children! But once again, Marian and I were traveling on—by ourselves (plus God—and that made the difference!). Our last month at Kamulila after graduation was kind of bittersweet. Marian and I were really looking forward to getting out of the Congo with all its strife and sorrow, but we were leaving Mom and Dad there. We were so looking forward to being back in civilization once again, but we knew that Mom and Dad would be facing hardships in the Congo. We spent every moment we could savoring the rapidly shrinking time with our parents.

We went into Bukavu from Kamulila on Thursday, June 2, 1960. The hotel we usually stayed at—and all the others we checked—was packed with Belgians, men sending their wives and children out of the Congo before Independence. We finally found a small room at a boarding house. There was a double bed in the room, and the owners brought in a cot for me and something that looked like a junior bed for Marian. Really cramped! But at least we had a place to sleep!

There was a sink in the bedroom, but we had to share bathroom facilities with other guests. The commode was in a small closet off the hallway—but no sink. In another room was a sink and a big bathtub. After traveling all day, that bathtub looked very inviting, so Mom sent Marian and me down there to clean up before we went out for supper. We felt very citified putting on our pretty graduation dresses. But then, we discovered that we were locked in. We couldn't get the skeleton key to work in the lock. Half an hour later, Mom knocked on the door and asked what was taking us so long—and then went to get Dad. He had us remove the skeleton key from the lock and shove it under the door. It took some finagling, but he finally got the door open. We decided we'd just wash thoroughly in the bedroom from that point on!

We ate in the hotel that night. The steaks and French fries were good. We even ate the salad and enjoyed every bite. But the music was loud and the crowd boisterous. Even though I was just a teenager, I could feel an undercurrent of desperation in the people all around us. Life was changing too rapidly!

On Friday, we spent most of the day shopping. Not knowing what would be happening, Mom and Dad still needed to order supplies for themselves and for others on the station. We had lunch at Le Gourmet, the delicatessen, and enjoyed ham sandwiches and Cokes. For supper, we chose a small restaurant that was much quieter than the hotel had been the night before.

On Saturday morning, we walked around town. Our room was too small to stay in, but we wanted to be doing something together. We had our last lunch at Le Gourmet and drove to the airport. We were the first ones there—but soon the tiny airport was filled with Belgian women and children, clinging to their loved ones. Fortunately, Dad had made our reservations months earlier, so our seats were guaranteed. The little Sabena planes were working overtime shuttling Belgian women and children out of the Congo to the big airport in Ruanda-Urundi.

The little gully-hopper to Usumbura was jammed. I'm surprised that it was even able to lift off the ground. This time, no one stared at Marian and me because we were crying. Everyone was.

We were only in Usumbura a short time before we boarded a big propeller plane for Brussels, Belgium. The seats were jammed together to hold as many people as possible. Small children sat on adults' laps. I don't know how the stewardesses managed to keep their cool with kids running in the aisles and babies crying. There were no stuffy businessmen complaining about the babies, however, because everyone was so anxious just to get out of the Congo. Marian and I ended up entertaining some of the kids until the lights went out for the night.

We stopped in Athens, Greece, to refuel sometime early in the morning, but since everything was quiet on the plane, we were not asked to deplane during the process—and the stewardesses made sure that the men refueling the plane kept quiet. They didn't want those children waking up yet!

We flew from Athens directly to Brussels, Belgium. I caught a few glimpses of the Alps below us, but we were flying too high above the clouds to see much of anything. And by the time the kids awakened, we were all busy watching after them. It was a noisy, harried trip, to say the least.

When we arrived in Brussels about 8:00 in the morning, we helped carry or hold the hands of some of the kids all the way into the terminal. Then, we had an eight-hour layover facing us. Dad knew that was a long time for us just to sit in the airport, so he had arranged for us to go on a tour of Brussels. We thought we would be on a bus with other tourists, so Marian and I were kind of concerned when we didn't see that kind of bus anywhere in sight. A young woman finally approached and asked if we were the American girls who were going on a tour. When I acknowledged we were, she said, "Your chauffeur and limousine are waiting over here." We were dumbfounded!

She led us to a very good-looking man with dark, curly hair. I felt kind of uneasy going off with the man, but the first thing he did was to open his billfold and show us photos of his wife and two little children. "Don't be afraid," he said in English. "I am safe."

So we two missionary kids, fresh out of the bush, were led to a big, black limousine and ushered into the back seat—and off we went to spend a day in Brussels. We saw old buildings, statues, all of the usual tourist interests, and all explained in our chauffeur's beautifully accented English. We visited a place where lace was made—and I bought a lace-trimmed handkerchief that I carried in my wedding two years later.

One little statue we saw was on a side street and aptly named, "Le Mannequin qui pis." The story goes that, one day one little Belgian prince managed to escape from the castle and had a high old time wandering around town. Everyone in the castle panicked, of course, and soldiers were sent out all over the city looking for the little prince. The king swore that he'd have a statue made of the little boy doing whatever he was engaged in when he was found. Sure enough, you can imagine what the little boy was doing - relieving himself! So a darling bronze statue of a boy—in a fountain—was set up on the street corner where the little prince was found.

We had lunch at a street café—included in the price of the tour—then went to visit the Atomium at the site of the 1958 World's Fair. Eight spheres, connected by escalators and an elevator, overlooked the city. It was kind of an eerily interesting experience.

By 2:00, our tour was finished, and our guide deposited us safely at the airport. But as we entered the terminal, we were suddenly surrounded by a number of Sabena World Airlines hostesses, chattering away in French. I finally got them to slow down and tell me what the problem was. Unfortunately, there had been no communication between Sabena and the tour operator—so Sabena was panicking over "losing" two American teenagers. They immediately escorted us back to the lounge for Sabena personnel, and there we stayed until we were escorted to the gate to board our plane for New York.

We left Brussels, Belgium, at 4:30 p.m. and arrived in New York's Idlewild Airport (now the J.F. Kennedy International Airport) at 7:30 p.m. Of course, several hours were swallowed up crossing the International Date Line. We even stopped in Shannon, Ireland, to refuel before crossing the Atlantic. Marian and I were both so exhausted that we were sound asleep, and the stewardesses didn't awaken us during refueling.

It was a good idea that we'd had a nap because life became very interesting in New York. We each had a little carry-on bag, plus a big suitcase with our clothes and also our accordion cases. The customs official wanted to see everything, of course. No contraband in the carry-on bags, nothing in the two big suitcases. Then, he pointed to the accordion cases—and I made a huge mistake. I shook my head and said, "You really don't want to open them." But, of course, he did!

As soon as the accordion cases were unlocked and opened, crinolines spewed out all over the place, leaving just the accordions in their cases. You should have heard the laughter of everyone else in the room! The customs official turned red, then marked the cases as okay. But that left Marian and me to try and corral all those yards of net back into the accordion cases. That was quite some job—and took a while before we were finally ready to go on our way.

We needed to find a shuttle bus to take us to LaGuardia Airport to catch our plane to St. Louis. When I inquired, I was told that the shuttles were not running after 8:00. But there was a silver lining. We were once again escorted out to a big, black limousine, and with several other passengers, we were driven across New York to LaGuardia Airport in New Jersey. There was so much to see—the tall buildings, the bright lights—that the time passed very quickly.

There were only a couple of hours to wait for our flight to St. Louis. Once again, Marian and I compared the treatment we received from the personnel at TWA to that of Sabena. It was obvious no one cared a hoot where we were—or even if we got on the right plane. Sabena had been so careful to make sure we were where we were supposed to be, but we were in America now!

But we made it onto the right plane all by ourselves, thank you. There were several stops between New York and St. Louis. At our first stop, Marian was sound asleep. The stewardess shook her head when I asked if we needed to deplane—and we stayed on board at every stop.

As we neared St. Louis, I awakened Marian, so she would have time to comb her hair and prepare for the landing. Our trip was almost over! Even at 5:00 a.m., St. Louis looked wonderful! The plane taxied up to the terminal, and we gathered our things together. No fear, no tears this time! And there they were, waiting for us—Grandma and Great-Aunt Minnie. We were home!

Marian's Comment: Hello, U.S.A.

Words cannot describe my happiness and anticipation as our family drove away from Katanti at the end of the school year in 1960. I knew we would never be returning to Katanti, the dorm, Berean Christian Academy, and our missionary friends there. For the most part, it had been a good school year with a lot of good memories. But knowing that Jeanette and I would be flying back to the United States, soon to be reunited with our family, was an overwhelming joy to me. I could hardly wait!

However, once Jeanette and I started packing on Kamulila to leave the Belgian Congo forever, we were filled with different emotions. There were goodbyes to be said to our Kamulila Africans. Goodbyes to Katindi and other houseboys we had grown to love and appreciate so much over the years. There were many hugs and tears as we bid farewell to Aunt Helen Gow, Aunt Iola Baker, and Aunt Evelyn Nickerson, the single missionary ladies on Kamulila who had become a big part of our family, as well as to the Petersen family. Then I had to say a final goodbye to my companion and pet monkey Chee Chee. Aunt Helen Gow promised she would take good care of Chee Chee like she did when I was away at school.

But the hardest goodbye of all came the day we said our tearful farewells to Dad and Mom at the airport in Bukavu. When we left, we assumed it would probably be three years before we saw them again. That's when they would have completed five years on the mission field, and it would be time for their furlough to the States for one year. But we also knew - without putting it into words - that their continued safety in the face of the Congolese rebels was a real concern. We had no idea as we boarded the plane, if we would actually ever see them again. Hugs were long as tears flowed. We all tried to smile but leaving Dad and Mom was truly the most difficult thing we had ever done.

My mind is a blur about our trip home so I am going to leave that part up to Jeanette to write about. She kept a good diary! For my part, I was just anxious to finally arrive at Lambert Airport in St. Louis, Missouri, again because I knew Grandma and Great-Aunt Minnie would be there waiting for us.

Our plane landed in St. Louis at 5:00 in the morning. We could hardly wait to walk down the steps of the plane and into the terminal. We ran into the loving arms of Grandma and Great-Aunt Minnie. It was so wonderful to see them again! For the first time in a long time, we felt safe. But our hearts were still heavy knowing Dad and Mom remained in the dense jungles of the Congo in the midst of rebel unrest.

I do believe Jeanette and I talked excitedly non-stop all the way from the airport to Grandma's house in East St. Louis, Illinois. We had so much to tell them. They probably were beginning to realize what having two teenage girls was going to do to their quiet, peaceful home!

The first thing we did when we walked into Grandma's beloved home, full of good memories of our childhood, was to see the rooms she had carefully prepared for us in the basement. Grandma had arranged a bedroom for us with a double bed, chest of drawers, dresser with a lovely, large mirror, and a place to hang our clothes. They also fixed up a sitting room with a couch, chair, and lamps so we could have space of our own and privacy. We loved every bit of it and squealed with delight!

The next thing Grandma did was fix us a wonderful breakfast. To be honest, Jeanette and I don't remember what we ate, but it was what we *drank* that thrilled us to no end. Jeanette started drinking glass after glass of pure, wholesome, white milk! You can't imagine how delicious that milk tasted after only having powdered milk (KLIM — milk spelled backwards!) mixed with boiled, filtered water in Africa. Yuk! For myself, I drank glass after glass of cold orange juice. After not having any for two years, I just couldn't seem to get enough of it. Now Grandma knew without a doubt that she would have two sick girls on her hands with stomachaches, but she didn't have the heart to tell us not to drink so much. She would deal with our stomachaches later!

Our first Sunday back at Edgemont Bible Church was marvelous. Pastor Wright had us stand up while everyone gave us a warm welcome. So many of these people had faithfully given financial support and prayed for us while we were on the mission field. They continued to do so for Dad and Mom. We received a lot of hugs after the service. We really knew we had come home.

However, that next Wednesday evening, the realization of our fear and anxiety for Dad and Mom became very personal to me. Jeanette had gone to choir practice with Grandma while I went to Prayer Meeting. Those of us who could kneel for prayer were doing so with Pastor Wright leading. One by one the dear folk at Edgemont began pouring out their hearts to the Lord and asking for mercy and safety for Dad and Mom. As I listened to their prayers, with many people crying, I suddenly felt terrified that my parents were going to die, and I would never see them again. I quickly got up, left the church, and ran the one block home to Grandma's house. I ran into the basement, throwing myself onto our bed and sobbed as if my heart would break in two. But our dear Great-Aunt Minnie heard me and came downstairs. She took me into her arms and just held me until I had no more tears. Then she told me that I must never cry alone because she had a big shoulder, and it was there for me to use. Then she started reminding me that God was with Dad and Mom each step of the way, and He would take care of them.

How I praise the Lord for family and friends who were faithful to hold our parents up in prayer. How thankful I am for Grandma and Great-Aunt Minnie who loved us, comforted us, and provided a home for us. And to God be the glory for His love and mercy in reuniting all of us again. But that story is still to come....

Jeanette's Comment: The Prelude to the Finale

The closer the time to Independence, the more difficult the situation became for the missionaries and the Africans on the Berean Mission stations. Groups of "politicians" arrived on the stations to hold rallies to support their particular candidates. Mission policy had been drawn up to steadfastly refuse the politicians access to any of the mission buildings. The Balega who lived in the mission station villages were free, of course, to go to meetings in nearby villages, but the politicians were not allowed to hold such meetings on mission property.

At the end of March 1960, the politicians finally arrived at Kamulila Station, even though it was so far off the main road. They were traveling the countryside, stopping near any vicinity where white people lived. Dad and Uncle Pete Peterson meet the group at the road leading up to Kamulila and told the politicians that they were Americans, not Belgians, and had no interest in politics. They emphasized that the mission's work was religious — and that the church was the House of the Lord, not a political arena. They also told the politicians that the mission villagers were totally free to go to any meeting they wished to hold in another village. The politicians tried to sass Dad, but he firmly escorted them off mission property.

The Africans from Kamulila station went to the meeting but weren't very impressed. But they did bring back a message from the politicians, demanding to meet face-to-face with the missionaries. Dad emphatically refused — and the politicians finally went on their way.

On June 21, 1960, after Marian and I were safely in the United States, Mom wrote to her sister's family about being on Katanti for the annual Field Conference — and the changes that would be coming with independence:

> There will be a few weeks when there will be no letters from us. Trucking is being suspended for nearly two weeks around Independence. Then the whole stamp system is being changed, and it may take us a while to catch up with it back here in the bush. We will keep on writing, but I don't know how much will come through. Just don't worry. We'll be all right.
>
> During this crisis period, we are to have daily communication by radio with our Belgian State man. He told us that if we have any difficulties in our area, paratroopers will be flown in. We are not trusting in troops or guns. God is our sufficient protection. The greatest anxiety comes not from the possibility of physical danger but from the way our Christians are reacting to Independence. All we hear from them is, "Give me! Give me!" They want money, houses, clothes, cars. A lot of us are wondering, "Is *this* what we came to Congo for?" We thought it was to preach the Gospel.
>
> I'm afraid this letter sounds discouraged. Our mission is really at a crossroads out here. Guess all Christian missions are. These are very difficult times with tremendous problems. We need to know God's will.

Life didn't get any easier. Shortly before Independence Day (June 30), Dad had to make a trip into Bukavu for some supplies for the mission. As usual, Katindi, our cook, went with Dad to help along the road, if needed.

Dad said there was no problem while he was in the main part of Bukavu. But as he departed, he had to go into the native section of town to pick up Katindi. Dad said he could really feel the hostility all around him.

He picked up Katindi at the appointed spot without incident. As they were leaving the area, however, a big, burly African in the uniform of a military man tried to wave Dad off the road. Katindi warned, "Do not stop, my father." So Dad swerved around the man and went on. He said his heart was really pounding. The man could have been a decoy — with others waiting in the shadows. He did know, however, that the man had no authority because the Belgians were still in control of the Congo.

The man might just have been wanting a ride back into town. But Dad and Katindi had no desire to go back into town. They were headed back home to Kamulila!

BEREAN MISSION, INC.	A F R I C A	Home Address:
3536 Russell Blvd.		563 North 86th Street
St. Louis, Missouri	The Dark Continent!	East St. Louis, Illinois

Prayer Letter	August 1960	No. 20

"God is our refuge and strength, a very present help in trouble" (Psalm 46:1).

Dear Praying Friends,

This prayer letter is being rushed to you in order that you may know that we are safely out of the Congo and have arrived in the United States. Just a few weeks ago we gathered together with our African Christians for the usual Sunday morning worship service at Kamulila Station. Independence Day (June 30) had passed without incident, and all was peaceful and quiet throughout the Congo. We were beginning to relax from the tension that had built up prior to Independence. Perhaps the transition of the Congo from a Belgian colony to an independent state was going to work out without the anticipated trouble.

We had been advised to refrain from travel on the roads for several days before and after Independence and were in daily radio contact with the local State authorities. Trouble was anticipated from the local populace because of the rising feeling of nationalism. But Independence Day had passed without a ripple of disturbance and the crisis seemed to be over.

Suddenly, on July 6, word was flashed around the world that the Congolese Army was in mutiny against their Belgian officers at Thyseville, a military camp, and were moving on the capitol city of Leopoldville. The next day the troops entered Leopoldville and began terrifying the white population. Europeans were rudely stopped on the streets with a rifle butt in the pit of the stomachs. Many were beaten and white women were subjected to the grossest indignities, which soon turned into the mass violation of white women and girls by the Congolese troops.

Some of the troops moved westward to the Congo River port of Matadi, wreaking havoc along the way. Baptist missionaries were maltreated and driven out of their stations; and a Catholic mission was attacked and twenty white nuns maliciously molested. This sort of terror broke out in many, widely-scattered areas. At Coquilhatville and at Stanleyville on the Congo River, the white population had to be rescued by Belgian paratroopers and airlifted out of the country. Some of the Disciples of Christ missionaries from Coquilhatville were aboard the jetliner on which we crossed the Atlantic and told us of the brutality of the Congolese soldiers in that area. A Salvation Army major told us of the terror and heroism in the fall of Stanleyville, which ended in the air evacuation of the white population.

At Luluabourg, capitol of the Kasai Province, southwest of our area, nearly 3,000 whites were under siege by 3,500 armed Congolese troops. The whites fought with what arms and ammunition they had while an airlift was organized to get them out. A few whites were killed, and many others wounded, beaten and raped before the last one was airlifted to safety.

In but a few days chaos had spread across Congo. Elisabethville had erupted to the far south of our Berean Mission stations. Goma, Bunia, Watsa, and other cities to the north of us were being pillaged. By this time mass evacuations by land, sea and air were taking place throughout the Congo. It is estimated that about ten thousand whites were being evacuated from the Congo per day.

We were glued to our short-wave radio sets, listening to all reports and keeping in constant touch with the State authorities and our own mission stations. We listened on our radios to the thrilling airlift evacuation by U. S. Army aircraft of the Methodist missionaries about 500 miles to the southwest of us as the Congolese troops from Luluabourg spread eastward. As other troops moved southeast out of Stanleyville, the Unevangelized Fields Mission, and Heart of Africa Mission began their evacuation. Due north of us the Africa Inland Mission and Conservative Baptist Mission were evacuating their stations one at a time with the advance of the troops.

Finally, as the Congolese soldiers laid siege to Kindu, about 200 miles to the west of our Berean Mission stations, the local State and mining personnel (white) began evacuation from our area. There was also danger that the city of Bukavu would fall to the Congolese thus cutting off our last way of escape, and so we were advised to get out as soon as possible. On July 12, our hospital station at Katshungu and also our Ikozi Station evacuated. Then, on July 14, those of us on Kamulila Station left. I was the only man on Kamulila at the time and had the responsibility for the safety of three women missionaries and three children, one of whom was a girl. I felt that to remain any longer would risk their falling into the hands of Congolese soldiers should a roadblock be thrown up in our path.

We had been preparing our African Christians for this eventuality, and so we called together as many of the local Christians as possible and told them that the time had come when we must go. We said that if God permitted we would come back to them. There were many tears on both white and black cheeks. The next day, the State man at Kasese notified our lone missionary family at Uku Station that they must evacuate immediately. He said to Rev. John Sanford, "Do you realize that your wife is the only white woman in all of Punia Territory? Get her out of here!" Congolese troops from Stanleyville were beginning to move into the area. And so our last two stations at Uku and Katanti were evacuated. We all drove into the neighboring territory of Ruanda Urundi, where we lived in native grass huts until it could be decided what next to do.

We made our exit from the Congo through the border city of Bukavu on July 18. Two days later the Congolese soldiers moved in and set up roadblocks. The Commissioner of Police was caught in the lobby of the main hotel where he was stripped of his clothing and brutally beaten. The other Belgians who attempted to rescue him had their heads split open with rifle butts. One of these men was aboard our airplane to Belgium. Throughout the city of Bukavu, first the soldiers and then the African populace began breaking into houses and stores and looting. All cars attempting to flee the city would be stopped at the roadblocks and their white occupants dragged out and beaten, the women violated, and all goods confiscated.

All 59 of our Berean missionaries and children escaped into Ruanda Urundi without harm. How we praise the Lord for His deliverance! Some of us drove to Usumbura on Lake Tanganyika from where we were flown to Brussels, Belgium, and then to New York and St. Louis. While in Usumbura we visited the huge refugee center where some 10,000 Congo refugees were housed. Mission doctors and nurses, who were helping take care of the victims of Congolese savagery, told us that at least 80 percent of the white women coming through the center had been brutally violated by the Congolese troops—some as many as 20 and 30 times. Many of them will be mental cases for the rest of their lives.

At the Brussels airport our plane was met by doctors and nurses and Red Cross personnel with wheel chairs and stretchers to care for the injured. Other missionaries are driving out to the east coast of Africa in order to ship their cars home. Many of us feel that it will be some time before it will be possible to return to the Congo, particularly with our wives and children. Some have elected to stay at other missions outside the Congo and wait for a while to see what conditions will be. Gertrude and I arrived in East St. Louis on Thursday, July 28, where we are staying with her mother. We are very weary and hope to rest here for a few weeks while we pray, seeking God's will for the future.

Every earthly possession, including our car, had to be abandoned in Africa. We left our car with a missionary in Urundi and told him to use it in the Lord's work. And so the future poses some difficult problems for us. We do not regret the loss of *things*; but rather, we simply praise the Lord for delivering us unharmed. Our greatest regret is leaving our African Christians. But Romans 8:28 is just as applicable to the black Christian as it is to the white Christian. And the Lord's promise, *"I will never leave thee, nor forsake thee"* applies to those whom we have left behind, as well as to us. So we confidently commit them *"unto Him that is able to do exceeding abundantly above all that we ask or think."*

We realize that you have been, and are, praying for us and that you are vitally interested in us as your missionaries. We do appreciate all you have done for us. If you will patiently bear with us for another month or two, while we wait on the Lord, we will then let you know of His leading for the future. May God bless you for your faithfulness to us as your missionaries to the Congo during these past years.

Yours in His never-failing grace,

Leslie and Gertrude Spainhower

Jeanette's Comment: The Rest of the Story

Dad and Mom's prayer letter only tells part of the story about their escape from the Congo. The letter is exciting enough—but there's more to their story.

Mom and Dad really didn't talk much about what happened when they left the Congo, preferring to rejoice that all of the Berean Mission families escaped unharmed and to remember those from other missions—and the Belgian state personnel—who suffered terribly during that time.

It was only a couple of years before he died that Dad finally told Marian and me the full story of what had happened during that momentous time in July 1960.

Dad was the chairman of Kamulila Station, so when both the Belgian state officials and the U.S. State Department told all Americans to get out of the Congo on July 14, he was the one who gathered the other missionaries on the station—three single women—and told them they had one hour to get ready to leave. But they immediately balked at leaving. They told Dad that they had come to the Congo to witness to the Balega, and they were willing to give their lives for them. Dad told them that's not what would happen. Many Balega would end up giving their lives to protect them—and he was not willing to give them that choice. One hour, and the missionaries would leave in caravan, each driving their own vehicles.

Because they had listened so closely to the news on their short-wave radio over the past few days, Mom and Dad were packed and ready to go at a moment's notice. However, they wanted to get Ngabo and Katindi and his family closer to their home territories. Katindi and his wife were from a different tribe, and it wouldn't have been safe for them to remain at Kamulila. Even Ngabo faced some danger because he was from a different area and clan. Dad told them they had one hour to gather their "bintu" (things) and be ready to leave. He would take them to the crossroads, and they could take the jungle trails back home.

Dad called the African elders and other Christians on the station together and told them the news. As Dad's letter indicates, tears flowed freely as the missionaries left the station. At the crossroads, tears flowed again as Dad and Mom parted from the two young men who had so faithfully worked for them for four years. Dad gave them all of his Congo francs, plus the clothing he wasn't taking with him.

There were tears in Dad's eyes again as he told us about watching them disappear down the jungle trails toward their home territories. Ngabo went one way with a suitcase balanced on his head. He turned once to wave a farewell. Katindi led the way down another trail with his family. His hand-cranked sewing machine was balanced on his head, and he carried a spear to protect his family. Behind him trudged his wife, a huge basket containing all their worldly goods strapped to her back, a baby in her arms, and little Maliana (named for Marian) running alongside. Mom and Dad had watched them out of sight, then climbed into their bright red carryall, Kasoga, and continued on toward Bukavu.

As Mom and Dad and the cars with the single women neared Bukavu, Dad decided to stop at Mushweshwe, just a few miles out of town, at a Conservative Baptist Mission station where the Bothwells were ministering. We had met them at the Summer Institute of Linguistics in Norman, Oklahoma, back in 1952 and generally saw them about once a year when we were in the Congo. Dad wanted to know if the Bothwells had any further information about the situation in the Congo and to make sure that the family was all right. The single women with the three children decided to go on ahead to Kumbya where the missionaries from Katshungu and Ikozi had already evacuated. Many of the missionaries had spent their vacations at the Bible Conference grounds in Kumbya and knew it was a good place of refuge outside of the Congo but also close enough in case things settled down and they could return to the Balega.

The news wasn't very good. The Congolese soldiers were headed for Bukavu—and that was the last escape route out of Congo to Ruanda-Urundi, a Belgian protectorate. So on July 18, Dad and Mom left Mushweshwe to join the other Berean missionaries at Kumbya.

They made it safely through Bukavu to the dirt road on the other side of town that led to Ruanda-Urundi. They finally could see the little bridge that separated the Congo from Ruanda-Urundi just a couple of blocks ahead. But then, their joy turned to terror! Suddenly, out of a huge cloud of dust coming toward them, they could see a large military convoy—trucks filled with Congolese soldiers. They knew what had happened to so many people when the soldiers had found whites alone on the road. Mom started praying aloud, and Dad kept on driving steadily forward to that bridge—and safety.

The trucks came closer and closer . . . they were right next to the carryall . . . they were passing . . . but not one soldier even looked their way. It was as if Kasoga, that bright red Chevy carryall, was totally invisible!

Dad said the incident brought the Bible story in 2 Kings, chapter 6, to life for him and Mom. In that instance, the king of Syria had decided to get rid of God's prophet Elisha because whatever the prophet foretold about Israel's battles with Syria came true—and Syria always lost. So the king of Syria determined to take out Elisha. He sent horses and chariots and a huge army to surround the city of Dothan where the prophet was staying. Everyone in the city was terrified, especially Elisha's servant—but Elisha was calm. He prayed to God, who opened the servant's eyes to see that, although the Syrian armies surrounded Dothan, the fiery armies of Heaven were protecting Elisha and the city.

In the case of Dad and Mom's evacuation, God threw of cloak of invisibility over that bright red carryall so that they were able to pass safely into Ruanda-Urundi.

They stayed at Kumbya for about four days, then had to leave for Usumbura to obtain passage back to the United States. The only housing at Kumbya were the grass huts on the conference grounds. Dad's allergies flared up so badly that they couldn't remain there, and he ended up with a bad sinus infection that didn't get treated until they arrived back in America.

Note: The name of the city, Usumbura, Urundi, was changed to Bujumbura, Burundi, when the country gained its independence in 1962.

Mom and Dad had to leave everything they owned in Africa—except for one suitcase apiece. Mom said that sometimes she would sigh a little over some of the things she'd had to leave in the Congo—but then, she knew they were only things. Others had lost far more.

At the time of the evacuation, Uncle Pete and Aunt Donelda Peterson and their family, usually stationed at Kamulila, were at the hospital station on Katshungu, awaiting the birth of their newest family member. They left with the first evacuation from that station and from Ikozi on July 12.

The Petersons suffered the greatest tragedy of all the Berean missionaries. Because of the stress and difficulty of traveling right at the end of her pregnancy, their baby was born dead shortly after the family reached safety. (I had complained in an earlier comment about how rough the Peterson's truck was when Uncle Pete took Marian and me, plus the Lindquist boys, back to school on Katanti in January 1960.) This was the third baby they'd lost in as many countries since leaving the United States. One baby was buried in Brussels, Belgium, where they had studied French; the second, in the Congo; the third, in Ruanda-Urundi. The first two were the result of SIDS (Sudden Infant Death Syndrome). The Petersons had two other small children, Roger and Faith, at the time of the evacuation.

While in Usumbura, Dad gave Kasoga to another missionary and told him to use it in the Lord's work. They'd brought out a few items, like the short-wave radio/record player to sell to help pay for their passage back home.

So they left Usumbura on July 26, 1960, and arrived back in St. Louis, July 28, totally exhausted and sick, with one suitcase apiece. When we opened the suitcases, we found two changes of clothing each. The rest of the suitcases were filled with their Bibles, curios, slides, and other irreplaceable memories of the Congo. "Clothing can be replaced," they said. "These things are priceless."

BEREAN MISSION, INC.	AFRICA	Home Address:
3536 Russell Blvd.		6202 State Street
St. Louis, Missouri	The Waking Continent!	East St. Louis, Illinois

Prayer Letter	October 1960	No. 21

Dear Friends,

Nearly three months have passed since we found it necessary to leave the Congo because of the political crisis. During this time the Congo has been in a state of anarchy and confusion, with a vying for power between various political factions and attempts to withdraw from the new Republic by the Katonga and Kasai Provinces. Tribal warfare has added to the confusion, and the country is in a state of political and economic chaos. The situation there has not improved, nor is there any real indication that law and order will be established in the foreseeable future.

Gertrude and I do not feel that the Lord would have us to return to the Congo under these conditions. Neither do I feel that I can take my wife back into the interior after the campaign of rape and brutality conducted by the Congolese troops.

For these reasons, we are resigning as missionaries to the Congo under Berean Mission as of October 31, 1960. It has been both a privilege and a pleasure to have labored together with God, and with all of you who have so faithfully supported us in the Berean family of missionaries, and we regret leaving that family.

Most of all we regret leaving our faithful African Christians who are so dear to our hearts. But our leaving is not a tragedy – it is a necessity if the Congolese Church is to become completely indigenous.

We have left behind several thousand Christians among the Balega tribe, as well as many stalwart elders, who through the Holy Spirit are capable of leading the "flock," and who have a burden for the salvation of their own people. Now, more than ever before, the burden of prayer rests upon you and us alike to *"pray without ceasing"* that our African brethren may be *"strong in the Lord and in the power of His might,"* and that they may be able to stand in these trying days that lie ahead for troubled Congo.

We want to thank each of you in the name of our Lord Jesus Christ for your faithful prayers, gifts, and support during these past years. We know that God will bless and reward you for your part in His great missionary program. We have always enjoyed fellowshipping with you via mail. We will not be sending out any more prayer letters, but please be assured that a letter from you will always gladden our hearts.

Sincerely yours in Christ Jesus,

Leslie and Gertrude Spainhower

Epilogue

This is the last picture of the Spainhower family in the Congo, taken on Jeanette's graduation day shortly before she and Marian left for the United States. Jeanette was 18 years old and a high school graduate; Marian was 15 and would be entering High School in the States.

As Marian and Jeanette returned to the United States, little did Dad and Mom know that their lives as missionaries to the Balega tribe in the jungles of the Belgian Congo would soon be drawing to a close. They knew that God had called them to this mission field and thought they would spend the rest of their lives serving the Lord in Congo. But that was not to be. During their years of ministry in the Congo, however, many men, women, and children had come to the saving knowledge of Jesus Christ. What was done for Christ is what matters.

When they first came home, Dad returned to work as a draftsman/engineer and eventually retired in 1980. As long as they were physically able, Dad and Mom faithfully served the Lord in church. First and foremost, they both were teachers of the Word. Dad set up and ran the PA system for their church. Mom became librarian of the large church library. Dad served on the official board, and Mom served on various committees. Their lives were centered on serving the Lord.

Our precious mother went Home to be with the Lord on October 21, 2000. Mom and Dad were one month away from celebrating their 64th wedding anniversary. Our dear father joined her on February 1, 2012. "Precious in the eyes of the Lord is the death of his saints" (Psalm 116:15).

To God be the Glory!

Finis

Appendixes

Appendix A
A Brief History of Berean Mission in the Belgian Congo

Berean Mission, Inc., was located in St. Louis, Missouri.

After negotiating with the Congo Protestant Council, which represented all Protestant missions in the Belgian Congo, five missionaries under Berean Mission (called the Berean African Missionary Society at that time) prepared to leave the United States to open the first mission station among the Balega tribe.

1938 — The first group of five missionaries arrive in the Kivu Province of the Belgian Congo. First row: Miss Amanda Johnson, Mrs. Beulah Amie, Mrs. Mamie Jansen. Standing: Irving Lindquist and Albert Jansen

1939 — Musuku Station is established, a dispensary opened, and the first school begins with 60 children enrolled.

1940 — A second station, Ikozi, is established. The Berean African Missionary Society is recognized by the Belgian Government. The first Balega church is organized with 28 charter members.

1943 — The first Kilega readers are printed and a second almost finished. A number of songs and hymns have been translated into Kilega. Mrs. Jansen begins work on a Kilega-English dictionary to help new missionaries as they arrive.

1944 — Musuku is moved and becomes Katanti Station. Several new missionaries are delayed in reaching the Belgian Congo because of World War II. Mrs. Jansen finishes work on the dictionary just before becoming seriously ill, necessitating that the Jansens return to the United States.

1948 — The dispensary at Ikozi receives state recognition. Balega teacher-evangelists are being sent out to the villages.

1951 — A number of new missionaries arrive. The manuscript for a Kilega songbook is sent to headquarters in St. Louis, Missouri, to be printed.

1952 — Irving Lindquist and his family open a new station on Kamulila. A Bible School begins on Katanti with 17 students.

1953 — A school for missionary children opens on Katanti.

1954 — The translation of the Kilega New Testament is finished. On March 12, the Belgian government awards Mrs. Beulah Amie a gold medal for her many years of meritorious service in the Congo. The Spainhower family arrive at Ikozi Station on August 4 and on Katanti on August 6.

1955 — Uku Station is established in the Bakumu tribe.

1956 — Hospital property at Katshungu is purchased from the Belgian government, and Dr. Zemmer and his family arrive on the field. The Spainhower family leaves on a medical emergency furlough and resigns from the mission.

1957 — After a final proofreading, the Kilega New Testament is sent to the British and Foreign Bible Society to be printed. The Spainhower family are reunited with Berean Mission.

1958 — First shipment of Kilega New Testaments arrive at Ikozi. Jeanette and Marian Spainhower arrive in the Congo on August 28; Les and Gertrude arrive on Kamulila Station on December 2.

1959 — Maranatha Hospital on Katshungu is completed.

1960 — Jeanette and Marian leave the Congo on June 4. Congo receives its independence from Belgium on June 30. Missionaries are evacuated by mid-July. Les and Gertrude Spainhower leave Kamulila on July 14 and arrive safely in St. Louis on July 28. They resign from Berean Mission on October 31.

1961-1973 — The work in what was then called Zaire is severely disrupted by riots and several more evacuations. In 1973, the Congolese government declares that all foreign missions are nonexistent and that all religious activities are to be delegated to local church bodies under the control and supervision of the government.

This is what Berean Mission reported in the May-June 1973, *Missiongrams* (Vol. 30, No. 3), the official organ of Berean Mission, Inc.:

> The present authorities, realizing the tremendous influence that Christianity and missions have had down through the years in influencing the minds of the people, have now "eliminated" all foreign mission organizations, setting up the Government approved and sponsored ECZ (Church of Christ in Zaire) and automatically including all national churches founded by missions. Unless God miraculously intervenes, the days of conservative Bible missionaries serving in Zaire may be numbered.

And that's exactly what happened.

In 1973, Berean Mission had stations all around the world — among the Navajo in New Mexico, one in Florida to minister to Cuban refugees, Ecuador, Brazil, Zaire, Kenya, Morocco, Barbados, Dominica, Grenada, and the Philippine Islands. There were more than 80 missionaries scattered among these various fields.

In 2000, Berean Mission merged with Unevangelized Fields Mission, which changed its name to CrossWorld in 2004

Appendix B

Berean Mission Stations

Below is a simple map showing the locations of Berean Mission's five missionary stations -- **Kamulila, Ikozi, Katshungu, Katanti,** and **Uku** -- that are mentioned throughout this book. Shabunda and Bukavu are also included for reference since there are stories related to those locations as well.

Using Katanti as a starting point, the mileages are as follows:
Katanti to Shabunda = 50 miles
Katanti to Ikozi = 75 miles
Katanti to Kamulila = 146 miles
Katanti to Uku = 77 miles
Katanti to Bukavu = 225 miles

About the Authors/Compilers

Jeanette Spainhower Rudder and her husband Larry spent many years in evangelistic work, traveling across the country. Jeanette played the piano and sang with Larry and conducted children's work while he ministered to the adults. They home-schooled their three children who traveled with them. Jeanette went to college at the same time as her daughter and graduated with an M.A. in English and American Literature. She was adjunct faculty at Southern Illinois University at Edwardsville and Belleville Area College for a number of years, then worked for almost 20 years as a writer and editor at Stephen Ministries in St. Louis, Missouri.

Jeanette and Larry have been married for more than 50 years. Their three children, Cynthia, Douglas, and Jonathan, delighted them by adding three more children to the family—John, Sheri, and Becky—by marriage. They have 6 grandchildren: James and Jeanette Deatherage (Idaho); Rebecca Rudder (Illinois); and Matt Lowe and Brenden and Ethan Rudder (Massachusetts).

Jeanette and Larry currently reside in Granite City, Illinois. They continue to sing together and minister to seniors at their congregation.

Marian Spainhower Ammons worked full-time after graduating from high school in East St. Louis, Il. She married Dolton Ammons, who was stationed at Scott Air Force Base, Illinois, in November 1966. She continued working while raising their daughter, Brenda, and son, Richard. After they were grown, Marian worked full-time but also received her BS Degree in Business Administration in 2003 by attending night classes for several years at Belleville Area College and then Greenville College, Greenville, Illinois.

Marian retired from Cardinal Glennon Children's Foundation in St. Louis, Missouri, in 2011, where she was the Director of Corporate and Foundation Giving, Assistant Director of Development, and Coalition Director for Reach Out and Read.

Marian and Dolton currently live in Caseyville, Illinois. They have been married for almost 50 years. Brenda and her husband Brian reside in Texas with children Ryan and Katy. Rich and Jackie live in Illinois, with their three sons, DJ, Cameron, and Dominic.

Now that Marian is retired, she enjoys attending Bible Study Fellowship, working as a volunteer with children for Good News Club in her church, having time to enjoy her hobby of quilting, and spending time with Dolton at their vacation home in southern Missouri.

www.ingramcontent.com/pod-product-compliance
Lightning Source LLC
Chambersburg PA
CBHW081829170426
43199CB00017B/2680